Biblical Hebrew: A Text and Workbook

Bonnie Pedrotti Kittel, Vicki Hoffer, and
Rebecca Abts Wright

Yale University Press
New Haven and London

Printed in the United States of America.

Library of Congress Cataloging-in-Publication Data
Kittel, Bonnie Pedrotti.
Biblical Hebrew: a text and workbook / Bonnie Pedrotti Kittel, Vicki Hoffer, and Rebecca Abts Wright.
p. cm. – (Yale language series)
English and Hebrew.
Includes index.
ISBN 0-300-04394-5 (alk. paper)
1. Hebrew language—Grammar—1950- 2. Hebrew language—Readers–Bible. I. Hoffer, Vicki, 1943- . II. Wright, Rebecca Abts, 1948- . III. Title. IV. Series.
PJ4567.3K5 1989
492.4'82421—dc19 88-28077
CIP

The paper in this book meets the guidelines for permanence and durability of the Committee on Production Guidelines for Book Longevity of the Council on Library Resources.

10 9 8 7 6 5 4 3 2 1

For Bonnie

May her memory be for a blessing

For Ron to whom she was devoted

And her sons, Mark and Daniel, about whom she spoke with pride and affection

Introduction

The purpose of this book is to get students reading Biblical Hebrew prose, and even a bit of poetry, as soon as possible. To effect this we take an uncommon approach by teaching (in descending order of frequency) the most common constructions, the most common verbs, the most common grammar and syntax. Because all Hebrew in the book - whether for teaching, illustration, or drill - is Biblical, from the very first students experience the joy of working with genuine material.

In each Lesson, a verse or segment generates the concepts to be taught and the workbook style of this grammar demands constant participation. To help students decipher words, explanations focus on key, recurring features rather than on historical and exceptional formations as the latter tend to spark interest and have value at a more advanced level of learning. Of course verb paradigms and other didactic necessities are not neglected. Conscientious study of this mixture equips students to approach passages with some analytic skill. Their embryonic skill is put to use early on, as extended Biblical passages are assigned for reading.

A major section of the book is devoted to annotations to the readings, but only very rarely do the comments translate; rather they identify potential difficulties, and guide the students through a reasoning process which consistently allows them to figure out such critical components as the root of the word, the part of speech, and the syntactical setting. At all times interpretive comments focus on the Hebrew idiom, alerting students to the fact that we are reading this text in a time and culture far removed from its origins and that we are working with a language which is built quite differently from English. If we can transmit an appreciation for the structure and beauty of the Hebrew text, then we will have succeeded in our task.

The only way we have to explain Biblical Hebrew grammar and syntax is to use English nomenclature. Common structures in English such as adjective, adverb, phrase, and sentence do not always function the same way in a Semitic language such as Hebrew. It is because of this disparity that we decided to develop the Glossary. Its entries focus on points of grammar as well as a vocabulary of terminology which is valuable in understanding the Biblical text.

A decision we made early on was to omit transliteration although there are many systems around. Some are highly phonetic; these make use of so many diacritical symbols, and require such a sophisticated knowledge of phonics in order to be comprehensible that it is almost like learning a third language to be able to read this Anglicized Hebrew. Other more literal methods are not standardized, and the easiest ones assume that Hebrew sounds are familiar to the English reader, which of course, they may not be. Practicing reading the Lesson sentences, and later the more lengthy passages, even if labored at first, should help the students develop some skill in reading Hebrew in Hebrew. For those who might find it useful, a tape for reading practice is available.

A necessary but regrettable omission is of accent marks in most places, most particularly in verb charts. Because of the design of the Hebrew font, the inclusion of the accent often obscured the visibility of a vowel. So the accent marks had to go.

The reader will surely notice that punctuation is missing in Hebrew-English segments of the text. We agonized over this decision. But where does one insert the punctuation when Hebrew is read in this direction: ⟵ and then one has to proceed in this direction: ⟶ There simply is no graceful way out of such a predicament and so we had to assume that readers would be flexible enough to adjust to compensatory measures. When switching from Hebrew to English, we left extra space to create a visual pause, and of course, a capital letter will signal the start of a new English sentence.

This book is an outgrowth of the elementary Biblical Hebrew course taught by Professor Bonnie Kittel during her tenure at the Yale Divinity School. Along with being an inspiring scholar, Bonnie was an exceptionally gifted and talented teacher. She transmitted her love and enthusiasm for Biblical Hebrew to her students. Not insignificantly, Bonnie was always sensitive to traditions not her own. Bonnie's untimely death was tragic, creating a great personal and professional loss. We hope that her creative style and ability to excite all of those who learned from her are reflected in this volume.

כִּי־קָרוֹב אֵלֶיךָ הַדָּבָר מְאֹד בְּפִיךָ וּבִלְבָבְךָ לַעֲשֹׂתוֹ Deuteronomy 30:14

Contents

Lesson 1

וַיֹּאמֶר יהוה

Lesson 2

וַיְדַבֵּר אֱלֹהִים אֶל־מֹשֶׁה וַיֹּאמֶר אֵלָיו אֲנִי יהוה

Lesson 3

וַיֵּלֶךְ דָּוִד מִשָּׁם

Lesson 4

וְלֹא־שָׁמַע הַמֶּלֶךְ אֶל־הָעָם

Lesson 5

דְּבַר־יהוה אֲשֶׁר הָיָה אֶל־הוֹשֵׁעַ

Lesson 6

וַיָּבֹאוּ עַד־הַיַּרְדֵּן הוּא וְכָל־בְּנֵי יִשְׂרָאֵל

Lesson 20 (continued)

Lesson 21

וַיִּקַּח יִשְׂרָאֵל אֵת כָּל־הֶעָרִים הָאֵלֶּה וַיֵּשֶׁב יִשְׂרָאֵל בְּכָל־עָרֵי הָאֱמֹרִי

Lesson 22

לֹא־תִקַּח אִשָּׁה לִבְנִי מִבְּנוֹת הַכְּנַעֲנִי אֲשֶׁר אָנֹכִי יֹשֵׁב בְּאַרְצוֹ

Lesson 23

אֶת־הָאָרֶץ אֲשֶׁר־יהוה אֱלֹהֵיכֶם נֹתֵן לָכֶם וִירִשְׁתֶּם אֹתָהּ וִישַׁבְתֶּם־בָּהּ

Lesson 24

אֲנִי וְהָאִשָּׁה הַזֹּאת יֹשְׁבֹת בְּבַיִת אֶחָד

Lesson 25

וְלֹא־נָתַן יהוה לָכֶם לֵב לָדַעַת וְעֵינַיִם לִרְאוֹת וְאָזְנַיִם לִשְׁמֹעַ
עַד הַיּוֹם הַזֶּה׃

Lesson 26

וְאַתֶּם רְאִיתֶם אֵת כָּל־אֲשֶׁר עָשָׂה יהוה אֱלֹהֵכֶם

Lesson 27

וְלֹא־שָׁבוּ אֶל־יהוה אֱלֹהֵיהֶם

Lesson 28

וְהַמֶּלֶךְ אָסָא הִשְׁמִיעַ אֶת־כָּל־יְהוּדָה

Lesson 29

וְהָיָה אֱלֹהִים עִמָּכֶם וְהֵשִׁיב אֶתְכֶם אֶל־אֶרֶץ אֲבֹתֵיכֶם

Lesson 40

גַּם עָשׂה תַעֲשֶׂה וְגַם יָכֹל תוּכָל

Lesson 41

נֵלֲכָה־נָּא דֶּרֶךְ שְׁלֹשֶׁת יָמִים בַּמִּדְבָּר

Lesson 42

יְהִי יהוה אֱלֹהֶיךָ בָּרוּךְ

Lesson 43

וְהָיָה בִּקְרָב־אִישׁ לְהִשְׁתַּחֲוֹת לוֹ וְשָׁלַח אֶת־יָדוֹ וְהֶחֱזִיק לוֹ וְנָשַׁק לוֹ׃

Lesson 44

אַתָּה הָרְאֵתָ לָדַעַת כִּי יהוה הוּא הָאֱלֹהִים אֵין עוֹד מִלְּבַדּוֹ׃

Readings

Glossary

Verb Charts

Vocabulary assignments

Lessons	words	Lessons	words
Lessons 1-8	1 - 50	Lessons 28-32	201 - 250
Lessons 9-12	51 - 75	Lessons 33-40	251 - 300
Lessons 13-17	76-100	Lessons 41-48	301-350
Lessons 18-22	101-150	Lessons 49-55	351-415
Lessons 23-27	151 - 200		

Symbols

⌴	Root letter
⌴ with dot	Root letter with dagesh
⊡	Letter with dagesh
___	Letter(s) but not necessarily root letters
|	Placed between Hebrew words (or phrases) to mark a break in thought
⟷	What is on one side of the arrow is equivalent to what is on the other
[ ]	Square brackets are used when a Hebrew letter is either the first or the last within parenthesis. (It just looks better that way)
*	Plain asterisk: Appears beside some exercise sentences to identify those which may be more difficult than the others
*****	**Bold Asterisk**: Seen only in the Glossary to identify a term which may be specific to this book
italics	Used when something is translated

The Hebrew Alphabet

Name	Sound	Letter	Name	Sound	Letter
lamed	l	ל	alef	silent	א
mem	m	מ ם	bet	b	בּ
nun	n	נ ן	(vet)	v	ב
sameḥ	s	ס	gimel	g	ג
ayin	silent	ע	dalet	d	ד
peh	p	פּ	heh	h	ה
(feh)	f	פ ף	vav	v	ו
tsadeh	ts	צ ץ	zayin	z	ז
qof	q	ק	ḥet	ḥ	ח
resh	r	ר	tet	t	ט
sin	s	שׂ	yod	y	י
shin	sh	שׁ	khof	k	כּ ךּ
tav	t	תּ	(ḥof)	ḥ	כ ך

Modern Hebrew equivalents are shown for the consonants. This will be true for the vowels as well. This is by far the simplest system for Hebrew pronunciation. Note the following:

א and ע were throat sounds which have been modified in the modern pronunciation system. They are most easily imitated by allowing a slight stoppage of breath (and sound) at the proper place in the word.

ג and גּ have the sound of "g" as in "gum."

ו now pronounced with a "v" sound, was originally pronounced as a "w" (the letter name is often written as "waw").

ח and כ a harsh "h" is an "h" sound with a strong puff of wind behind it. Say "h" with the mouth open while blowing sound from the back of the throat. This sound will be designated by "ḥ."

ט ת and תּ are all simple "t" sounds.

ס and שׂ are both "s" sounds.

צ is most closely approximated in English by the sound of "ts" as in hi**ts**.

ק has a hard "q" sound close to "k," never the sound of our "qu."

Hebrew is read from right to left; books (such as the Bible) begin at the "back." Note that some letters have two forms. The second is called the **final form**, as it is used only at the end of a word. The first form is used at the beginning and middle of a word. Locate both forms of each letter in the examples below:

tsadeh	peh	nun	mem	khof
צדק	פּנים	נפל	מה	כּל
ארץ	כּסף	בּן	שׁם	מלך

Vowel Points

Sign	Sound	Name	Vowel Class
◌ָ	a (f**a**ther)	qamets	"A"
◌ַ	a (f**a**ther)	pataḥ	
◌ֵי	e (pr**e**y)	tsere (plene)	"E" and "I"
◌ֵ	e (pr**e**y or p**e**n)	(defectiva)	
◌ֶ	e (m**e**t)	segol	
◌ִי	i (mach**i**ne)	hireq (plene)	
◌ִ	i (mach**i**ne or h**i**t)	(defectiva)	
וֹ	o (h**o**pe)	holem (plene)	"O" and "U"
◌ֹ	o (h**o**pe)	(defectiva)	
◌ָ	o (h**o**ld)	qamets ḥatuf	
וּ	u (fl**u**te)	shureq	
◌ֻ	u (fl**u**te)	qibbuts	
◌ְ	no sound	simple shewa (silent)	Shewa vowels
◌ְ	slight sound (M'Coy)	(vocal)	
◌ֳ	o (**o**bstruct)	composite shewa	
◌ֲ	a (**a**round)		
◌ֱ	e (**e**ffect)		

Note the following:

More than one vowel may have the same sound, e.g.: shureq וּ and qibbuts ◌ֻ are both heard as "u" in fl**u**te.

Qamets and qamets ḥatuf are represented by the same symbol but are pronounced differently. Their distinguishing characteristics are discussed in Lesson 6.

The composite shewas are pronounced like the corresponding full vowel, only shorter.

The following words show the Hebrew pointing system. Note the position of the vowels — above, beneath, and to the side of the consonants. Find an example of each of the vowels on the chart, so that you are aware of their position:

holem only vowel above ↓ ↓

הוֹלֵךְ אֱלֹהִים יִשְׂרָאֵל כָל־ וַיִּשְׁמְעוּ בְּנֵי אֲשֶׁר וְאִם חֳלִי אָב

The Hebrew alphabet is the oldest in the world still in use today; our own alphabet is a descendant of it by a circuitous route. The text of the Hebrew Bible we use today reflects several periods of development. Originally only the consonants were used. By the time of the Israelite kingdoms, some consonants י ו ה were used to indicate certain vowels:

ה "a"   י "i" or "e"   ו "o" or "u"

These letters continued to be used as consonants as well. Much later, in the Middle Ages, a system of dots and dashes was devised to indicate every vowel. This was done by scholars we call Masoretes. By that time, the text was so sacred that the vowel letters י ו ה could not be removed, so the dot-dash system was used <u>in addition</u> to the vowel letters. For example:

Long "e" (pr**e**y) can be represented by either	◌ֵי	or	◌ֵ
Long "i" (mach**i**ne) can be represented by	◌ִי	or	◌ִ
Long "o" (h**o**pe) can be represented by either	וֹ	or	◌ֹ
Long "u" (fl**u**te) is represented by	וּ	or	◌ֻ

The spellings <u>with</u> the vowel letters are considered to be long or longer than those without the vowel letters. Spelling rules during the period in which the texts were written varied a good deal, and the vagaries were usually preserved by the Masoretes. That is why you may see the same word spelled different ways in the text. For example: יֹשֵׁב and יוֹשֵׁב
To distinguish the forms we have two terms: יֹשֵׁב is **defectiva** spelling and יוֹשֵׁב is **plene** (or full) spelling. Sometimes, then, the use of vowel letters represents different spellings of one word, and may also represent a slightly different vowel quality in various districts. If a word is usually written with a vowel letter, however, it means that the vowel is long and that it is basically unchangeable, whatever else is added to a word.

Each consonant in Hebrew, except the last, must have a vowel point with it. The proper way to sound out a word is to sound the first consonant, then the vowel with it, then the next consonant and vowel combination, and so on. The last consonant most often has no vowel sound and rounds off (closes) the syllable.

אֱ|לֹ|הִים   מֶ|לֶךְ   דָ|בָר

אֱ ← no sound for א
↑ pronounce the vowel

Usually, the final syllable in a word is accented or stressed. In most cases, printed texts mark the accented syllables. Stress rules become complicated as the language is inflected. Conventions affecting pronunciation will be discussed during the progress of the course as various examples come up.

Where no vowel sound was heard, the shewa ְ was used. Either it has no sound (**silent shewa**) or a very slight sound (**vocal shewa**) to link the consonants together. A shewa is heard as a slight "uh" sound (vocal shewa) when:

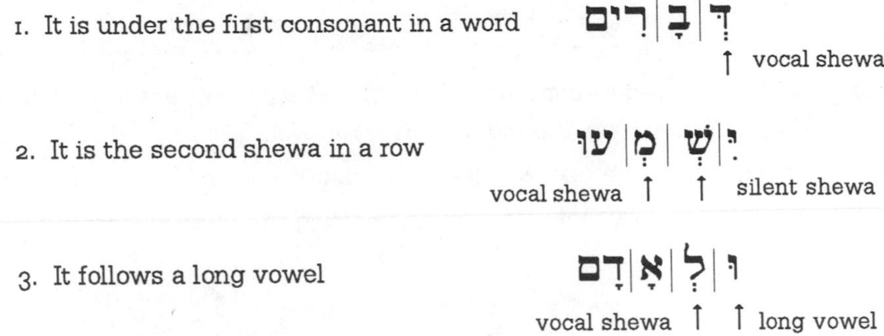

1. It is under the first consonant in a word
דְ|בָ|רִים
vocal shewa
2. It is the second shewa in a row
יִשְׁ|מְ|עוּ
vocal shewa
silent shewa
3. It follows a long vowel
וּ|לְ|אָ|דָם
vocal shewa
long vowel

Aside from the vowel signs, another mark was used to indicate more precisely how certain consonants were pronounced. This mark, called a **dagesh**, is simply a dot in the center of a letter. The dagesh was also used in certain grammatical constructions you will learn, and so can be found in most letters. In some letters it always indicates different pronunciation as well:

with dagesh		without dagesh	
b	בּ	v	ב
p	פּ	f	ף פ
k	ךּ כּ	ḥ	ך כ

Three other letters ת ד ג were distinguished by different pronunciation when dagesh appeared in them but these distinctions are no longer made in modern Hebrew pronunciation, where these letters have only one sound each. We will follow this practice in pronunciation, but the dagesh will still be written in these three letters.
These six consonants ת פ כ ד ג ב are known as the **BeGaDKePHaT** letters.

Some letters do not take dagesh. These are the **gutturals** ע ח ה א and the letter ר

Some letters become **quiescent**, that is, they drop out of pronunciation altogether. This happens if a silent letter would have a simple shewa ְ under it. In these cases, the consonant is written (remember, it is part of the sacred text), but the shewa is not:

וַיֹּאמֶר

consonant, no shewa

Using the simple guidelines presented so far, practice pronunciation with the words below.

אַף בָּא בִּי בּוֹ בָּם בֵּן

גַּם אָב אֶל אִם אֵת אָח

כֵּן יָד חַג זֶה עִם דָּג

עַד רֹב בַּת נָא מִי לֹא

טוֹב חוּץ הִיא הוּא בּוֹא אִישׁ

מוּת שָׁמַע עָשָׂה אֶחָד כּוֹל יוֹם

רִיב רָאָה פֶּה שְׁבוּ עַם סוּס

הָיָה דָּוִד דָּבָר בַּ֫יִת אֲשֶׁר אֶ֫רֶץ

גָּזֵל כֶּ֫סֶף דֶּ֫רֶךְ נָתַן לָקַח יָצָא

פָּנִים אַבְרָהָם יִשְׂרָאֵל אֱלֹהִים יְהוּדָה הַשָּׁמַ֫יִם

Here is what the Hebrew letters look like written by hand. Practice writing them.

אבגדהוזחטיכךלמםנןסעפףצץקרששת

Lesson 1

Genesis 3:13 **וַיֹּ֫אמֶר יהוה**

1.1a Read

Referring to the alphabet and vowel listings, (pp. 1-2) pronounce these two words, reading from right to left: consonant, vowel, consonant, etc. Most Hebrew words have the stress on the final syllable. (p. 3) When a word in the Lesson sentence[1] has the accent elsewhere, as in וַיֹּ֫אמֶר an accent mark will be used.

1.1b The vowels of the second word יהוה have been omitted intentionally. This is the sacred four-letter name for God. For religious reasons this word sometimes appears in the Hebrew Bible with the vowel markings for another divine name. Some think that an approximation of the original sound of the name is "Yahweh." If you do not wish to say the name, you may substitute "Adonai" ("LORD" in English) whenever you see יהוה

1.2 Count the Consonants וַיֹּ֫אמֶר

In most aspects Hebrew is a very simple language. Almost every word contains a root of three consonants. The first step in finding the root is to count the consonants in a word. So, ו = 1 consonant. Notice the dot in the yod: יּ A dot in a consonant is called a **dagesh**.

> If there is a vowel immediately preceding the letter containing the dagesh, the dagesh is a **dagesh forte** (or strong dagesh), and has the effect of doubling the letter in which it appears.

Here the יּ is preceded by a vowel (the pataḥ ַ under the ו is the preceding vowel), so the dagesh is a dagesh forte. יּ = יי Thus, ו = 1 consonant, יּ = 2 consonants, א = 1 consonant, מ = 1 consonant, and ר = 1 consonant, for a total of 6 consonants.

1.3 Find the Root

You must separate three consonants from the word in order to identify the root. Since the root consonants will appear together, you can expect to find the non-root consonants at either the beginning (right) or the end (left) of the word.

1.3a A ו at the beginning of a word means *and* regardless of the vowel which appears with it. It cannot stand by itself as a word in Hebrew.

---

1 Especially in the early Lessons, you will rarely have a complete Biblical verse as the "Lesson sentence." Terminology is also tricky here: while "sentence" is a clearly defined concept in English grammar, it is not so clear in Biblical Hebrew. However, for convenience of reference we may use the terms "verse" and "sentence" interchangeably.

1.3b When such a ו is followed by a pataḥ ַ and a dagesh appears in the next letter וַ◻ the construction is called **vav conversive**.

1.3c A vav conversive indicates:

1. The word is a verb.
2. The subject of the verb, a pronoun, is indicated by the consonant following the vav, which here is י When such a pronoun subject precedes the root, this pronoun is called a prefix, and we say that the verb has **prefix form**.
3. The verb should be translated in the past tense.

1.3d Having accounted for וַיּ you are left with three letters אמר which you can assume are the root.

1.4 Verb Analysis

You now have: וַ◻ = vav conversive
י = prefix (pronoun subject)
אמר = root (meaning *say, command*)

As an aid to translation you make a chart for verbs:

Root	Stem	Form	Person, Gender, Number			Special Features
אמר	Qal	prefix	3	m.	sg.	vav conversive

1.4a **Stem**: indicates whether there has been some change in the basic meaning of the root. Variations from the basic meaning are indicated by additions to the root. When there are no additional letters or other indicators, the meaning is that closest to the root. This is the case here: once you have found the vav conversive and the pronoun, only the root is left. The name of this basic, unaugmented stem is **Qal**. You may write "Qal" or "Q" in the Stem column.

1.4b **Form**: In this column write "prefix" indicating prefix form. In this part of the analysis you are identifying the aspect or type of action of the verb. More will be said of this later.

1.4c **Person, Gender, Number**: We said that י is the prefix, the pronoun subject. י as a prefix indicates the third person, masculine subject of the verb. In this case, the number of the subject is singular, *he* (for the plural, a special ending is added to the word). So you may write "third masculine singular" (3 m. sg.) in this column. In the Special Features column write "vav conversive."

1.5 Translation

Reading the analysis chart from right to left you can translate:

vav conversive	=	*and* (followed by past tense translation)
3 m. sg. prefix	=	*he*
Qal	=	basic meaning of root
אמר	=	*say*

Translation: *and-he-said*

1.6 יהוה This is the sacred four-letter name for God. (See 1.1b) וַיֹּאמֶר יהוה is literally: *and-he-said-Lord.*

In Biblical Hebrew, the normal word order is verb - subject. So the "he" contained in the verb refers to the subject, יהוה and you can properly translate, *And the Lord said.* (You now know about 4% of the Hebrew Bible's vocabulary.)

1.7 Assignment:

A. Start learning the words from the vocabulary list. You will be responsible for the particles plus the first 50 words for Lessons 1-8.

Exodus 6:2 וַיְדַבֵּר אֱלֹהִים אֶל־מֹשֶׁה וַיֹּאמֶר אֵלָיו אֲנִי יהוה

2.1 Pronounce the words in the above verse. This is assumed to be the first step in all subsequent Lessons.

2.2 Count the Consonants וַיְדַבֵּר

ו = 1

יּ = 2 What kind of dagesh is in the י ______ (1.2)

ד = 1

בּ = ___ What kind of dagesh is this? ______ (1.2)

ר = 1

7 total

2.3 Verb Analysis

2.3a What is the initial ◻ וַ ______ (1.3b)

2.3b What is the י ______ Form? ______

Person, Gender, Number? ______ (1.3c, 1.4c)

2.3c This leaves four consonants דבבר from which you must extract the root:

> The doubling of the middle letter of a root by a dagesh forte indicates a change or augment to the root, and thus a change in stem. We call this stem the **Pi`el**.

דבר is thus the root of three consonants. In general the Pi`el yields a transitive or intensive meaning of the root, although it doesn't show in this verb. דבר is one of the Pi`els thought to be denominative, that is, built from an original noun. The Pi`el of דבר means *speak*. (This verb is used almost exclusively in the Pi`el. Examples of verbs used in both Qal and Pi`el stems will be studied later.)

2.3d You have accounted for all 7 letters of the word, so you can fill in the analysis:

Root	Stem	Form	Person/Gender/Number	Special Features

2.3e Translation

Using the analysis chart you can translate:

vav conversive	=	*and* (plus past tense translation) (1.3c)
3 m. sg. prefix	=	*he* (1.5)
Pi`el	=	denominative meaning
דבר	=	*speak*

Translation: *and he spoke*

2.4 אֱלֹהִים means *Elohim* or *God.* What is the relationship of *God* to the verb? ______ ____________________ (1.6) Note that this appears to be the longest word in the verse. Nouns, like verbs, are built primarily on three letter roots. Here the root has a masculine plural ending ִים The word can, and does, mean *gods.* But most often in the Bible it is used for God, with 3 m. sg. verbs. So *God* is the subject referred to by the 3 m. sg. prefix pronoun.

Translation: *and God spoke*

2.5 אֶל־ is a preposition meaning *to, unto, into.* The dash, called a **maqqef** merely indicates that this word is closely related to and pronounced with the next word without a separate stress.

2.6 מֹשֶׁה pronounced "Mo-shéh," is the name *Moses*: *and God spoke to Moses*

2.7 וַיֹּאמֶר Referring, if necessary, to 1.2-1.4, fill in the chart:

Root	Stem	Form	Person/Gender/Number	Special Features

2.8 Using the chart and reading from right to left, translate: ____________________ (1.5)

2.9 אֵלָיו

2.9a Notice the אֵל in this word. Here it means the same thing as אֶל in 2.5.

> A ו at the end of a word is the third person masculine singular pronoun suffix.

2.9b **Suffixes are either objective** (*him*) **or possessive** (*his*). A suffix attached to a preposition is the object of that preposition, and therefore objective. The י connects this preposition and the suffix. Translation: *to him*

2.10 אֲנִי יהוה

2.10a אֲנִי means *I*. יהוה means ______________________ (1.1b)

2.10b

> In Hebrew two nouns (or a noun and a pronoun) can be linked by writing them together. In English we usually link nouns by writing some form of the verb *to be* between them. Such a Hebrew construction (in which *to be* is understood) is called a **noun sentence.**

Translation: *I am the Lord*

2.11 Translation of verse: *And God spoke to Moses and he said to him, "I am the Lord."*

2.12 Special Note:

In the Masoretic Text the first word of our verse appears with a slight spelling difference. It is spelled וַיְדַבֵּר (without the dagesh in the yod) rather than וַיְּדַבֵּר This was the preferred pointing because the shewa under the yod י caused a stoppage of sound and the doubled consonant could no longer be heard. This happens with some frequency in the Bible, and you must learn to recognize this exceptional form of the vav conversive. All further examples in this workbook follow the Masoretic practice.

2.13 Assignment:

The exercises throughout this workbook will rarely be of a complete Biblical verse, but will be limited to those grammatical constructions and vocabulary you have learned. Therefore, what you translate may be only a phrase or a clause.

A. Translate:

1. וַיֹּאמֶר יהוה אֵלָיו Hosea 1:2
2. וַיְדַבֵּר יהוה אֶל־מֹשֶׁה וְאֶל אַהֲרֹן Exodus 6:13
3. וַיֹּאמֶר מֹשֶׁה אֶל־אַהֲרֹן Exodus 32:21
4. וַיֹּאמֶר מֶלֶךְ Judges 11:13

I Samuel 22:1 וַיֵּלֶךְ דָּוִד מִשָּׁם

3.1 Count the Consonants וַיֵּלֶךְ

There is a total of five consonants. As you now know ☐וַ is a ______________ ______________ (1.3b) and י is a ______________ (1.3c, 1.4c) You are thus left with only two consonants לך Since you need three for the root, one consonant is missing. You can determine where the letter is missing (beginning, middle, or end), and which letter is missing, by the vowel underneath the prefix pronoun: וַיֵּלֶךְ
↑

> When a root letter is missing from a prefix form of the verb, the position of the missing letter and also which letter is missing is indicated by the vowel under the prefix consonant. If this vowel is tsere ֵ then the root letter is missing from the beginning of the root and will usually be a י

In one exceptional case ☐לך the missing letter is ה So the root is הלך meaning *go, walk*.

3.1a ך is the one consonant that never appears without a vowel of its own. If it has no vowel, a shewa is inserted: ךְ

3.2 Verb Analysis

Based on the above information, you should be able now to fill in the verb chart:

Root	Stem	Form	Person/Gender/Number	Special Features

The stem should be no problem, for no letters have been added to the root, and missing letters do not affect the stem determination. So the stem is Qal (basic meaning).

3.2a Translation:

Reading the analysis chart from right to left you can translate:

vav conversive	=	________________
3 m. sg. prefix	=	________________
Qal	=	basic meaning
הלך	=	*go*

Translation: *and he went*

3.3 דָּוִד is *David*, in case you had not guessed. Notice the dagesh in the first ד Since it is not immediately preceded by a vowel, it is not a dagesh forte. We call this dagesh a **dagesh lene** (weak dagesh). A dagesh lene may affect pronunciation but has no grammatical significance. (Review Vocalization, p. 4, for information on pronunciation changes with dagesh.)

> A dagesh in a consonant which is not immediately preceded by a full vowel is a **dagesh lene.**

The normal order of the Hebrew sentence is ________________ (1.6) So the first two words of this Lesson sentence are translated: ________________

3.3a

	Dagesh Forte	**Dagesh Lene**
In what letters	All except א ה ח ע ר	Only ב ג ד כ פ ת
Preceded by full vowel?[1]	Yes	No

3.4 מִשָּׁם

3.4a What kind of dagesh is in the שּׁ ________________

3.4b In Hebrew a number of small words are always or frequently fused to the following word. The most frequent of these particles, or short words, is וְ which you have already met. (1.3a) Another is the particle מִן However, this particle undergoes a change when it is attached to a word. The ן drops out and a dagesh forte takes its

[1] A silent shewa is not considered a vowel. Vocal shewas and composite shewas are not considered full vowels.

place in the following letter. In grammatical terms, we say that the ן has been assimilated to (come to sound like) the following letter, causing a doubling of that letter to take place.

> ☐מִ attached to the beginning of a word is the particle מִן which means *from, away from.*

3.4c שָׁם means *there.* So מִשָּׁם means *from there.*

3.4d This assimilation of letters, or the dropping out of one and the doubling of its neighbor, can be seen in many places in English.

in + mobile	→	**im**mobile
in + mature	→	**im**mature
in + logical	→	**il**logical
in + legal	→	**il**legal
in + reverent	→	**ir**reverent
in + rational	→	**ir**rational

3.5 Translation of verse: ______________________________

3.6 Assignment:

A. Translate:

1 וַיֵּלֶךְ אַבְרָהָם Genesis 22:13

2 וַיְדַבֵּר אֱלֹהִים אֶל־נֹחַ Genesis 8:15 [נֹחַ famous arkitect]

3 וַיֵּלֶךְ אֵלָיו 1 Samuel 15:32

4 וַיֵּלֶךְ מִשָּׁם יִצְחָק Genesis 26:17 [son of אַבְרָהָם⟵יִצְחָק [יִצְחָק

5 וַיֹּאמֶר שְׁלֹמֹה 2 Chronicles 1:18 [son of דָּוִד⟵שְׁלֹמֹה [שְׁלֹמֹה

וְלֹא־שָׁמַע הַמֶּלֶךְ אֶל־הָעָם I Kings 12:15

4.1 וְלֹא־שָׁמַע הַמֶּלֶךְ

4.1a וְלֹא What does וְ at the beginning of a word mean? ______________ (1.3a)
לֹא means *not*.

4.2 Verb Analysis שָׁמַע

4.2a Since there are only three letters, you can assume that שמע is the root.

Root	Stem	Form	Person/Gender/Number	Special Features

Is there any indication of a change in the basic meaning of the root? ___________

What do you call this stem? ______________ (1.4a) Previous verb forms examined were prefix, in which the pronoun subject was attached to the front of the verb. (1.3c) There is a second form of the verb in which the pronoun is placed after the root.

> The form of the verb with the pronoun subject indicated at the end is called **affix form**; and this pronoun subject is called the affix.[1]

Notice the vowel under the שׁ in שָׁמַע

> A qamets ָ under the first root consonant of a verb is a sign of both the Qal stem and the affix form.

You may write "affix" in the Form column.

In the affix form, the pronoun subject comes at the end of the word, after the root:

___ שמע

affix pronoun goes here ↑ root

[1] Don't confuse the term "affix" with "suffix." (See: Glossary)

4.2b For one person, gender, and number (PGN), the pronoun is lacking. In this case you can identify the stem and form of the verb by the vowels under the root letters, but the PGN can be identified only by the fact that there is no pronoun ending. This happens only in the 3 m. sg. affix form; all other affix PGNs have a pronoun following the root. You may write 3 m. sg. in the PGN column. Look carefully at this form, for it is very common.

3 m. sg.	**Qal Affix**	2 m. sg.
שָׁמַע		שָׁמַעְתָּ
root		pronoun ↑ root

4.2c Translation

An affix form of a verb is normally translated in the past tense, so you may translate, using the analysis chart: *he listened*, or *he did listen.*

4.2d A negative statement is formed by putting לֹא in front of the verb, as we have here. The whole phrase becomes then: *and he did not listen.*

4.3 הַמֶּלֶךְ

How many letters? ______ What kind of dagesh is in the מּ ______________ (1.2)

> The combination הַ◻ּ at the beginning of a word means *the.*

מֶלֶךְ is a noun meaning *king.* What is the relationship of this word to the verb?

______________________ (1.6) Translation: ______________________

4.4 Pronunciation

4.4a The sound of כ is quite different from that of כּ and is notoriously difficult for English speakers. The sound of כּ is close to English "k." כ is a harsh "ḥ," close to what we have suggested for the letter ח (p.1) Thus, מֶלֶךְ is pronounced "meh leḥ."

Although the ךְ in מֶלֶךְ has dots in it, they are a shewa, and not a dagesh plus a hireq. In a few exceptional cases a final ך will have both a dagesh and a shewa, but they will be written separately:

Genesis 50:1 וַיֵּבְךְּ *and he wept*

4.4b There is a group of nouns which is pronounced with the accent on the first, rather than the last syllable. Since many of these nouns have two segols ֶ ֶ for their vowels, they are called segolates. מֶלֶךְ is a segolate noun, so it is accented מֶ֫לֶךְ

4.5 אֶל־הָעָם

4.5a אֶל־ means ____________ (2.5)

4.5b הָעָם

What does הָ mean? It sounds like הַ◻ּ in 4.3, but you will notice a difference between this ה and the one in 4.3. The change in vowel takes place because ע cannot accept a dagesh. It was difficult or impossible to produce a doubled ע The vowel with the definite article was lengthened in compensation. So הָ before some gutturals = הַ◻ּ in meaning. עָם is a noun meaning *people*.

4.6 Write the translation for the entire sentence: ____

____

4.7 Extra Grammar

You have been introduced to the 3 m. sg. Qal affix, which is vocalized אָמַר
The 3 m. sg. Pi`el affix looks like this: דִּבֵּר

Pi`el		Qal
ר ב ד	Root	ר מ א
⎵ ⎵ּ ⎵	Stem indicator	no augment
⎵ ⎵ּ ⎵ִ	Regular vowel	⎵ ⎵ ⎵ָ
ר בֵּ דִּ	Affix	ר מַ אָ

Fill in the prefix + vav conversive for the 3 m. sg. in the chart below:

Pi`el		Qal
ר ב ד	Root	ר מ א
⎵ ⎵ּ ⎵	Stem indicator	no augment
⎵ ⎵ּ ⎵ ְ	Regular vowel	not regular
⎵ ⎵ ⎵ ___	Prefix + vav conversive	⎵ ⎵ ⎵ ___

4.8 Assignment:

A. Put each of the following verbs in the two columns according to form and stem. You do not need to translate them. Indeed, one of the purposes of this exercise is to show you that you do not need to know what the root means in order to analyze a verb.

Form	Stem	
Prefix/vav conversive or Affix	Qal or Pi`el	
		וַיֹּאמֶר
		נִסָּה
		אָהַב
		וַיַּחֲבֹשׁ
		וַיְבַקַּע
		וַיֵּלֶךְ
		וַיַּעֲרֹךְ
		וַיְדַבֵּר
		וַיִּשְׁלַח
		וַיְשַׁלַּח
		וַיִּקְרָא
		יָדַע
		חָשַׁךְ

B. Translate:

1 וְלֹא שָׁמַע אֵלָיו Jeremiah 37:14

2 הָלַךְ דָּוִד 1 Kings 9:4

3 לֹא־דִבֶּר יהוה 1 Kings 22:28

4 דִּבֶּר יהוה אֶל־הָעָם Jeremiah 36:7

5 עַם יָצָא Numbers 22:5

I. Vocabulary

Remember you are responsible for the first 50 words in the vocabulary list. Vocabulary is not repeated here.

II. Translate Hebrew to English

Note: Many of the verses include proper names. This is to provide you with even more practice in pronouncing Hebrew. If you don't know the traditional English spellings, transliteration is fine.

Verb forms:

וַיְדַבֵּר וַיֵּלֶךְ אָמַר דִּבֶּר וַיֹּאמֶר שָׁמַע וַיִּשְׁמַע הָלַךְ

Verses:

1 הַמֶּלֶךְ לֹא רָאָה 2 Samuel 14:24

2 דִּבֶּר הָאִישׁ Genesis 42:30 (review 4.5 if necessary)

3 וַיִּשְׁמַע הַמֶּלֶךְ־יְהוֹיָקִים Jeremiah 26:21

4 וַיהוה לֹא דִבֵּר Ezekiel 22:28

5 וַיִּשְׁלַח. . .אֶל־הַמֶּלֶךְ חִזְקִיָּהוּ 2 Kings 18:17

6 וַיֵּלֶךְ אַבְרָם כַּאֲשֶׁר דִּבֶּר אֵלָיו יהוה [*as* כַּאֲשֶׁר] Genesis 12:4

7 וַיֹּאמֶר הַמֶּלֶךְ אֲחַשְׁוֵרוֹשׁ Esther 8:7

8 נָתַן הַמֶּלֶךְ אַרְתַּחְשַׁסְתְּא לְעֶזְרָא Ezra 7:11

[לְ is a preposition (see vocabulary list "particles.") עֶזְרָא is a name.]

9 כִּי־שָׁמַע הָעָם 2 Samuel 19:3

10 וַיִּקְרָא יהוה לְמֹשֶׁה Exodus 19:20

11 וַיִּשְׁמַע אַבְרָהָם אֶל־עֶפְרוֹן Genesis 23:16

12 וַיִּקְרָא שָׁם אַבְרָם Genesis 13:4

III. Translate English to Hebrew:

Verb forms: Use vav conversive forms where "and" appears; use affix forms for verbs without "and."

he spoke and he said and he heard he went he said and he walked

Sentences:

1. The king did not go from there.
2. The people did not listen to God.
3. And God heard.
4. And God spoke to Abraham.
5. And David said to the people, "I am David."
6. And Moses listened to the people.
7. The LORD said.
8. The king spoke to him.

Hosea 1:1 דְּבַר־יהוה אֲשֶׁר הָיָה אֶל־הוֹשֵׁעַ

5.1 דְּבַר־יהוה

5.1a What kind of dagesh is in the ד ________________ (3.3a)

5.1b דְּבַר

דְּבַר is related to the root דבר which you encountered in Lesson 2. The verb root means ____________ (2.3c) In this case, you have a noun rather than a verb. What might a noun from this same root mean? If you guessed *word*, you are catching on to the way Hebrew is built. דָּבָר means *word, thing, event.*

יהוה means ____________

Notice the maqqef (2.5) linking דְּבַר and יהוה The Masoretes used the maqqef in their accentual system to indicate that the first word in the phrase did not receive a separate stress. It can be a great help to beginning students, since such accent combinations can occur only where grammatical relationships are close. In this particular case we call this relationship a **construct chain**.

We can diagram it like this:

יהוה	דָּבָר

our two nouns are separate links

By putting the links together in Hebrew, one after the other, we get a chain:

דְּבַר־יהוה

To render this chain in English, we must link the individual words with *of:*

word-of-the-Lord

5.1c In some cases the vowel(s) of the word in the construct are shortened, as is the case with the first word in the Lesson sentence: דָּבָר becomes דְּבַר when it is in construct relationship to another word.

5.1d Translation: *word of the* L*ORD*

5.2 There is another aspect of construct chains that is important. To use our phrase as an example, we can label the words:

יהוה	דְּבַר
(last link) **absolute**	**construct** (first link)

In Hebrew, the definite article [*the* ◻הַ], which you met in 4.3, can be attached only to the absolute, never to the construct. The construct can never carry components which make a noun definite, but the absolute may carry these components.

5.2a

> A noun can be definite (specific) in several ways:
> 1. If it has the definite article
> 2. If it is a proper noun (a name)
> 3. If it has a possessive pronoun (*my*, *his*, etc.)

Of our two nouns, which is definite? ____________________

Why? ____

> In a construct chain, if the absolute is definite, the whole chain is definite — in translating you can place the definite article *the* in front the whole chain.

Translation of our chain: *the word of the* LORD

5.3 אֲשֶׁר הָיָה

5.3a אֲשֶׁר means *which, who.* It is the all purpose **relative pronoun** in Hebrew and never changes.

5.3b הָיָה is a new verb, but you studied its form in Lesson 4. The landmark vowel is the ָ under the first root letter.

Root	Stem	Form	Person/Gender/Number	Special Features

Is הָיָה a prefix form? ________ (1.3c) Is it an affix form? ________ (4.2a) What is the stem? ________ (4.2a)

Translation of the phrase: *which (it) happened*

5.3c Hebrew does not have a neuter gender, but you can supply a neuter pronoun in English when that makes an appropriate translation. Notice that in good English you do not have to say the pronoun *he* or *it* in this phrase — *which* takes its place.

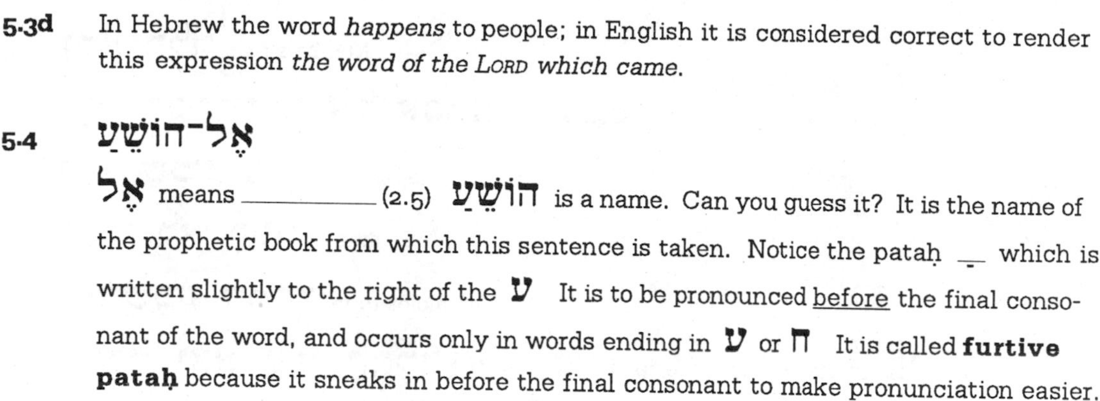

5.3d In Hebrew the word *happens* to people; in English it is considered correct to render this expression *the word of the* Lord *which came.*

5.4 אֶל־הוֹשֵׁעַ

אֶל means __________ (2.5) הוֹשֵׁעַ is a name. Can you guess it? It is the name of the prophetic book from which this sentence is taken. Notice the pataḥ ַ which is written slightly to the right of the ע It is to be pronounced before the final consonant of the word, and occurs only in words ending in ע or ח It is called **furtive pataḥ** because it sneaks in before the final consonant to make pronunciation easier.

5.5 Write your translation of the Lesson sentence: ______________________________

____

5.6 Identify each of the following words and phrases as definite or indefinite. You do not need to be able to translate them in order to determine this; you simply need to know the "rules" in 5.2a. For those which are definite, be able to tell how you know they are definite. The proper names are not difficult ones.

הַדְּבָרִים	הָעִיר	(1.3a) וּבֶגֶד
אַבְרָהָם	רַגְלָיו	(2.9a) מַלְכּוֹ
הַמָּקוֹם	צֹאן	מַצֵּבָה
עֵינָיו	שְׁנֵי נְעָרָיו	וְהַנַּעַר
שֵׁם	הַמַּאֲכֶלֶת	הַר
הַשֶּׂה	מָקוֹם	הַיּוֹם
סֻלָּם	שֵׁם־הַמָּקוֹם	הַשֶּׁמֶשׁ
בֵּית אֱלֹהִים	הָאָרֶץ	שַׁעַר הַשָּׁמָיִם

Assignment:

A. Translate:

1 הַדָּבָר אֲשֶׁר הָיָה אֶל־יִרְמְיָהוּ Jeremiah 11:1

2 וְלֹא־שָׁמַע יהוה Deuteronomy 1:45

3 דְבַר־יהוה אֵלָיו Genesis 15:4

4 וְלֹא־הָלַךְ Numbers 24:1

5 הָיָה דְבַר־יהוה אֶל־אַבְרָם Genesis 15:1

6 וְלֹא שָׁמַע מֶלֶךְ Judges 11:17

7 אֲשֶׁר לֹא הָלַךְ Psalms 1:1

8 לֹא־שָׁמַע הַמֶּלֶךְ 2 Chronicles 10:16

9 הַדָּבָר יָצָא מִפִּי הַמֶּלֶךְ Esther 7:8 [פִּי is the construct form of פֶּה *mouth*]

10 שָׁמַע אֱלֹהִים Genesis 21:17

Joshua 3:1 וַיָּבֹאוּ עַד־הַיַּרְדֵּן הוּא וְכָל־בְּנֵי יִשְׂרָאֵל

6.1 Verb Analysis **וַיָּבֹאוּ**

Root	Stem	Form	Person/Gender/Number	Special Features

By now you should be able to recognize almost immediately the way in which the verb begins, and you can fill in the Form column and the Special Features column on the chart.

The prefix pronoun י is what person and gender? ____________ (1.4c) Notice the ו___ at the end of the verb. When this is added to a prefix form, and the prefix י is used, the verb is no longer 3 masculine singular, but 3 masculine plural:

3 m. sg.	3 m. pl.
[**root**] וַיִּ	וּ [**root**] וַיִּ
↑ prefix pronoun	↑ prefix complement ↑ prefix pronoun

> The letter(s) indicating PGN which occur after the root in prefix form verbs are called the **prefix complement**.

Fill in the PGN column. How many letters are left now? ____________ Where do you look for the indication of the missing letter in such a case? ____________ ____________ (3.1)

6.1a

> When the vowel under the prefix pronoun is qamets ָ the missing root letter will be in the middle of the root and will be וּ or וֹ or יִ. This type of verb is called a **hollow verb**.

In this case, **ביא** does not exist, so **בוא** [pronounced **בּוֹא**] is our root. Is there any indication of a stem change? ________ So the stem will be ____________ (1.4a)

Translation of verb: ____________

6.2 עַד־הַיַּרְדֵּן

הַיַּרְדֵּן | הַ ☐ is the ________________ meaning ________________ (4.3)

יַרְדֵּן is the major river in Palestine: ________________ What kind of dagesh is in the י ________________ What kind of dagesh is in the ד ________________ (3.3a)

6.3 הוּא וְכָל־בְּנֵי יִשְׂרָאֵל

הוּא means *he* (the independent pronoun for 3 m. sg.)

וְכָל | וְ means ________________ (1.3a) כָל or כּוֹל means *all, every*.

6.3a Pronunciation

כָּל | כּוֹל is the second most frequent word in the Hebrew Bible, and one whose pronunciation, when there is no dagesh, may be difficult for English speakers. It is common in all four possible forms: construct, absolute, and both with and without the dagesh lene.

	Absolute	Construct
With dagesh	כֹּל כּוֹל	כָּל
Without dagesh	כֹל כוֹל	כָל

Refer back to 4.4a for a discussion of the pronunciation of כ The following section discusses the pronunciation of the vowel.

6.3b Qamets ḥatuf

How can you tell the qamets ḥatuf from the qamets? They look exactly the same, but a qamets ḥatuf is really a short holem. When the ambiguous vowel ָ is in a closed, unaccented syllable, it is a qamets ḥatuf and pronounced close to the "o" in "h**o**ld;" otherwise (and by far the most often), it is qamets and pronounced as in the "a" of "f**a**ther."

	Accented	Unaccented
Open	הָאָרֶץ	שָׁמַע
Closed	מִשָּׁם	וְכָל־בְּנֵי[1] ↑ qamets ḥatuf

---

[1] The maqqef connects the words so closely that they are said to have only one accent as a whole unit; neither syllable of וְכָל is accented; the accent falls on the word after the maqqef, which here is בְּנֵי

The form of כּוֹל with ◌ָ is a construct form, so וְכָל begins a ____________________ ____________________ (5.1b) The dagesh in בְּנֵי is a ____________________ (3.3a)

6.3c Notice the ◌ֵי on the end of this word.

> The occurrence of ◌ֵי at the end of a word is the sign of a masculine plural noun that is in construct relationship with the noun that follows.

Often the addition of a construct ending will cause a change (shortening) of other vowels in the word, as is the case with בְּנֵי

6.3d יִשְׂרָאֵל means ____________________ The final noun of a construct chain is called the ____________________ (5.2) How are the words of the chain linked in English? ____________________ (5.1b) Is the absolute definite? ____________________ (5.2a) So the whole chain is ____________________ Translation of the whole chain (3 members): ____________________

6.3e How does this entire phrase הוּא וְכָל־בְּנֵי יִשְׂרָאֵל relate to the verb? ____________________ (1.6) Note that this is what we call a **compound subject** and it requires a plural verb. Also note that the prepositional phrase עַד־הַיַּרְדֵּן is inserted between the verb and its subject. This construction is frequently found in Hebrew.

6.4 Translation of verse: ____________________

____

6.5 Construct and Absolute

6.5a בֵּן is a masculine singular noun. This form, found in the vocabulary list and in the lexicon, is the absolute form. Nouns are always listed in dictionaries in the singular absolute. In this Lesson you have learned the masculine plural construct form בְּנֵי Obviously there are two other forms of בֵּן which you have not yet seen: the singular construct and the plural absolute.

Here are the four possible forms for בֵּן

	Absolute	Construct
Singular	בֵּן	בֶּן
Plural	בָּנִים	בְּנֵי

For the singular construct, no special ending is added, but vowel changes (shortening) usually take place. Compare the two singular forms of דָּבָר in the box below. In the masculine plural noun, you can tell the difference between construct and absolute by the ending. (There are vowel changes as well.) The plural absolute ending is ________ Consulting the forms of בֵּן above, fill in the endings for the plural forms of דָּבָר in the box.

	Absolute	Construct
Singular	דָּבָר	דְּבַר
Plural	___דְּבָר	___דִּבְר

You have already learned one noun that is almost always used in the masculine plural, though its meaning may be in the singular: אֱלֹהִים Circle the plural ending. (Don't forget that the hireq ִ is part of the ending.) The construct form will be __________ (In this case there are no vowel changes except in the ending itself.)

6.5b Noun endings give information about **N**umber and **G**ender. As a mnemonic device, we will refer to them as endiNGs.

6.6 Extra Grammar

הוּא the third masculine singular independent pronoun has several important functions.

1. הוּא can be one of the elements in a noun sentence. Often the best translation in this case is *it*, or sometimes *that*, *that one*, *he*.

Genesis 24:65 וַיֹּאמֶר הָעֶבֶד הוּא אֲדֹנִי

And the servant said, "He [or that one] is my master."

2. Often הוּא simply emphasizes the subject pronoun of the verb.

Exodus 4:16 וְדִבֶּר־הוּא לְךָ

And he will speak to you.

3. Sometimes הוּא appears between two nouns that form a noun sentence; it is called a copula in this case and provides the same linking function as the verb *to be* in such a sentence, in addition to its emphatic function as in #2.

Deuteronomy 4:35 יהוה הוּא הָאֱלֹהִים

The Lord he is God.

6.7 Assignments:

A. Translate:

Extra Vocabulary: דֶּרֶךְ *way, road, journey*

1 וַיָּבֹא עַד־חֶבְרוֹן Numbers 13:22

2 וַיָּבֹאוּ עַד־חָרָן Genesis 11:31

3 וַיְדַבְּרוּ בְּנֵי יוֹסֵף Joshua 17:14

4 וְלֹא הָלַךְ בְּדֶרֶךְ יהוה 2 Kings 21:22

[בּ is a preposition. See vocabulary section "particles."]

5 וַיֵּלְכוּ וַיָּבֹאוּ אֶל־מֹשֶׁה Numbers 13:26

6 דְּבַר־יהוה אֲשֶׁר הָיָה אֶל־מִיכָה Micah 1:1

7 וַיֹּאמֶר אֵלָיו מֶלֶךְ־יִשְׂרָאֵל 1 Kings 20:40

8 אָמַר יהוה אֱלֹהֵי יִשְׂרָאֵל Exodus 5:1

9 דִּבְרֵי יִרְמְיָהוּ בֶּן־חִלְקִיָּהוּ Jeremiah 1:1

10 וַיִּשְׁמְעוּ אֵלָיו בְּנֵי־יִשְׂרָאֵל Deuteronomy 34:9

11 וַיֹּאמְרוּ אֶל־מֹשֶׁה Exodus 20:19

B. Analyze in chart form:

יָבֹאוּ הָלַךְ וַיְדַבְּרוּ וַיָּבֹא וַיֵּלְכוּ

וַיֹּאמְרוּ אָמַר וַיִּשְׁמְעוּ הָיָה

Genesis 25:5 וַיִּתֵּן אַבְרָהָם אֶת־כָּל־אֲשֶׁר־לוֹ לְיִצְחָק

7.1 Verb Analysis וַיִּתֵּן

7.1a What kind of dagesh is in the י ________________ What kind of dagesh is in the ת ________________

Root	Stem	Form	Person/Gender/Number	Special Features

You should be able to determine immediately the form (1.3b and 1.3c) and the PGN. (1.4c) In so doing you have accounted for וַיִּ How many letters are left? ________ What are they? ________________ [Be sure you take account of the dagesh forte in the תּ] This is the proper number for a Hebrew root, but no Hebrew root ever begins with two identical letters. So the root cannot be תתן

> Whenever a root appears to begin with two identical letters, due to the use of a dagesh forte, the first root letter is actually a נ which has been assimilated to (come to sound like) the second root letter.

The real root here, therefore, is נתן

What is the stem? ________________ (Remember, you have accounted for the dagesh forte by the assimilated נ rule, so this cannot be a Pi`el.)

> A dagesh never does "double duty;" it never stands for more than one consonant at a time.

7.1b Translation of phrase וַיִּתֵּן אַבְרָהָם

What is the relation of these two words? ________________________ (1.6)

Translate the phrase: ________________________

7.2 אֶת־כָּל־אֲשֶׁר־לוֹ

אֶת is the sign of the **definite direct object (DDO)**. It is not translated; it merely indicates that the word or words that follow:

1. are the object of the verb action and
2. are definite.

7.2a When not joined by a maqqef to the following word, the vowel is ֵ rather than ֶ

אֶת־כָּל־ אֵת כָּל־

7.2b כָּל means ________________ (6.3) אֲשֶׁר means ________________ (5.3a)

7.2c לוֹ short as it is, is made up of two parts: וֹ and ל

לְ means *to, for*; and like וְ *and*, it must always be connected with some other element. וֹ = ו at the end of a word, and thus means ________________ (2.9a) So לוֹ means *to him*. ל is also often used to indicate possession, so that לוֹ could mean *his*.

Do not confuse this לוֹ with לֹא or לוֹא *not*.

Notice that this whole phrase is tied together by maqqefs. This indicates close relationship of the words. In this case the whole phrase is the direct object of the verb. (Usually the direct object is only one noun.) This object is also definite. Review what makes a noun definite. (5.2a) These rules apply in determining definiteness for the verb object too. So this accounts for the use of אֶת. In order to make good English of this phrase you must treat it as a noun sentence and add a form of the verb *to be*.

Translation: ________________________

7.3 לְיִצְחָק

לְ at the beginning of a word can mean ________________ (7.2c)

Translation: ________________________

7.4 Translation of verse: ____

____

7.5 Extra Grammar

לְ is used with great frequency. It can be synonymous in meaning with אֶל and the two are often (but not always) interchangeable in grammatical constructions. Two uses of ל are seen in the verse just studied:

1. It is regularly used to indicate possession and is the equivalent of the English verb *have*, in the sense of *own*. בֵּן לוֹ *he has a son*, etc.

2. It often indicates the indirect object of the verb, the one who receives the action of the direct object. Our Lesson sentence consists of:

indirect object [noun + prep.]	⟵ direct object [noun or noun clause]	⟵ subject [noun]	⟵ verb
לְיִצְחָק	אֶת־כָּל־אֲשֶׁר־לוֹ	אַבְרָהָם	וַיִּתֵּן

While in English the preposition before an indirect object is sometimes left out, it will invariably be present in Hebrew. So you can also describe לְיִצְחָק as a prepositional phrase, and יִצְחָק as the object of the preposition.

7.6 Sort the following masculine nouns into the appropriate categories. It is not necessary to be able to translate them. (Note: At this point you are not equipped to recognize construct singular nouns out of context. If the nouns below have no special endiNGs, you may assume they are absolute singular.)

Absolute singular　　Absolute plural　　Construct plural

דְּבָרִים

בֵּן

הָרִים

שְׁנֵי

הַמָּקוֹם

וְהָעֵצִים

עֲצֵי

בְּנֵי

Absolute singular	Absolute plural	Construct plural	
			יָד
			מֶלֶךְ
			אִישׁ
			אֱלֹהֵי
			מְלָכִים
			דִּבְרֵי

7.6a Assignment:

A. Translate:

1 וְיַעֲקֹב נָתַן לְעֵשָׂו לֶחֶם [לֶחֶם *bread, food*] Genesis 25:34

2 אֲשֶׁר־נָתַן אֱלֹהִים לְאַבְרָהָם Genesis 28:4

3 וַיִּשְׁמְעוּ כָל־יִשְׂרָאֵל 1 Kings 3:28

4 וַיִּתֶּן־לוֹ אֶת־רָחֵל Genesis 29:28[1]

5 וַיִּשְׁמְעוּ...אֵת הַדְּבָרִים Jeremiah 26:10

6 וַיֹּאמְרוּ לוֹ Judges 15:13

7 וַיִּשְׁמְעוּ אֶת־דְּבַר יהוה 1 Kings 12:24

1 She was worth 50 shekels of silver or seven sheep plus change.

Remember:

וֹ____ at the end of a word can be either a possessive or an objective pronoun. When attached to a noun, it is possessive; attached to a verb or preposition it is objective.

דִּבְּרוֹ *he spoke it* דְּבָרוֹ *his word*

(As is often the case, there are vowel changes in the word when the suffix is added.)

I. Chart and Translate:

וַיִּתֵּן	וַיֵּלְכוּ	וַיִּשְׁמְעוּ
וַיְדַבְּרוּ	וַיִּתְּנוּ	הָלַךְ
הָיָה	וַיֹּאמְרוּ	וַיָּבוֹאוּ

II. Translate:

כָּל־בְּנֵי יִשְׂרָאֵל	דֶּרֶךְ דָּוִד
אֱלֹהֵי יִשְׂרָאֵל	בֶּן־מֶלֶךְ
בְּנֵי אַבְרָהָם	דַּרְכֵי הַבֵּן
כָּל־מַלְכֵי־יִשְׂרָאֵל	יַד יהוה
דִּבְרֵי מֹשֶׁה	עַם־הָאָרֶץ

1 וַיֵּלֶךְ בְּכָל־הַדֶּרֶךְ אֲשֶׁר־הָלַךְ אָבִיו [אָבִיו *his father*] 1 Kings 21:21

2 וַיֵּלֶךְ בְּכָל־דֶּרֶךְ דָּוִד אָבִיו 2 Kings 22:2

(Note in sentences 1 and 2, the different ways of making the construct chain definite.)

3 וַיִּשְׁמְעוּ אֶת־דִּבְרֵי יהוה 2 Chronicles 11:4

4 וַיִּקְרְאוּ אֶל־לוֹט וַיֹּאמְרוּ לוֹ Genesis 19:5

5 וַיְדַבֵּר אֶת־כָּל־הַדְּבָרִים Genesis 20:8

6 וַיִּשְׁמַע אֶת־דִּבְרֵי בְנֵי־לָבָן Genesis 31:1

7 יהוה אֲשֶׁר עָשָׂה אֶת־מֹשֶׁה וְאֶת־אַהֲרֹן 1 Samuel 12:6

8 וַיָּבֹאוּ עַד־חָרָן וַיֵּשְׁבוּ שָׁם Genesis 11:31

9 וַיֵּלֶךְ בְּדַרְכֵי מַלְכֵי יִשְׂרָאֵל 2 Chronicles 28:2

10 וַיִּשְׁמַע מֹשֶׁה אֶת־הָעָם Numbers 11:10

11 וַיְדַבֵּר אֱלֹהִים אֵת כָּל־הַדְּבָרִים Exodus 20:1

12 וַיִּשְׁמַע שְׁמוּאֵל אֵת כָּל־דִּבְרֵי הָעָם 1 Samuel 8:21

13 רָאָה יַעֲקֹב אֶת־רָחֵל Genesis 29:10

14 אַבְרָם יָשַׁב בְּאֶרֶץ־כְּנָעַן Genesis 13:12

15 וַיִּשְׁמְעוּ אֵלָיו בְּנֵי יִשְׂרָאֵל Numbers 34:9

16 לֹא־לָקַח יִשְׂרָאֵל אֶת־אֶרֶץ מוֹאָב Judges 11:15

17 אֲשֶׁר לָקַח מִיַּד יְהוֹאָחָן 2 Kings 13:25

18 וַיְדַבְּרוּ אֵלָיו אֵת כָּל־דִּבְרֵי יוֹסֵף אֲשֶׁר דִּבֶּר Genesis 45:27

19 וַיִּשְׁמַע פַּרְעֹה אֶת־הַדָּבָר Exodus 2:15

III. Translate English to Hebrew:

the kings of Israel	in the way of Israel	all the words of Moses
the son of the king	God of Abraham	the ways of God
to the people of Israel		

1. I am the king of Israel.
2. And Moses spoke to the people all which God said to him.
3. The LORD did not listen to the sons of David.
4. And all Israel came to the Jordan.
5. God gave a king to the people.
6. And he went to the king who was in Israel.

Jeremiah 16:21 וְיָדְעוּ כִּי־שְׁמִי יהוה

8.1 Verb Analysis וְיָדְעוּ

8.1a What does an initial וְ mean? __________ (1.3a) Is this a vav conversive? ______ (1.3b)

8.1b You need to locate the root, and you have some help:

> וּ___ is a plural verb ending, and וּ___ rarely ends anything except a verb form.

8.1c Since this is not a vav conversive form, the chance that י is part of the root, rather than the prefix pronoun, is greatly increased. What consonants are thus the probable root? __________

Root	Stem	Form	Person/Gender/Number	Special Features

What is the stem? __________ (4.2a) What is the form? __________ (4.2a)

You will remember that the third person masculine singular affix has no pronoun element at the end, but that the other pronoun subjects will be written at the end of the affix forms. In this case, the simple ending וּ___ gives us the third person plural, both masculine and feminine. Compare this third person common plural affix form (3 c. pl.) with the 3 m. pl. prefix form:

Affix Form	Prefix Form
ידע וּ	י שמע וּ
root; affix pronoun (וּ)	prefix pronoun (י); root; prefix complement (וּ)

8.1d An affix form is normally translated in the past tense in English. (4.2b)

> An initial ו used with an affix form verb forms a construction often best rendered by the English future tense. For convenient reference we will call this construction the **vav reversive**.

On the chart indicate this with "vav rev." in the Special Features column.

יָדַע means ______ Translation of the verb: ______

8.1e Note the small vertical line to the left of the vowel under the י It is called a **meteg** and indicates a slight hesitation in pronunciation between the vowel and the following consonant. The meteg keeps the vowel from being a qamets ḥatuf (6.3c) and shows that the following shewa is a vocal shewa.

8.2 כִּי means ______

8.3 שְׁמִי יהוה

ִי at the end of a noun is normally the first person singular suffix.

Suffixes are possessive or object pronouns. (2.9b) שֵׁם is a noun meaning ______

A suffix attached to a noun is a possessive pronoun.

שְׁמִי means *my name.* Notice that the vowels of the noun change when a possessive suffix is added.

8.3a יהוה means ______ The two word phrase means ______ (2.10b)

8.4 Translation of verse: ______

______

8.5 Vowel changes

You have seen that vowel changes (shortening) can occur under the following circumstances:

1. a masculine singular noun is in construct (5.1c) בֵּן ⟵ בֶּן
2. a masculine plural noun is in constuct (6.3d) בָּנִים ⟵ בְּנֵי
3. a maqqef ties a word to another word (7.2a) אֵת ⟵ אֶת־
4. a suffix is added to a word (8.3) שֵׁם ⟵ שְׁמִי

8.6 For each ו in the words below, tell whether the ו is a plain conjunction, vav conversive, vav reversive, possessive suffix, object suffix, prefix complement, affix pronoun, or part of the root of the word.

וְהָאֱלֹהִים	יהוה
חֲמֹרוֹ	וַיֹּאמֶר
יוֹם	וַיַּחֲבֹשׁ
לוֹ	הוּא
וְכָל	וַיֵּדְעוּ
וַיֹּאמְרוּ	יוֹסֵף
נְעָרָיו	שָׁמְעוּ
אֵלָיו	בְּנוֹ

8.7 Assignment:

A. Translate the following. From now on, a few sentences will be marked with an asterisk. These have elements that are more "challenging." (In other words, they're hard.) Do try to figure them out before looking them up.

1 דָּוִד לֹא יָדָע 1 Kings 1:11

2 לֹא יָדְעוּ אֶת־יהוה 1 Samuel 2:12

3 וַיָּבֹאוּ כָל־עַם הָאָרֶץ 2 Kings 11:18

4 הוּא אֱלֹהֵי הָאֱלֹהִים Deuteronomy 10:17

*5 וְהָיָה יהוה לִי לֵאלֹהִים Genesis 28:21

*6 אֲנִי יהוה הוּא שְׁמִי Isaiah 42:8

7 כִּי־לֹא־מֶלֶךְ יִשְׂרָאֵל הוּא 1 Kings 22:33

*8 וַיֵּדְעוּ כָל־הָעָם וְכָל־יִשְׂרָאֵל 2 Samuel 3:37

9 וְאָמְרוּ אֶל־כָּל־אִישׁ יִשְׂרָאֵל Deuteronomy 27:14

10 וַיִּתֵּן יהוה לְיִשְׂרָאֵל אֶת־כָּל־הָאָרֶץ Joshua 21:43

11 בְּנֵי־יִשְׂרָאֵל לֹא־שָׁמְעוּ אֵלַי Exodus 6:12 [אֵלַי ⟵ אֶל + 1 c. sg. suffix]

Genesis 42:23 וְהֵם לֹא יָדְעוּ כִּי שֹׁמֵעַ יוֹסֵף

9.1 וְהֵם Initial וְ means ________ הֵם means *they*.

הֵם is the 3 m. pl. independent pronoun.

9.2a לֹא יָדְעוּ | לֹא means ________ (4.1)

9.2b Verb Analysis יָדְעוּ

Root	Stem	Form	Person/Gender/Number	Special Features

What tense will you use in translation? ________ (4.2b)

Translation of the first phrase: ________

9.3 כִּי שֹׁמֵעַ יוֹסֵף

כִּי means ________

שֹׁמֵעַ has an "extra" vowel at the end to facilitate pronunciation; it is called ________ (5.4)

9.3a Verb Analysis שֹׁמֵעַ

Root	Stem	Form	Person/Gender/Number	Special Features

שמע means ________ What is the stem? ________ (1.4a)

Is the form prefix? ________ Is the form affix? ________ (It is useful when determining form to ask these two questions first.)

In the Qal stem, holem וֹ or ˙ after the first root letter indicates the **participle** form.

You may write "participle" in the Form column. Participles function as nouns and adjectives as well as verbs. Participles have noun endiNGs. Where there is no extra endiNG, the participle is masculine singular, as it is here. Participles have no person (no pronouns for 1st, 2nd, or 3rd person), but they modify nouns and pronouns. In the PGN column write "m. sg."

9.3b Many students mistakenly believe that all participles in English end in "-ing," and conversely that all words ending in "-ing" are participles. Neither statement is true. Because participles may be used in verb clauses or as nouns or adjectives, the appropriate translation must make use of syntactical clues and context.

Let us first consider our Lesson phrase שֹׁמֵעַ יוֹסֵף

יוֹסֵף is a name, *Joseph*. The participle modifies the noun Joseph. In this simple phrase the participle provides the action, the verbal component. You can translate: *Joseph was listening* or *Joseph is listening*. The tense will be decided by the main verb of the verse. Other possible translations exist for this construction, but this will suffice for the moment.

Sometimes the participle is used in a construction as a noun. A hypothetical phrase might be:

יוֹסֵף הַשֹּׁמֵעַ דִּבֵּר *Joseph, the listener, spoke*
Joseph, the one who heard, spoke
Joseph, who was listening, spoke

Again, the larger context and syntax of the verse would help us decide on the translation (and a more exact description of the function of the participle). Whether used as verbal action or as a noun, the **participle** always involves someone doing something. Frequently you will be helped by having a noun or pronoun in the immediate vicinity of the participle, and you will remember this rule.

The participle never stands for the action of the verb in the abstract.

That is, for example, the participle of שׁמע would never mean the act of listening as in *listening is an art*.

9.4 Translation of verse: ______________________________

____

9.5 Extra Grammar

To identify the Qal participle, you must look for the holem after the first root letter. Remember, this vowel can be written two ways in Hebrew: וֹ and ֹ Thus two spellings are possible for the Qal participle. For example:

defectiva	**plene**
שֹׁמֵעַ	שׁוֹמֵעַ

9.5a For hollow verbs (verbs which are missing the middle root letter in the vav conversive form), there is an irregular participle form. In this case the 3 m. sg. affix and the masculine singular participle are identical in the Qal: בָּא can be either the 3 m. sg. affix or the m. sg. participle.

Three hints can help you decide on the form used:

1. You have a participle if the ambiguous form is combined with another participle.

Joshua 6:1 אֵין יוֹצֵא וְאֵין בָּא

ambiguous regular

None went out and none came in.

2. You have a participle if the ambiguous form is combined with an independent pronoun or a pronoun attached to הִנֵּה (See Lesson 10)

Exodus 3:13 [אֲנִי←אָנֹכִי] אָנֹכִי בָא אֶל־בְּנֵי יִשְׂרָאֵל

I am coming to the children of Israel.

3. You have a participle if the definite article is attached to the ambiguous form, since the affix cannot be combined with the definite article.

Psalms 118:26 [בָּרוּךְ *blessed* (adj.)] בָּרוּךְ הַבָּא בְּשֵׁם יהוה

Blessed is he who comes in the name of the Lord.

9.6 Assignments:

A. For lessons 9-12, learn words 51-75 from the vocabulary list.

B. Analyze the following verbs:

יוֹדֵעַ וְאָמַר הַנֹּתֵן וְשָׁמַע הֹלֵךְ

C. Translate:

Be able to tell whether בָּא is a participle or an affix form in the verses below.

1 אֲנִי הֹלֵךְ אֵלָיו 2 Samuel 12:23

2 וְשָׁמַע הַשֹּׁמֵעַ וְאָמַר 2 Samuel 17:9

3 וַיָּמָת יוֹסֵף...וְכֹל הַדּוֹר [דּוֹר *generation*] 6.1a [וַיָּמָת] Exodus 1:6

4 וְלֹא־בָא שְׁמוּאֵל הַגִּלְגָּל 1 Samuel 13:8

*5 כִּי זֶה הַיּוֹם אֲשֶׁר נָתַן יהוה אֶת־סִיסְרָא בְּיָדֶךָ Judges 4:14
[בְּיָדֶךָ *into your hand*]

6 הוּא־בָא עַד־לֶחִי Judges 15:14

7 דּוֹר הֹלֵךְ וְדוֹר בָּא Qohelet 1:4

8 זֶה־הַיּוֹם עָשָׂה יהוה Psalms 118:24

9 בָּא אִישׁ הָאֱלֹהִים 2 Kings 8:7

10 כִּי־יוֹדֵעַ יהוה דֶּרֶךְ צַדִּיקִים [צַדִּיקִים *righteous ones*] Psalms 1:6

11 הֵם יָצְאוּ אֶת־הָעִיר Genesis 44:4

*12 וַיִּקְרָא שֵׁם הָעִיר כְּשֵׁם בְּנוֹ Genesis 4:17

Genesis 27:18 וַיָּבֹא אֶל־אָבִיו וַיֹּאמֶר אָבִי וַיֹּאמֶר הִנֶּנִּי

10.1 וַיָּבֹא אֶל־אָבִיו

10.1a Verb Analysis וַיָּבֹא (1.3b, 1.3c, 6.1a)

Root	Stem	Form	Person/Gender/Number	Special Features

10.1b אֶל means ______________ In אָבִיו | אָב is a noun meaning *father*. The ו____ at the end of the word is a ________________ meaning ______________ (2.9b) What kind of suffix is this? ________________ אָבִיו means *his father*. Note the extra י connecting the noun and suffix. אָב has some irregular forms, and is one of only two nouns which require this extra connecting link before a suffix.

Translate the whole first clause: ____

10.2 וַיֹּאמֶר אָבִי

10.2a Verb Analysis וַיֹּאמֶר (1.4)

Root	Stem	Form	Person/Gender/Number	Special Features

10.2b אָבִי You should recognize the same noun you had just above: ________________ Again there is a suffix on the word. What are the components of the suffix? ________ Which person, gender, and number is it? ____________ (8.3) Note that this time there is no connecting י between the noun and the suffix.

אָבִי means ________________________

10.2c Biblical Hebrew does not use quotation marks (or any other familiar punctuation marks). Sometimes it is difficult to tell where a speech begins. In this case, אָבִי is <u>what</u> he said, not the noun subject of the verb. This is clear from the larger context of the story. This context is the only clue you will have in deciding the structure of similar verses (unless you later memorize the whole accentual system).

10.2d Notice the ֑ under אָבִ֑י This mark, called **atnaḥ**, indicates a break in the verse or sentence, equivalent to the break we mark with a period or semi-colon. It indicates that the next word begins a new phrase, and it is one of the few helps you will have in punctuating a Hebrew verse in the Bible.

10.3 וַיֹּאמֶר הִנֶּנִּי

10.3a The new phrase begins with a familiar verb. וַיֹּאמֶר means ______________

10.3b הִנֶּנִּי

הִנֵּה is a word that cannot be classed as either noun or verb. It is called a **predicator of existence**, emphasizing presence; we have no comparable word function in English. *Here* and *now* are both acceptable translations for beginning students to use for this word, though you will need broader understanding of the syntactical usage of this word later. When suffixes are added to this word — which happens frequently — the final ה is lost. נִי____ or נִּי____ is a first person singular suffix. So הִנֶּנִּי is made up of two components; it can be translated *here I am*. Compare this word with אָבִי which also has a first person singular suffix. Can you think of a reason why the suffixes are different? Nouns and most prepositions take ִי__ Verbs, particles like הִנֵּה and a few prepositions take נִי____

10.4 Translation of verse: ______________________________

____

10.5 Assignment:

A. Translate and note how the function of the word הִנֵּה changes in the various verses.

1 הִנֵּה בְנֵי־הַמֶּלֶךְ בָּאוּ 2 Samuel 13:35

*2 הִנְנִי־בָא Zechariah 2:14

*3 וְעַתָּה הִנְנִי הוֹלֵךְ לְעַמִּי Numbers 24:14

4 הִנְנִי נֹתֵן לוֹ אֶת־בְּרִיתִי [בְּרִית covenant] Numbers 25:12

5 וַיֹּאמֶר מֹשֶׁה מֹשֶׁה וַיֹּאמֶר הִנֵּנִי Exodus 3:4

6 וַיָּבֹא יַעֲקֹב אֶל־יִצְחָק אָבִיו Genesis 35:27

7 וְהִנֵּה אִישׁ מִבְּנֵי יִשְׂרָאֵל בָּא Numbers 25:6

I. Chart and translate the following verbs:

וְדִבְּרוּ	שָׁמְעוּ	יָדְעוּ
נָתְנוּ	וְהָלְכוּ	אָמְרוּ
יָדַע	בָּאוּ	וְיָדַע
הוֹלֵךְ	אֹמֵר	שׁוֹמֵעַ
וַיִּשְׁלַח	נֹתֵן	בָּא

II. Translate:

1 יהוה הוּא הָאֱלֹהִים 1 Kings 18:39

*2 וּמֹשֶׁה עָלָה אֶל־הָאֱלֹהִים וַיִּקְרָא אֵלָיו יהוה מִן־הָהָר Exodus 19:3
(For help with וּמֹשֶׁה see 1.3a and for הָהָר see 4.5b)

3 אֶרֶץ כְּנַעַן אֲשֶׁר־אֲנִי נֹתֵן לִבְנֵי יִשְׂרָאֵל Numbers 13:2

*4 וְגַם הִנֵּה־הוּא יֹצֵא Exodus 4:14

5 וַיֹּאמְרוּ לֹא־הוּא Jeremiah 5:12

6 הוּא מֹשֶׁה וְאַהֲרֹן Exodus 6:27

7 הוּא הַלֶּחֶם אֲשֶׁר נָתַן יהוה [לֶחֶם *bread, food*] Exodus 16:15

8 לַיהוה הָאָרֶץ Psalms 24:1

9 הַלֶּחֶם אֲשֶׁר־הוּא אוֹכֵל Genesis 39:6

*10 וְאֵלָיו הוּא נֹשֵׂא אֶת־נַפְשׁוֹ Deuteronomy 24:15

11 כִּי־יָדַע כָּל־יִשְׂרָאֵל 2 Samuel 17:10

12 כִּי אֶת־כָּל־הָאָרֶץ אֲשֶׁר־אַתָּה רֹאֶה לְךָ אֶתְּנֶנָּה Genesis 13:15
[לְךָ אֶתְּנֶנָּה *to you I will give (it)*]

*13 אֱלֹהִים עִמְּךָ בְּכֹל אֲשֶׁר־אַתָּה עֹשֶׂה Genesis 21:22
[2 m. sg. object pronoun + עִם ⟵ עִמְּךָ]

III. Translate from English to Hebrew:

I am going	they entered	and he knew
he is walking	and they will know	

1. And he said, "My father, here I am."
2. The LORD is God. (two ways of saying this)
3. The earth is mine.
4. Here was the man of God coming on his way.
5. For my name is in (over) all the earth.
6. And God gave a covenant to Israel.

Genesis 12:5 וַיֵּצְאוּ לָלֶכֶת אַרְצָה כְּנַעַן וַיָּבֹאוּ אַרְצָה כְּנָעַן

II.1 Verb Analysis וַיֵּצְאוּ

Root	Stem	Form	Person/Gender/Number	Special Features

How do you determine the root? ________________ (3.1) Where is the missing letter? ________________ What will it be? ________________ (3.1) What are the components of the PGN? ________________

Translation: ________________

II.2 לָלֶכֶת

II.2a You need to separate at least one letter from the word to find the root. But there are two possibilities. An initial ל can be a preposition meaning *to, for*, but ת___ is frequently a special ending as well. In this case, both are present. Why can you eliminate ללך immediately as the root? (7.1a) Whenever לכ is left, the root is הלך

II.2b Verb Analysis לָלֶכֶת

Root	Stem	Form	Person/Gender/Number	Special Features

As in English, *to* before a verb form usually indicates the infinitive. ת___ is a special infinitive ending for some verbs. As in English, Hebrew infinitives have no PGN. What is the stem? ____________ In the Special Features column, put "preposition, ל" Are any letters left unaccounted for? ____________

II.3 אַרְצָה כְּנַעַן

אֶרֶץ means ____________ כְּנַעַן means *Canaan.*

Notice the ה‍ָ on the end of ארץ

> An extra, final ה ָ on a noun can be added to denote motion toward a place, and is called a ה- **directive**. It is usually translated *to* or *toward.*

What is the relationship of אַרְצָה to כְּנַעַן ______________________ (5.1b)

Is כְּנַעַן definite?________ (5.2a) Is the chain definite or indefinite? ____________

Note that the ה- directive can be placed on the construct noun just as any other preposition could be placed on the front of that noun.

Translate the phrase: ______________________________

II.4 Verb Analysis וַיָּבֹאוּ

Root	Stem	Form	Person/Gender/Number	Special Features

II.5 Translation of the whole verse: ______________________________

____

II.6 Assignments:

A. Analyze the following verbs:

וַיָּבֹא　　יֵצְאוּ　　וַיֵּצֵא　　וַיֵּלְכוּ

B. Translate:

*1 וַיֵּלְכוּ וַיָּבֹאוּ הָהָרָה [הָהָרָה is composed of three elements] Joshua 2:22

2 וַיֵּצֵא לָלֶכֶת לְדַרְכּוֹ Judges 19:27

3 יָצְאוּ מִן־הָעָם Exodus 16:27

4 וַיָּבֹא עַד־הַיַּרְדֵּן וִיהוּדָה בָּא הַגִּלְגָּלָה 2 Samuel 19:16
[Read וִיהוּדָה as if it were written וְ + יְהוּדָה]

5 וַיֵּלְכוּ בְנֵי־רְאוּבֵן...לָלֶכֶת אֶל־אֶרֶץ הַגִּלְעָד Joshua 22:9

6 וְכָל־הָעָם יָצְאוּ 2 Samuel 18:4

1 Kings 18:39 וַיַּרְא כָּל־הָעָם וַיִּפְּלוּ עַל־פְּנֵיהֶם

12.1 Verb Analysis וַיַּרְא

Root	Stem	Form	Person/Gender/Number	Special Features

Only the root is a problem. Under what letter do you look for the clue to the missing letter? ______________________

> When any vowel other than ֵ (tsere) or ָ (qamets) appears under the prefix pronoun, the missing letter is at the end of the root and is always ה

12.2 כָּל־הָעָם

הָעָם means ______________________ (4.5b) The relationship of this phrase to the first verb is ______________________ Note that *people* as a collective noun regularly takes a singular verb in Hebrew, rather than a plural verb.

12.3 Verb Analysis וַיִּפְּלוּ

Root	Stem	Form	Person/Gender/Number	Special Features

What rule do you use to find the root? ______________________ (7.1a) You may be wondering why the "missing letter" rules weren't used here, why the root isn't פלה which is a rare, but perfectly good, Biblical Hebrew root. The missing letter rules come into play only when a letter is completely missing. Assimilated letters leave a "footprint" behind by means of the dagesh forte. Always check for such a "footprint dagesh" before trying the missing letter rules.[1]

נפל means *fall.*

---

[1] The missing letter rules can be found in Lessons 3.1, 6.1a, and 12.1.

12.3a We said in 12.2 that עָם regularly takes a singular verb. It is also not unusual for it to take a plural verb. Such mixing of singular and plural within a verse is not at all uncommon in Biblical Hebrew.

12.4 פְּנֵיהֶם

הֶם____ is the 3 m. pl. possessive or objective suffix.

Compare with the independent subject pronoun in 9.1. When you remove the suffix, you are left with פְּנֵי Notice the similarity to בְּנֵי in 6.3c. The absolute form of בְּנֵי is ______________________ So the absolute form of פְּנֵי will have the endiNG ________

פָּנִים means *face, faces*. Like אֱלֹהִים (2.4) <u>almost</u> without exception it is the plural of this noun which is used in Hebrew.

12.5 Translate the verse: ____

____

12.6 Extra Grammar

פָּנִים is frequently used idiomatically. This word in its construct form פְּנֵי combines most frequently with the preposition לְ ⟶ לִפְנֵי Literally this combination means *to (the) faces of.* In its present compound form this word is equivalent to our preposition *before* or *in the presence of.*

Exodus 6:12 וַיְדַבֵּר מֹשֶׁה לִפְנֵי יהוה

And Moses spoke in the presence of the Lord*.*

It is common in Hebrew to combine prepositions to create new prepositions. Thus the preposition מִן (3.4b) can be combined with לִפְנֵי to form a new preposition meaning <u>*away from*</u> *(the presence of)*:

Genesis 4:16 וַיֵּצֵא קַיִן מִלִּפְנֵי יהוה

And Cain went out from the presence of the Lord*.*

12.7 Assignments:

A. Analyze these verbs:

וַיִּרְאוּ   רָאָה   וַיָּבֹא   וַיְדַבְּרוּ   יוֹצֵא

B. Translate:

1 וַיַּרְא־שָׁם אִשָּׁה Judges 16:1

2 וַיְדַבְּרוּ לִפְנֵי מֹשֶׁה Numbers 36:1

3 וַיָּבֹא אֶל־הַר הָאֱלֹהִים חֹרֵבָה Exodus 3:1

4 וּשְׁמוּאֵל רָאָה אֶת־שָׁאוּל 1 Samuel 9:17

5 וַיִּרְאוּ אֵת אֱלֹהֵי יִשְׂרָאֵל Exodus 24:10

6 וַיִּפְּלוּ עַל־פְּנֵיהֶם אָרְצָה Judges 13:20

*7 כִּי־הוּא יוֹצֵא וָבָא לִפְנֵיהֶם 1 Samuel 18:16

8 וַיֵּצֵא יוֹסֵף מִלִּפְנֵי פַרְעֹה Genesis 41:46

9 וַיִּפֹּל...לִפְנֵי אֲרוֹן יהוה [אֲרוֹן *ark of the covenant*] Joshua 7:6

*10 וַיִּרְאוּ הַשֹּׁמְרִים אִישׁ יוֹצֵא מִן־הָעִיר Judges 1:24

Review and Drill 4

I. Referring to the Lesson if necessary, write the Qal prefix with vav conversive, 3 m. sg. and 3 m. pl., for each of the following verbs.

	3 m. sg.	3 m. pl.
אמר (1)	__ __ __ ____	____ __ __ __ ____
הלך (3)	__ __ ____	____ __ __ ____
שׁמע	__ __ __ ____	____ __ __ __ ____
בוא (6)	__ __ __ ____	____ __ __ __ ____
נתן (7)	__ __ ____	____ __ __ ____
ידע (3)	__ __ ____	____ __ __ ____
ראה (12)	__ __ ____	____ __ __ ____
יצא (3)	__ __ ____	____ __ __ ____

These verb forms are at the top of the list in frequency, and are the key to analyzing most of the other regular and irregular prefix forms. Memorize them!

II. Write the Qal affix 3 m. sg. and 3 c. pl. for the following verbs. If you need help, for 3 m. sg. see 4.2a; for 3 c. pl. see 8.1c. The Qal affix is much more regular than the prefix. All you need here are the two sample forms listed to obtain the vowel pattern.

	3 m. sg.	3 c. pl.
אמר	__ __ __	____ __ __ __
הלך	__ __ __	____ __ __ __
שׁמע	__ __ __	____ __ __ __
נתן	__ __ __	____ __ __ __
ידע	__ __ __	____ __ __ __
יצא	__ __ __	____ __ __ __

Note that יצא uses ָ under the second root letter rather than ַ in the 3 m. sg. This will be the case for every strong verb whose third root letter is either א or ה

III. For דבר write the Pi'el prefix 3 m. sg. __ __ __ 3 m. pl. ____ __ __ __ ____ and the affix 3 m. sg. __ __ __ 3 c. pl. ____ __ __ __ This verb also is used over 1000 times in the Hebrew Bible, and these are its most frequent forms. Memorize them.

IV. Write the Qal m. sg. participle form (9.3a) for:

נתן אמר הלך ידע (5.4) שמע בוא (9.5a)

V. Make up 20 construct chains using the following information:

Construct forms:

שֵׁם אֲבִי אֶרֶץ בֶּן דְּבַר עַם מֶלֶךְ אֱלֹהֵי

Absolute forms:

דָּוִד אָב יִשְׂרָאֵל עַם מֶלֶךְ יהוה אֱלֹהִים

Identify each chain as definite or indefinite.

VI. Turn to your Hebrew Bible. Read Exodus 6:12-13 aloud. You will notice that some of the letters look slightly different in print from our script, and you will see many dots and lines in addition to the vowels. These are part of an elaborate accent system devised by the Masoretes. Many of these need not concern you at this stage. Each of these signs marks the syllable of the word which you must accent — as you read the verses aloud, check to see if you are accenting the proper syllable. Two marks are useful to learn at this stage: ֑ **atnaḥ** occurs at the main pause in almost every verse in the Bible, roughly in the middle. You can think of it as equivalent to a period, semi-colon, or important comma. (10.2d) Locate the atnaḥ in both verses here, and read them again with a pause at the atnaḥ. The final accent in a verse, usually on the last word, is ֽ called **silluq**, and is followed by ׃ **sof passuq**, marking the end of the verse.

verse 12: שְׂפָתָֽיִם׃

verse 13: מִצְרָֽיִם׃

Translate the verses. Vocabulary you need:

saying (made up of what two elements?)	לֵאמֹר
how?	אֵיךְ
to bring forth	לְהוֹצִיא
and he charged them	וַיְצַוֵּם
uncircumcised lips	עֲרַל שְׂפָתַיִם

You have been learning various forms of the verb in these first 12 Lessons. You have learned how to abstract a root, how to conjugate various roots in specific PGNs by changing vowels, adding letters, and so forth. You have expanded the pattern you learned with וַיֹּאמֶר and שָׁמַע to other verbs, for example, so that at this point you should be able to parse almost any 3 m. sg. Qal prefix or affix verb in the language. But you may feel at sea when it comes to larger patterns of the verb; there are still stems, forms, and PGNs you have not studied. The following paragraphs will give you an overview of the verbal system to sustain you while allowing your grasp of the forms to grow more slowly.

Roots: All of the Semitic languages build on triconsonantal and biconsonantal roots. There is disagreement as to whether the two letter or the three letter root is more primary in the emergence of these languages. Though many common words have only two letters, and cannot be traced back to three letter roots, all verbal roots are considered to have three letters, and must be sought in the lexicon under the hypothetical triliteral root. The "missing letter" verbs represent three types of verbs where only two strong letters are present. In some instances there is a strong case for arguing their derivation from three letters; in other cases there is not.

Each of the "missing letter" classes has its own designation. Verbs with the pattern of בּוֹא are called **hollow** verbs, because of the disappearing middle letter. Another way to describe the verbs is to identify the place where the weak letter occurs by number, and then the weak letter: 1st י means "a verb with י in the first position." 3rd ה means "a verb with ה in the third position." An older system accomplishes the same thing by using a paradigm verb פָּעַל in its designations. Any verb can be described by using פ ע and ל as equivalent to 1, 2, 3.

3	2	1
ל	ע	פ
ב	שׁ	י

In ישׁב the י occurs in the פ position, שׁ in the ע position, and ב in the ל position. ישׁב falls into the class of פ/י (peh-yod) verbs. Other weak classes include ע/ו (ayin-vav) and ל/ה (lamed-heh). In this book the former system (1st י etc.) is used; however many paradigm charts use the older system, and you should understand this terminology as well.

Stems: Also characteristic of Semitic languages is the modification of the root meaning of verbs by the addition of letters (more properly, morphemes) at the beginning or within the word. The modification patterns are similar within the Semitic language group, but Hebrew uses only four of the "families" of stems. These modifications are identified in two ways: descriptively and with an invented name. For example, the most basic stem, closest to the root itself, we can describe as having no augment, only a set of characteristic vowels in each of its forms; or we can call it **Qal**, which is the name given this stem by classical grammarians of the Middle Ages. Qal is an appropriate name for this stem since it means "light," and was given to the pattern that had no additions. The other stem names were derived by these same grammarians by using the sound of the 3 m. sg. affix form of a sample verb in each family of modifications. Unfortunately the verb they chose for this honor was <u>not</u> a regular verb; it was פָּעַל and the ע cannot take a dagesh. This meant that, while the names bear a relation to regular verbs in some stems, the names for the family in which the middle root letter is doubled are of little aid to the student. However, the system took hold and is now part of the shorthand terminology needed in studying Hebrew. Here is how the system works:

Stem Name		Description	Meaning change	Regular verb example
פָּעַל	**Qal**	simple stem	basic	פָּקַד
פִּעֵל	**Pi`el**	doubled middle root letter - in sample verb, doubling can't take place, so the vowel before ע is often lengthened	intensive, denominative, privative	פִּקֵּד
פֻּעַל	Pu`al	doubled middle root letter ֻ under 1st root letter	intensive passive	פֻּקַּד
הִפְעִיל	**Hif`il**	ה added before root	causative	הִפְקִיד
הָפְעַל	Hof`al	ה + ֻ or ָ following	passive causitive	הָפְקַד
נִפְעַל	**Nif`al**	נ sound added before root	passive, reflexive occurs most for verbs used basically in Qal	נִפְקַד

Stems related to the Pi`el system

הִתְפַּעֵל	Hitpa'el	prefixed ה + infixed ת and doubled middle root letter	reflexive, passive, iterative	הִתְפַּקֵּד
פֹּלֵל	Pol`el (+ Pol`al)	These are rather infrequent;		
הִתְפֹּלֵל	Hitpol`el	occur with verbs having		
פִּלְפֵּל	Pilp`el	only two strong letters		

You have studied verbs only in the Qal and Pi`el systems so far, and will not be studying the Hif`il or Nif`al systematically for some time yet. However, you should memorize the material in this chart now, especially if you are studying Biblical passages while learning grammar. Although the various stems are usually identified with specific meaning changes from the Qal, some things must be remembered about the whole system:

1. Not every pattern is complete. Very few verbs in Biblical Hebrew occur in every stem.
2. Not every verb meaning seems to "fit" every stem in which it occurs. So, for example, although the Hif`il stem generally seems to yield a causative or transitive meaning, it does not always. And of course, the subtleties of meaning of the various stems may be lost in translation.

One further problem in terminology: the modification of the root system which is so marked a characteristic of Semitic languages is quite variously named. Besides "stems," this same phenomenon is sometimes termed theme, conjugation, or pattern.

Forms: To use the term "form" for this part of the verb classification scheme admittedly is not precise. The stem modifications just described could as easily be called forms as the patterns about to be described. Most often, however, "form" is used by grammarians in describing the various patterns which result when a verb is conjugated with a subject pronoun within a stem system. In Hebrew there are five of these forms:

affix prefix imperative participle infinitive

Attention has so far been devoted primarily to the prefix and affix forms. Notice that we do not say that the prefix and affix are present or past tenses, but only that we translate them in certain situations as English present or past tenses. Hebrew (and other Semitic languages) in the classical period did not use a tense system; rather the prefix and affix represent aspects of action.

Prefix forms without vav conversive presented ongoing, incomplete action.

Prefix forms with vav conversive presented completed action, temporal sequence, or result.

Affix forms presented completed action or description of state or condition.

The practical differences between the Hebrew system and our own must be absorbed. The prefix and affix forms cover a wide range of tenses in English, not always neatly divided between the two forms in Hebrew:

שָׁמַע	can mean	*he heard*	
		he has heard	completed actions
		he had heard	

יִשְׁמַע	can mean	*he hears, he is hearing* *he will hear* *he will have heard* *he would hear* (constantly)	on-going actions
אָהֵב	can mean	*he loved* *he had loved*	completed action
		he loves *he would have loved*	describing a state of being

The **vav conversive** with the prefix form was originally a separate form of the verb, a preterite conveying completed action. Before the classical Biblical period, however, this form had fallen together with the prefix form, so that for regular verbs, the prefix form is the same with or without the vav conversive. Hollow verbs and 3rd ה verbs have differences between the prefix form alone and the prefix form with vav conversive attached. Students should bear in mind that this form, like the other prefix and affix forms, has a broad range of translational possibilities because of syntactic variations.

The **vav reversive** arose by analogy to the vav conversive forms, and does not represent an originally separate aspect. While any ◌ַ ו can be identified as a vav conversive, not every וְ is a vav reversive. Remember that:

1. vav reversive occurs only with the affix.
2. vav reversive has no unique marker. וְ with an affix form can also be "plain vav."

As is often the case, the context will give indications of which translation is to be preferred.

Identify the stem (Qal, Pi`el, Nif`al, Hif`il, or Hitpa`el) of each verb below and the root:

Root	Stem	Verb	Root	Stem	Verb
		יֵֽדְעוּ			נֶאֱחַז
		הִתְבָּֽרְכוּ			יְחַלֵּק
		וַיִּשָּׂא			שִׁלַּח
		יָלַד			שִׁבְּרוּ
		נִשְׁמְרוּ			הִתְהַלֵּךְ
		שָֽׁמְרוּ			הִקְטִירוּ

Give a possible translation for each of the augmented forms:

ברך *bless*	הִתְבָּֽרְכוּ	______
	נִבְרְכוּ	______
שבר *break*	שִׁבֵּר	______
קטר *burn*	הִקְטִירוּ	______
שפך *pour out*	נִשְׁפַּךְ	______
לבש *dress*	הִלְבִּישׁ	______
	נִלְבַּשׁ	______
בוא *come*	הֵבִיא	______
בנה *build*	נִבְנָה	______
	הִתְבַּנָּה	______
	בִּנָּה	______

וַיֹּאמֶר הִנְנִי כִּי קָרָאתָ לִי 1 Samuel 3:8

13.1 וַיֹּאמֶר means ______________

13.2 הִנְנִי means ______________ (10.3b) נִי_ is a ______________ meaning ______________ What is the relationship between the first two words of this verse? ______________ (10.2c) After וַיֹּאמֶר or וַיְדַבֵּר you must learn to watch for **direct speech**, as we have here. Where will the speech end? In Biblical stories the appearance of another third person verb, often with vav conversive, will signal the resumption of the narrative.

13.3 כִּי קָרָאתָ לִי

כִּי means ______________ קָרָאתָ is a verb. The stem and form are likely to be ______________ because under the first root consonant there is a ______ (4.2a) In all affix forms except 3 m. sg., a pronoun will be found ______________

> תָ_ is the second masculine singular pronoun (2 m. sg.) in the affix form.

Root	Stem	Form	Person/Gender/Number	Special Features

קָרָא means ______________ לִי means ______________ (7.2c, 8.3)

13.4 Translation of the verse: ______________

____

13.5 Extra Grammar

It is now time to learn how to conjugate a verb in the Qal affix in all persons, genders, and numbers. We are using פקד as the paradigm verb because it is a **strong verb**. That means that all three of its root letters will always be present and each of them is able to receive a dagesh. We also chose it because it is one of the few verbs which is attested in Biblical Hebrew in all 7 stems.

Reminder:

The sign of the Qal affix is qamets ָ under the first root letter.

Qal Affix Strong Verb

3 m. sg.	פָּקַד	3 c. pl.	פָּֽקְדוּ	
3 f. sg.	פָּֽקְדָה			
2 m. sg.	פָּקַדְתָּ	2 m. pl.	פְּקַדְתֶּם	⟵
2 f. sg.	פָּקַדְתְּ	2 f. pl.	פְּקַדְתֶּן	⟵
1 c. sg.	פָּקַדְתִּי	1 c. pl.	פָּקַדְנוּ	

13.5a We strongly suggest that you memorize the basic patterns as they are presented and then the variations on those patterns.

13.5b Notice how regular the vowels under the root letters stay as the different pronouns are added. The arrows point to the places where a vowel change takes place in the stem pattern. In each case the pattern vowel has become a shewa. The change is due to the tendency of the vowels at the beginning of a word to shorten when these pronouns are added at the end.

13.5c Each dagesh in <u>this</u> paradigm is a dagesh lene. (3.3) Look at the 3 f. sg. and 3 c. pl. forms. You might expect such a dagesh in the ד because it follows a shewa ְ But this is a vocal shewa due to the meteg (8.1e) preceding it, and therefore a dagesh lene is not required. Remember that dagesh lene affects only pronunciation and there are a number of factors which can influence its appearance, or nonappearance for that matter.

13.6 Variations on the strong verb pattern

In the terminology of this book, a verb which shows all three root letters but which has different vowels from the strong (regular) verb pattern (13.5), is said to be a **variation** on the strong pattern. We are reserving the term **weak** for verbs which do not show all three root letters in each stem. Verbs which don't seem to follow a pattern, or which are sometimes one way and sometimes another, we will call **irregular**. The landmark signs (such as qamets ָ under the first root letter for the Qal affix) will <u>usually</u> be seen in variations of the strong verb, and in weak and irregular verbs.

13.6a Variation: 3rd א

A verb like קרא which ends in א is regular in the Qal affix except for three small changes:

1. dagesh lene cannot stand in the affixed pronouns. (3.3)
2. no shewa is written under the א
3. the second vowel in the stem pattern will be ָ rather than ַ

strong	2 m. sg.	3rd א
		↓ 2nd vowel ָ
פָּקַדְתָּ		קָרָאתָ
		no dagesh↑ ↑no shewa

13.6b Variation: **1st Guttural**

Verbs like אמר הלך or עבד which begin with a guttural normally do not take simple shewa under the first root letter. A composite shewa ֲ is therefore used in the 2 m. pl. and 2 f. pl. forms.

strong	2 m. pl.	1st Guttural
פְּקַדְתֶּם		הֲלַכְתֶּם
		↑composite shewa

13.6c Most verbs are regular in the Qal affix, following 13.5 or the pattern of קרא or הלך Two types of verbs that are not regular are hollow verbs [like בוא] and verbs ending in ה These will be discussed in detail later. Complete paradigms for each type of variation and weak verb are given in the back of the book.

13.7 Referring to the paradigm for the strong verb in 13.5 and the variations noted in 13.6a and b, fill in the chart for the following verbs:

Qal Affix 3rd א

3 m. sg.	נָשָׂא	3 c. pl.	נָשְׂא ___
3 f. sg.	נָשְׂא ___		
2 m. sg.	___ ⎵ ⎵ ⎵	2 m. pl.	___ ⎵ ⎵ ⎵ ⟵
2 f. sg.	___ ⎵ ⎵ ⎵	2 f. pl.	___ ⎵ ⎵ ⎵ ⟵
1 c. sg.	___ ⎵ ⎵ ⎵	1 c. pl.	___ ⎵ ⎵ ⎵

Qal Affix 1st Guttural

3 m. sg.	עָ בַ ד	3 c. pl.	___ ـ ـ ـ
3 f. sg.	___ ـ ـ ـ		
2 m. sg.	___ ـ ـ ـ	2 m. pl.	עֲ בַ דְ תֶּם ←
2 f. sg.	___ ـ ـ ـ	2 f. pl.	___ ـ ـ ـ ←
1 c. sg.	___ ـ ـ ـ	1 c. pl.	___ ـ ـ ـ

13.8a Assignments:

A. For Lessons 13-17 learn words 76-100 from the vocabulary list.

B. Memorize the paradigm for the Qal affix of the strong verb, and the variations for 3rd א and 1st Guttural.

C. Write out the Qal affix conjugation for:

קרא　　יצא　　ידע　　אמר　　הלך

D. Read and translate Genesis 22:1-2

Each Lesson from now on will have a reading assignment with it. If you can read the assigned verses in your Hebrew Bible without further assistance, great. If you need help, annotations begin on p. 232

E. Translate the following verses:

1 נָתְנָה־לִּי מִן־הָעֵץ [עֵץ *tree*] Genesis 3:12

2 יָדַעְתִּי כִּי־נָתַן יהוה לָכֶם אֶת־הָאָרֶץ [לָכֶם *to you* m. pl.] Joshua 2:9

3 כִּי־לֹא שָׁמַעְתָּ בְּקוֹל יהוה [בְּ + שׁמע *listen to*] Deuteronomy 28:45

4 הָלַכְתָּ לְפָנַי [לְפָנַי ⟵ לִפְנֵי + ־ִי] 1 Kings 8:25

5 וְאָמַרְתָּ אֶל־אַהֲרֹן Exodus 7:9

6 וְלֹא־הָלְכוּ בָנָיו בִּדְרָכוֹ [בִּדְרָכוֹ Read the last word as if it were בִּדְרָכָיו] 1 Samuel 8:3

7 וְלֹא שְׁמַעְתֶּם בְּקֹלוֹ Deuteronomy 9:23

8 שָׁמַעְנוּ אֶל־מֹשֶׁה Joshua 1:17

9 וַיֹּאמֶר לֹא קָרָאתִי 1 Samuel 3:5

10 וּקְרָאתֶם בְּשֵׁם אֱלֹהֵיכֶם [כֶם__ *your* m. pl.] I Kings 18:24

11 עַל־כֵּן אָמַרְתִּי לִבְנֵי יִשְׂרָאֵל [עַל־כֵּן *therefore*] Leviticus 17:12

A good Hebrew grammar for students beginning the study is still a desideratum. Our writers of Hebrew grammars have aimed to write for scholars rather than for students. They have been ambitious on most points to say all that could be said, without studying to say only that which is needful to be said.

"Hermeneutics and Homiletics"
Methodist Quarterly, 48 (1866), 372

כִּי־תִשְׁמֹר אֶת־כָּל־הַמִּצְוָה הַזֹּאת לַעֲשֹׂתָהּ Deuteronomy 19:9

14.1 כִּי־תִשְׁמֹר

For the first time you meet a prefix verb form without a vav conversive. Once you memorize all the prefix subject pronouns these will not be too difficult to recognize, even though you do not have the help of the vav.

> תּ is the prefix pronoun for the second person masculine singular.

Root	Stem	Form	Person/Gender/Number	Special Features

> Without the vav conversive, a prefix form is translated in a future or present tense, as the context suggests.

שׁמר means ____________ כִּי means ____________

Translation of the first phrase: ____________

14.2 אֶת־כָּל־הַמִּצְוָה הַזֹּאת

14.2a אֶת is ____________ (7.2) Which is the noun that is definite? ____________
כָּל means ____________ Note that this word functions here as a noun, as the first member of a construct chain. Why is it spelled here כָּל instead of כּוֹל
(See 6.3b if you're not sure of the answer.)

14.2b הַמִּצְוָה begins with ____________ (4.3) Thus the noun itself is מִצְוָה
This is a feminine noun, and its gender is signaled by the accented ָה ending.

> ָה is the regular feminine singular absolute noun ending.

מִצְוָה means *commandment*.

14.2c הַזֹּאת This word also begins with ________________ (4.3) When you remove this article, you are left with זֹאת which means *this.* זֹאת is the feminine singular demonstrative adjective; its masculine counterpart is זֶה Demonstrative adjectives must agree with the noun they modify in gender and number. זֹאת must be used here rather than זֶה because מִצְוָה is feminine. In addition, when the adjective modifies a noun directly, it must follow the noun and agree with it in definiteness as well. We call this kind of adjective an **attributive adjective**.

> An attributive adjective modifies a noun directly; it follows the noun and agrees with it in gender, number, and definiteness.

Here מִצְוָה is definite, so זֹאת must also be definite — both therefore have the definite article. We would translate הַמִּצְוָה הַזֹּאת *this commandment.*

In a construct chain the absolute noun may be modified by an attributive adjective, but construct nouns cannot be so modified.

14.3 לַעֲשֹׂתָהּ

ל is a preposition here; it means __________ ָהּ at the end of a word is the third feminine singular suffix *her.* Note the dot in the הּ This is not a dagesh, but a **mappiq** (which you may remember as the "feminine period"), and it marks this as a consonant rather than a vowel letter. Masoretic usage conventions are helpful here, because the mappiq is confined almost entirely to marking this pronoun — hence this pronoun cannot be confused with the feminine singular noun endiNG ָה (as in 14.2b) which never has a mappiq.

14.3a This leaves עֲשֹׂת (The dot for the שׂ is also functioning as the vowel holem.) You must locate the root. The ע and שׂ must be part of the root, but according to what you have learned so far, ת___ could be either part of the root or an ending. (11.2a) In this case ת___ is part of an ending: ֹת or וֹת is the regular Qal infinitive ending for verbs ending in ה So the root is עשׂה Fill in the chart.

Root	Stem	Form	Person/Gender/Number	Special Features
			See 11.2b	

> Verbs whose root ends in ה regularly lose the ה and have ת‍ִ_ or ו‍ֹת_ in the Qal infinitive.

This infinitive can be translated literally ______________ The *her* refers back to what noun? ______________ In English, nouns of this sort are considered neuter and thus you can use the pronoun *it* in your translation of this Hebrew word.

14.4 Verse translation: ____

____

14.5 Extra Grammar

Once again you are ready to conjugate a verb more fully, this time in the Qal prefix system. Unfortunately there are far fewer regular verbs in the prefix than in the affix. All of the "missing letter" verbs: 1st י 3rd ה and hollow are weak, as are 1st נ verbs. However, the regular form is an important base from which to build, so you must memorize its pattern first:

Qal Prefix Strong Verb

3 m. sg.	יִפְקֹד		3 m. pl.	יִפְקְדוּ	←
3 f. sg.	תִּפְקֹד		3 f. pl.	תִּפְקֹדְנָה	
2 m. sg.	תִּפְקֹד		2 m. pl.	תִּפְקְדוּ	←
2 f. sg.	תִּפְקְדִי	←	2 f. pl.	תִּפְקֹדְנָה	
1 c. sg.	אֶפְקֹד	←	1 c. pl.	נִפְקֹד	

First of all, circle the pronoun elements lightly. Be sure to circle the prefix pronoun at the beginning <u>and</u> the prefix complement at the end of the verb. (6.1) These pronoun elements (the consonants but not the vowels) remain the same in all prefix forms of the verb, regardless of stem, and recognizing them will help you to parse verbs even when you do not fully understand the vowel pattern of the verb.

Notice that the vowel pattern changes more in the Qal prefix than in the Qal affix. The arrows point to the forms that diverge from the common pattern. In addition, the third vowel in the pattern (here holem) changes depending on the type of verb used. To conjugate a verb correctly in the prefix, you must see one of its PGNs to ascertain this vowel.

14.5a For the strong verb the vav conversive form can be created simply by adding ⊡וַ to the forms on the chart. And conversely, the simple prefix for such a verb can be derived by removing ⊡וַ from a form. The one exception will be the first person singular. You cannot add ⊡וַ to אֶפְקֹד because the א cannot take a dagesh. (3.3b) The vav conversive for this PGN will be וָאֶפְקֹד As you can see, removing the וָ leaves the proper prefix form. This is the only circumstance in which vav conversive is not pointed וַ

14.6 Exercises:

A. In addition to the endiNG of 2 f. pl. and 3 f. pl. prefix form verbs, you have now seen a number of things represented by ָה 3 f. sg. affix, 3 m. sg. affix of 3rd ה verbs, f. sg. nouns, and ה- directive. The following words which end in ָה should be familiar to you from your vocabulary list and your reading in Genesis 22. Identify each ָה

אַרְצָה	וַתֹּאמַרְנָה	הַמֹּרִיָּה
שָׁמְרָה	הָיָה	בָּנָה
שָׁנָה	נִסָּה	אַתָּה
נָתְנָה	עֹלָה	תֵּלַכְנָה
הָלְכָה	עָלָה	אִשָּׁה

B. Conjugate שלח in the Qal prefix form. The pattern is begun for you:

Qal Prefix שלח

3 m. sg.	יִ שְׁ לַ ח	3 m. pl.	יִ שְׁ לְ ח וּ
3 f. sg.	_ _ _ _	3 f. pl.	תִּ שְׁ לַ חְ נָה
2 m. sg.	_ _ _ _	2 m. pl.	_ _ _ ְ _ _
2 f. sg.	_ _ _ ְ _ _	2 f. pl.	_ _ _ _ _
1 c. sg.	אֶ _ _ _	1 c. pl.	_ _ _ _

Conjugate מלך in the Qal prefix form. The 3 m. sg. יִמְלֹךְ gives you the pattern to follow.

Qal Prefix מלך

3 m. sg.	י ִ מְ ל ֹ ךְ	3 m. pl.	י ִ מְ לְ כ וּ
3 f. sg.	___ ___ ___ ___	3 f. pl.	תִּ מְ ל ֹ כְ נָה
2 m. sg.	___ ___ ___ ___	2 m. pl.	___ ___ ___ ְ ___ ___
2 f. sg.	___ ___ ְ ___ ___ ___	2 f. pl.	___ ___ ___ ___ ___
1 c. sg.	אֶ ___ ___ ___	1 c. pl.	___ ___ ___ ___

14.6a Assignments:

A. Memorize the paradigm for the Qal prefix of the strong verb 14.5

B. Read and translate Genesis 22:3-5

C. In the following verses, "missing letter" verbs will be found as well as a few regular prefix forms. The missing letter rules work with the simple prefix forms as well as with vav conversive forms. Translate the verses, then analyze each prefix form verb.

1 וַתֹּאמֶר הָאִשָּׁה אֶל־שָׁאוּל I Samuel 28:12

2 וָאָבוֹא אֶל־יְרוּשָׁלִַם [The city name is regularly spelled without the 2nd י]
Nehemiah 2:11

3 כִּי תָבֹאוּ אֶל־אֶרֶץ כְּנַעַן אֲשֶׁר אֲנִי נֹתֵן לָכֶם [כֶם — *you* m. pl.]
Leviticus 14:34

4 בְּדֶרֶךְ הַמֶּלֶךְ נֵלֵךְ Numbers 21:22

5 בְּזֹאת תֵּדַע כִּי אֲנִי יהוה Exodus 7:17

*6 כֵּן יִהְיֶה דְבָרִי אֲשֶׁר יֵצֵא מִפִּי [כֵּן *thus* פִּי *my mouth*] Isaiah 55:11

7 וַיַּעַל אַבְרָם מִמִּצְרַיִם Genesis 13:1 (12.1)

*8 וַתִּתֵּן לָהֶם אֶת־הָאָרֶץ הַזֹּאת Jeremiah 32:22

9 וַיִּשְׁלַח יַעֲקֹב וַיִּקְרָא לְרָחֵל וּלְלֵאָה Genesis 31:4

10 וְהִנֵּה אֶשְׁלַח אֶת־הַנַּעַר [נַעַר *youth*] 1 Samuel 20:21

11 לֹא־תִרְאוּ פָנַי [ַ־י *my*] Genesis 43:3

12 כִּי־נִשְׁמֹר לַעֲשׂוֹת אֶת־כָּל־הַמִּצְוָה הַזֹּאת Deuteronomy 6:25

*13 וָאֶעֱבֹר אֶל־שַׁעַר הָעִיר [שַׁעַר הָעִיר *fountain gate*] Nehemiah 2:14

14 וַיֹּאמֶר לֹא תַעֲבֹר Numbers 20:20

*15 לֹא־תֵדַע לְשֹׁנוֹ וְלֹא תִשְׁמַע מַה־יְדַבֵּר [לָשׁוֹן *language*] Jeremiah 5:15

Isaiah 39:8 וַיֹּאמֶר חִזְקִיָּהוּ אֶל־יְשַׁעְיָהוּ טוֹב דְּבַר־יהוה אֲשֶׁר דִּבַּרְתָּ

15.1 וַיֹּאמֶר חִזְקִיָּהוּ אֶל־יְשַׁעְיָהוּ

חִזְקִיָּהוּ is a proper name, functioning as the ____________________ of the sentence.

יְשַׁעְיָהוּ is another proper name.

Translation: ____

Note the similarity in the endings of these names. Many Hebrew names are compounds with God's name יהוה as יָהוּ____ or יָה____ as one element.

חָזַק means *be strong;* יָשַׁע means *rescue, save, deliver.* How might the two names be "translated:" ____

15.2 What do you expect to follow the first phrase? ____________________ (13.2)

טוֹב is an adjective meaning *good* and דְּבַר־ is a noun. But this time the adjective precedes the noun. You cannot translate *the good word [of the* LORD*]* because an attributive adjective must ____________________ the noun (14.2c) This new type of adjective which <u>precedes</u> the noun we call the predicate adjective.

> A **predicate adjective** usually precedes the noun. It must agree with its noun in gender and number but not necessarily in definiteness.

A phrase consisting of an adjective preceding a noun or construct phrase is treated like a noun sentence (2.10b): you need to insert a form of the verb *to be.*

Translate the phrase: ____

15.3 אֲשֶׁר דִּבַּרְתָּ

אֲשֶׁר is the relative pronoun. (5.3a) The only new grammatical element in this sentence is the final verb: דִּבַּרְתָּ

Root	Stem	Form	Person/Gender/Number	Special Features

You should have no trouble finding the root, form, and PGN for this verb. Refer to 13.5

if necessary. Is this stem Qal? What is the stem indicator for the Qal affix? ________

________________________ This is the other stem you have seen in the Lessons.

What is its stem indicator? (2.3c) ______________________________

Translation of the whole verse: ______________________________

____

15.4 Pi`el Affix

The major **stem** indicator of the Pi`el is the dagesh forte in the middle root letter:

＿ ＿̇ ＿

The major **form** indicator for the Pi`el affix is hireq ִ under the first root letter:

＿ ＿̇ ＿ִ

The subject pronoun endings you have learned for the Qal Affix are the same ones used in the Pi`el; <u>these endings are used in the affix form of every stem</u>. If you haven't memorized them yet, do so **now**.

Pi`el Affix Strong Verb

3 m. sg.	דִּבֵּר	3 c. pl.	דִּבְּרוּ
3 f. sg.	דִּבְּרָה		
2 m. sg.	דִּבַּרְתָּ	2 m. pl.	דִּבַּרְתֶּם
2 f. sg.	דִּבַּרְתְּ	2 f. pl.	דִּבַּרְתֶּן
1 c. sg.	דִּבַּרְתִּי	1 c. pl.	דִּבַּרְנוּ

What kind of dagesh is in the first root letter of our example? You can see that much of the rest of the pointing is regular throughout the paradigm. This will be the case for most Pi`el verbs.

15.4a Pi`el Affix for middle א ה ח ע ר

These letters cannot take a dagesh. The form (and stem) indicator for this group of verbs in the Pi`el affix is tsere ֵ under the first root letter ＿ ＿ ＿ֵ One way to remember this is to think of the dagesh forte as having gone from the middle root letter to join the expected hireq under the first root letter. There are many cases where a dagesh which cannot stand where it "should" will "move" to join the preceding vowel. We will call this the case of the **travelling dagesh**.

Complete the following paradigm using 15.4 as a guide.

Pi'el Affix for middle א ה ח ע ר

3 m. sg.	בֵּ רַ ךְ	3 c. pl.	___ ⌴ ⌴ְ ⌴
3 f. sg.	___ ⌴ ⌴ְ ⌴		
2 m. sg.	___ ⌴ ⌴ ⌴	2 m. pl.	___ ⌴ ⌴ ⌴
2 f. sg.	___ ⌴ ⌴ ⌴	2 f. pl.	___ ⌴ ⌴ ⌴
1 c. sg.	___ ⌴ ⌴ ⌴	1 c. pl.	___ ⌴ ⌴ ⌴

15.5 Pi'el Prefix

You construct the Pi'el prefix the same way as the Qal prefix. <u>The prefix pronouns and prefix complements are the same for every stem of the verb</u>.

> The form indicator for the Pi'el prefix is shewa ְ under the prefix pronoun. ⌴ ⌴̇ ⌴ | ְ

Fill in the chart for the Pi'el prefix of דבר Where something deviates from the regular pattern, it has been filled in for you.

Pi'el Prefix Strong Verb

3 m. sg.	יְ דַ בֵּ ר	3 m. pl.	___ ⌴ ⌴ְ ⌴ —
3 f. sg.	⌴ ⌴ ⌴ —	3 f. pl.	___ ⌴ ⌴ ⌴ —
2 m. sg.	⌴ ⌴ ⌴ —	2 m. pl.	___ ⌴ ⌴ְ ⌴ —
2 f. sg.	___ ⌴ ⌴ְ ⌴ —	2 f. pl.	___ ⌴ ⌴ ⌴ —
1 c. sg.	⌴ ⌴ ⌴ אֲ	1 c. pl.	⌴ ⌴ ⌴ —

Can you explain the composite shewa under the prefix pronoun for the 1 c. sg.? (13.6b)

15.5a Pi`el Prefix for middle ר ע ח ה א

The stem indicator for the Pi`el prefix of this group of verbs is shewa ְ under the prefix pronoun (the same as for verbs with dagesh forte in the middle root letter). To compensate for the lack of doubling of the middle root letter, the vowel under the first root letter is lengthened, this time from pataḥ ַ to qamets __ __ ָ | —

doubled middle root letter	middle root letter cannot double
↓	↓
יְפַקֵּד	יְבָרֵךְ
pataḥ ↑ ↑ landmark shewa	qamets ↑ ↑ landmark shewa

Complete this paradigm using the 3 m. sg. as a model and refer to 15.5 if necessary.

Pi`el Prefix for middle ר ע ח ה א

3 m. sg.	יְבָרֵךְ	3 m. pl.	___ ְ ___
3 f. sg.	___	3 f. pl.	___
2 m. sg.	___	2 m. pl.	___ ְ ___
2 f. sg.	___ ְ ___	2 f. pl.	___
1 c. sg.	___ ֲ	1 c. pl.	___

15.6 Meanings of the Pi`el Stem

You have learned that the Qal Stem is the simple or basic meaning of the verb. (1.4a) The change from the Qal to the Pi`el varies from one verb to another but there are a few common relationships:

A. **Transitives**: Many verbs which are intransitive in the Qal have a transitive force in the Pi`el.

Qal		Pi`el	
אָבַד	*perish*	אִבֵּד	*destroy*
לָמַד	*learn*	לִמֵּד	*teach*

A subcategory of these verbs is called **factitive**. An adjective complement is needed to complete the meaning of the verb.

Qal	Pi`el
צָדַק *be just, righteous*	צִדֵּק *declare just*

B. **Denominatives**: Some Pi`els seem to have been formed from nouns. You are already familiar with one of the most common of these: דִּבֵּר and its related noun דָּבָר

Noun	Pi`el
סֵפֶר *book, record*	סִפֵּר *recount, narrate*

A subgroup of these denominatives is called **privative**: the verb relates to taking away or injuring the noun, in either a literal or figurative sense.[1]

Noun	Pi`el
חֵטְא *sin*	חִטֵּא *free from sin*

C. **Strengthening, repetition**, or **intensification** of action ("pluralization") seems to be the pattern in other Pi'el verbs.

Qal	Pi`el
שָׁאַל *ask*	שִׁאֵל *beg*
Genesis 23:4 וְאֶקְבְּרָה מֵתִי	I Kings 11:15 לְקַבֵּר אֶת־הַחֲלָלִים
that I may bury my dead (1 person)	*to bury the slain* (many people)

D. **Others**: There are some Pi`el verbs for which Biblical Hebrew has no Qal. In other cases, Qal and Pi`el forms are both extant, but we do not know how to express the intended difference, if any, between the two.

No Qal	Pi`el
בקשׁ _____	בִּקֵּשׁ *seek*
הלל _____	הִלֵּל *praise, commend*

Qal	unidentified nuances	Pi`el
Qohelet 2:8 כָּנַסְתִּי לִי גַּם־כֶּסֶף וְזָהָב		Psalms 147:2 נִדְחֵי יִשְׂרָאֵל יְכַנֵּס
I also gathered for myself silver and gold		*he gathers the outcasts of Israel*

[1] The grammar of English food preparation has several of these noun/verb pairs: *skin, bone, seed, peel*, and so forth.

15.7 Hebrew Names

It is often intriguing to delve into a name either to learn the Hebrew root, as in the names in our Lesson sentence, or to discover a cultural influence. The name of Sarah's maidservant הָגָר (Genesis 21) may be from an Arabic root *forsake, retire.* It could also be a play on the word גֵּר *stranger.*

Hebrew proper names, both of people and of places, are often compounds. Many town names include the word בֵּית as in בֵּית אֵל and בֵּית לֶחֶם How would you "translate" these? ____________________

In some cases particular names are given for theological purpose. Hosea is told to name two of his children לֹא רֻחָמָה (Hosea 1:6) and לֹא עַמִּי (Hosea 1:9) The first name is *Not Pitied.* What is the second? ____________________

Many times, especially on the occasion of naming or changing the name of an individual, a reason for the name is given. Look at the poignant lines in Ruth 1:20. The names bespeak the difficulties Naomi has suffered.

וַתֹּאמֶר אֲלֵיהֶן אַל־תִּקְרֶאנָה לִי נָעֳמִי קְרֶאןָ לִי מָרָא
כִּי־הֵמַר שַׁדַּי לִי מְאֹד׃

"Then she said to them, 'Do not call me נָעֳמִי [root: נעם *pleasant, delightful*], *call me* מָרָא [root: מרר *bitter*], *because God has made much bitterness for me.'"*

There are stories in which the names themselves set up our reactions to the characters. The story of David [root: דוד *beloved*] and Nabal [root: נבל *foolish*] (1 Samuel 25) is such an illustration. Look especially at 1 Samuel 25:25.
Of course every name is not pregnant with overtones, but in many cases names add dimensions of meaning and enjoyment to our reading of the text.

15.8 Assignments:

A. Memorize the Pi`el affix and prefix paradigms for the strong verb and verbs whose middle root letter is א ה ח ע ר

B. Read and translate Genesis 22:6-8

C. Translate the following verses:

Vocabulary to learn: נָבִיא *prophet*

חזק Qal: *be strong, hard* Pi`el: *strengthen, harden*

1 וַיְשַׁמַּע שָׁאוּל אֶת־כָּל־הָעָם I Samuel 23:8

2 אֲחַזֵּק אֶת־לִבּוֹ וְלֹא יְשַׁלַּח אֶת־הָעָם [לִבּוֹ ⟷ לֵב + וֹ] Exodus 4:21

3 וַיֹּאמֶר פַּרְעֹה אָנֹכִי אֲשַׁלַּח אֶתְכֶם [אֶתְכֶם ⟷ 2 m. pl. object suffix + אֵת] Exodus 8:24

4 וַיְחַזֵּק יהוה אֶת־לֵב פַּרְעֹה וְלֹא שִׁלַּח אֶת־בְּנֵי־יִשְׂרָאֵל מֵאַרְצוֹ
Exodus 11:10 (Find the travelling dagesh in this verse. It <u>isn't</u> in a Pi`el verb this time.)

5 וְלֹא שִׁלַּח אֶת־הָעָם Exodus 8:28

6 וְנִשְּׂאוּ אֶת־הָעָם וְאֶת־בֵּית־הָאֱלֹהִים Ezra 8:36

7 וְשִׁלַּחְתֶּם אֹתוֹ וְהָלָךְ [אֹתוֹ ⟷ DDO marker + 3 m. sg. obj. pronoun] I Samuel 6:8

*8 כְּכֹל הַדְּבָרִים הָאֵלֶּה וּכְכֹל הֶחָזוֹן הַזֶּה כֵּן דִּבֶּר נָתָן אֶל־דָּוִיד׃
I Chronicles 17:15 [חָזוֹן *vision*]

9 וַיֹּאמֶר לָהֶם הִנֵּה בֶן־הַמֶּלֶךְ יִמְלֹךְ כַּאֲשֶׁר דִּבֶּר יהוה
עַל־בְּנֵי דָוִיד 2 Chronicles 23:3

10 זֶה הַדָּבָר אֲשֶׁר דִּבֶּר יהוה אֶל־מוֹאָב Isaiah 16:13 [predicate adjective]

11 כִּי יהוה דִּבֶּר אֶת־הַדָּבָר הַזֶּה Isaiah 24:3 [attributive adjective]

12 וַיִּשְׁלְחוּ וַיִּקְרְאוּ־לוֹ וַיָּבֹא יָרָבְעָם וְכָל־יִשְׂרָאֵל וַיְדַבְּרוּ
אֶל־רְחַבְעָם 2 Chronicles 10:3

13 וְלֹא אֲדַבֵּר עוֹד בִּשְׁמוֹ Jeremiah 20:9

14 וְלֹא תִשְׁמַע מַה־יְדַבֵּר Jeremiah 5:15
[Can the "tenses" be rendered in more than one way here?]

15 וְאֶל־צִדְקִיָּה מֶלֶךְ־יְהוּדָה דִּבַּרְתִּי כְּכָל־הַדְּבָרִים הָאֵלֶּה Jeremiah 27:12

Genesis 50:1 וַיִּפֹּל יוֹסֵף עַל־פְּנֵי אָבִיו וַיֵּבְךְּ עָלָיו וַיִּשַּׁק־לוֹ׃

16.1 From now on, atnaḥ ֑ and sof passuq ׃___ (See Review and Drill 4, section VI.) will be inserted in full verses.

16.1a וַיִּפֹּל יוֹסֵף

Root	Stem	Form	Person/Gender/Number	Special Features

After accounting for the וַיִּ how many consonants are left for the root? ____________

If you forget why the root can't be פפל review 7.1a.

If you forget why the root isn't פלה review 12.3.

The root is ____________ What is the stem? ____________ It cannot be Pi`el because you have already accounted for the dagesh forte in the פ It is the assimilated נ of the root. Remember: a dagesh forte cannot stand for two letters simultaneously. (7.1a)

Besides, if this were a Pi`el form, what vowel would you expect under the י ___ (15.5) You should be able to fill in the rest of the chart.

נָפַל means *fall*. Translation of the phrase: ____________

16.2 עַל־פְּנֵי אָבִיו

If you have trouble with this phrase, check the idioms in 12.6.

Translation: ____________

16.3 וַיֵּבְךְּ עָלָיו

16.3a וַיֵּבְךְּ

Root	Stem	Form	Person/Gender/Number	Special Features

The PGN, stem, and form of this verb are straightforward; the trouble comes in determining the root. The י you see cannot be part of the root because וַיִּ begins a vav conversive construction, and therefore the י is a prefix pronoun.

No letter of an affix pronoun, prefix pronoun, or prefix complement will ever assimilate.

That means that a footprint dagesh as in וַיִּפֹּל or a missing letter as in וַיֵּבְךְּ will always be telling you something about a <u>root</u> letter in a verb form.
According to 12.3, this is a time when the missing letter rules can be used.
According to the appropriate rule, the root needs __________ in the __________ position. But this is one of the 5% or so of cases where the convention for identifying the missing letter simply doesn't work.[1]
The root here is בָּכָה which means *weep*. Sometimes בָּכָה will follow the missing letter rule [וַיִּבְכּוּ Gen. 33:4], sometimes it won't [וַתֵּבְךְּ Gen. 21:15].
There are a few other 3rd ה verbs which <u>sometimes</u> take the prefix pronoun vowel of a 1st י The non-conforming instances tend to be in the 2 m. sg., 3 m. sg., and 1 c. pl.

<u>Verb</u>		<u>Expected Pointing</u>		<u>Ambiguous Pointing</u>	
שתה	*drink*	וַיִּשְׁתֶּה	1 Kings 19:8	וַיֵּשְׁתְּ	Genesis 9:21
נטה	*stretch out, extend*	יִטֶּה	Job 15:29	וַיֵּט	Genesis 12:8
רעה	*pasture, tend*	יִרְעֶה	Isaiah 30:23	יֵרַע	Job 20:26

16.3b עָלָיו This is a preposition and object suffix you have seen before.
Translation of phrase: ______________________________

16.4 וַיִּשַּׁק־לוֹ

Root	Stem	Form	Person/Gender/Number	Special Features

[1] The vowels used reflect <u>pronunciation</u>, not a thoroughly consistent grammatical system. The "rules" of grammar we use are really observations which were made much later and from outside the language.

וַיִּפֹּל יוֹסֵף עַל־פְּנֵי אָבִיו וַיֵּבְךְּ עָלָיו וַיִּשַּׁק־לוֹ׃

16.4a לוֹ Without any context, this would be translated *to him* or *for him*. In this sentence, it would make awkward English to say *he kissed to/for him.* This is an idiomatic use of the preposition לְ where we might expect אֶת It shouldn't be given a strictly literal English translation.

Translation of the whole verse: ______________________________

____

16.5a The Qal affix of a 1st נ verb is completely regular, exactly like the pattern you learned in 13.5. Conjugate the Qal affix of נפל

Qal Affix נפל

3 m. sg.	___ ___ ___	3 c. pl.	___ ___ ___ ___
3 f. sg.	___ ___ ___ ___		
2 m. sg.	___ ___ ___ ___	2 m. pl.	___ ___ ___ ___ ←
2 f. sg.	___ ___ ___ ___	2 f. pl.	___ ___ ___ ___ ←
1 c. sg.	___ ___ ___ ___	1 c. pl.	___ ___ ___ ___

16.5b Qal Prefix of 1st נ

Because the prefix pronoun causes the assimilation of the נ the Qal prefix does not follow exactly the pattern you learned in 14.5. However, the prefix pronouns and prefix complements themselves are the same.

Qal Prefix נפל

3 m. sg.	יִ פֹּ ל	3 m. pl.	___ ___ ___ ___
3 f. sg.	___ ___ ___	3 f. pl.	___ ___ ___ ___
2 m. sg.	___ ___ ___	2 m. pl.	___ ___ ___ ___
2 f. sg.	___ ___ ___ תִּ	2 f. pl.	___ ___ ___ ___
1 c. sg.	___ ___ אֶ	1 c. pl.	___ ___ ___

Just as is the case with strong verbs, the second vowel in the Qal prefix is not the same for every verb which is 1st נ The other pattern, pataḥ _ under the second root letter, can be seen with נגשׁ *draw near, approach.* Using the 3 m. sg. as a guide, finish this paradigm. Remember the dagesh forte.

Qal Prefix נגשׁ

3 m. sg.	יִ גַּ שׁ	3 m. pl.	___ ___ ___ ___
3 f. sg.	___ ___ ___	3 f. pl.	___ ___ ___ ___
2 m. sg.	___ ___ ___	2 m. pl.	___ ___ ___ ___
2 f. sg.	___ ___ ___ תִּ	2 f. pl.	___ ___ ___ ___
1 c. sg.	___ ___ ___	1 c. pl.	___ ___ ___

The 1 c. pl. needs careful consideration. The נ you see is the prefix pronoun. The footprint of the first root letter is found in the dagesh forte of the middle root letter.

16.5c Some common 1st נ verbs which appear in the Qal are:

נתן	*give, permit*	נסע	*set out, journey*
נשׂא	*lift, carry*	נגשׁ	*draw near, approach*
נפל	*fall*	נשׁק	*kiss*
נגע	*harm, reach, touch*		

16.6 נָתַן

The most frequent of all the 1st נ verbs is נתן It is "irregular," not simply "weak," because its third root letter is a ן which behaves as its first נ does. That is, this ן also assimilates when it is between two strong letters.[2] Therefore, the Qal affix forms will not look exactly like the paradigms in 16.5a in those PGNs in which the

[2] **Strong letter**: does not assimilate, does not elide, can take a dagesh:

ב ג ד ו ז ט י כ ל מ נ ס פ צ ק שׂ שׁ ת

Rebellious letter: appears but cannot take a dagesh, may cause changes in the vowels of neighboring letters:

א ה ח ע ר

Weak letter: a strong or rebellious letter is weak when, because of its position in a word, it assimilates, elides, or quiesces.

א ה ו י ל נ

affix begins with a strong letter. In these cases the footprint dagesh in the first letter of the affix pronoun will alert you to the identity of the unseen root letter. This is the only root that ends in a nun ן which acts this way.

In the following paradigm, the arrow indicates those forms in which the third root letter has assimilated.

Pay special attention to the 3 c. pl. נָתְנוּ and the 1 c. pl. נָתַנּוּ How can they be distinguished?

Qal Affix נתן

3 m. sg.	נָתַן	3 c. pl.	נָתְנוּ
3 f. sg.	נָתְנָה		
2 m .sg.	נָתַתָּ ⟵	2 m. pl.	נְתַתֶּם ⟵
2 f. sg.	נָתַתְּ ⟵	2 f. pl.	נְתַתֶּן ⟵
1 c. sg.	נָתַתִּי ⟵	1 c. pl.	נָתַנּוּ ⟵

The prefix forms are regular according to 1st נ patterns, showing the second and third root letters in every case. Thus the root can be identified after accounting for the dagesh forte which represents ______________________

Fill in the Qal Prefix paradigm yourself, or ask a friend to do it.

Qal Prefix נתן

3 m. sg.	יִתֵּן	3 m. pl.	___ ___ ___ ___
3 f. sg.	___ ___ ___	3 f. pl.	___ ___ ___ ___
2 m. sg.	___ ___ ___	2 m. pl.	___ ___ ___ ___
2 f. sg.	___ ___ ___ ___	2 f. pl.	___ ___ ___ ___
1 c. sg.	___ ___ ___	1 c. pl.	___ ___ ___

The participle is regular: ______________________

16.7 Extra Grammar

Idiomatic usage of certain verbs with certain prepositions.

16.7a Preposition instead of **את**

There are times when what we would consider a DDO is preceded not by the DDO marker but by a preposition. One such case occurs in the Lesson sentence:

וַיִּשַּׁק־לוֹ

Another verb which commonly takes a preposition, this time **בְּ** is **בחר** *choose:*

לֹא־בָחַרְתִּי בְעִיר 1 Kings 8:16

I did not choose a city

16.7b Sometimes a preposition will change the meaning of the verb it accompanies from what the verb usually means without the preposition. At times different prepositions express different nuances; sometimes they seem to be interchangeable.

קרא *call, proclaim*

קָרָא לְ or **קָרָא בְּ** *call, give a name to, call unto, read*

וַיִּקְרָא אֱלֹהִים לָאוֹר יוֹם Genesis 1:5

and God called (named) the light Day

וַיִּקְרָא בְּסֵפֶר תּוֹרַת הָאֱלֹהִים Nehemiah 8:18

and he read in the book of the Torah of God

שמע *hear, listen*

שָׁמַע אֶל/לְ or **שָׁמַע בְּ** *listen to*

לֹא־שָׁמְעוּ בְּקוֹל־יהוה...וְלֹא שָׁמְעוּ וְלֹא עָשׂוּ 2 Kings 18:12

They did not listen to (obey) the voice of the Lord...and they did not hear (listen) and they did not do.

וְלֹא־שָׁמְעוּ אֶל־מֹשֶׁה Exodus 16:20

and they did not listen to Moses

16.8 Assignments:

A. Memorize the Qal affix and prefix conjugations of נפל נגשׁ נתן

B. Read and translate Genesis 22:9-11

C. Translate:

1 וְאֶת־כָּל־אֶחָיו נָתַתִּי לוֹ לַעֲבָדִים Genesis 27:37

[3 m. sg. possessive suffix + אָח⟷אֶחָיו]

2 וַיָּבֹא יְהוּדָה וְאֶחָיו בֵּיתָה יוֹסֵף...וַיִּפְּלוּ לְפָנָיו אָרְצָה Genesis 44:14

3 וַתָּבֹא וַתִּפֹּל עַל־רַגְלָיו...וַתִּשָּׂא אֶת־בְּנָהּ וַתֵּצֵא [רֶגֶל *foot*] 2 Kings 4:37

*4 דָּבָר שָׁלַח אֲדֹנָי בְּיַעֲקֹב וְנָפַל בְּיִשְׂרָאֵל׃ Isaiah 9:7

[בְּ can mean *against* here.]

*5 וַיִּפֹּל הַבַּיִת עַל־הַסְּרָנִים וְעַל־כָּל־הָעָם אֲשֶׁר־בּוֹ Judges 16:30

[הַסְּרָנִים *the princes*]

6 וְאֶת־כָּל־יְהוּדָה אֶתֵּן בְּיַד מֶלֶךְ־בָּבֶל Jeremiah 20:4

7 וַיִּגַּשׁ דָּוִד אֶת־הָעָם 1 Samuel 30:21

8 וַתִּתֶּן־לוֹ בֵן 1 Kings 3:6

9 וְהִנֵּה־יָד נָגְעָה בִּי [נָגַע בְּ *touch*] Daniel 10:10

10 וּמִי יִתֵּן אֶת־הָעָם הַזֶּה בְּיָדִי Judges 9:29

יהוה לִי לֹא אִירָא מַה־יַּעֲשֶׂה לִי אָדָם׃ Psalms 118:6

17.1 יהוה לִי

The preposition לְ was introduced in 7.2c where you learned that it often acts as a marker of the indirect object [לוֹ *to* or *for him*] or as an indicator of the possessive [מֶלֶךְ לוֹ *he has a king*]. In the phrase here, either use of לְ would make sense.

Translation: ________________________

17.2 לֹא אִירָא

Root	Stem	Form	Person/Gender/Number	Special Features

אִירָא shows four consonants. When faced with too many consonants it is often helpful to begin by removing any vowel letters. That won't work here because:

אָרא is not a root.

A prefix pronoun is never followed by a plene hireq.

Take off the prefix pronoun and you are left with ירא which are the three root letters of the verb *fear.*

Translation of phrase: ________________________

The 1st י verbs you have already studied in the Qal prefix (Lessons 3 and 11) are distinguished by the elision of the י of the root. The tsere ֵ under the prefix pronoun is the clue to the identity and location of the missing root letter.[1] You are familiar with forms such as יֵצֵא and יֵשֵׁב.

A second group of 1st י verbs is conjugated like אִירָא in the Qal prefix. In these, the י of the root quiesces (that is, it appears but it has no vowel of its own) and the vowel hireq ִ is under the prefix pronoun.

---

1 Remember הלך follows the pattern of these first י verbs.

17.3 מַה־יַּעֲשֶׂה לִי אָדָם

17.3a יַּעֲשֶׂה

Root	Stem	Form	Person/Gender/Number	Special Features

What letter is not part of the root? ________________ The root is __________

There are two unusual things about יַּעֲשֶׂה First is the vowel under the prefix pronoun.

> Roots that begin with the gutturals ע ח or ה have the vowel pataḥ ַ under the prefix pronoun in the Qal prefix except for the first person singular whose prefix pronoun is also a guttural letter. In that case the vowel is usually segol ֶ

17.3b Second, did you notice the dagesh in the י It is called a **euphonic dagesh**. What its original melodic function was, we do not know. It has no effect according to today's pronunciation conventions and has no apparent grammatical function. You will recognize one of these only by process of elimination; its most common occurrence is in the first consonant of a word following a final ה

The subject of this part of the verse is ________________

17.3c לִי is the ________________

17.3d אָדָם is most frequently used in the generic sense meaning *mankind, humanity* as opposed to אִישׁ *man* which has a feminine counterpart אִשָּׁה *woman.*

Although the Qal prefix form may be translated as a simple present or future, it needn't be restricted to one of those "tenses." Remember, the prefix connotes incomplete action rather than a strict time period. A few other acceptable possibilities for יַּעֲשֶׂה are *can do, might do,* or *could do.*

17.3e Translation of phrase: ________________________

17.4 Translation of entire verse: ________________________

____

17.5 Following the pattern of אִירָא finish conjugating ירא in the Qal prefix. Remember to make the adjustments which a 3rd א requires. (13.6a)

Qal Prefix ירא

3 m. sg.	_ _ _ _	3 m. pl.	___ _ _ְ _ _
3 f. sg.	_ _ _ _	3 f. pl.	___ _ _ֶ _ _
2 m. sg.	_ _ _ _	2 m. pl.	___ _ _ְ _ _
2 f. sg.	___ _ _ְ _ _	2 f. pl.	___ _ _ֶ _ _
1 c. sg.	אִ י רָ א	1 c. pl.	_ _ _ _

Following the pattern of אֵשֵׁב finish conjugating ישב in the Qal prefix.

Qal Prefix ישב

3 m. sg.	_ _ _	3 m. pl.	___ _ _ְ _
3 f. sg.	_ _ _	3 f. pl.	___ _ְ _ַ _
2 m. sg.	_ _ _	2 m. pl.	___ _ _ְ _
2 f. sg.	___ _ _ְ _	2 f. pl.	___ _ְ _ַ _
1 c. sg.	אֵ שֵׁ ב	1 c. pl.	_ _ _

17.6 Extra Grammar

17.6a Roots containing weak letters have several unusual characteristics, many of which are demonstrated in the Qal. Much of the grammar presented so far has dealt with recognizing the Qal affix and prefix forms of these verbs. But aside from their deviating from the pattern of the strong verb, they have some other features worth noting.

17.6b A weak root may have more than one pattern for a particular form of a verb: שִׂים and שָׂם are both 3 m. sg. Qal affix forms of the hollow root שׂים

17.6c A verb with a weak letter may mimic a verb with a different weak letter. וַיֵּבְךְּ (16.3a) is an example of a 3rd ה verb which looks like some 1st י verbs. There are some 1st י verbs which act like 1st נ verbs in the Qal prefix: the י assimilates into the second root letter: וַתִּצֹּק *and she poured* from the root יצק (giving yet a third pattern for 1st י verbs).

These observations do not mean to imply that you should abandon the identification landmarks. Only if a form does not yield to analysis on the basis of the general "rules" you have learned should you consider these secondary possibilities to help find the root.

If you look over your vocabulary list you will see that many of the most common verbs contain weak letters and many are "doubly weak," containing two weak letters. A significant number are "weak and rebellious" like ירא the verb for this Lesson. It is vital to watch for changes from the pattern of the strong verb that might be due to these types of consonants.

17.7 Qal Affix Vowel Patterns

ירא differs from verbs you have seen so far not only in the Qal prefix but also in the Qal affix. Most of the verbs you have seen have either ָ or ַ as their second vowel in the 3 m. sg. Qal affix: אָמַר and קָרָא They are called "A" class verbs because the sound of the second vowel approximates the sound of an English "a" as in f**a**ther. (A better reason is that ַ and ָ are known as the "A" vowels.)

Two other patterns exist. "E" class verbs have tsere ֵ [2] as their second vowel, and "O" class verbs have holem וֹ in the second vowel position. These patterns correspond to the three classes of vowels as listed in the section Vowel Points (p. 2). Except for hollow verbs, the Qal affix will always have its landmark ָ under the first root letter, regardless of the second vowel.

Many of these "E" and "O" class verbs are intransitive and describe a state of being rather than an action. For example, יָרֵא means *be in awe, fear,* and קָטֹן means *be small.* Some textbooks refer to them as "statives." But some "E" or "O" class verbs are transitive or otherwise do not seem to fit a stative definition, and many "A" class verbs are intransitive. Therefore, we do not use that terminology here.

---

[2] That ֵ sounds more like an English "a" than either ָ or ַ is true, but it is an "E" vowel nonetheless.

Qal Affix vowel patterns

"A" class		"E" class	"O" class
יָצָא	שָׁמַע	יָרֵא	גָּדֹל
2nd vowel ◌ָ	2nd vowel ◌ַ	2nd vowel ◌ֵ	2nd vowel וֹ

Below are Qal affix conjugations of verbs representative of these two other patterns.

Qal Affix "E" class כָּבֵד [3]

3 m. sg.	כָּבֵד	3 c. pl.	כָּבְדוּ
3 f. sg.	כָּבְדָה		
2 m. sg.	כָּבַדְתָּ	2 m. pl.	כְּבַדְתֶּם
2 f. sg.	כָּבַדְתְּ	2 f. pl.	כְּבַדְתֶּן
1 c. sg.	כָּבַדְתִּי	1 c. pl.	כָּבַדְנוּ

Qal Affix "O" class גָּדֹל [4]

3 m. sg.	גָּדֹל	3 c. pl.	גָּדְלוּ	
3 f. sg.	גָּדְלָה			
2 m. sg.	גָּדֹלְתָּ	2 m. pl.	גְּדָלְתֶּם	←
2 f. sg.	גָּדֹלְתְּ	2 f. pl.	גְּדָלְתֶּן	←
1 c. sg.	גָּדֹלְתִּי	1 c. pl.	גָּדֹלְנוּ	

3 In the Qal affix only the 3 m. sg. demonstrates the "E" class vowel.

4 Notice that in גָּדֹל the holem וֹ (written defectiva in our example) becomes a qamets ḥatuf in a closed unaccented syllable. (6.3b)

17.7a Assignments:

A. Learn the Qal affix paradigms of the "E" and "O" class verbs.

B. Read and translate Genesis 22:12-14

C. Read Genesis 21:1-7 and find the following:

A verb in the Pi`el ____________________

A DDO ____________________

A Qal 3 m. sg. affix form ____________________

A verb whose third root letter is ה ____________________

A dagesh lene ____________________

A proper noun ____________________

A preposition ____________________

A prefix pronoun ____________________

V:2 A noun in the absolute ____________________

A noun with a possessive suffix ____________________

A vav conversive ____________________

A 1st י verb ____________________

V:3 A 3 f. sg. affix form ____________________

A construct chain ____________________

A 3 m. sg. Qal prefix form ____________________

The relative pronoun ____________________

V:4 A noun which is present twice ____________________

A verb that looks like a hollow verb ____________________

A m. pl. noun in the absolute ____________________

A Pi`el affix form ____________________

V: 5 A conjunction ________________

V:6 A 3 m. sg. Qal prefix form ________________

A 3 m. sg. affix form ________________

A 3 f. sg. prefix form ________________

A m. sg. Qal participle ________________

A 1 c. sg. pronominal suffix ________________

V:7 A 1 c. sg. affix form ________________

A dagesh forte ________________

Deuteronomy 6:4 שְׁמַע יִשְׂרָאֵל יהוה אֱלֹהֵינוּ יהוה אֶחָד׃

18.1 Verb Analysis שְׁמַע

Root	Stem	Form	Person/Gender/Number	Special Features

18.1a Is the form prefix? __________ Is it affix? __________ What is the sign of the Qal affix? ____________________ (4.2a) Is the form participle? ______________ What is the sign of the Qal participle? ______________________________ (9.3a) Is the form infinitive? ________ What letter might you expect to see in front of the root if it were an infinitive? ____________ (11.2a) There is one other form: the **imperative** (command), which we have here. Its indicators in the Qal are less distinctive than those marking other forms.

> Often the masculine singular Qal imperative can be recognized by the shewa under the first root letter ___ ___ ___ְ

18.1b If the first root letter is a guttural, you can expect a composite shewa: אֱמֹר

18.1c Imperatives are always in the second person. When no other indication is attached to the end of the imperative, the gender is masculine and the number is singular. Write 2 m. sg. in the PGN column.

18.2 יִשְׂרָאֵל means ________________ Here it is the one addressed by the command: *(You) hear, O Israel!* This is called a **vocative**. Note that no special endings are used for the vocative. You can recognize its use only by the context.

18.3 יהוה אֱלֹהֵינוּ יהוה אֶחָד

18.3a יהוה means ______________________

18.3b אֱלֹהֵינוּ

> נוּ___ at the end of a word (noun or preposition) is the first person plural suffix (*us, our*).

אֱלֹהֵי is the form אֱלֹהִים takes when a suffix is attached. Note that the form that takes the suffix pronoun is like the construct form. (6.5a) אֱלֹהֵינוּ means ____________________

יהוה אֱלֹהֵינוּ can be translated as a phrase: ______________________________ (2.10b)

18.3c יהוה אֶחָד | אֶחָד means *one* [feminine form: אַחַת]. Numbers can be nouns or adjectives in Hebrew. This phrase can be translated *one* LORD with *one* as an adjective. What kind of adjective? ______________________ (14.2c) Or it can be translated as a noun sentence: *the* LORD *is one*. Our entire phrase then has at least two possible translations. *the* LORD *is our God, one* LORD or *the* LORD *is our God, the* LORD *is one*. Actually there are some other possibilities here, and you should notice at this point that we cannot always be sure there is a single "correct" translation.

18.4 Verse translation: ____

________________________ (This is the most important verse in the Hebrew Bible.)

18.5 Extra Grammar

You have now seen both attributive (14.2c) and predicate (15.2) adjectives. Descriptive adjectives (*good, bad, old, tall* etc.), demonstratives (*this, that, these, those*), and numbers can act as either attributive or predicate adjectives. The following chart should help you to sort out these distinctions.

	Attributive	Predicate
Descriptive (definite)	הָאָרֶץ הַטּוֹבָה	טוֹבָה הָאָרֶץ
Descriptive (indefinite)	אֶרֶץ טוֹבָה	וְהַמֶּלֶךְ...זָקֵן[1]
Demonstrative	הָאָרֶץ הַזֹּאת	זֹאת הָאָרֶץ אֵלֶּה אֱלֹהֶיךָ
Numbers[2]	יהוה אֶחָד	יהוה אֶחָד

[1] One could argue that זָקֵן is either the m. sg. Qal affix of an "E" class verb (17.7) or a m. sg. adjective. They look the same.

[2] Numbers, in Hebrew, can function in a few ways. This example demonstrates only their attributive and predicate possibilites.

In addition to translating the following verses, identify the relationship of each occurrence of אֶרֶץ with its modifiers.

1 מִן־הָאָרֶץ הַהִוא אֶל־אֶרֶץ טוֹבָה Exodus 3:8

2 מֵעַל הָאָרֶץ הַטֹּבָה אֲשֶׁר יהוה נֹתֵן לָכֶם Deuteronomy 11:17

[ל + 2 m. pl. object suffix ⟷ לָכֶם   מֵעַל *from off*]

3 וַיֹּאמְרוּ טוֹבָה הָאָרֶץ אֲשֶׁר־יהוה אֱלֹהֵינוּ נֹתֵן לָנוּ Deuteronomy 1:25

4 וְנָתַתִּי אֶת־הָאָרֶץ הַזֹּאת לְזַרְעֲךָ Genesis 48:4 [זֶרַע *seed, descendants*]

5 וַיֹּאמֶר לְזַרְעֲךָ אֶתֵּן אֶת־הָאָרֶץ הַזֹּאת Genesis 12:7

18.6 Assignments:

A. Review vocabulary words 1-100 and add words 101-150 for Lessons 18-22

B. Read and translate Genesis 28:10-12

C. Translate:

1 שֵׁם הָאֶחָד פֶּלֶג Genesis 10:25

2 שְׁמַע בְּקוֹל הָעָם לְכֹל אֲשֶׁר־יֹאמְרוּ אֵלֶיךָ 1 Samuel 8:7

3 שְׁמַע לְקוֹל דִּבְרֵי יהוה 1 Samuel 15:1

4 שְׁלַח־לִי אִישׁ־חָכָם 2 Chronicles 2:6 [חָכָם *wise*]

5 אֱמֹר אֶל־בְּנֵי־יִשְׂרָאֵל Exodus 33:5 [אֱמֹר 18.1b]

6 שֵׁם אַחַת חַנָּה 1 Samuel 1:2

7 וּשְׁמַע אֵת כָּל־אֲשֶׁר יֹאמַר יהוה אֱלֹהֵינוּ Deuteronomy 5:24 (27)

8 קְרָא שְׁמוֹ יִזְרְעֶאל Hosea 1:4

9 קוֹל אֹמֵר קְרָא Isaiah 40:6

10 שְׁמֹר אֶת־הָאִישׁ הַזֶּה 1 Kings 20:39

11 אֱמֹר אֶל־כָּל־עַם הָאָרֶץ וְאֶל הַכֹּהֲנִים Zechariah 7:5

Review: shewa ְ can be an identifier of a Pi'el form. Which form? What is its position?

וְאָמַרְתָּ דַּבֵּר יהוה כִּי שֹׁמֵעַ עַבְדֶּךָ 1 Samuel 3:9

19.1 Verb Analysis וְאָמַרְתָּ

What kind of dagesh is in the תּ ________________

Root	Stem	Form	Person/Gender/Number	Special Features

Don't forget to note the type of vav in the Special Features column. (8.1d)

Translation: ______________________________

19.2 דַּבֵּר יהוה

19.2a Verb Analysis דַּבֵּר

Root	Stem	Form	Person/Gender/Number	Special Features

What kind of dagesh is in the בּ ________________ The dagesh forte in the middle root letter indicates ________________ (2.3c) Is the form affix? ________ (4.2a) What vowel would be under the first root letter if this were an affix? ______

> In the Pi`el, pataḥ under the first root letter ___ ּ ___ ַ indicates the imperative form.

What will be the PGN? ____________ (18.1c)

19.2b יהוה means ____________ How is it related to the imperative just preceding it? ______________________ (18.2)

Translate the entire phrase: ______________________________

19.3 כִּי שֹׁמֵעַ עַבְדֶּךָ

19.3a Verb Analysis שֹׁמֵעַ

Root	Stem	Form	Person/Gender/Number	Special Features

Review 9.3a if you need help.

19.3b עַבְדֶּךָ

ךָ___ is the second person masculine singular possessive suffix for nouns and prepositions.

עֶבֶד means ______________

Translation of phrase: ______________

19.4 Sentence translation: ______________

____

19.5 Extra Grammar

The word עַבְדֶּךָ in the Lesson sentence usually reads עַבְדְּךָ but here it is **in pause**. That means the word falls at a major disjunctive accent which may cause a change in pointing and stress. You can see that with עַבְדֶּךָ the second shewa ְ has become a segol ֶ and the stress has moved from the last syllable to the second to last.

noun	noun with suffix	noun with suffix (in pause)
עֶבֶד	עַבְדְּךָ	עַבְדֶּךָ
דָּבָר	דְּבָרִי	דְּבָרָי
כֶּסֶף	כַּסְפְּךָ	כַּסְפֶּךָ׃

preposition	preposition with suffix	preposition with suffix (in pause)
לְ	לְךָ	לָךְ
מִן	מִמְּךָ	מִמֶּךָּ

19.6 Exercise:

Often it's the little words that will trip you up. Be sure you're confident of these, which may either look or sound similar.

שָׁם	שֵׁם	
לוֹ	לֹא	
אַל	עַל	אֶל
עִם	אִם	עַם
בַּיִת	בַּת	
דָּבָר	דִּבֵּר	
הִיא	הוּא	
יָם	יוֹם	
מָה	מִי	
עַיִן	אַיִן	
אַתָּא	עַתָּה	
צָוָה	צָבָא	
רָעָה	רָאָה	יָרֵא
נָשָׂא	אִשָּׁה	

Assignments:

A. Read and translate Genesis 28:13-15

B. Translate:

1 שְׁמַע יַעֲקֹב עַבְדִּי Isaiah 44:1

2 וַיֹּאמֶר מֹשֶׁה כֵּן דִּבַּרְתָּ Exodus 10:29

3 מַה דִּבַּרְתָּ אֶל־הַמֶּלֶךְ Jeremiah 38:25

4 דַּבֵּר אֶל־בְּנֵי יִשְׂרָאֵל וְאָמַרְתָּ אֲלֵהֶם Leviticus 1:2

5 כִּי־לֹא שָׁמַעְתָּ בְּקוֹל יהוה אֱלֹהֶיךָ Deuteronomy 28:45

6 שַׁלַּח אֶת־בְּנִי Exodus 4:23

7 דַּבֵּר אֶל־פַּרְעֹה מֶלֶךְ מִצְרַיִם Exodus 6:29

*8 שַׁלַּח לַחְמְךָ עַל־פְּנֵי הַמָּיִם [לֶחֶם *bread*] Qohelet 11:1

9 עֲמֹד בְּשַׁעַר בֵּית יהוה וְקָרָאתָ שָּׁם אֶת־הַדָּבָר הַזֶּה Jeremiah 7:2

10 וַיֹּאמֶר יהוה אֶל־מֹשֶׁה עֲבֹר לִפְנֵי הָעָם Exodus 17:5

11 שְׁמֹר וְשָׁמַעְתָּ אֵת כָּל־הַדְּבָרִים הָאֵלֶּה Deuteronomy 12:28

*12 וְעַתָּה יהוה אֱלֹהֵי יִשְׂרָאֵל שְׁמֹר לְעַבְדְּךָ דָוִד אָבִי אֵת אֲשֶׁר
דִּבַּרְתָּ לּוֹ 1 Kings 8:25

Exodus 10:24 וַיִּקְרָא פַרְעֹה אֶל־מֹשֶׁה וַיֹּאמֶר לְכוּ עִבְדוּ אֶת־יהוה

20.1 וַיִּקְרָא פַּרְעֹה אֶל־מֹשֶׁה

Verb analysis וַיִּקְרָא

Root	Stem	Form	Person/Gender/Number	Special Features

קרא means ______________

Translation of phrase: ____

20.2 וַיֹּאמֶר means ______________________

20.3 לְכוּ

This word begins the quotation — what Pharaoh said to Moses. Direct address of one person to another frequently means that imperatives will be used. Such is the case here. לְכוּ is a plural imperative.

> וּ___ is the second person masculine plural imperative ending.

This leaves only two letters for the root, and here there is no prefix with its vowel to help in determining the root. This situation will occur in the imperative with all types of roots in which the first letter is lost or assimilated in the prefix form. It can also occur with hollow verbs, and in feminine and plural forms of 3rd ה verbs. You must guess the root, but the possibilities will be significantly reduced by your knowledge of the missing letter rules. That is, you are familiar with which letters can be missing from which positions. You know that אלך בלך גלך and so forth are not serious contenders. Here the possibilities would be נלך הלך ילך לכה ליך לוך Which root is familiar? In this case, you may also remember from 11.2a that whenever the remaining two root letters are לכ the root is הלך Fill in the chart:

Root	Stem	Form	Person/Gender/Number	Special Features

20.4 Analyze **עִבְדוּ**

Is this an affix form? ________ Which form is it? (on the basis of elimination and context) ____________________

Root	Stem	Form	Person/Gender/Number	Special Features

This is the regular vowel pattern for the Qal plural imperative for verbs having three more or less strong root letters. Translate: ______________________________

20.5 Translate the verse: ______________________________

____

20.6 Extra Grammar

20.6a The imperative is a derivative of the prefix form. This may not be apparent in all four imperatives of every verb, but it is useful to note this feature as an aid in recognition and memorization.

Qal Imperatives

	Strong	3rd א	1st Guttural
m. sg.	שְׁמַע	קְרָא	עֲבַד
f. sg.	שִׁמְעִי	קִרְאִי	עִבְדִי
m. pl.	שִׁמְעוּ	קִרְאוּ	עִבְדוּ
f. pl.	שְׁמַעְנָה	קְרֶאנָה	עֲבַדְנָה

	1st י ישׁב	1st י ירא	3rd ה
m. sg.	שֵׁב	יְרָא	רְאֵה
f. sg.	שְׁבִי	יִרְאִי	רְאִי
m. pl.	שְׁבוּ	יִרְאוּ	רְאוּ
f. pl.	שֵׁבְנָה	יְרֶאנָה	רְאֶינָה

Qal Imperatives (continued)

Hollow[1]

m. sg.	קוּם	בּוֹא	שִׂים
f. sg.	קוּמִי	בּוֹאִי	שִׂימִי
m. pl.	קוּמוּ	בּוֹאוּ	שִׂימוּ
f. pl.	קֹמְנָה ←	בֹּאנָה ←	שֵׂמְנָה ←

	1st נ	1st נ[2]	נתן
m. sg.	גַּשׁ	נְפֹל	תֵּן
f. sg.	גְּשִׁי	נִפְלִי	תְּנִי
m. pl.	גְּשׁוּ	נִפְלוּ	תְּנוּ
f. pl.	גַּשְׁנָה	נְפֹלְנָה	תֵּנָּה

20.6b **Pi`el Imperatives**

	Strong	3rd Guttural	Mid Guttural/ר
m. sg.	דַּבֵּר	שַׁלַּח	בָּרֵךְ
f. sg.	דַּבְּרִי	שַׁלְּחִי	בָּרְכִי
m. pl.	דַּבְּרוּ	שַׁלְּחוּ	בָּרְכוּ
f. pl.	דַּבֵּרְנָה	שַׁלַּחְנָה	בָּרֵכְנָה

[1] The imperatives of hollow verbs whose middle letter is ו or י can be written plene or defectiva. Watch for spellings such as בָּא and קָם Note the deviation from the pattern of the f. pl.

[2] Some 1st נ verbs lose the נ of the root in the imperative form and some act like strong verbs with all root letters present.

20.7 Exercises:

A. Write the four Qal imperatives for the verbs listed below:

	הלך	עמד	שׁמר
m. sg.			
f. sg.			
m. pl.			
f. pl.			

B. Write the root for each of the following Qal imperative forms:

דְּעִי	עֲנִי	עֲשֵׂה
עֲלוּ	מְצָא	בְּנֵה
קְרָא	שְׂאוּ	מֻת
צְאוּ	שְׁמַעְנָה	רֵד

20.8 Assignments:

A. Learn the imperatives presented in 20.6a and 20.6b

B. Read and translate Genesis 28:16-18

C. Translate:

1 קוּם צֵא מִן־הָאָרֶץ Genesis 31:13

2 לְכִי וּבֹאִי אֶל־הַמֶּלֶךְ דָּוִד 1 Kings 1:13

3 לֵךְ וְאָמַרְתָּ אֶל־עַבְדִּי 2 Samuel 7:5

4 תְּנוּ־לָנוּ מַיִם Exodus 17:2

5 דְּעוּ אֶת־יהוה Jeremiah 31:34

6 בֹּא דַבֵּר אֶל־פַּרְעֹה מֶלֶךְ מִצְרָיִם וִישַׁלַּח אֶת־בְּנֵי־יִשְׂרָאֵל
מֵאַרְצוֹ׃ Exodus 6:11 [Read וִישַׁלַּח as if it were written וְ + יְשַׁלַּח]

7 דַּבְּרוּ אֶל־בְּנֵי יִשְׂרָאֵל Leviticus 11:2

8 דְּעוּ כִּי־יהוה הוּא אֱלֹהִים Psalms 100:3

וַיִּקַּח יִשְׂרָאֵל אֵת כָּל־הֶעָרִים הָאֵלֶּה וַיֵּשֶׁב יִשְׂרָאֵל בְּכָל־עָרֵי הָאֱמֹרִי

Numbers 21:25

21.1 וַיִּקַּח יִשְׂרָאֵל

Verb analysis וַיִּקַּח

Root	Stem	Form	Person/Gender/Number	Special Features

You should be able to fill in all but the root column. What kind of dagesh is in the ק ________ For root letters then, we have קקח ⟷ קח You would expect the root to be נקח but this is the one instance where a footprint dagesh of an assimilated first root letter represents not a נ but a ל So the root is ________

21.2 אֵת is the sign of ________ (7.2a) Where is the direct object? ________

21.3 כָּל־הֶעָרִים הָאֵלֶּה

21.3a כָּל means ________ Look at the next word, הֶעָרִים What kind of endiNG does it have? ________ (6.5a) If you take off the noun endiNG, you still do not have the root, however. The הֶ at the beginning is the definite article. Usually before a guttural it is pointed הָ (4.5b) but הֶ or sometimes even הַ is a possibility. Now you have עָר left — this is a form of the noun עִיר one of a small group of irregular nouns. עָרִים is the plural form. This is all the more unusual because עִיר is a feminine noun (even though it lacks the feminine endiNG in the singular), and it takes the masculine plural noun endings. הֶעָרִים will mean ________

21.3b הָאֵלֶּה | הָ means ________ The dagesh associated with the definite article is lost because ________ (4.5b) אֵלֶּה is a demonstrative adjective meaning *these*. While you must choose the correct form, זֶה or זֹאת in the singular, אֵלֶּה is used for the plural with both masculine and feminine nouns. What do you call the type of adjectival construction in this phrase? ________ ________ (14.2c)

Translation of the whole phrase: ________

21.4 וַיֵּשֶׁב יִשְׂרָאֵל

Verb analysis וַיֵּשֶׁב

Root	Stem	Form	Person/Gender/Number	Special Features

Left with only שׁב for the root, how do you determine the missing letter?

________________ (3.1)

____

______

a word indicates ________________ (6.3c)

this word is ________ and means ________

ite (to be construed in a collective sense).

ord phrase? ________________

____

____

21.7 Extra Grammar

21.7a לקח is a common irregular verb. But in the Qal affix it follows the pattern of the strong verb. You should be able to fill in the chart below:

Qal Affix לקח

3 m. sg.	לָ ק ח	3 c. pl.	___ ___ ___
3 f. sg.	___ ___ ___ ___		
2 m. sg.	___ ___ ___ ___	2 m. pl.	___ ___ ___ ___
2 f. sg.	___ ___ ___ ___	2 f. pl.	___ ___ ___ ___
1 c. sg.	___ ___ ___ ___	1 c. pl.	___ ___ ___ ___

21.7b The Qal prefix of לקח follows the pattern of נגשׁ (16.5b) Complete the chart:

Qal Prefix לקח

3 m. sg.	יִ קַּ ח	3 m. pl.	___ ___ ___ ___
3 f. sg.	___ ___ ___	3 f. pl.	___ ___ ___ ___
2 m. sg.	___ ___ ___	2 m. pl.	___ ___ ___ ___
2 f. sg.	___ ___ ___ ___	2 f. pl.	___ ___ ___ ___
1 c. sg.	___ ___ אֶ	1 c. pl.	___ ___ ___

21.7c The Qal imperatives of לקח also follow the pattern of נגשׁ Complete the chart:

Qal Imperative לקח

m. sg.	קַ ח	m. pl.	___ ___ ___
f. sg.	___ ___ ___	f. pl.	___ ___ ___

21.7d The m. sg. Qal participle of לקח is לֹקֵחַ The _ is a furtive pataḥ. (5.4)

21.8 Assignments:

A. Memorize the paradigms for the Qal of לקח

B. Read and translate Genesis 28:19-22

C. Translate:

1 וַיֵּצְאוּ כְּאִישׁ אֶחָד I Samuel 11:7

2 וְלֹא־לָקַחְתָּ מִיַּד־אִישׁ מְאוּמָה [מְאוּמָה *anything*] I Samuel 12:4

3 וְלֹא־יָשַׁב אָדָם שָׁם Jeremiah 2:6

4 וַיָּבֹא שָׁאוּל עַד־עִיר עֲמָלֵק I Samuel 15:5

5 וְהוּא יוֹשֵׁב בְּאֶרֶץ הַנֶּגֶב Genesis 24:62

6 וְיָשַׁבְתָּ בְאֶרֶץ־גֹּשֶׁן Genesis 45:10

7 וַיַּרְא וְהִנֵּה הָעָם יֹצֵא מִן־הָעִיר Judges 9:43

8 וְדָוִד יוֹשֵׁב בִּירוּשָׁלִָם 2 Samuel 11:1

9 קַח אֶת־אַהֲרֹן וְאֶת־בָּנָיו Leviticus 8:2

10 וַיִּבְנוּ אֶת־הֶעָרִים וַיֵּשְׁבוּ בָּהֶם Judges 21:23

11 כִּי־בָנָה יהוה צִיּוֹן [note absence of אֶת] Psalms 102:17

12 שְׁבוּ בָאָרֶץ וְעִבְדוּ אֶת־מֶלֶךְ בָּבֶל 2 Kings 25:24

Can't walk? Take לקח

לֹא־תִקַּח אִשָּׁה לִבְנִי מִבְּנוֹת הַכְּנַעֲנִי אֲשֶׁר אָנֹכִי יֹשֵׁב בְּאַרְצוֹ

Genesis 24:37

22.1 Verb לֹא־תִקַּח

Root	Stem	Form	Person/Gender/Number	Special Features

You should be able to analyze this verb. (21.7b) The tense of the verb translation will be _______________ (14.1) Translate the verb phrase: ____________________

22.2 אִשָּׁה means _______________ Relationship of noun to verb phrase: _______________

22.3 לִבְנִי There are three parts to this word; can you break it down? לְ means ______ בֵּן means ______________ ִי means ___________ (8.3) Notice the vowel changes in the noun when it is combined in such a phrase. Translate the word: ______________

22.4 מִבְּנוֹת | מִ ☐ means _____________ (3.4b) בְּנוֹת means *daughters.* Minus the endiNG וֹת____ is the familiar root בֵּן The feminine singular of בְּנוֹת is בַּת an irregular noun.

וֹת____ is the feminine plural noun endiNG, for both the construct and absolute plural.

22.4a We can now make a chart for feminine nouns as we did for masculine nouns in 6.5a. שָׁנָה means *year.*

	Absolute	Construct
Singular	שָׁנָה	שְׁנַת
Plural	שָׁנוֹת	שְׁנוֹת

In the singular absolute ָה or ַת is a common endiNG for feminine nouns. In the singular construct these nouns will all end in ַת

Fill in the appropriate endiNGs (consonants and vowels) in the chart below. מַלְכָּה means *queen.*

	Absolute	Construct
Singular	___ מַלְכּ	___ מַלְכּ
Plural	___ מְלָכ	___ מַלְכ

22.5 הַכְּנַעֲנִי

☐הַ in front of a word means ________ כְּנַעֲנִי is related to a place name you have already seen. The ending is equivalent to -ite in English. הַכְּנַעֲנִי means *the Canaanite.*

How are מִבְּנוֹת and הַכְּנַעֲנִי related? ______________________ (5.1b)

Translation: ______________________

22.6 אֲשֶׁר אָנֹכִי יֹשֵׁב

אֲשֶׁר means __________ (5.3a) אָנֹכִי ⟷ אֲנִי which means ________

Verb analysis יֹשֵׁב

Root	Stem	Form	Person/Gender/Number	Special Features

Translation of phrase: ______________________

22.7 בְּאַרְצוֹ

Again there are three parts to this word. בְּ means ______ אֶרֶץ means ______ וֹ ⟷ ו as a suffix pronoun. Translation: ______________________

22.8 Sentence translation: ______________________

____

22.8a Notice the way this subordinate אֲשֶׁר clause is constructed. It is a clause which further describes the Canaanite. In the clause in Hebrew a pronoun is used which repeats this antecedent noun:

הַכְּנַעֲנִי אֲשֶׁר אָנֹכִי יֹשֵׁב בְּאַרְצוֹ

the ***Canaannite, which*** *I am dwelling in* ***his*** *land*

This is a very common syntactical construction in Hebrew. In good English you may combine the אֲשֶׁר...וֹ and say:

the Canaanite in ***whose*** *land I am dwelling*

22.9 Extra Grammar

You know from 5.3a that the relative particle אֲשֶׁר never changes. That is, its form will always be the same, regardless of what it modifies. It can fill any one of several functions, and can be translated in many different ways, depending on its particular use in each instance. You have seen several of these uses in the readings from Genesis 22 and 28. In addition to what we usually think of as "relative" functions, אֲשֶׁר can be the subject of a verb, the object of a verb – with or without את – or it can be the object of a preposition.

A. אֲשֶׁר as the subject of a verb:

וַיֵּרַע בְּעֵינֵי יהוה אֲשֶׁר עָשָׂה Genesis 38:10

and it was evil in the eyes of the Lord *— what he had done*

and what he had done was evil in the eyes of the Lord[1]

B. אֲשֶׁר as the direct object of a verb:

1. Definite direct object with את

עָשִׂיתִי אֵת אֲשֶׁר־דִּבַּרְתִּי לָךְ Genesis 28:15

I have done (that about) which I had spoken to you

2. Direct object without את

אֲשֶׁר־אָהַבְתָּ Genesis 22:2

whom you love

[1] Often the English will have different word order from the Hebrew, though the translation itself is straightforward. Here we are giving a literal translation followed by a more idiomatic rendering.

C. אֲשֶׁר as the object of a preposition:

1. With a resumptive object suffix:

Genesis 28:13 הָאָרֶץ אֲשֶׁר אַתָּה שֹׁכֵב עָלֶיהָ

the land which-you-are-dwelling-on-it

the land upon which you are dwelling

2. Without a resumptive suffix:

Genesis 28:20 בַּדֶּרֶךְ הַזֶּה אֲשֶׁר אָנֹכִי הוֹלֵךְ

in this way which I am walking

D. אֲשֶׁר expressing a relative relationship:

m. sg. antecedent — Genesis 29:9 הַצֹּאן אֲשֶׁר לְאָבִיהָ

the flock which was her father's

f. sg. — Genesis 28:18 וַיִּקַּח אֶת־הָאֶבֶן אֲשֶׁר שָׂם

and he took the stone which was there

m. pl. — Genesis 20:9 מַעֲשִׂים אֲשֶׁר לֹא־יֵעָשׂוּ

things which should not have been done

f. pl. — Deuteronomy 4:2 אֶת־מִצְוֹת...אֲשֶׁר אָנֹכִי מְצַוֶּה אֶתְכֶם

the commandments ...which I am commanding you

22.10 Assignments:

A. Read and translate Genesis 29:1-3

B. Translate:

1 וַתְּדַבֵּר אֵלָיו כַּדְּבָרִים הָאֵלֶּה [כַּ ⟵⟶ כְּ + הַ] Genesis 39:17

2 תֵּדַע כִּי לַיהוה הָאָרֶץ Exodus 9:29

3 וְלָקַחְתָּ אִשָּׁה לִבְנִי מִשָּׁם Genesis 24:7

4 הֵן גּוֹי לֹא־תֵדַע תִּקְרָא [הֵן ⟵⟶ הִנֵּה] Isaiah 55:5

5 כִּי־תָבֹא אֶל־הָאָרֶץ אֲשֶׁר יהוה אֱלֹהֶיךָ נֹתֵן לָךְ Deuteronomy 17:14

6 יָבֹאוּ בְּנֵי הָאֱלֹהִים אֶל־בְּנוֹת הָאָדָם Genesis 6:4

7 וַיֹּאמֶר יהוה אֶל־אַבְרָם לֶךְ־לְךָ מֵאַרְצְךָ...אֶל־הָאָרֶץ
אֲשֶׁר אַרְאֶךָּ [*I will show you* אַרְאֶךָּ] Genesis 12:1

*8 וַיֹּאמֶר דָּוִיד אֶל־הָאֱלֹהִים חָטָאתִי מְאֹד אֲשֶׁר עָשִׂיתִי
אֶת־הַדָּבָר הַזֶּה [*sin* חטא *exceedingly* מְאֹד] 1 Chronicles 21:8

9 יִצְחָק אֲשֶׁר תֵּלֵד לְךָ שָׂרָה Genesis 17:21

10 וַיִּקְרְאוּ אֶל־לוֹט וַיֹּאמְרוּ לוֹ אַיֵּה הָאֲנָשִׁים אֲשֶׁר־בָּאוּ אֵלֶיךָ
[*where?* אַיֵּה   אִישׁ plural of ⟷ אֲנָשִׁים] Genesis 19:5

*11 אֶל כָּל־הַמָּקוֹם אֲשֶׁר נָבוֹא שָׁמָּה אִמְרִי־לִי אָחִי הוּא Genesis 20:13

12 וַיָּקָם מֶלֶךְ־חָדָשׁ עַל־מִצְרָיִם אֲשֶׁר לֹא־יָדַע אֶת־יוֹסֵף׃ Exodus 1:8
[*new* חָדָשׁ]

13 וָאֹמַר אֲלֵכֶם בָּאתֶם עַד־הַר הָאֱמֹרִי אֲשֶׁר־יהוה אֱלֹהֵינוּ נֹתֵן לָנוּ׃
Deuteronomy 1:20

14 וְלוֹ־אֶתֵּן אֶת־הָאָרֶץ אֲשֶׁר דָּרַךְ־בָּהּ וּלְבָנָיו Deuteronomy 1:36
[דֶּרֶךְ verb related to ⟷ דָּרַךְ]

15 כִּי עִמְּךָ יהוה אֱלֹהֶיךָ בְּכֹל אֲשֶׁר תֵּלֵךְ Joshua 1:9

אֶת־הָאָ֫רֶץ אֲשֶׁר־יהוה אֱלֹהֵיכֶם נֹתֵן לָכֶם וִירִשְׁתֶּם אֹתָהּ וִישַׁבְתֶּם־בָּהּ

Deuteronomy 11:31

23.1 אֶת־הָאָ֫רֶץ אֲשֶׁר־יהוה אֱלֹהֵיכֶם נֹתֵן לָכֶם

23.1a There is only one new element here: the suffix on the noun אֱלֹהֵי and on the preposition לְ

כֶם___ is the second person masculine plural suffix for nouns, prepositions, and verbs.

What form of the noun is אֱלֹהֵי ______________________________

Suffixes are usually attached to the ______________ form of a noun.

23.1b You should be able to analyze נֹתֵן

Root	Stem	Form	Person/Gender/Number	Special Features

Participles take on "tense" from the context in which they occur. Here the sense may be present: *is giving*, or of imminent future: *is about to give*.

23.1c Translation: ______________________________

23.2 וִירִשְׁתֶּם אֹתָהּ וִישַׁבְתֶּם־בָּהּ

23.2a תֶּם___ is the sign of which PGN and which form? ______________ וִישַׁבְתֶּם should yield a familiar root. What is it? ______________ Is there any augment to the root to suggest a stem other than Qal? ______________ So you would expect the first root letter to be pointed with a ______ (13.5) But יְ + וְ (here for a vav reversive) makes a difficult vowel combination at the beginning of a word and so וְיְ becomes the diphthong וִי

When the conjunction וְ is followed by a letter other than י that is pointed with a shewa, the conjunction becomes וּ e.g. וּלְיַעֲקֹב

ירשׁ means *inherit*.

23.2b אֹתָהּ is an interesting construction. It consists of אֶת the sign of the DDO combined with a pronoun, here הּ___ When the DDO sign combines with pronouns, the segol ֶ usually becomes a holem וֹ or ֹ

1 c. sg.	אֹתִי	1 c. pl.	אֹתָנוּ
2 m. sg.	אֹתְךָ	2 m. pl.	← אֶתְכֶם
2 f. sg.	אֹתָךְ	2 f. pl.	← אֶתְכֶן
3 m. sg.	אֹתוֹ	3 m. pl.	אֹתָם
3 f. sg.	אֹתָהּ	3 f. pl.	← אֶתְהֶן

Such a combination is the form a pronoun takes if it stands as a direct object of the verb.

In our phrase, what is the antecedent for the pronoun הּ ______________________

23.2c There is a circumstance in which the mappiq may be missing from the feminine singular suffix. If the final ה is already consonantal because it has its own vowel, then a mappiq is not needed to give it that force.

Numbers 30:8 וְקָמוּ נְדָרֶיהָ וֶאֱסָרֶהָ אֲשֶׁר־אָסְרָה עַל־נַפְשָׁהּ יָקֻמוּ

mappiq ↑ f. sg. affix ↑ no mappiq ↑ ↑ no mappiq

and her vows will stand and her bonds which she bound on her life will stand

23.2d Translate the phrase: ____

23.3 Translate the verse: ____

____

23.4 Assignments:

A. For Lessons 23-27 learn vocabulary words 151-200

B. Memorize the chart of DDO marker plus pronominal suffixes in 23.2b

C. Read and translate Genesis 29:4-7

D. No sentences. Night off. וְהָיִיתָ אַךְ שָׂמֵחַ (Deuteronomy 16:15b)

אֲנִי ·וְהָאִשָּׁה הַזֹּאת יֹשְׁבֹת בְּבַ֫יִת אֶחָד I Kings 3:17

24.1 אֲנִי וְהָאִשָּׁה הַזֹּאת

Translate the first three words of this sentence: ______________________________

24.2 יֹשְׁבֹת

Root	Stem	Form	Person/Gender/Number	Special Features

This word contains a root you have seen a number of times: ____________ (17.5, 21.4)

The ending וֹת___ however is used on what kind of words? ______________ (22.4)

Only one verb form can take noun endiNGs — the participle. Up until now you have seen only masculine singular participles, which have no special endiNGs, just as masculine singular nouns have no special endiNGs. But all other participles must take the appropriate noun endiNGs which tell us the gender and number of the participle. This participle is what gender and number? ______________

How do participles use these endiNGs? They must agree with the noun(s) or pronoun(s) they modify. What words are modified by this participle? ____________

____

Is the noun definite? ____________ Is the participle? ____________ Then what sort of adjective must it be in this case? ________________________ (15.2)

How do you fit this phrase together? Review 9.3b, and then translate the whole first phrase of the sentence: ______________________________

24.3 בְּבַ֫יִת אֶחָד | בְּ means ________ בַּ֫יִת means ________ אֶחָד means ________

(18.3c and 18.5) The type of grammatical construction you have here is called

____

Translate the phrase: ______________________________

24.4 Sentence translation: ______________________________

____

24.5 Extra Grammar

24.5a The Qal participle of almost every verb is regular and can be recognized by the holem (written plene or defectiva) after the first root letter plus the appropriate noun endiNG. Complete the chart below:

Qal Participle

m. sg.	יֹשֵׁב	א מֵ ר	נ פֵ ל
f. sg.	יֹשְׁבָה[1]	___ ˍ ˍְ ˍ	___ ˍ ˍ ˍ
m. pl.	יֹשְׁבִים	___ ˍ ˍְ ˍ	___ ˍ ˍ ˍ
f. pl.	יֹשְׁבוֹת	___ ˍ ˍְ ˍ	___ ˍ ˍ ˍ

24.5b Qal participle of hollow verbs

The Qal participle of hollow verbs does not have holem וֹ after the first root letter. You learned in 9.5a that the m. sg. participle of a hollow verb looks exactly like the 3 m. sg. affix form. There is the same ambiguity between the f. sg. participle and the 3 f. sg. affix form of hollow verbs. The same clues given in 9.5a for removing the ambiguity of בָּא will also work for בָּאָה The plural forms can be recognized by the noun endiNGs.

Qal Participle Hollow Verbs

	בּוֹא	קוּם	שִׂים
m. sg.	בָּא	קָם	שָׂם
f. sg.	בָּאָה	קָמָה	שָׂמָה
m. pl.	בָּאִים	קָמִים	שָׂמִים
f. pl.	בָּאוֹת	קָמוֹת	שָׂמוֹת

24.5c Participles, as verbal nouns, can have not only the definite article, but also any of the attached prepositions that a noun can have. Participles may occur in the construct or absolute states. Translate the words or phrases below:

כָּל־יוֹצְאֵי שַׁעַר עִירוֹ   הַיֹּצֵא   יֹצֵא   לַיּוֹצֵא   וְהַיּוֹצֵאת

[1] The f. sg. participle may also end in ת__ e.g. יוֹשֶׁבֶת

24.6 Assignments:

A. Read and translate Genesis 29:8-11

B. Translate:

1 וַיִּרְאוּ הַשֹּׁמְרִים אִישׁ יוֹצֵא מִן־הָעִיר [וַיִּרְאוּ ≠ וַיִּירְאוּ] Judges 1:24

2 וְהִנֵּה רִבְקָה יֹצֵאת [Remember ת___ is a f. sg. participle endiNG] Genesis 24:15

3 הִנֵּה שֶׁבַע שָׁנִים בָּאוֹת [*7 years* שֶׁבַע שָׁנִים] Genesis 41:29

4 קוֹל דְּבָרִים אַתֶּם שֹׁמְעִים [אַתֶּם pl. of אַתָּה] Deuteronomy 4:12

*5 וַיֹּאמֶר הַמֶּלֶךְ זֹאת אֹמֶרֶת זֶה־בְּנִי 1 Kings 3:23

6 וּמַלְכַּת־שְׁבָא שֹׁמַעַת אֶת־שֵׁמַע שְׁלֹמֹה 1 Kings 10:1
[שֵׁמַע *report* מַלְכַּת review 22.4]

7 וּבְנֵי יִשְׂרָאֵל הַיֹּצְאִים מֵאֶרֶץ מִצְרָיִם Numbers 26:4

*8 שִׁמְעוּ אֵלַי יֹדְעֵי צֶדֶק [צֶדֶק *righteousness*] Isaiah 51:7

9 הִנֵּה בֵית־יִשְׂרָאֵל אֹמְרִים Ezekiel 12:27

10 קָרְאוּ...וְכָל־הָעָם הַבָּאִים מֵעָרֵי יְהוּדָה Jeremiah 36:9

11 הִנֵּה־עָם יוֹרֵד מֵרָאשֵׁי הֶהָרִים [רֹאשׁ vocabulary word] Judges 9:36

*12 וְיָרַדְתָּ לְפָנַי...וְהִנֵּה אָנֹכִי יֹרֵד אֵלֶיךָ 1 Samuel 10:8

13 אָנֹכִי כֹּרֵת אֶת־הַבְּרִית הַזֹּאת Deuteronomy 29:13
[כָּרַת בְּרִית *make a convenant*]

14 וְשָׂרָה שֹׁמַעַת פֶּתַח הָאֹהֶל [פֶּתַח *opening*] Genesis 18:10

*15 כִּי כֹה אָמַר־יהוה אֶל־שַׁלֻּם בֶּן־יֹאשִׁיָּהוּ מֶלֶךְ יְהוּדָה הַמֹּלֵךְ
תַּחַת יֹאשִׁיָּהוּ אָבִיו אֲשֶׁר יָצָא מִן־הַמָּקוֹם הַזֶּה לֹא יָשׁוּב
שָׁם עוֹד׃ Jeremiah 22:11

In the last few Lessons you have been introduced to an assortment of nouns, both masculine and feminine, with a confusing array of endings, and we must attempt some order. At this point it is necessary to summarize the forms of the noun in Hebrew. Some of this material is best memorized immediately; other pieces of information can be assimilated more gradually.

With each noun we must determine three things:

Gender:	masculine or feminine
Number:	singular or plural
State:	absolute or construct (5.1b)

The following chart shows the endiNGs which help in determining these three things:

	Masc. Absolute	Masc. Construct	Fem. Absolute	Fem. Construct
singular	— no special endiNGs —		___ָה ___ת	___ַת
	דָבָר	דְבַר	חַטָּאת בְּרָכָה	חַטַּאת בִּרְכַּת
plural	___ִים	___ֵי	___וֹת	___וֹת
	דְבָרִים	דִבְרֵי	חַטָּאוֹת בְּרָכוֹת	חַטֹּאות בִּרְכוֹת

In addition to the help given by the endiNGs, you will observe that vowel changes take place within a word when the number or state is changed.

These vocalic changes make Hebrew quite a different type of language from English, where the vowel sounds within a word are relatively fixed. (Note, however, that even in English, vowels in words are often shortened in speech when words are strung together in long phrases and spoken quickly.) In Hebrew, the addition of the endiNGs, or the use of a construct phrase, causes the accent to shift away from the syllable accented in the singular absolute. The vowels in the early syllables of a word are reduced or shortened when this happens, since the accent is on the last syllable. Certain regular patterns are found in nouns as the number and state change, but the number of patterns is quite large, and there are many exceptions to the basic patterns. This makes it difficult for a beginning student, since each noun requires separate pattern memorization. Remember, however, that the <u>root consonants</u> do not change, and the endiNGs will help you to identify gender, number, and state.

It helps most students to divide mastery of nouns into two parts: first, to identify the gender, number, and state of the noun, its root, and any additions to it; then after some experience, to study nouns with more attention so that the more basic patterns can be remembered, and nouns can be classified by type.

A. You may usually assume that a noun is masculine unless it ends in ָה or ת or unless it falls into one of the following exceptional classes. Two common feminine nouns that do not have these endiNGs are אֶרֶץ *land* and עִיר *city*. [עִיר even takes masculine plural endiNGs.]

If a noun ends in ֶה it is masculine. Common examples are פֶּה *mouth*, שָׂדֶה *field*, מַטֶּה *staff, tribe.*

While sometimes there seems to be no reason behind gender assignment, there are classes of objects that tend to fall into a particular gender:

Not only is אֶרֶץ feminine, but so are similar words such as אֲדָמָה *ground*, and תֵּבֵל *world.*

Pottery items are always feminine, but containers of wood are usually masculine. Boats, however, are feminine and have the ָה endiNG.

B. Many parts of the body — especially those occurring in pairs — are feminine even if they do not end in ָה

יָד	*hand*	אֹזֶן	*ear*
עַיִן	*eye*	רֶגֶל	*foot*
בֶּטֶן	*belly*	נֶפֶשׁ	*self, soul*
רוּחַ	*breath, spirit*	שֵׁן	*tooth*

A notable exception to the rule of paired body parts being feminine is the masculine שַׁד *breast*. A few body parts, like לֵב *heart*, are considered masculine, but use feminine plural endiNGs.

A special plural is used for these pairs: ַיִם the dual ending.

dual absolute		dual and plural construct	
עֵינַיִם	אָזְנַיִם	עֵינֵי	אָזְנֵי

C. Many nouns have more (or less) than three letters. Yet many lexicons require you to establish the hypothetical three letter root in order to look up the noun. It is helpful, therefore, to learn to find the root base of any noun.[1]

[1] Nouns of two letters and three letter nouns whose root may be difficult to determine will be discussed later in the Lessons.

1. Nouns may be formed from three letter roots simply by adding ה at the end:

ברך *bless* — בְּרָכָה *blessing*

צדק *be righteous* — צְדָקָה *righteousness*

2. Nouns may be formed from three letter roots by placing a מ in front of the root:

שפט *judge* — מִשְׁפָּט *judgment, justice*

קום *arise* — מָקוֹם *place*

3. Nouns may be formed by adding a ת in front of the three letter root:

ירה *teach* — תּוֹרָה *law, instruction*

D. Many masculine nouns have feminine counterparts which can be easily guessed or remembered:

בֵּן *son* — בְּנוֹת *daughters* [sg. בַּת]

אָח *brother* — אָחוֹת *sister*

מֶלֶךְ *king* — מַלְכָּה *queen*

אָדָם *man* — אֲדָמָה *earth*

(If this last pair seems strange to you, look at Genesis 2:7.)

E. Family relationships of nouns may be both helpful and confusing. For example, consider these nouns related to the root מלך

מֶלֶךְ *king* מַלְכָּה *queen* מַמְלָכָה *kingdom* מַלְכוּת *reign*

Again, ability to pick out the root is an important asset in such times of confusion, since you can then use a lexicon to untangle the meanings.

F. One common noun pattern is the segolate noun, so called because the two syllable nouns of this class nearly always have segol as their second vowel. They are always accented on the <u>first</u> syllable in the singular absolute, not the second. Nouns of this class are easy for most students to memorize, especially since the vowels are the same in both the absolute and construct singular. Some common examples are

אֶרֶץ *land* מֶלֶךְ *king* כֶּסֶף *silver* סֵפֶר *book* בֹּקֶר *morning*

A few relatively common nouns – whose middle letter is a guttural – are considered segolates, even though the segol doesn't appear. They follow the other patterns of this class however, in that the accent is on the first syllable and the vowels in the absolute and construct singular remain the same:

נַ֫עַר *lad, youth* בַּ֫עַל *Baal, master, owner, lord* נַ֫חַל *stream, wadi, torrent*

G. When pronoun suffixes are added to nouns, other endiNGs are changed. Many times (though certainly not always) the form of the noun to which the pronoun is added is similar to the construct form:

Absolute	Construct	Suffixed Form
דָּבָר	דְּבַר	דְּבָרְנוּ
תּוֹרָה	תּוֹרַת	תּוֹרָתִי
אֱלֹהִים	אֱלֹהֵי	אֱלֹהֵינוּ
דְּבָרִים	דִּבְרֵי	דְּבָרֵינוּ

It follows from the above observation that it is possible to tell whether a noun with a suffix is singular or plural; masculine plural nouns can be recognized by the ֵי___ of the plural construct endiNG which will be present between the noun root and the suffix. Feminine plural nouns use both וֹת___ (the plural endiNG) and a connecting י

דִּבְרֵי *words of* דְּבָרֵינוּ *our words*

תּוֹרוֹת *laws* תּוֹרוֹתֵינוּ *our laws*

This rule is infallible for distinguishing singular and plural nouns with suffixes, with only two exceptions:

1. אָב *father* and אָח *brother* have irregular constructs in the singular using י___ (See section H below)

2. With the first person singular suffix, the vowel alone tells you whether the noun is singular or plural:

יָדִי *my hand* יָדַי *my hands*

H. Some very common nouns have irregular forms that occur a great deal. <u>It is well worth memorizing all of these</u>.

Sg. Absolute	Sg. Construct	Pl. Absolute	Pl. Construct
אִישׁ *man*	אִישׁ	אֲנָשִׁים	אַנְשֵׁי
אִשָּׁה *woman*	אֵשֶׁת	נָשִׁים	נְשֵׁי
בַּיִת *house*	בֵּית	בָּתִּים	בָּתֵּי
בַּת *daughter*	בַּת	בָּנוֹת	בְּנוֹת
אָב *father*	אֲבִי	אָבוֹת	אֲבוֹת
אָח *brother*	אֲחִי	אַחִים	אֲחֵי
יוֹם *day*	יוֹם	יָמִים	יְמֵי
עִיר *city*	עִיר	עָרִים	עָרֵי

Attempting to classify nouns by patterns of formation, and then again by gender, and finally by variations to vowels caused by silent letters (and gutturals), produces well over one hundred different patterns for nouns. This does not count the nouns that are simply downright irregular. Eventually you will want, and need, to know more about the forms or morphology of Hebrew nouns, but for now the information in this excursus should serve as a basic introduction.

וְלֹא־נָתַן יהוה לָכֶם לֵב לָדַעַת וְעֵינַיִם לִרְאוֹת וְאָזְנַיִם לִשְׁמֹעַ
עַד הַיּוֹם הַזֶּה׃ Deuteronomy 29:3

25.1 וְלֹא־נָתַן יהוה לָכֶם

25.1a Analyze נָתַן

Root	Stem	Form	Person/Gender/Number	Special Features

25.1b לָכֶם | לָ means ________ כֶם means ________

Translation of phrase: ____________________

25.2 לֵב לָדַעַת

לֵב means ____________ לָדַעַת is a verb form. Can you analyze it?

Root	Stem	Form	Person/Gender/Number	Special Features

The key to the form is the ל in front of the root. Which form of the verb usually occurs with the preposition *to?* ____________ ת is the infinitive ending of one type of verb (see 11.2b). Do you remember a root with the letters דע in it?

____

> When a verb root begins with י the Qal infinitive construct usually drops the י and adds ת on the end.

Translation of phrase: ____________________

25.3 וְעֵינַיִם לִרְאוֹת

25.3a וְעֵינַיִם Initial וְ means ____________

וְלֹא־נָתַן יהוה לָכֶם לֵב לָדַעַת וְעֵינַיִם לִרְאוֹת וְאָזְנַיִם לִשְׁמֹעַ עַד הַיּוֹם הַזֶּה׃

> ַיִם is the dual ending on nouns. This ending is used instead of the simple plural for referring to two of a noun, or for things that occur in pairs. (Review The Noun B.)

עַיִן means __________ so עֵינַיִם means __________ Note that there is a similarity between this dual ending and the masculine plural endiNG. The dual ending can occur with either gender, but is most likely to be seen with feminine nouns, since it is used most often with parts of the body, and body parts occurring in pairs are most often feminine. The dual construct is like the masculine plural construct and the possessive suffixes are added to this construct ending.

25.3b לִרְאוֹת

Root	Stem	Form	Person/Gender/Number	Special Features

> 3rd ה verbs in the Qal infinitive drop the ה and add וֹת___

25.4 וְאָזְנַיִם לִשְׁמֹעַ

What kind of endiNG is on וְאָזְנַיִם __________ אֹזֶן means *ear.*
אָזְנַיִם means __________

Analyze לִשְׁמֹעַ

Root	Stem	Form	Person/Gender/Number	Special Features

> A holem after the second root letter indicates the Qal infinitive of the regular verb.

Translate phrase: ____________________

וְלֹא־נָתַן יהוה לָכֶם לֵב לָדַעַת וְעֵינַיִם לִרְאוֹת וְאָזְנַיִם לִשְׁמֹעַ
עַד הַיּוֹם הַזֶּה׃

25.5 עַד הַיּוֹם הַזֶּה

What do you call this kind of adjective construction? ______________________

Translate phrase: ______________________

25.6 Translation of verse: ______________________

____

25.7 Here is a summary of the **Qal infinitive construct.**[1]

Regular Infinitive שְׁמֹעַ With attached preposition, לִשְׁמֹעַ

The Qal infinitive of a regular verb has a ______________________ (25.4)

1st י דַּעַת With attached preposition, ______________ לָ

Verbs beginning with a י usually form their infinitives by ______________________

______________________ (25.2)

This pattern extends to other verbs whose first root letter is weak.

קַחַת ← לקח and לֶכֶת ← הלך

Some 1st נ verbs follow this rule as well: גֶּשֶׁת ← נגשׁ while some follow the rule for regular verbs: נְפֹל ← נפל

Note the differences in interior vocalization of the examples given.

1st י verbs which retain the י of the root in the prefix, (17.5) usually follow the pattern of the regular infinitive יְרֹא ← ירא

3rd ה רְאוֹת With attached preposition ______________ לִ

Roots ending in ה form the infinitive by ______________________ (25.3b)

Hollow verbs קוּם With attached preposition ______________ לָ

That is, hollow verbs retain the י or ו in the Qal infinitive.

נתן

The infinitive of נתן is תֵּת With an attached preposition, לָתֵת

[1] A second type of infinitive, the infinitive absolute, will be studied later.

וְלֹא־נָתַן יהוה לָכֶם לֵב לָדַעַת וְעֵינַיִם לִרְאוֹת וְאָזְנַיִם לִשְׁמֹעַ
עַד הַיּוֹם הַזֶּה׃

25.8 Assignments:

A. Memorize the Qal infinitive patterns in 25.7

B. Translate Exodus 3:1-3

C. Translate:

1 וַיָּקָם הָאִישׁ לָלֶכֶת Judges 19:7

2 וַיִּשְׁלַח הַמֶּלֶךְ לִקְרֹא אֶת־אֲחִימֶלֶךְ 1 Samuel 22:11

3 לֹא אַתָּה תִּבְנֶה־לִּי הַבַּיִת לָשָׁבֶת׃ 1 Chronicles 17:4

*4 וַיִּמְלְאוּ יָמֶיהָ לָלֶדֶת [יָמֶיהָ *her days*] Genesis 25:24

5 וַיְדַבֵּר אֱלֹהִים אֶל־נֹחַ לֵאמֹר׃ Genesis 8:15

6 וַיֵּרֶד יהוה לִרְאֹת אֶת־הָעִיר Genesis 11:5

7 עֵינַיִם לָהֶם לִרְאוֹת וְלֹא רָאוּ אָזְנַיִם לָהֶם לִשְׁמֹעַ וְלֹא שָׁמֵעוּ
Ezekiel 12:2

8 וַיֹּאמֶר שְׁלֹמֹה לִבְנוֹת בַּיִת לְשֵׁם יהוה 2 Chronicles 1:18

9 וַיֵּלְכוּ...לָלֶכֶת לָבוֹא מִצְרָיִם Jeremiah 41:17

10 וַיִּשְׁלַח שָׁאוּל מַלְאָכִים לָקַחַת אֶת־דָּוִד [מַלְאָךְ *messenger*] 1 Samuel 19:14

11 אֲנִי יהוה אֱלֹהֵיכֶם אֲשֶׁר־הוֹצֵאתִי אֶתְכֶם מֵאֶרֶץ מִצְרַיִם לָתֵת
לָכֶם אֶת־אֶרֶץ כְּנַעַן [הוֹצֵאתִי אֶתְכֶם *I brought you*] Leviticus 25:38

12 עֵת לָלֶדֶת וְעֵת לָמוּת [עֵת vocabulary] Qohelet 3:2

*13 כִּי אֲנִי יָדַעְתִּי אֲשֶׁר עֲבָדֶיךָ יוֹדְעִים לִכְרוֹת עֲצֵי לְבָנוֹן 2 Chronicles 2:7

14 עַתָּה עִם־לְבָבִי לִכְרוֹת בְּרִית לַיהוה אֱלֹהֵי יִשְׂרָאֵל 2 Chronicles 29:10

(Note the two very different uses of כרת in 14 and 15.)

15 וַיָּקָם יְהוֹשֻׁעַ וְכָל־עַם הַמִּלְחָמָה לַעֲלוֹת הָעָי Joshua 8:3

16 וַיָּשֶׂם חֲזָאֵל פָּנָיו לַעֲלוֹת עַל־יְרוּשָׁלָיִם 2 Kings 12:18

17 וַיֹּאמֶר יוֹסֵף אֶל־אֶחָיו אֲנִי יוֹסֵף...וְלֹא יָכְלוּ אֶחָיו לַעֲנוֹת Genesis 45:3
אֹתוֹ [יכל *be able*]

Joshua 23:3 וְאַתֶּם רְאִיתֶם אֵת כָּל־אֲשֶׁר עָשָׂה יהוה אֱלֹהֵיכֶם

26.1 וְאַתֶּם | וְ means ________

> אַתֶּם is the second person masculine plural independent pronoun.

When an independent pronoun is followed by a verb in the same person, gender, and number, it is used for emphasis.

26.2 Verb analysis רְאִיתֶם

Root	Stem	Form	Person/Gender/Number	Special Features

תֶּם____ is the 2 m. pl. affix ending. The root must therefore be found in the letters ראי However, **no root ends in** י

> When a verb root ends in a י before an affix pronoun, the last letter of the root is actually ה

What is the stem? ____________ The form is Qal affix, even though ָ is not used. The change in pointing is due to the "heavy" ending תֶּם____ which causes vowel shifts in the first part of the word. (Review 13.5) Translate verb: ____________

26.3 אֵת כָּל־אֲשֶׁר עָשָׂה יהוה אֱלֹהֵיכֶם

This whole segment is the DDO of the main verb, but it is made up of three grammatical components. What are they? ____________

____

Analyze עָשָׂה

Root	Stem	Form	Person/Gender/Number	Special Features

26.4 Translate verse: ____

____

26.5 Extra Grammar

3rd ה verbs present one of the very few irregular patterns in the Qal affix. The following chart shows how the ending of the root is affected by the addition of each affix pronoun.

26.5a

Qal Affix 3rd ה

3 m. sg.	בָּנָה	3 c. pl.	בָּנוּ ⟵
3 f. sg.	בָּֽנְתָה ⟵		
2 m. sg.	בָּנִיתָ	2 m. pl.	בְּנִיתֶם
2 f. sg.	בָּנִית	2 f. pl.	בְּנִיתֶן
1 c. sg.	בָּנִיתִי	1 c. pl.	בָּנִינוּ

Note especially the 3 f. sg. and the 3 c. pl., which are unlike the others in the pattern. The chart uses בנה which has two strong letters at the beginning of the root. The most common 3rd ה verbs עשׂה עלה היה ראה are composed of weak and guttural letters, and thus may have other irregular vowel markings as well as those connected with the final ה

26.5b The Qal prefix of 3rd ה verbs loses the ה of the root before a prefix complement is added. In some PGNs, a י takes its place.

Qal Prefix 3rd ה

3 m. sg.	יִבְנֶה	3 m. pl.	יִבְנוּ
3 f. sg.	תִּבְנֶה	3 f. pl.	תִּבְנֶינָה
2 m. sg.	תִּבְנֶה	2 m. pl.	תִּבְנוּ
2 f. sg.	תִּבְנִי	2 f. pl.	תִּבְנֶינָה
1 c. sg.	אֶבְנֶה	1 c. pl.	נִבְנֶה

26.5c The Qal imperative of 3rd ה verbs was presented in 20.6a. Fill in the chart for בנה

Qal Imperative 3rd ה

m. sg.	___ ___ ___
f. sg.	___ ___ ___
m. pl.	___ ___ ___
f. pl.	___ י___ ___

26.5d The Qal participle for 3rd ה verbs can be recognized by the usual feature for Qal participles: ______________________ The interior vocalization is different for the m. sg. and f. sg., and as is the way with 3rd ה forms, the ה of the root is lost before endiNGs are added.

Qal Participle 3rd ה

m. sg.	בֹּנֶה
f. sg.	בֹּנָה
m. pl.	בֹּנִים
f. pl.	בֹּנוֹת

26.5e You already learned the Qal infinitive for 3rd ה verbs. (14.3a, 25.7)
The Qal infinitive construct for בנה is ____________ and with an attached preposition ____________

26.6 Assignments:

A. Memorize the 3rd ה Qal paradigm. (26.5a-e)

B. Read and translate Exodus 3:4-6

C. Translate:

1 וְעָשִׂינוּ עִמְּךָ חָסֶד׃ Judges 1:24

2 וּרְאִיתֶם אֶת־הָאָרֶץ Numbers 13:18

3 וְהָיִינוּ לְעַם אֶחָד Genesis 34:16

4 וּבָנִים לֹא־הָיוּ לָהֶם Numbers 3:4

5 כִּי רָאִיתִי אֵת כָּל־אֲשֶׁר לָבָן עֹשֶׂה לָּךְ Genesis 31:12

6 מַה־זֹּאת עָשִׂיתָ לִּי Genesis 12:18

*7 וַיִּקְרָא יַעֲקֹב שֵׁם הַמָּקוֹם פְּנִיאֵל כִּי־רָאִיתִי אֱלֹהִים פָּנִים
אֶל־פָּנִים וַתִּנָּצֵל נַפְשִׁי׃ [נַפְשִׁי, i.e., *it is preserved*, תִּנָּצֵל] Genesis 32:31

8 וַיִּקְרָא אֲבִימֶלֶךְ לְאַבְרָהָם וַיֹּאמֶר לוֹ מֶה־עָשִׂיתָ לָּנוּ
וּמֶה־חָטָאתִי לָךְ [מֶה ⟷ מַה] Genesis 20:9

9 וְאַתֶּם רְאִיתֶם אֵת כָּל־אֲשֶׁר עָשָׂה יהוה אֱלֹהֵיכֶם לְכָל־הַגּוֹיִם
הָאֵלֶּה מִפְּנֵיכֶם Joshua 23:3

10 וּבְנֵי רְאוּבֵן בָּנוּ אֶת־חֶשְׁבּוֹן Numbers 32:37

11 בַּת־שְׁלֹמֹה הָיְתָה לּוֹ לְאִשָּׁה 1 Kings 4:11

12 וְאֶרֶץ הַגִּלְעָד הָיְתָה לִבְנֵי־מְנַשֶּׁה Joshua 17:6

13 אַתֶּם רְאִיתֶם אֲשֶׁר עָשִׂיתִי לְמִצְרָיִם Exodus 19:4

14 וַיֹּאמֶר לָהֶם יוֹסֵף מָה־הַמַּעֲשֶׂה הַזֶּה אֲשֶׁר עֲשִׂיתֶם Genesis 44:15

15 וְאֵלֶּה הַכֹּהֲנִים וְהַלְוִיִּם אֲשֶׁר עָלוּ עִם־זְרֻבָּבֶל בֶּן־שְׁאַלְתִּיאֵל
Nehemiah 12:1 [Can you tell why there is a dagesh in וְהַלְוִיִּם]

16 וַיִּקְרָא מֹשֶׁה אֶל־כָּל־יִשְׂרָאֵל וַיֹּאמֶר אֲלֵהֶם אַתֶּם רְאִיתֶם אֵת
כָּל־אֲשֶׁר עָשָׂה יהוה לְעֵינֵיכֶם בְּאֶרֶץ מִצְרַיִם לְפַרְעֹה
וּלְכָל־עֲבָדָיו וּלְכָל־אַרְצוֹ׃ Deuteronomy 29:1 [Note the nuances of the use of לְ]

17 אַךְ בַּת־פַּרְעֹה עָלְתָה מֵעִיר דָּוִד אֶל־בֵּיתָהּ אֲשֶׁר בָּנָה־לָהּ
1 Kings 9:24 [אַךְ *surely, only*]

18 וַיֵּרֶד יהוה לִרְאֹת אֶת־הָעִיר וְאֶת־הַמִּגְדָּל אֲשֶׁר בָּנוּ בְּנֵי הָאָדָם׃
Genesis 11:5 [מִגְדָּל *tower*]

19 וּבָנִיתָ שָּׁם מִזְבֵּחַ לַיהוה אֱלֹהֶךָ Deuteronomy 27:5

Hosea 7:10 וְלֹא־שָׁבוּ אֶל־יהוה אֱלֹהֵיהֶם

27.1 וְלֹא־שָׁבוּ

Analyze שָׁבוּ

Root	Stem	Form	Person/Gender/Number	Special Features

The only difficulty with this verb is finding the root since there is no prefix pronoun to help you. However, a short rule will aid you here: 1st י and 1st נ verbs are regular in the Qal affix; 3rd ה verbs are irregular and you have just studied their forms. Of our major classes of irregular verbs, only hollow verbs are unaccounted for.

> In the Qal affix, **hollow verbs** use only the two strong letters of the root, plus the affix pronouns. This form is distinct from most two letter imperative forms because either ָ or ַ will appear under the first root letter.

Once you know this is an affix form, it should not be difficult to fill in all the columns of the chart.

Translate phrase: ______________________________

27.2 אֶל־יהוה אֱלֹהֵיהֶם

All the components of this phrase have been seen several times.

27.3 Translate the verse: ______________________________

____

27.4 Extra Grammar

While the third person forms of hollow verbs use the characteristic stem vowel for the Qal affix, note what happens to the vowel in other PGNs.[1]

---

[1] The Qal affix vowel pattern for שׁוּב is also applied to hollow verbs whose middle letter is וֹ or ִי.
So you will see בּוֹא → 3 m. sg. בָּא 3 f. sg. בָּאָה etc., and for שִׂים → 3 m. sg. שָׂם 3 f. sg. שָׂמָה etc.

27.4a **Qal Affix Hollow שׁוּב**

3 m. sg.	שָׁב	3 c. pl.	שָׁבוּ
3 f. sg.	שָׁבָה		
2 m. sg.	שַׁבְתָּ	2 m. pl.	שַׁבְתֶּם
2 f. sg.	שַׁבְתְּ	2 f. pl.	שַׁבְתֶּן
1 c. sg.	שַׁבְתִּי	1 c. pl.	שַׁבְנוּ

27.4b The Qal prefix of hollow verbs is regular,[1] except for the 3 f. pl. and the 2 f. pl.

Qal Prefix Hollow שׁוּב

3 m. sg.	יָ שׁ וּ ב	3 m. pl.	___ ⌴ ⌴ ⌴ _
3 f. sg.	⌴ ⌴ ⌴ _	3 f. pl.	___ בְ שׁ תָּ ←
2 m. sg.	⌴ ⌴ ⌴ _	2 m. pl.	___ ⌴ ⌴ ⌴ _
2 f. sg.	___ ⌴ ⌴ ⌴ _	2 f. pl.	___ ⌴ ⌴ _ ←
1 c. sg.	⌴ ⌴ ⌴ אָ	1 c. pl.	⌴ ⌴ ⌴ _

27.4c The Qal Imperative of hollow verbs is regular (that is, it is formed by removing the prefix pronoun from the corresponding 2nd person prefix form). Review 20.6a if necessary, then fill in the chart:

Qal Imperative Hollow

	שׁ וּ ב	א וֹ ר	בּ י ן
m. sg.	⌴ ⌴ ⌴	⌴ ⌴ ⌴	⌴ ⌴ ⌴
f. sg.	___ ⌴ ⌴ ⌴	___ ⌴ ⌴ ⌴	___ ⌴ ⌴ ⌴
m. pl.	___ ⌴ ⌴ ⌴	___ ⌴ ⌴ ⌴	___ ⌴ ⌴ ⌴
f. pl.	___ ⌴ ⌴	___ ⌴ ⌴	___ נָּ ⌴

[1] That means the middle letter of the root remains so בּוֹא → 3 m. sg. יָבוֹא 3 f. sg. תָּבוֹא and שִׂים → 3 m. sg. יָשִׂים 3 f. sg. תָּשִׂים The 2 and 3 f. pl. are pointed with a shortened interior vowel.

27.4d The Qal participle of hollow verbs is not regular. Review 24.5b and fill in the chart:

Qal Participle Hollow

	שׁ ו ב	ב ו א	בּ י ן
m. sg.	___ ___	___ ___	___ ___
f. sg.	____ ___ ___	____ ___ ___	____ ___ ___
m. pl.	____ ___ ___	____ ___ ___	____ ___ ___
f. pl.	____ ___ ___	____ ___ ___	____ ___ ___

27.4e The Qal infinitive of hollow verbs is formed by removing the prefix pronoun from the 3 m. sg. Review 25.7, then fill in the chart using the 3 paradigm verbs just above:

Qal Infinitive Hollow

	With attached preposition
___ ___ ___	לָ ___ ___ ___
___ ___ ___	לָ ___ ___ ___
___ ___ ___	לָ ___ ___ ___

27.5 Assignments:

A. Memorize the Qal forms of the hollow verb 27.4a-e

B. Read and translate Exodus 3:7-9

C. Translate:

*1 כִּי הָעֲמָלֵקִי וְהַכְּנַעֲנִי שָׁם לִפְנֵיכֶם וּנְפַלְתֶּם בֶּחָרֶב כִּי־עַל־כֵּן
שַׁבְתֶּם מֵאַחֲרֵי יהוה וְלֹא־יִהְיֶה יהוה עִמָּכֶם׃ Numbers 14:43
[כִּי־עַל־כֵּן *because* מֵאַחֲרֵי *from after*]

2 וַיָּשׁוּבוּ הַמַּלְאָכִים אֵלָיו וַיֹּאמֶר אֲלֵיהֶם מַה־זֶּה שַׁבְתֶּם׃ 2 Kings 1:5

3 וְשַׂמְתִּי מָקוֹם לְעַמִּי לְיִשְׂרָאֵל 2 Samuel 7:10

4 שִׂים יְמִינְךָ עַל־רֹאשׁוֹ [יָמִין *right hand*] Genesis 48:18

5 וַתֹּאמֶר נָעֳמִי...לֵכְנָה שֹׁבְנָה Ruth 1:8

6 וְנִחְיֶה וְלֹא נָמוּת Genesis 43:8

7 וְרוּחַ יהוה סָרָה מֵעִם שָׁאוּל [מֵעִם *from*] 1 Samuel 16:14

*8 קוּמִי שְׂאִי אֶת־הַנַּעַר Genesis 21:18

9 וַיָּשָׁב אַבְרָהָם אֶל־נְעָרָיו וַיָּקֻמוּ וַיֵּלְכוּ יַחְדָּו אֶל־בְּאֵר שָׁבַע
וַיֵּשֶׁב אַבְרָהָם בִּבְאֵר שָׁבַע׃ [יַחְדָּו *together*] Genesis 22:19

Hint: the most common vowel letter in hollow verbs is וּ The rarest is וֹ

וְהַמֶּלֶךְ אָסָא הִשְׁמִיעַ אֶת־כָּל־יְהוּדָה 1 Kings 15:22

28.1 וְהַמֶּלֶךְ means ______________________ אָסָא is a name: ________________

28.2 Verb Analysis הִשְׁמִיעַ

Root	Stem	Form	Person/Gender/Number	Special Features

Here you encounter a new stem. It is called **Hif'il**, and is formed by adding ה before the root letters and by using a characteristic set of vowels. The key vowel to watch for comes between the second and third root letters and will usually be
ִי ִ ֵ or ֶ (an "I" or "E" vowel) which you can refer to as a **dot vowel**.
This vowel does not occur in every PGN and form in the Hif'il, but is in the most frequent ones.

> The Hif'il gives a causative meaning to roots.

If you add the words "to cause" or "to make" before the Qal meaning you will get the rough equivalent of the Hif'il in most cases. Sometimes a verb in the Hif'il may not transmit a causative sense into English but may be translated as a simple transitive verb. Some Hif'ils do not convey to us their reason for being in that stem. Such are the problems of translation and ignorance of the full nuances of the Hebrew.

The root in this case, once you have dealt with the signs of the Hif'il, is ____________
This form, in which the ה clearly stands in front of the root, is the affix. As in the Qal, the affix is most clearly recognizable by the use of the affix pronouns you have seen, but the 3 m. sg. has no added pronoun.

28.3 אֶת־כָּל־יְהוּדָה means ______________________________________

28.4 Sentence translation: ______________________________________

____

28.5 A chart summarizing the regular Hif`il affix may be helpful:

Hif`il Affix גדל

3 m. sg.	הִגְדִּיל	3 c. pl.	הִגְדִּילוּ
3 f. sg.	הִגְדִּילָה		
2 m. sg.	הִגְדַּלְתָּ	2 m. pl.	הִגְדַּלְתֶּם
2 f. sg.	הִגְדַּלְתְּ	2 f. pl.	הִגְדַּלְתֶּן
1 c. sg.	הִגְדַּלְתִּי	1 c. pl.	הִגְדַּלְנוּ

Note that the vowels we have said are characteristic of the Hif`il are actually found only in the third person singular and plural forms. These forms make up the bulk of Biblical usage, however, so the rule will still be valuable due to the frequency of these forms.

גדל in the Qal means *be great* or *be big.* In the Hif`il it means ____________________

28.6 Extra Grammar: Interrogative ה

There is yet something else ה on the front of a word can be. You have seen two ways of indicating a question in Hebrew: use of interrogative words, מָה or מִי for example, and inverted word order. Another way is to use the interrogative particle ה which is placed on the first word of a clause or phrase. This ה can be distinguished from the sign of the Hif`il and from the definite article by its <u>usual</u> pointing: הֲ [It is sometimes pointed הַ and occasionally הֶ]

הֲ at the beginning of the first word of a phrase is the interrogative ה

הֲ can be attached to: a particle — Exodus 4:11 הֲלֹא אָנֹכִי יהוה

a noun or pronoun — Genesis 29:6 הֲשָׁלוֹם לוֹ

a verb — 1 Samuel 23:11 הֲיֵרֵד שָׁאוּל

a participle — Genesis 4:9 הֲשֹׁמֵר אָחִי אָנֹכִי

28.7 Assignments:

A. For Lessons 28-32, review words 1-200 and learn vocabulary words 201-250

B. Memorize the regular Hif'il affix presented in 28.5

C. Read and translate Exodus 3:10-13

D. Translate:

*1 וְהִשְׁמִיעוּ עָלַיִךְ בְּקוֹלָם Ezekiel 27:30

[עַל takes a connecting י before a suffix, which here is 2 m. sg. For בְּקוֹלָם see 16.7a.]

2 וְהִקְרִיב אֹתוֹ לִפְנֵי יהוה Leviticus 3:7

3 הִגְדִּיל יהוה לַעֲשׂוֹת עִמָּנוּ Psalms 126:3

4 כִּי הִגְדַּלְתָּ עַל־כָּל־שִׁמְךָ Psalms 138:2

*5 וַיָּבֶן דָּוִד כִּי מֵת הַיָּלֶד וַיֹּאמֶר דָּוִד אֶל־עֲבָדָיו הֲמֵת הַיֶּלֶד

וַיֹּאמְרוּ מֵת 2 Samuel 12:19 [מֵת *is dead*]

6 אַתָּה הִמְלַכְתָּ אֶת־עַבְדְּךָ תַּחַת דָּוִד אָבִי 1 Kings 3:7

7 מִשָּׁמַיִם הִשְׁמַעְתָּ דִּין Psalms 76:9 [דִּין *judgment*]

8 הִקְרִיבוּ עֹלוֹת לֵאלֹהֵי יִשְׂרָאֵל Ezra 8:35

9 וְהִקְרַבְתֶּם עֹלָה לַיהוה Numbers 29:8

10 וַיְהִי מֵאָז הִפְקִיד אֹתוֹ בְּבֵיתוֹ וְעַל כָּל־אֲשֶׁר יֶשׁ־לוֹ וַיְבָרֶךְ יהוה

אֶת־בֵּית הַמִּצְרִי בִּגְלַל יוֹסֵף Genesis 39:5

[אָז *at that time* בִּגְלַל *for the sake of*]

11 וַיִּשְׁמְעוּ כָל־שָׂרֵי הַחֲיָלִים אֲשֶׁר בַּשָּׂדֶה הֵמָּה וְאַנְשֵׁיהֶם כִּי־הִפְקִיד

מֶלֶךְ־בָּבֶל אֶת־גְּדַלְיָהוּ בֶן־אֲחִיקָם בָּאָרֶץ Jeremiah 40:7

Genesis 48:21 וְהָיָה אֱלֹהִים עִמָּכֶם וְהֵשִׁיב אֶתְכֶם אֶל־אֶרֶץ אֲבֹתֵיכֶם

29.1 Verb Analysis וְהָיָה

Root	Stem	Form	Person/Gender/Number	Special Features

אֱלֹהִים means ____________ עִמָּכֶם means ____________ (23.1a)

Translation of this phrase: ____________

29.2 Verb analysis וְהֵשִׁיב

Root	Stem	Form	Person/Gender/Number	Special Features

A ה in front of a verb form can indicate ____________ stem. (28.2) You see that the ִי which usually accompanies Hif'il forms is present, but then that leaves you only two root letters.

> In hollow verbs, the characteristic Hif'il stem vowel will appear in its place in Hif'il forms, and thus in the middle of the verb.

29.3 You have had all the components of the remaining phrase. If you need help with אֲבֹתֵיכֶם review The Noun H. Note the form used when the plural endiNG וֹת___ is combined with a possessive pronoun:

כֶם | י | אֲבוֹתֵ

pronoun plural ends in וֹת___

All nouns using וֹת___ plurals have this extra ֵי___ between the noun and the pronoun suffix.

29.4 Sentence Translation: ____________

____

29.5 Extra Grammar

Verbs with weak letters[1] and 1st gutturals may deviate from the pattern of the strong verb in the Hif`il. The changes at the end of 3rd ה verbs are similar to those in the Qal (review 26.5). 1st נ verbs have an assimilation of the נ into the second root letter, but can be recognized easily: הִגִּישׁ 1st gutturals show all letters but the preformative ה may be pointed הֶ as in הֶחֱזִיק The changes in the hollow verb are slightly more complicated and are shown below.

Hif`il Affix Hollow שׁוּב

3 m. sg.	הֵשִׁיב	3 c. pl.	הֵשִׁיבוּ
3 f. sg.	הֵשִׁיבָה		
2 m. sg.	הֲשִׁיבוֹתָ	2 m. pl.	הֲשִׁיבוֹתֶם
2 f. sg.	הֲשִׁיבוֹת	2 f. pl.	הֲשִׁיבוֹתֶן
1 c. sg.	הֲשִׁיבוֹתִי	1 c. pl.	הֲשִׁיבוֹנוּ

Note the addition of the ו between the root and the affix pronouns in first and second person forms. These forms appear much less frequently than the third person forms, which are more regular; and בּוֹא does not use the extra ו at all.

29.6 Exercises:

You have now seen four uses of a ה at the beginning of a word. One is "first root letter." What are the other three?

________________________ (4.3)

________________________ (28.2)

________________________ (28.6)

What are some of the ways you can determine the function of the ה and what are some possible ambiguities?

____

____

---

1 The Hif`ils of 1st י verbs are covered separately.

Identify the initial ה in the following words, and describe your reasoning process in each case, unless you don't have one; then just do the first part:

הָאָרֶץ	הַהוּא	הֵשִׁיב
הַבָּשָׂר	הָיָה	הָאֱלֹהִים
הֲקִימֹתִי	הִגִּישׁ	הִגִּידָה
הֲשֹׁמֵר	הֲשַׁמְתָּ	הַשָּׁלוֹם
הָלַךְ	הֲהֹלֵךְ	הָהֹלֵךְ

29.7 Assignments:

A. Memorize the Hif`il affix paradigm of the Hollow verb. (28.5)

B. Read and translate Exodus 3:14-17

C. Translate:

1 וְהֵבִיאָה אֹתָם אֶל־הַכֹּהֵן Leviticus 15:29

*2 יהוה הֶעֱלִיתָ מִן־שְׁאוֹל נַפְשִׁי Psalms 30:4

3 וְהֵבֵאתִי אֶתְכֶם אֶל־אַדְמַת יִשְׂרָאֵל Ezekiel 37:12

4 וַהֲשִׁבֹתִי אֶתְכֶם דָּבָר כַּאֲשֶׁר יְדַבֵּר יהוה אֵלָי Numbers 22:8

5 וְהִפַּלְתִּי אֶת־הַחֶרֶב מִיָּדוֹ Ezekiel 30:22

6 הֵשִׁבוּ פְלִשְׁתִּים אֶת־אֲרוֹן יהוה [אֲרוֹן vocabulary word] I Samuel 6:21

7 וְהֶעֱמִיד הַכֹּהֵן אֶת־הָאִשָּׁה לִפְנֵי יהוה Numbers 5:18

*8 וְהִנֵּה הֶרְאָה אֹתִי אֱלֹהִים גַּם אֶת־זַרְעֶךָ Genesis 48:11

*9 וְיִתֵּן אֶת־יִשְׂרָאֵל בִּגְלַל חַטֹּאות יָרָבְעָם אֲשֶׁר חָטָא וַאֲשֶׁר הֶחֱטִיא
אֶת־יִשְׂרָאֵל׃ [בִּגְלַל *on account of* חַטֹּאות super plene spelling] I Kings 14:16

10 יהוה אֱלֹהֵיכֶם הִרְבָּה אֶתְכֶם Deuteronomy 1:10

11 וַיֹּאמֶר יִתְרוֹ בָּרוּךְ יהוה אֲשֶׁר הִצִּיל אֶתְכֶם מִיַּד מִצְרַיִם וּמִיַּד
פַּרְעֹה אֲשֶׁר הִצִּיל אֶת־הָעָם מִתַּחַת יַד־מִצְרָיִם׃ Exodus 18:10
[בָּרוּךְ⟷m. sg. Qal passive participle of ברך]

הַגִּידָה לִּי מֶה עָשִׂיתָה 1 Samuel 14:43

30.1 הַגִּידָה

Here we have another form of the Hif`il. Therefore the ה at the beginning of the word will be ______________________________ and not a letter of the root. (28.2)
How many letters are left? ________ What other letter is part of the characteristic Hif`il pattern? __________ Locating this tells you something important, for this combination comes ____ (28.2)
So the final ה must be some special ending, and you have the second and third letters of the root. What will the first letter be? ______ (7.1a)
Note the vowel under the first ה In the affix form the usual vowel under the ה indicator of the stem was ◌ִ (Review 29.5 for variations.)

Pataḥ ◌ַ under the ה stem indicator is the sign of the imperative form in the Hif`il.

30.1a We have accounted now for all the letters except the final ה This is **not** a PGN ending (review imperative endings in 20.6a if necessary), but is usually called the emphatic ה It occurs at the end of imperatives and imperative-like forms sometimes but not always. The actual function of this ending is still a matter of speculation.

Analyze הַגִּידָה

Root	Stem	Form	Person/Gender/Number	Special Features

נגד means *be conspicuous.* In the Bible it is used exclusively in the Hif`il and we translate it *tell, declare.*

30.2 לִּי What kind of dagesh is in the ל ____________________ (17.3b)
Translate phrase: ______________________________

30.3 מֶה עָשִׂיתָה

מֶה ⟷ מָה and so means ______________

Analyze עָשִׂיתָה

Root	Stem	Form	Person/Gender/Number	Special Features

What is the PGN? If you remember, the rule states that a final ה becomes י before all affix pronouns except 3 f. sg. and 3 c. pl. (26.5a) The pronoun must begin with the ת therefore, so the final ה cannot be the 3 f. sg. pronoun. תָה ⟷ תָ here; the PGN is ________ Once again this is an extra lengthening of the pronoun ending, a rather infrequent phenomenon.

30.4 Translate sentence: ______________________________

30.5 The sign of the Hif`il imperative, preformative הַ is constant for most types of verbs. One exception is Hollows, whose preformative is usually pointed הָ

30.6 Give the form and PGN of the following Hif`ils:

Form	PGN		Form	PGN	
		הֶאֱכַלְתֶּם			הַרְאֶנָה
		הָבֵא			הַעֲלֵה
		הַשְׁמִיעוּ			הִשְׁלַכְתִּי
		וְהִגַּדְתָּ			הַגִּידוּ
		וַהֲקִימֹתִי			הֶעֱלוּ
		הַקְרֵב			הָשְׁבוּ
		הַעַל			וְהֵקִים

30.8 Assignments:

A. Read and translate Genesis 37:1-4

B. Translate:

*1 וַיֹּאמֶר דָּוִד מֶה עָשִׂיתִי עָתָּה הֲלוֹא דָּבָר הוּא I Samuel 17:29

2 הַשְׁמִיעוּ זֹאת Isaiah 48:20

3 וְאַתָּה הַקְרֵב אֵלֶיךָ אֶת־אַהֲרֹן אָחִיךָ וְאֶת־בָּנָיו Exodus 28:1

4 הָבֵא אֶת־הָאֲנָשִׁים הַבָּיְתָה Genesis 43:16

5 הֲלוֹא טוֹב לָנוּ שׁוּב מִצְרָיְמָה Numbers 14:3

6 הָשִׁיבוּ נָא לָהֶם [נָא particle of politeness] Nehemiah 5:11

7 הַעַל אֶת־הָעָם הַזֶּה Exodus 33:12

8 עֲלֵה הָקֵם לַיהוה מִזְבֵּחַ 2 Samuel 24:18

9 וְהֵקִים יהוה לוֹ מֶלֶךְ עַל־יִשְׂרָאֵל I Kings 14:14

10 וַתֹּאמֶר אֵלָיו הֲלֹא צִוָּה יהוה אֱלֹהֵי־יִשְׂרָאֵל Judges 4:6

*11 וַיֹּאמֶר הַמֶּלֶךְ אֶל־הַכּוּשִׁי הֲשָׁלוֹם לַנַּעַר לְאַבְשָׁלוֹם וַיֹּאמֶר
הַכּוּשִׁי יִהְיוּ כַנַּעַר אֹיְבֵי אֲדֹנִי הַמֶּלֶךְ וְכֹל אֲשֶׁר־קָמוּ עָלֶיךָ
לְרָעָה׃ 2 Samuel 18:32

12 וַהֲקִמֹתִי אֶת־בְּרִיתִי אִתָּךְ [אִתָּךְ with you] Genesis 6:18

הֵם הַמְדַבְּרִים אֶל־פַּרְעֹה מֶלֶךְ־מִצְרַיִם לְהוֹצִיא אֶת־בְּנֵי־יִשְׂרָאֵל מִמִּצְרָיִם Exodus 6:27

31.1 הֵם הַמְדַבְּרִים

הֵם means ______________ הַמְדַבְּרִים is a verb form – a new one, but one which contains many familiar elements if you break it down.

Root	Stem	Form	Person/Gender/Number	Special Features

הַ means ________ The endiNG ִים is ________ Only one verb form takes noun endiNGs: it is the ____________________ form. (9.3a) Out of the five (count them) letters left, do you see a familiar root? ________________ What stem will this be? Note the doubled root letter.

> The Pi`el participle uses a מְ preformative in front of the root, in which the middle letter is doubled מְ_ _ּ_ _

Translation of phrase: ____

31.2 Verb Analysis לְהוֹצִיא

Root	Stem	Form	Person/Gender/Number	Special Features

The form is easy to identify because ל is used before it. The stem is not Qal but ______________ because of ____________________ (28.2) The root letters appear to be וצא and this actually was the root in a more archaic Hebrew. Later the ו became י in Qal forms, so that we know the root as יצא which means ____________________ In the Hif`il (and other derived stems) the ancient ו takes the place of י in the infinitive forms in most verbs now beginning with י The Hif`il meaning of יצא will be ____________________________ or more simply *bring forth.*

הֵם הַֽמְדַבְּרִים אֶל־פַּרְעֹה מֶלֶךְ־מִצְרַיִם לְהוֹצִיא אֶת־בְּנֵי־יִשְׂרָאֵל מִמִּצְרָיִם

31.3 The rest of this sentence contains familiar words. Translate the whole sentence:

____

____

31.4 Extra Grammar

The Hif`il infinitive of a 1st י verb looks the same as the 3 m. sg. affix form. So הוֹצִיא could be translated *to bring out* or *he brought out*. How will you know which is meant? The infinitive usually has an attached preposition, and of course the context will tell you which makes more sense. The other 1st י Hif`il affix PGNs can be identified by הוֹ at the front of the verb and an affix pronoun at the end. Speaking of the Hif`il affix, try your skills by filling in the chart below. There is a vowel change caused by יצא being a 3rd א A tsere ֵ occurs where pataḥ ַ appears in the strong verb. There is no infixed י in those PGNs in either case. (28.5) One more thing, don't forget to consider the א when you add the affix pronouns. (13.6a)

Hif`il Affix יצא

3 m. sg.	ה וֹ צִי א	3 c. pl.	___ ___ ___ ___ ___
3 f. sg.	___ ___ ___ ___ ___		
2 m. sg.	___ א צֵ ___ ___	2 m. pl.	___ ___ ___ ___ ___
2 f. sg.	___ ___ ___ ___ ___	2 f. pl.	___ ___ ___ ___ ___
1 c. sg.	___ ___ ___ ___ ___	1 c. pl.	___ ___ ___ ___ ___

31.5 Exercise:

Give the root and form of the following Hif`ils:

Root	Form		Root	Form	
		וְהוֹדַעְתֶּם			וְהוֹדַעְתָּ
		וְהִזְכַּרְתֶּן			הוֹתַרְתִּי
		וְהוֹשִׁיבוּ			הִזְכִּיר

הֵם הַמְדַבְּרִים אֶל־פַּרְעֹה מֶלֶךְ־מִצְרַיִם לְהוֹצִיא אֶת־בְּנֵי־יִשְׂרָאֵל מִמִּצְרָיִם

Root	Form		Root	Form	
		הוֹתִיר			הוֹלִיד
		לְהָבִיא			לְהַקְרִיב
		לְהַמְלִיךְ			הֲשִׂימִי
		הִקְרִיב			הֵבִיאוּ
		הַזְכִּיר			הֲקִימֹתִי
		הֵקִימוּ			הָקֵם

31.7 Assignments:

A. Read and translate Genesis 37:5-8

B. Translate:

1 וְהוֹדַעְתָּ לָהֶם אֶת־הַדֶּרֶךְ Exodus 18:20

2 וְהוֹדַעְתִּי לְךָ אֵת אֲשֶׁר תַּעֲשֶׂה 1 Samuel 10:8

3 הִנְנִי מְשַׁלֵּחַ בָּם אֶת־הַחֶרֶב Jeremiah 29:17

4 שְׁמַע אֵת אֲשֶׁר־אֲנִי מְדַבֵּר אֵלֶיךָ Ezekiel 2:8

5 וְהוֹצֵאתָ לָהֶם מַיִם Numbers 20:8

6 כִּי־אֲנִי־הוּא הַמְדַבֵּר הִנֵּנִי Isaiah 52:6

7 הוֹצֵאתִי אֶתְכֶם מֵאֶרֶץ מִצְרָיִם Leviticus 19:36

8 וְחַנָּה הִיא מְדַבֶּרֶת עַל־לִבָּהּ [See 24.5a[1] for endiNG מְדַבֶּרֶת] 1 Samuel 1:13

9 וְהוֹצִיאוּ מִשָּׁם אֶת־הָאִשָּׁה וְאֶת־כָּל־אֲשֶׁר־לָהּ Joshua 6:22

10 וְהוֹדַעְתֶּם אֶת־בְּנֵיכֶם Joshua 4:22

11 וְהוֹצִיאוּ אֹתוֹ אֶל־זִקְנֵי עִירוֹ [elder זָקֵן] Deuteronomy 21:19

12 וְעָמְדוּ לְפָנַי לְהַקְרִיב לִי חֵלֶב וָדָם [fat חֵלֶב] Ezekiel 44:15

13 בָּאוּ חֶבְרוֹנָה לְהַמְלִיךְ אֶת־דָּוִיד עַל־כָּל־יִשְׂרָאֵל 1 Chronicles 12:39

14 הַמֶּלֶךְ אֲחַשְׁוֵרוֹשׁ אָמַר לְהָבִיא אֶת־וַשְׁתִּי הַמַּלְכָּה לְפָנָיו Esther 1:17

15 וַיֹּאמֶר לִבְנֵי אַהֲרֹן הַכֹּהֲנִים לְהַעֲלוֹת עַל־מִזְבַּח יהוה 2 Chronicles 29:21

Exodus 19:9 וַיַּגֵּד מֹשֶׁה אֶת־דִּבְרֵי הָעָם אֶל־יהוה

32.1 Analyze וַיַּגֵּד

Root	Stem	Form	Person/Gender/Number	Special Features

The focus of this Lesson is on this first word of the sentence. Obviously we have here a prefix form of the verb. What is the root? ____________ (7.1a) The stem is neither Qal nor Pi`el, but Hif`il. Where is the ה that marks the Hif`il stem? It has been elided (squashed) out of the word:

וַיַּגֵּד ⟵ וַיְהַגֵּד original form

The ה sound, merely a breath, was easily slid over and eventually dropped out altogether in the Hif`il prefix form. Only its vowel was left – pataḥ – which now stands under the prefix pronoun.

> The Hif`il prefix can be recognized by two characteristic vowels: pataḥ ַ under the prefix pronoun and ִ ֵ or ִי ("dot vowel") between the second and third root letters.

32.2 The remainder of this sentence is quite simple; translate the whole sentence:

____

32.3 Fill in the chart for the Hif`il prefix of גדל Why is there a dagesh in the ד

Hif`il Prefix גדל

3 m. sg.	יַ גְ דִּי ל	3 m. pl.	___ ___ ___ ___ ___
3 f. sg.	___ ___ ___ ___	3 f. pl.	___ גְ דֵּ לְ ___
2 m. sg.	___ ___ ___	2 m. pl.	___ ___ ___ ___ ___
2 f. sg.	___ ___ ___ ___	2 f. pl.	___ ___ ___ ___ ___
1 c. sg.	___ ___ ___ ___	1 c. pl.	___ ___ ___ ___

32.3a Extra Grammar

The verb for this Lesson וַיַּגֵּד demonstrates a feature of some Hif`ils with vav conversive: **the shortened form.**[1] That means וַיַּגֵּד ← יַגִּיד The ◌ֵ ← ◌ִי
There is another pattern: וַתַּגֵּד ← תַּגִּיד The ◌ֶ ← ◌ִי

BUT note, the pataḥ under the prefix pronoun and dot vowel remain as faithful stem indicators.

Shortened forms with vav conversive also run through the **Qal**. This is most evident in the 2nd and 3rd persons singular of 1st י hollow, and 3rd ה verbs. So you should expect to see:

יָשִׂים ← וַיָּשֶׂם	יָשׁוּב ← וַיָּשָׁב	יֵשֵׁב ← וַיֵּשֶׁב
תִּבְנֶה ← וַתִּבֶן	יַעֲשֶׂה ← וַיַּעַשׂ	יִרְאֶה ← וַיַּרְא

32.3b וַיַּרְא and וַיַּעַשׂ forms just listed, bring us into conflict with the recognition feature of the Hif`il prefix. A 3rd ה prefix form + vav conversive may look identical in the Qal and Hif`il. Your only clue to the correct stem in such a case is context. The Hif`il will tend to be transitive.

Another problem: 1st gutturals in the Qal prefix may have ◌ַ under the prefix pronoun. (17.3a) The stem of these verbs can be determined by going to the secondary key feature of the form. The Hif`il will have a dot vowel between the 2nd and 3rd root letters. Qal יַעֲמֹד Hif`il יַעֲמִיד (The ambiguity remains, alas, with 1st Guttural/3rd ה verbs in some PGNs. See יַעֲשֶׂה just above.)

32.4 Assignments:

A. Make sure you are confident of all the Hif`il signs presented so far. To learn this stem more thoroughly, consult the verb charts at the back of the book.

B. Read and translate Genesis 37:9-12

C. Analyze:

תַּקְרִיב	תַּקְרִיבוּ	וַיַּקְרֵב	אַגִּיד
הַגֵּד	וַיַּגִּדוּ	וַיִּשְׁמְעוּ	תַּשְׁמִיעַ
תִּשְׁמַע	תָּשִׁיב	תָּשׁוּב	הִשִּׁיא
וַיָּשָׁב	הוּשַׁבְתָּ	הָשֵׁב	וַתֵּשֶׁב

[1] If you are at a social gathering and wish to impress the cognoscenti, you would refer to these as "apocopated forms."

D. Translate:

1 וְכֹל אֲשֶׁר בִּלְבָבְךָ אַגִּיד לָךְ 1 Samuel 9:19

2 הוּא יַגִּיד לָךְ מַה־יִּהְיֶה לַנָּעַר 1 Kings 14:3

3 וַיֵּלְכוּ וַיַּגִּדוּ לַמֶּלֶךְ דָּוִד 2 Samuel 17:21

4 וְאֶת־אַהֲרֹן וְאֶת־בָּנָיו תַּקְרִיב אֶל־פֶּתַח אֹהֶל מוֹעֵד Exodus 29:4
[פֶּתַח *entrance, opening*]

5 לֹא תַקְרִיבוּ אֵלֶּה לַיהוה Leviticus 22:22

*6 וְיַשְׁמִעוּ דְבָרַי אֶת־עַמִּי [דְּבָרַי is functioning as a DO] Jeremiah 23:22

7 וַיַּקְרֵב אֹתְךָ וְאֶת־כָּל־אַחֶיךָ Numbers 16:10

8 וַתַּגֶּד־לוֹ אִשְׁתּוֹ אֶת־הַדְּבָרִים הָאֵלֶּה 1 Samuel 25:37

9 וְלֹא־תַשְׁמִיעוּ אֶת־קוֹלְכֶם Joshua 6:10

וָאוֹצִיא אֶת־אֲבוֹתֵיכֶם מִמִּצְרַיִם Joshua 24:6

33.1 Analyze וָאוֹצִיא

Root	Stem	Form	Person/Gender/Number	Special Features

Can the וָ here be a vav conversive? ________ Why or why not? ________________

________________________________ (14.5a) What is the stem? ________________

The clue here is the ִי between the second and third letters of the root. (32.1) The root of the verb is ____________ because in the Hif'il the original first root letter was ________ (31.2) א is the prefix for which PGN? ________

Translate: ____

Holem וֹ after a prefix pronoun, combined with a dot vowel after the middle root letter, is the sign of the Hif'il prefix in this group of 1st י verbs.

33.2 אֶת־אֲבוֹתֵיכֶם means ________________________

מִמִּצְרַיִם means ________________________

33.3 Translate the whole sentence: ____

____

33.4 Most deviant from the regular Hif'il vocalization patterns are 1st י verbs. However, they are consistently characterized by having וֹ between the preformative or prefix pronoun and the root. This pattern can be seen in the participle as well. The Hif'il participle can be recognized by a מ preformative, usually pointed ____ מַ (pataḥ being the favorite vowel for Hif'il preformatives) but for 1st י verbs it is ____ מוֹ

33.5 In the chart below, the (3) m. sg. pronoun is used even though its vocalization may not be the most representative for the form, but other PGNs have affix pronouns, prefix pronouns and/or complements, or endiNGs to help with identification.

Hif'il Synopsis

	Regular	Hollow	Ist י
Affix	הִ__ __ִי__	הֵ__ִי__	הוֹ__ִי__
Prefix	יַ__ __ִי__	יָ__ִי__	יוֹ__ִי__
Prefix/vav conv.	וַיַּ__ __ֵ__	וַיָּ__ֶ__	וַיּוֹ__ֶ__
Imperative	הַ__ __ֵ__	הָ__ֵ__	הוֹ__ֵ__
Participle	מַ__ __ִי__	מֵ__ִי__	מוֹ__ִי__
Infinitive	הַ__ __ִי__	הָ__ִי__	הוֹ__ִי__

33.6 Assignments:

A. For Lessons 33-40 learn words 251-300 from your vocabulary list.

B. Learn the Hif'il synopsis.

C. Read and translate Genesis 37:13-16

D. Translate:

1 יוֹדִיעַ דְּרָכָיו לְמֹשֶׁה Psalms 103:7

2 וַיּוֹשֶׁב שָׁם אֶת־בְּנֵי יִשְׂרָאֵל 2 Chronicles 8:2

3 וְאֶת־שֵׁם קָדְשִׁי אוֹדִיעַ בְּתוֹךְ עַמִּי יִשְׂרָאֵל Ezekiel 39:7

4 כִּי־תוֹלִיד בָּנִים וּבְנֵי בָנִים Deuteronomy 4:25

5 וַיּוֹצִא אֶת־בֶּן־הַמֶּלֶךְ 2 Kings 11:12

6 נָתַתִּי רוּחִי עָלָיו מִשְׁפָּט לַגּוֹיִם יוֹצִיא Isaiah 42:1

7 תּוֹצִיא הָאֲדָמָה Haggai 1:11

8 וַיּוֹרִידוּ אֶת־הַמֶּלֶךְ מִבֵּית יהוה וַיָּבוֹאוּ דֶּרֶךְ־שַׁעַר 2 Kings 11:19

9 וְעֹבֵד הוֹלִיד אֶת־יִשָׁי וְיִשַׁי הוֹלִיד אֶת־דָּוִד׃ Ruth 4:22

10 וַיּוֹרֶד אֶת־הָעָם אֶל־הַמָּיִם Judges 7:5

11 וַתֵּלֶד שָׂרָה לְאַבְרָהָם בֵּן לִזְקֻנָיו Genesis 21:2

12 וְכִי אוֹצִיא אֶת־בְּנֵי יִשְׂרָאֵל מִמִּצְרָיִם Exodus 3:11

*13 וְיָרְשׁוּ בֵּית יַעֲקֹב אֵת מוֹרָשֵׁיהֶם Obadiah 17

וַיַּכּוּ אֶת־גְּדַלְיָהוּ בֶן־אֲחִיקָם בֶּן־שָׁפָן בַּחֶרֶב וַיָּמֶת אתו Jeremiah 41:2

34.1 Analyze וַיַּכּוּ

Root	Stem	Form	Person/Gender/Number	Special Features

You may wonder, after you have dealt with the vav conversive and the PGN of this verb, whether you have been too drastic in your surgery, but a little thought will help you find the root. The first root letter will be ______ because the dagesh forte in the כ indicates ________ (7.1a) The final letter of the root must be ______ (use the missing letter rule in 12.1). There are only a few verbs like this in Hebrew, but one or two occur with some frequency.

> When only one consonant (doubled or not) shows for a root, you probably have a combination 1st נ 3rd ה verb.

What is the stem? Here we have real difficulties, because according to the discussion in 32.3b, this could be Qal or Hif`il. The PGNs in which this ambiguity appears are 3 m. sg., 2 m. pl., and 3 m. pl. In all other cases, you should watch for both characteristic vowels in the Hif`il prefix. The fact that a DDO follows the verb indicates that it is transitive and so the stem is more likely to be Hif`il.

34.2 אֶת־גְּדַלְיָהוּ בֶן־אֲחִיקָם בֶּן־שָׁפָן means ________________________________

________________________________ Now "translate" the names.

שָׁפָן means *rock badger* (!) ________________________________

34.3 בַּחֶרֶב means ________________________

34.4 וַיָּמֶת אתו

Analyze וַיָּמֶת

Root	Stem	Form	Person/Gender/Number	Special Features

Determining stem: with hollow verbs, the vowel under the prefix letter continues to be ָ in the Hif'il (following the missing letter rule of 6.1a). In this case, you must use the characteristic dot vowel to help you determine the stem. מוּת in the Qal means __________ so ____________ in the Hif'il.

34.5 Translate sentence: ____

____

34.6 Extra Grammar

The verb מוּת is a hollow "E" class verb. It will follow the pattern for hollow verbs in the derived stems; however, the pattern in the Qal affix is not regular and so a chart will be helpful. Note that the "E" vowel shows only in the third person.

Extra credit: why there is a dagesh forte in the ת of some PGNs?

Qal Affix Hollow "E" class

3 m. sg.	מֵת	3 c. pl.	מֵתוּ
3 f. sg.	מֵתָה		
2 m. sg.	מַתָּה	2 m. pl.	מַתֶּם
2 f. sg.	מַתְּ	2 f. pl.	מַתֶּן
1 c. sg.	מַתִּי	1 c. pl.	מַתְנוּ

34.7 Assignments:

A. Learn the Qal affix of מוּת (34.6)

B. Read and translate Genesis 37:17-20

C. Translate:

*1 וְנָבִא לְבַב חָכְמָה Psalms 90:12

2 לָמָּה תָּבִיאוּ אֹתוֹ אֵלָי 1 Samuel 21:15

3 וַיַּרְא אֹתָם אֶת־בֶּן־הַמֶּלֶךְ 2 Kings 11:4

4 וַיָּבִיאוּ אֶת־הַנַּעַר אֶל־עֵלִי 1 Samuel 1:25

5 וְאַתָּה תַּעֲלֶה אֹתָם יְרוּשָׁלִָם 2 Chronicles 2:15

6 וַיַּעֲלוּ הַכֶּסֶף בְּיָדָם Judges 16:18

7 וַיַּעַל דָּוִד עֹלוֹת לִפְנֵי יהוה 2 Samuel 6:17

8 וַיָּבֹא יוֹסֵף וַיַּגֵּד לְפַרְעֹה Genesis 47:1

*9 וַתָּקֶם אֶת־דְּבָרֶיךָ כִּי צַדִּיק אָתָּה Nehemiah 9:8

10 וַיָּקֶם יהוה אֶת־דְּבָרוֹ אֲשֶׁר דִּבֵּר 1 Kings 8:20

11 וַיָּשֶׁב־יהוה לִי כְצִדְקִי Psalms 18:25

12 וְלֹא־יָשִׁיב אֶת־הָעָם מִצְרַיְמָה Deuteronomy 17:16

13 וַיָּשִׁבוּ אוֹתָם דָּבָר Joshua 22:32

14 וְאֶת־בְּרִיתִי אָקִים אֶת־יִצְחָק [אֶת means *with* here] Genesis 17:21

15 וַיַּכֶּה יְהוֹשֻׁעַ אֶת־כָּל־הָאָרֶץ Joshua 10:40

16 אַעֲלֶה אֶתְכֶם מִמִּצְרַיִם וָאָבִיא אֶתְכֶם אֶל־הָאָרֶץ Judges 2:1

17 כִּי אַתָּה תָּבִיא אֶת־בְּנֵי יִשְׂרָאֵל אֶל־הָאָרֶץ Deuteronomy 31:23

18 וַתִּשָּׂא אֹתִי רוּחַ וַתָּבֵא אֹתִי אֶל־שַׁעַר בֵּית־יהוה Ezekiel 11:1

19 וַיִּקַּח אֶת־לֵאָה בִתּוֹ וַיָּבֵא אֹתָהּ אֵלָיו Genesis 29:23

20 וָאָקִים מִבְּנֵיכֶם לִנְבִיאִים Amos 2:11

I Chronicles 11:2 בִּהְיוֹת שָׁאוּל מֶלֶךְ אַתָּה הַמּוֹצִיא וְהַמֵּבִיא אֶת־יִשְׂרָאֵל

35.1 בִּהְיוֹת שָׁאוּל מֶלֶךְ

35.1a Analyze בִּהְיוֹת

Root	Stem	Form	Person/Gender/Number	Special Features

The key to analyzing this form is the בּ What part of speech is this? ____________ Only one form of the verb regularly is found with a preposition, although usually it is the preposition ל What is this form? ______________________________ (11.2b) This analysis is confirmed by the וֹת____ ending. This is the regular infinitive ending for what sort of root? ______________________ (14.3a)

The translation of this infinitive is obviously different from the translation of one employing ל The infinitive, used alone, names the action of the verb; the best way of achieving this in English is to add "–ing" to the meaning:

היה *be* הֱיוֹת *be-ing*

When an infinitive is used in this way, it can have a subject and object.

35.1b שָׁאוּל is a name. In the phrase we are studying, it is the subject of the infinitive. מֶלֶךְ is the object of the infinitive. Literally, with no attention to other grammatical facets, we have "in-being-Saul-king." If we work with the idea of the infinitive as a verb with a subject and object we can translate:

subject	verb	object of verb
in Saul's	*being*	*(a) king*

35.1c When either בּ or כּ is used with the infinitive, the best translation is usually "when" + the past tense of the verb (infinitive):

***when** Saul **was** king*

In other words, the infinitive with a subject and object represents an idiomatic expression in Hebrew, one which yields to simple analysis, but which may take you a few moments to work out.

35·2 **אַתָּה הַמּוֹצִיא**

אַתָּה means ______________

Analyze **הַמּוֹצִיא** (33.4)

Root	Stem	Form	Person/Gender/Number	Special Features

You have seen the elements of this form before. The stem is __________ because the vowels are ______________________ (33.4) The root is therefore ______________

□הַ is the ____________________ and this can occur only with a verb used as a noun, so the form is probably ____________________ (9.3b) The מ here is ____________________

____

Translate phrase: ____

35·3 Analyze **וְהַמֵּבִיא**

Root	Stem	Form	Person/Gender/Number	Special Features

What is the root? ______________ With hollow verbs in the Hif'il, the Hif'il vowels regularly occur ____ (29.2)

35·4 Sentence translation: ____

____

35·5 Exercise:

Analyze the following forms:

מוֹשִׁיבִים	מֵקִים	הֵשִׁיב
שִׁמְעוּ	כִּשְׁמֹעַ	הַמַּעֲלֶה
הָעֹלֶה	רוֹאוֹת	וְשִׂים
וַיַּשְׁמַע	מַשְׁמִעַ	הַמַּגִּיד

35.6 Assignments:

A Read and translate Genesis 37:21-24

B. Translate:

1 אֲנִי מֵשִׁיב אֶל־הַמָּקוֹם הַזֶּה אֶת־כָּל־כְּלֵי בֵּית יהוה Jeremiah 28:3

2 וַאֲנִי הִנְנִי מֵקִים אֶת־בְּרִיתִי אִתְּכֶם וְאֶת־זַרְעֲכֶם אַחֲרֵיכֶם׃ Genesis 9:9
[אִתּ + suffix means *with.* The dagesh differentiates it from the sign of the DDO.]

3 הִנֵּה אָנֹכִי מֵבִיא רָעָה אֶל־הָעָם הַזֶּה Jeremiah 6:19
[רעה represents different roots.]

4 כִּי יהוה אֱלֹהֵינוּ הוּא הַמַּעֲלֶה אֹתָנוּ וְאֶת־אֲבוֹתֵינוּ מֵאֶרֶץ מִצְרַיִם
מִבֵּית עֲבָדִים Joshua 24:17

5 וַיְהִי כִּשְׁמֹעַ כָּל־יִשְׂרָאֵל כִּי־שָׁב יָרָבְעָם וַיִּשְׁלְחוּ וַיִּקְרְאוּ אֹתוֹ
1 Kings 12:20

6 לָכֵן הִנְנִי מֵבִיא רָעָה אֶל־בֵּית יָרָבְעָם 1 Kings 14:10

7 שְׁמַע וְשִׂים לִבְּךָ לְכֹל אֲשֶׁר־אֲנִי מַרְאֶה אוֹתָךְ Ezekiel 40:4

8 אֲנִי יהוה הַמַּעֲלֶה אֶתְכֶם מֵאֶרֶץ מִצְרַיִם לִהְיֹת לָכֶם לֵאלֹהִים
Leviticus 11:45

9 וַיֹּאמֶר דָּוִד אֶל־הַנַּעַר הַמַּגִּיד לוֹ 2 Samuel 1:5

10 אַף אֵין־מַגִּיד אַף אֵין מַשְׁמִיעַ [אַף *surely*] Isaiah 41:26

11 אֲנִי יהוח מְקַדִּשְׁכֶם׃ הַמּוֹצִיא אֶתְכֶם מֵאֶרֶץ מִצְרַיִם Leviticus 22:32-33

Psalms 5:13 כִּי־אַתָּה תְּבָרֵךְ צַדִּיק יהוה

36.1 כִּי means ________ Note that כִּי frequently begins sentences in Biblical Hebrew, sentences that describe the result of preceding actions. כִּי may sometimes also be translated as *but, surely,* when it introduces a phrase which contrasts with a preceding statement.

36.2 אַתָּה means ________ What do you call this kind of pronoun? ________

36.3 Verb Analysis תְּבָרֵךְ

Root	Stem	Form	Person/Gender/Number	Special Features

תּ is the prefix pronoun for ________ (14.1) ברך appears almost always in the Pi`el stem. However, as you have learned, ר is a letter which cannot take the dagesh required in the formation of the Pi`el: the "r" sound was one which was not doubled. As a result, there is compensation for the missing dagesh in the previous vowel. (15.4a) Not all mid gutturals demand compensation. In those cases, watch for the regular Pi`el vowels minus the mid dagesh forte.

The following synopsis shows the usual changes which take place in various forms:

36.3a

	Pi`el regular	**mid guttural / ר**	**no compensation**
Affix	דִּבֵּר	בֵּרַךְ בֵּרֵךְ	נִהַג
Prefix	יְדַבֵּר	יְבָרֵךְ	יְנַהֵג
Imperative	דַּבֵּר	בָּרֵךְ	נַהֵג
Participle	מְדַבֵּר	מְבָרֵךְ	מְנַהֵג
Infinitive	דַּבֵּר	בָּרֵךְ	נַהֵג

36.3b When the middle root letter of a Pi`el is pointed with a shewa ְ the dagesh forte may not appear, in which case there is no compensation for the missing dagesh: תְּבַקְשֶׁנּוּ (Gen. 43:9) but תְּבַקְשֶׁנָּה (Gen. 31:39). Your clue to the stem will be the usual vocalization for the particular Pi`el form.

36.4 צַדִּיק means ____________________ This word is an adjective, but is used here as a noun, *righteous one.*

36.5 יהוה is related to the sentence in what way? ____________________ (18.2)

36.6 Sentence translation: ____

36.7 Extra Grammar

Independent subject pronouns are often used in Biblical Hebrew for emphasis, as is the case in this Lesson sentence. They are also used as:

1. the subject of a noun sentence: אֲנִי יהוה (Genesis 15:7)
2. the subject in a participial clause: כִּי־עֹשֶׂה אֲנִי (Judges 15:3)

Independent Subject Pronouns

1 c. sg.	אֲנִי אָנֹכִי	1 c. pl.	אֲנַחְנוּ
2 m. sg.	אַתָּה	2 m. pl.	אַתֶּם
2 f. sg.	אַתְּ	2 f. pl.	אַתֵּן אַתֵּנָה
3 m. sg.	הוּא	3 m. pl.	הֵם הֵמָּה
3 f. sg.	הִיא	3 f. pl.	הֵן הֵנָּה

36.8 Exercise:

Analyze the following verbs:

קָרְבוּ	קֵרַבְתִּי	אֹכֵל
יִשְׁאַל	רַבָּה	אָכְלוּ
בָּרֲכִי	וַיְבָרֵךְ	גֹּאֵל
שִׁחֵת	שַׁחֵת	וְיֵסְפָה
בָּרְכוּ	יָכִין	וַיָּגֶל
מְצָאתָ	יֶחֱטָא	הוֹשִׁיעַ

36.9 Assignments:

A. Make sure you can identify all Pi`el forms for regular and mid guttural/ר verbs.

B. Memorize the chart of independent subject pronouns. (36.7)

C. Read and translate Deuteronomy 6:1-5

D. Translate:

1 אַתָּה יָדַעְתָּ אֶת־הָעָם Exodus 32:22

2 וַיהוה בֵּרַךְ אֶת־אַבְרָהָם בַּכֹּל Genesis 24:1

*3 וְעַתָּה אֲדֹנָי יהוה אַתָּה־הוּא הָאֱלֹהִים 2 Samuel 7:28

4 וַיְבָרֲכוּ אֱלֹהִים בְּנֵי יִשְׂרָאֵל Joshua 22:33

(Note absence of DDO marker. How will you determine the subject?)

5 קָדֹשׁ יִהְיֶה־לָּךְ כִּי קָדוֹשׁ אֲנִי יהוה Leviticus 21:8

6 כִּי עַם קָדוֹשׁ אַתָּה לַיהוה אֱלֹהֶיךָ בְּךָ בָּחַר יהוה אֱלֹהֶיךָ
לִהְיוֹת לוֹ לְעַם סְגֻלָּה מִכֹּל הָעַמִּים אֲשֶׁר עַל־פְּנֵי הָאֲדָמָה
Deuteronomy 7:6 [סְגֻלָּה *possession, treasure*]

7 רוּחַ יהוה דִּבֶּר בִּי 2 Samuel 23:2

8 וּבָרֵךְ אֶת־בֵּית עַבְדְּךָ לִהְיוֹת לְעוֹלָם לְפָנֶיךָ כִּי־אַתָּה אֲדֹנָי
יהוה דִּבַּרְתָּ 2 Samuel 7:29

9 הִנְנִי נֹתֵן בּוֹ רוּחַ 2 Kings 19:7

*10 וּלְעוֹלָם כָּל־מִשְׁפַּט צִדְקֶךָ Psalms 119:160

(Treat as a noun sentence + construct chain.)

11 כִּי הַמִּשְׁפָּט לֵאלֹהִים הוּא Deuteronomy 1:17

12 צַדִּיק יהוה בְּכָל־דְּרָכָיו Psalms 145:17

*13 בָּרְכִי נַפְשִׁי אֶת־יהוָה וְכָל־קְרָבַי אֶת־שֵׁם קָדְשׁוֹ׃ Psalms 103:1

14 וְיָשַׁב שָׁם עַד־עוֹלָם 1 Samuel 1:22

15 וְאַתָּה תִּהְיֶה עַל־בֵּיתִי Genesis 41:40

16 וַיַּרְא דָוִד כִּי־יָצָא שָׁאוּל לְבַקֵּשׁ אֶת־נַפְשׁוֹ 1 Samuel 23:15

17 הִנֵּה בָּרְכוּ אֶת־יהוה כָּל־עַבְדֵי יהוה Psalms 134:1

Psalms 118:23 מֵאֵת יהוה הָיְתָה זֹּאת

37.1 מֵאֵת יהוה

We have here a compound prepositional phrase. The first component is ________

אֵת is not the sign of the definite direct object here, but a preposition meaning *with*. Since this אֵת is identical in many cases to the sign of the DDO, you must decide by the context which you have. Here there is no problem — the sign of the DDO could never combine with a preposition.

Literal translation of the phrase: ______________________________

37.1a When the preposition אֵת combines with a pronoun, it can usually be differentiated from the sign of the DDO + pronoun (23.2b) by its being accompanied by a dagesh.

אֹתִי *me* אִתִּי *with me*

37.2 הָיְתָה זֹּאת

הָיְתָה is a verb. Can you determine the root? There is one type of weak verb in which the 3 f. sg. affix looks like תָה__ __ When other affix endings are added to 3rd ה roots, the final ה either drops off or changes to י (26.5a)

Root	Stem	Form	Person/Gender/Number	Special Features

37.2a הָיָה is not a hollow verb. Its middle root letter is י but the letter before it has a vowel and the י has its own vowel; therefore, the י is functioning as a consonant. This י will not be lost in any stems or forms of היה The other letter which can be either the middle letter of a hollow verb or a consonant is ______ If the letter preceding it has a vowel already, the ו must be a consonant and will be pronounced "v." The confusion comes in a word like מִצְוָה in which ו is ו + dagesh and not the vowel shureq.

37.2b זֹאת is the feminine counterpart of זֶה What is its relation to the verb? __________ ______________________________ Note the order of the elements in this sentence.

37.3 Literal translation: ______________________________

English order: ______________________________

37.4 Exercises:

In the following words, identify each י or ו as a consonant or vowel letter:

וְעַתָּה סוּר יַיִן
וַיֹּאמֶר קָדוֹשׁ צִוָּה
אוֹר יִהְיֶה גְּבוּל
מוּת אִישׁ אַיִן
וָאֶחְיֶה הֵיכָל מָוֶת
וּלְאָדָם הַמִּצְוֹת מִצְוֹת

Analyze:

וְתִהְיֶינָה הָיוּ רֶבְתָה
וְהָיִינוּ הָיִיתָ תִּהְיִי
רָאֲתָה רָאִינוּ יִרְאֶה
וַיֵּשְׁבָה וּבָנִיתָ חִיָּה
יִשָּׂא וְהֵלְכָה אֶמְרָה
נֶתְנָה וַתּוֹצֵא עֲשֵׂה

37.5 Assignments:

A. Review the Qal affix of 3rd ה verbs. (26.5a)

B. Read and translate Deuteronomy 6:6-10

C. Translate:

1 וְרָחֵל בָּאָה עִם הַצֹּאן Genesis 29:9
2 כִּי־יָצְאָה בִי יַד־יהוה Ruth 1:13
3 הִיא נָתְנָה־לִּי מִן־הָעֵץ וָאֹכֵל Genesis 3:12
4 וּלְדָוִד וּלְזַרְעוֹ וּלְבֵיתוֹ...יִהְיֶה שָׁלוֹם עַד־עוֹלָם 1 Kings 2:33
5 וַיֵּצֵא הַשָּׂטָן מֵאֵת פְּנֵי יהוה [just transliterate שָׂטָן] Job 2:7
6 יִשָּׂא בְרָכָה מֵאֵת יהוה Psalms 24:5

7 וְלֹא־הָיִיתָ כְּעַבְדִּי דָוִד 1 Kings 14:8

8 וַתֹּאמֶר הָאִשָּׁה הַזֹּאת אָמְרָה אֵלַי 2 Kings 6:28

*9 עַיִן לֹא־רָאָתָה Isaiah 64:3

10 כִּי־הָיוּ יָדָיו כִּידֵי עֵשָׂו Genesis 27:23

11 וּבָנִיתָ בֵּית יהוה אֱלֹהֶיךָ 1 Chronicles 22:11

12 וְיָשְׁבָה הָעִיר־הַזֹּאת לְעוֹלָם Jeremiah 17:25

13 וְגַם־בְּנֵי עֲנָקִים רָאִינוּ שָׁם Deuteronomy 1:28

14 וְיָצְאָה מִבֵּיתוֹ וְהָלְכָה וְהָיְתָה לְאִישׁ אַחֵר Deuteronomy 24:2

15 כָּזֹאת וְכָזֹאת דִּבְּרָה הַנַּעֲרָה אֲשֶׁר מֵאֶרֶץ יִשְׂרָאֵל 2 Kings 5:4

16 הֲלוֹא רָאִיתָ מָה־הָעָם הַזֶּה דִּבְּרוּ Jeremiah 33:24

17 וְאָמַרְתָּ לְבִנְךָ עֲבָדִים הָיִינוּ לְפַרְעֹה Deuteronomy 6:21

18 וּבָנוּ בָתִּים וְלֹא יֵשֵׁבוּ וְנָטְעוּ כְרָמִים וְלֹא יִשְׁתּוּ אֶת־יֵינָם Zephaniah 1:13
[יַיִן *wine* כֶּרֶם *vineyard*]

וַיִּקָּחֵהוּ שָׁאוּל בַּיּוֹם הַהוּא וְלֹא נְתָנוֹ לָשׁוּב בֵּית אָבִיו׃ I Samuel 18:2

38.1 Verb analysis וַיִּקָּחֵהוּ

Root	Stem	Form	Person/Gender/Number	Special Features

For help in determining the root, see 21.7b

הוּ__ at the end of a verb is another form of the 3 m. sg. suffix.

It is easy to confuse this with the plural prefix and affix ending. Always look to see if a ה precedes ו If so, the chances are very good that you have a suffix (object of the verb).

Translation of phrase: ____________________

38.2 בַּיּוֹם הַהוּא

38.2a What is the initial בַּ ____________ Notice the vowel under the בַּ Pataḥ represents the definite article *the* הַ◻ which has been elided (slid over) so that only the vowel of the definite article and the dagesh forte remain.

Thus, בְּהַ◻ ⟶ בַּ◻ *in the* יוֹם means ____________

38.2b הַהוּא

What is the initial הַ ____________ (21.3a) הוּא besides being the 3 m. sg. independent pronoun, is also used as a demonstrative adjective (*that*). The adjective construction בַּיּוֹם הַהוּא is called ____________

38.2c Summary of the Demonstrative Adjectives

	this	*that*
masculine	הַיּוֹם הַזֶּה	הַיּוֹם הַהוּא
feminine	הָאִשָּׁה הַזֹּאת	הָאִשָּׁה הַהִיא

	these	*those*
masculine	הַיָּמִים הָאֵלֶּה	הַיָּמִים הָהֵם
feminine	הַנָּשִׁים הָאֵלֶּה	הַנָּשִׁים הָהֵן

38.3 Verb Analysis וְלֹא נְתָנוֹ

וְלֹא means __________

Root	Stem	Form	Person/Gender/Number	Special Features

Until now, all the suffixes we have studied have been on nouns (possessive suffixes) or on prepositions (object suffixes). Verbs can also have suffixes – object suffixes (receive the action of the verb). What is the suffix here? ________ (7.2c)

The root is then ________ Enter this on the chart and place the PGN of the suffix in the Special Features column: 3 m. sg. suffix. נתן means __________
When a suffix is added to a verb, the regular vowels associated with the forms change as the stress in the word shifts. This happens in nouns too. (8.5) When a suffix causes the regular vowels of a verb to change, you must determine the form by other hints. Is the form prefix? Is the form imperative? (Look at the context.) What form fits the context best? The stem will be Qal, since there are no other changes in the verb. So we have a verb: 3 m. sg. Qal affix, with a 3 m. sg. suffix.

38.4 Verb Analysis לָשׁוּב

Root	Stem	Form	Person/Gender/Number	Special Features

38.5 בֵּית אָבִיו is a ________________ It means ________________
Note that the context demands a preposition in front of the phrase. Occasionally there is no preposition in Biblical Hebrew with nouns toward which, or in which, action takes place. Supply the preposition when you translate.

38.6 Translate sentence: ____________________________________

____

38.7a Extra Grammar

You have seen two ways of expressing a verb + pronominal DDO. One is by using the verb followed by את + pronoun: וַיָּמִתוּ אֹתוֹ (23.2b) The other way we have seen in this Lesson: the object pronoun can be attached directly to the conjugated form of the verb. Below is a chart showing the most common suffixes.

Verb Suffixes

1 c. sg.	־נִי	1 c. pl.	־נוּ
2 m. sg.	־ךָ	2 m. pl.	־כֶם
2 f. sg.	־ֵךְ	2 f. pl.	־כֶן
3 m. sg.	־הוּ ־וֹ ־ו	3 m. pl.	־ם ־הֶם
3 f. sg.	־ה ־הּ	3 f. pl.	־ן ־הֶן

38.7b As you have seen, there can be vocalization changes in the verb when a suffix is added. This does not mean that all identification keys totally disappear. Affix pronouns, prefix pronouns, and complements will remain and so will any augmentation to the root. Most of the problems occur in the Qal.

1. Vowels at the beginning of the word may shorten:

3 m. sg. Qal affix	3 m. sg. Qal affix + 3 f. sg. suffix
שָׁמַר	שְׁמָרָהּ

2. Affix pronouns may lose their characteristic vocalization:

2 m. sg. Qal affix	2 m. sg. Qal affix + 1 c. sg. suffix
שָׁמַרְתָּ	שְׁמַרְתַּנִי

3. There may be an extra syllable in the word to facilitate pronunciation:

3 m. sg. Qal prefix	3 m. sg. Qal prefix + 1 c. sg. suffix
יִשְׁמֹר	יִשְׁמְרֵנִי

4. In cases of ambiguity context should help:

3 m. sg. Qal affix + 2 m. sg. suffix	Qal infinitive + 2 m. sg. suffix
שְׁמָרְךָ	שֹׁמְרְךָ

וַיִּקָּחֵהוּ שָׁאוּל בַּיּוֹם הַהוּא וְלֹא נְתָנוֹ לָשׁוּב בֵּית אָבִיו׃

38.8 If you can analyze these verbs with confidence, or even with difficulty, you are well on your way to mastery of Hebrew verbs.

פְּקַדְתִּים	פְּקַדְתִּיו	פָּקַדְתִּי
יִפְקְדֵם	פָּקְדוּ	פְּקַדְתֶּם
הִפְקַדְתִּיךְ	וַיַּפְקִידוּ	פּוֹקֵד
תְּבִיאֶנָּה	וַיָּבֹאוּ	וַתָּבֵא
וַתְּבִיאֵם	הֲבִיאֹתַנִי	בְּבוֹא
וַיָּשְׁבוּ	אָשִׁיב	וָאָבִיא
יֵשֵׁב	יָשַׁב	וַיָּשׁוּבוּ
וָאַעֲלֶה	אֲשִׁיבְךְ	אוֹשִׁיבְךְ
תַּעֲלֶה	וַיַּעֲלוּ	וַיַּעֲלֵהוּ
מָצָאתִי	יַרְאֵהוּ	יוֹרִידֵנִי
נֹתְנִים	נְתַתִּים	מְצָאתִיו
נְתָנַנִי	נְתַתִּיהוּ	נְתַתִּיו
צִוָּה	צִוָּהוּ	נְתָתָנִי
בֵּרְכוּנִי	בֵּרַכְנוּ	בֵּרְכוּ
וִיבָרְכֵנוּ	וַיְבָרְכֵהוּ	יְבָרְכֵנוּ
יַעֲשֶׂה	בָּרְכוּ	תְּבָרֲכֵנִי
יַעֲשׂוּ	יַעֲשֶׂהָ	יַעֲשֵׂהוּ
וַיַּעֲשׂוּנִי	עָשׂוּ	עֲשׂוּ
עֲשִׂיתַנִי	עֲשִׂיתִיו	עָשִׂיתִי
עֲשִׂיתָנִי	עֲשִׂיתִים	וַעֲשִׂיתִיהוּ
עָשָׂהוּ	עָשְׂתָה	עֲשִׂיתָהּ
עָשׂוּנִי	עָשִׂינוּ	עָשָׂנוּ
שְׁלָחַנִי	שְׁלָחָנוּ	עָשׂוּהוּ
תְּשַׁלְּחוּם	שִׁלַּחְתָּנוּ	שְׁלַחָנוּ

38.9 Assignments:

A. Learn the verb suffixes in 38.7a

B. Read and translate Deuteronomy 6:11-15

C. Translate:

1 וַיִּרְאֶהָ יְהוּדָה Genesis 38:15

2 בַּיָּמִים הָהֵם אֵין מֶלֶךְ בְּיִשְׂרָאֵל Judges 17:6

3 אֲשֶׁר לְקָחָהּ לוֹ לְאִשָּׁה Deuteronomy 24:3

4 וַיָּשָׁב בַּיּוֹם הַהוּא עֵשָׂו לְדַרְכּוֹ Genesis 33:16

5 וַיִּשָּׂאוּם בְּנֵי־קִישׁ אֲחֵיהֶם 1 Chronicles 23:22

6 כֹּה אָמַר יהוה שַׁבְתִּי אֶל־צִיּוֹן Zechariah 8:3

7 וַיִּשְׁלַח יָדוֹ וַיִּקָּחֶהָ Genesis 8:9

8 וַיִּתְּנֵהוּ יהוה אֱלֹהֵינוּ לְפָנֵינוּ Deuteronomy 2:33

9 וְרוּחַ נְשָׂאַתְנִי וַתִּקָּחֵנִי וָאֵלֵךְ Ezekiel 3:14

10 וַיִּתְּנָהּ אֶל־הַכֹּהֲנִים בְּנֵי לֵוִי Deuteronomy 31:9

11 וּנְתַתִּיךָ בְּיַד מְבַקְשֵׁי נַפְשֶׁךָ Jeremiah 22:25 (36.3b)

12 וּנְתַתִּיו לַיהוה כָּל־יְמֵי חַיָּיו 1 Samuel 1:11

[חַיָּיו construct pl. of חַיִּים *life* + suffix]

13 לָמָּה זֶּה שְׁלַחְתָּנִי Exodus 5:22

וַיְצַו מֹשֶׁה וַיַּעֲבִ֫ירוּ קוֹל בַּמַּחֲנֶה לֵאמֹר אִישׁ וְאִשָּׁה אַל־יַעֲשׂוּ־עוֹד
מְלָאכָה לִתְרוּמַת הַקֹּ֫דֶשׁ Exodus 36:6

39.1 וַיְצַו מֹשֶׁה

Verb Analysis וַיְצַו

Root	Stem	Form	Person/Gender/Number	Special Features

According to the missing letter rule in 12.1, what is the missing root letter? ________
The tricky part of this analysis is the stem. The vowel under the prefix pronoun is what we need to look at to help determine that feature of the verb. What stem routinely has shewa ְ under the prefix pronoun? ____________ (15.5) Where then is the supporting dagesh forte to confirm this stem?

> Omission of dagesh forte occurs, almost always, at the end of a word.

צוה is a common verb and in the Bible is found almost exclusively in the Pi`el. Because it is a 3rd ה it may lose its third root letter in some forms; therefore, it will lose the dagesh forte when ו appears as the last letter.

Translation of the phrase: ____

39.2 וַיַּעֲבִירוּ קוֹל בַּמַּחֲנֶה לֵאמֹר

39.2a Verb Analysis וַיַּעֲבִירוּ

Root	Stem	Form	Person/Gender/Number	Special Features

Does the vowel under the prefix pronoun create an ambiguity? ____________ (32.3b)
Where will you look next to determine the stem? Pay particular attention to the PGN of this verb. A literal translation would be ____________________
How is קוֹל related to וַיַּעֲבִירוּ ____________________

You should be able to translate the next word in this phrase, but if you can't, where would you look in the dictionary? ________________ (The Noun section C.)

39.2b Verb Analysis **לֵאמֹר**

Root	Stem	Form	Person/Gender/Number	Special Features

What is the form of the verb ____________________ and how is it being used? (35.1a)

________________________________ Compare this to the uses of the participle. (9.3b)

לֵאמֹר often comes immediately before a direct quotation and functions as "aural quotation marks."

Literal translation of the whole phrase: ______________________________

____

39.3 **אִישׁ וְאִשָּׁה אַל־יַעֲשׂוּ־עוֹד מְלָאכָה**

39.3a The compound subject of this phrase is composed of a masculine and a feminine noun: **אִישׁ וְאִשָּׁה** In such a case, you can expect a masculine verb. The conjunction linking the two nouns need not be translated *and*. After working out the verb, see how you can best link the subject to it.

אִישׁ can mean, in addition to *a man, each man,* or *every man.* By extension, then, the phrase here is an idiom meaning *each man and woman.*

39.3b **אַל־יַעֲשׂוּ**

Root	Stem	Form	Person/Gender/Number	Special Features

> **אַל** is a negative particle, used with a prefix form of the verb to express a negative command (*Don't. . .*)

In the Special Features column write "negative imperative."

The problem with analyzing the verb is determining the stem. What are the possibilities? ________________________ (32.3b) Can you resolve the ambiguity in this case? עוֹד is an adverb meaning ________________ To find the root of מְלָאכָה take out the consonant cluster which must be part of the root.

Translation of the phrase: ____

____

39-4 לִתְרוּמַת הַקֹּדֶשׁ

One thing to be determined about לִתְרוּמַת is whether it is a noun or a verb. In either case, which letter will be extraneous? ________ Of the letters left is there a pattern which can confirm or eliminate one syntactical possibility? (prefix pronoun/prefix complement, or noun preformative and state indicator.)

What part of speech is הַקֹּדֶשׁ ______________ It means ______________

קֹדֶשׁ may be a synecdoche (the naming of a part to represent the whole; not to be confused with a city in upstate New York) referring to the sanctuary.

39-5 Translation of the verse: ____

____

____

39-6 In the sampling of translations below, you can see how editors handled what they perceived as idiom or awkward language in this verse. Consider whether you think such liberties as change in voice, and change in placement of the negative are justified. Then there is the matter of some of the words themselves. Does צוה mean more than *command?* It may carry with it a military connotation, or by translating it *give a charge* it may connote the transmission of a sense of responsibility. קוֹל and וַיַּעֲבִירוּ are other words which may have an idiomatic sense of which we are unaware and which some of the editors tried to capture by using the colloquial speech of their day.

And Moses gave commandment, and they caused it to be proclaimed throughout the camp, saying, "Let neither man nor woman make any more work for the offering of the sanctuary."

Jewish Publication Society of America, 1917
King James Version
New King James Version

וַיְצַו מֹשֶׁה וַיַּעֲבִירוּ קוֹל בַּמַּחֲנֶה לֵאמֹר אִישׁ וְאִשָּׁה אַל־יַעֲשׂוּ־עוֹד מְלָאכָה לִתְרוּמַת הַקֹּדֶשׁ

So Moses sent word round the camp that no man or woman should prepare anything more as a contribution for the sanctuary.

New English Bible

So Moses bade the crier give out that no man or woman should offer any more for the needs of the sanctuary.

Knox

So Moses sent a command throughout the camp that no one was to make any further contribution for the sacred Tent.

T E V American Bible Society

Moses thereupon had this proclamation made throughout the camp: "Let no man or woman make further effort toward gifts for the sanctuary."

The Torah, A Modern Commentary

39.7 Assignments:

A. Read and translate Deuteronomy 6:16-20

B. Translate:

1 הִנֵּה הַנְּבִאִים אֹמְרִים לָהֶם לֹא־תִרְאוּ חֶרֶב וְרָעָב לֹא־יִהְיֶה
לָכֶם כִּי־שְׁלוֹם אֱמֶת אֶתֵּן לָכֶם [אֱמֶת *truth*] Jeremiah 14:13

2 וְכָל־הָעָם רֹאִים אֶת־הַקּוֹלֹת Exodus 20:18

3 וַיְהִי קוֹל הַשּׁוֹפָר הוֹלֵךְ וְחָזֵק מְאֹד Exodus 19:19

4 וַתֹּאמֶר בַּת־שֶׁבַע טוֹב אָנֹכִי אֲדַבֵּר עָלֶיךָ אֶל־הַמֶּלֶךְ׃ 1 Kings 2:18

5 וַיֹּאמֶר יהוה אֵלַי אַל־תֹּאמַר נַעַר אָנֹכִי כִּי עַל־כָּל־אֲשֶׁר
אֶשְׁלָחֲךָ תֵּלֵךְ וְאֵת כָּל־אֲשֶׁר אֲצַוְּךָ תְּדַבֵּר׃ אַל־תִּירָא
מִפְּנֵיהֶם כִּי־אִתְּךָ אֲנִי לְהַצִּלֶךָ נְאֻם־יְהוָה׃ Jeremiah 1:7-8

6 וְעַתָּה בָנִים שִׁמְעוּ־לִי וְאַל־תָּסוּרוּ מֵאִמְרֵי־פִי׃ Proverbs 5:7

Review question: Give 3 reasons why the dagesh forte may be missing from the middle root letter of a Pi'el.

גַּם עָשֹׂה תַעֲשֶׂה וְגַם יָכֹל תּוּכָל I Samuel 26:25

40.1 גַּם means ______________ It can also be used to stress a particular word, as in גַּם אֵלֶּה *even these.*

Paired with a negative, it can mean *neither:*

לֹא יָדַעְתִּי אֶת־יהוה וְגַם אֶת־יִשְׂרָאֵל לֹא אֲשַׁלֵּחַ Exodus 5:2

Used as it is here גַּם...וְגַם is often translated *both...and.*

40.2 עָשֹׂה תַעֲשֶׂה

40.2a What do you notice about these two words? We hope the fact that the root is repeated stands out to you. The first word uses the root alone, the second word is a prefix form of the verb; together they form an emphatic phrase — we translate this type of construction with the word *surely* plus the verb used in the proper tense. If you are sharply observant, you will see the first word is like an infinitive without the ל It is actually a special type of the infinitive, the **infinitive absolute** (here, in the Qal) and this is its major use in Hebrew prose. Note the difference between the infinitive construct and the infinitive absolute for a verb like עשה (25.7)

> The infinitive absolute + verb (usually prefix) is an emphatic construction conveyed in English by adding the word *surely* to the verb employed.

40.2b Analyze עָשֹׂה (14.3a comments on the vocalization)

Root	Stem	Form	Person/Gender/Number	Special Features

In the Special Features column note the type of infinitve.

40.2c Analyze תַעֲשֶׂה

Root	Stem	Form	Person/Gender/Number	Special Features

40.3 **וְגַם יָכֹל תּוּכָל**

You can see here a repetition of the previous construction. יכל has several meanings: *be able, have power, prevail, endure.*

40.4 Translate the verse: ____________________

____

40.5 יכל does not follow a 1st י pattern. Below are charts of its extant forms in the Bible.

Qal Affix יכל

3 m. sg.	יָכֹל	3 c. pl.	יָֽכְלוּ
3 f. sg.	יָֽכְלָה		
2 m. sg.	יָכֹלְתָּ	2 m. pl.	----
2 f. sg.	----	2 f. pl.	----
1 c. sg.	יָכֹלְתִּי	1 c. pl.	----

Qal Prefix יכל

3 m. sg.	יוּכַל	3 m. pl.	יוּכְלוּ
3 f. sg.	תּוּכַל	3 f. pl.	-----
2 m. sg.	תּוּכַל	2 m. pl.	תּוּכְלוּ
2 f. sg.	----	2 f. pl.	-----
1 c. sg.	אוּכַל	1 c. pl.	נוּכַל

Qal Infinitives יכל

Construct	יְכֹלֶת	Absolute	יָכֹל

40.6 Assignments:

A. Read and translate Deuteronomy 6:21-25

B. Translate:

1 כִּי עָשֹׂה אֶעֱשֶׂה עִמְּךָ חֶסֶד 2 Samuel 9:7

2 וַאֲנַחְנוּ לֹא נֵדַע מַה־נַּעֲשֶׂה כִּי עָלֶיךָ עֵינֵינוּ 2 Chronicles 20:12

3 אָכוֹל תֹּאכְלוּ אֹתָהּ בַּקֹּדֶשׁ כַּאֲשֶׁר צִוֵּיתִי Leviticus 10:18
[בַּקֹּדֶשׁ See 39.4]

4 בֹּא־יָבֹא מֶלֶךְ־בָּבֶל וְהִשְׁחִית אֶת־הָאָרֶץ הַזֹּאת Jeremiah 36:29

5 וְכִי תֹאמְרוּ מַה־נֹּאכַל Leviticus 25:20

6 הֲלֹא אַהֲרֹן אָחִיךָ הַלֵּוִי יָדַעְתִּי כִּי־דַבֵּר יְדַבֵּר הוּא Exodus 4:14

7 אֶת־בְּנֹתָם נִקַּח־לָנוּ לְנָשִׁים וְאֶת־בְּנֹתֵינוּ נִתֵּן לָהֶם Genesis 34:21

8 וְעֹזְבֵי יהוה יִכְלוּ Isaiah 1:28

9 יָצֹא אֵצֵא גַּם־אֲנִי עִמָּכֶם 2 Samuel 18:2

10 וַיֹּאמֶר יְהוּדָה מַה־נֹּאמַר לַאדֹנִי מַה־נְּדַבֵּר Genesis 44:16

11 וּצְדָקָה תִּהְיֶה־לָּנוּ כִּי־נִשְׁמֹר לַעֲשׂוֹת אֶת־כָּל־הַמִּצְוָה הַזֹּאת
לִפְנֵי יהוה אֱלֹהֵינוּ כַּאֲשֶׁר צִוָּנוּ׃ Deuteronomy 6:25

12 אַל־תַּעֲמֹד בְּדָבָר רָע Qohelet 8:3

13 וְנֵצֵא אֶל־מֶלֶךְ יִשְׂרָאֵל אוּלַי יְחַיֶּה אֶת־נַפְשֶׁךָ 1 Kings 20:31
[אוּלַי *perhaps*]

14 כִּי מֵרָעָה אֶל־רָעָה יָצָאוּ וְאֹתִי לֹא־יָדָעוּ Jeremiah 9:2

15 וְגַם־אֲנַחְנוּ נִהְיֶה לַאדֹנִי לַעֲבָדִים Genesis 44:9

16 פֶּן־תִּכְרֹת בְּרִית לְיוֹשֵׁב הָאָרֶץ וְזָנוּ אַחֲרֵי אֱלֹהֵיהֶם וְזָבְחוּ
לֵאלֹהֵיהֶם וְקָרָא לְךָ וְאָכַלְתָּ מִזִּבְחוֹ׃ [פֶּן *lest* זנה *whore*] Exodus 34:15

17 כִּי־כָלִינוּ בְאַפֶּךָ Psalms 90:7

18 כִּי אָמַרְתִּי יֶשׁ־לִי תִקְוָה גַּם הָיִיתִי הַלַּיְלָה לְאִישׁ וְגַם
יָלַדְתִּי בָנִים [תִּקְוָה *hope*] Ruth 1:12

Exodus 3:18 נֵלֲכָה־נָּא דֶּרֶךְ שְׁלֹשֶׁת יָמִים בַּמִּדְבָּר

41.1 Verb Analysis נֵלֲכָה־נָּא

Root	Stem	Form	Person/Gender/Number	Special Features

In the first word נֵ is ______________ Thus the root will be __________ The ending ָה can be an emphatic verb ending. (30.3) When, however, it is combined with a 1st person prefix pronoun, it is a sign of a specialized form of the prefix.

> A first person prefix, singular or plural, may be used in a specialized construction called the **cohortative**.

The cohortative is a type of command — to oneself:

"Let us do such and such."

"I shall do. . ."

"We shall do such and such." (not future, an exercise of will)

41.1a נָא is a particle attached almost exclusively to imperatives, cohortatives, and jussives (see next Lesson). Use this helpful bit of information to assist in locating these forms. It is sometimes also attached to הִנֵּה | נָא is frequently translated as *please*, and just as frequently not translated at all! Some scholars treat it as a "modal particle," indicating action arising out of a preceding statement (translation: *now, as a result*). While this explanation will not work in every case, נָא usually has the force of *now* in the English, "Now finish your milk!"

41.1b The cohortative ה is usually ָה It is not added to a verb which already ends in ה So in a form like נַעֲלֶה the mood has to be inferred from the context.

41.2 דֶּרֶךְ שְׁלֹשֶׁת יָמִים

דֶּרֶךְ means ____________________ שְׁלֹשֶׁת is a form of שָׁלֹשׁ *three.* יָמִים means ______________________ (The Noun H) Note the endiNGs on these words. Do they agree?

41.2a Numbers are the grand exception to all our adjective rules in Hebrew. In fact they themselves do not follow one consistent scheme. The basic number words (cardinals) for the numbers from 1-10 are shown below. Note that the form given is identified as the word modifying masculine or feminine nouns – the words themselves often appear to be in the gender opposite to the noun modified.

	Modifying masculine nouns		Modifying feminine nouns	
	before or after	before only	before or after	before only
One	אֶחָד		אַחַת	
Two	שְׁנַיִם	שְׁנֵי	שְׁתַּיִם	שְׁתֵּי
Three	שְׁלֹשָׁה	שְׁלֹשֶׁת	שָׁלֹשׁ	שְׁלֹשׁ
Four	אַרְבָּעָה	אַרְבַּעַת	אַרְבַּע	
Five	חֲמִשָּׁה	חֲמֵשֶׁת	חָמֵשׁ	חֲמֵשׁ
Six	שִׁשָּׁה	שֵׁשֶׁת	שֵׁשׁ	
Seven	שִׁבְעָה	שִׁבְעַת	שֶׁבַע	שְׁבַע
Eight	שְׁמֹנָה	שְׁמֹנַת	שְׁמֹנֶה	
Nine	תִּשְׁעָה	תִּשְׁעַת	תֵּשַׁע	תְּשַׁע
Ten	עֲשָׂרָה	עֲשֶׂרֶת	עֶשֶׂר	

Rules on use:

The number **one** always agrees with its noun, and the same word is used in front of or after the noun. When in front, the word may be part of a construct chain.

Two has a dual ending ַ־יִם in both masculine and feminine forms. The noun used with the number two is plural. BUT if an item occurs in a pair, only the dual ending is used with the noun, without the use or the word *two.*

From **three** to **ten** the plural of the noun is used with the number word.

Note the construction of this three word phrase. We have here a ________________
This also helps in our understanding how the number can be singular and the noun plural. Is the chain defininte or indefinite? ________________________
Translate phrase: ____________________________ בַּמִּדְבָּר means ________________

41.3 Translate verse: ____

41.4 You have seen that there are many things that הַ at the end of a word can be:

רָאָה	part of verb root
פָּקְדָה	3 f. sg. affix pronoun
תִּרְאֶינָה	2 and 3 f. pl. prefix complement
שְׁמֹרְנָה	feminine plural imperative
נֵלְכָה	cohortative ה
הַגִּידָה	optional m. sg. imperative ending
עָשִׂיתָה	emphatic verb form
שָׁנָה	part of feminine singular noun
טוֹבָה	feminine singular adjective endiNG
פֹּקְדָה	feminine singular participle endiNG
עָרֶיהָ	feminine singular possessive suffix (consonantal)[1]
אַתָּה	part of another sort of word (pronoun, adverb, etc.)
אַרְצָה	location/direction

Some clues to help you determine what the הַ is:

It may be part of a whole word you should recognize as it stands: אַתָּה

In other cases, you need to find the root. If it is a noun, knowing your vocabulary will be a great help

If it is a verb form:

a. holem וֹ after the first root letter is probably a sign of ____________

b. shewa ְ under the first root letter and נ immediately before the הַ could be an indication of ____________

c. a prefix pronoun, combined with נ immediately before the הַ could indicate ____________

What other hints can you think of to identify other things? ("Context" counts!)

---

[1] Admittedly, הָ is not the same as הַ but it is included because it may cause visual ambiguity.

41.5 Identify the function of the הָ‎ in each of the following words. In some cases there is more than one possibility. In such potentially ambiguous cases, tell how you would decide among the options.

רָעָה	וְאָֽבְדָה	הַיַּרְדֵּנָה
עֲשָׂרָה	בְּהֵמָה	הַבָּאָה
תִּרְאֶינָה	שְׁמֹרְנָה	וַיַּצִּילֶהָ
נֹאבְדָה	שְׂדֹתֶיהָ	טוֹבָה
רָאֲתָה	מִצְרַיְמָה	שִׁבְעָה
הֹלְכָה	מֵאָה	עֵדָה
הַשְׁלֵכְנָה	עָשִׂיתָה	שֻׁפְּטָה
גִּלָּה	מִלְחָמָה	הִרְבְּתָה
שָׁמָּה	שִׁשָּׁה	שׁוֹפְטָה
עַתָּה	אֶשְׁמְרָה	דַּבֵּרְנָה
הֶרְאָה	צִוָּה	מִשְׁפָּחָה
שִׁכְבָה	גָּלָה	נָבוֹאָה
וְנָשׁוּבָה	לָמָּה	תַּשְׁלֵכְנָה
אִמְרָה	מִנְחָה	וָאֹמְרָה
הָאֹמְרָה	אֱמֹרְנָה	אֱמְרָה
עֹלָה	גֳּדְלָה	וְהַגְּדוֹלָה
חָכְמָה	הֶרְשָׁעָה	הִטָּה
שְׁלַחְנָה	עָנָה	נַחֲלָה
אַמָּה	זֶרָה	לַיַּמָּה
אֲדָמָה	וַתֹּאבַדְנָה	מְצֶאנָה
חַיָּה	מַלְכָּה	מָֽלְכָה
הַשְׁמַעְנָה	רָבָה	תִּכְלֶינָה
שָׁתָה	עֲלֶינָה	יֵכְלָה

41.6 Assignments:

A. For Lessons 41-48 learn vocabulary words 301-350

B. Learn the numbers from 1-10 (41.5)

C. Read and translate 1 Kings 17:1-5

D. Translate. Then identify the form and mood of each 1st person verb:

1 וְאָבוֹאָה אֶל־מִזְבַּח אֱלֹהִים Psalms 43:4

2 שִׁבְעַת יָמִים מַצּוֹת תֹּאכֵלוּ Exodus 12:15

3 וַנֹּאמֶר בֹּאוּ וְנָבוֹא יְרוּשָׁלַםִ Jeremiah 35:11

4 וָאֲבָרֵךְ אֶת־יהוה אֱלֹהֵי אֲדֹנִי Genesis 24:48

5 שָׂמַחְתִּי בְּאֹמְרִים לִי בֵּית יהוה נֵלֵךְ Psalms 122:1

6 וַיִּקַּח סֵפֶר הַבְּרִית וַיִּקְרָא בְּאָזְנֵי הָעָם וַיֹּאמְרוּ כֹּל אֲשֶׁר־דִּבֶּר
יהוה נַעֲשֶׂה וְנִשְׁמָע׃ Exodus 24:7

7 וַיַּעֲשׂוּ־חָג שִׁבְעַת יָמִים Nehemiah 8:18

8 לְעוֹלָם אֶשְׁמָר־לוֹ חַסְדִּי Psalms 89:29

9 וַנִּקַּח בָּעֵת הַהִיא אֶת־הָאָרֶץ מִיַּד שְׁנֵי מַלְכֵי הָאֱמֹרִי Deuteronomy 3:8

10 וַיִּגְּשׁוּ אֶל־זְרֻבָּבֶל וְאֶל־רָאשֵׁי הָאָבוֹת וַיֹּאמְרוּ לָהֶם נִבְנֶה עִמָּכֶם
Ezra 4:2

11 וָאֶבְנֶה הַבַּיִת לְשֵׁם־יהוה 1 Kings 8:20

*12 הִנֵּה־נָא לִי שְׁתֵּי בָנוֹת אֲשֶׁר לֹא־יָדְעוּ אִישׁ אוֹצִיאָה־נָּא אֶתְהֶן
אֲלֵיכֶם וַעֲשׂוּ לָהֶן כַּטּוֹב בְּעֵינֵיכֶם Genesis 19:8

13 שְׁנֵי אֲנָשִׁים הָיוּ בְּעִיר אֶחָד 2 Samuel 12:1

14 שֵׁשֶׁת יָמִים תַּעֲבֹד Deuteronomy 5:13

15 וַיִּהְיוּ־שָׁם שְׁלֹשָׁה בְּנֵי צְרוּיָה 2 Samuel 2:18

16 וַיֹּאמְרוּ לָנוּ עֶשֶׂר פְּעָמִים Nehemiah 4:6

17 אֶת־יהוה אֱלֹהֵינוּ נַעֲבֹד וּבְקוֹלוֹ נִשְׁמָע Joshua 24:24

18 אֶעְבְּרָה־נָּא וְאֶרְאֶה אֶת־הָאָרֶץ הַטּוֹבָה Deuteronomy 3:25

יְהִי יהוה אֱלֹהֶיךָ בָּרוּךְ 1 Kings 10:9

42.1 Verb Analysis יְהִי

Root	Stem	Form	Person/Gender/Number	Special Features

Analyzing the verb on the chart should not be difficult. We have here a different form syntactically, however. This form is called the **jussive**.

A third person prefix form, singular or plural, may be used as a jussive, a command given in the third person.

Examples of jussives:

"May he do such and such"

"Let them do such and such"

42.1a The jussive form is ordinarily identical to the prefix form. However, if there are two forms of the prefix, as happens with 3rd ה verbs — יִהְיֶה and יְהִי — the jussive will use the shorter or **apocopated** form. (Apocopated refers to subtraction from the end of a word.) We have seen examples of this apocopated form until now only with the vav conversive. (32.3a) Without this vav conversive, the apocopated form must be a jussive.

42.2 יהוה אֱלֹהֶיךָ is related to the verb ____________

Translation of the first three words: ____________

42.3 בָּרוּךְ

Do you see a familiar root here? This form, in which a וּ appears between the second and third letters of the root is called the **Qal passive participle**. In the Bible it is regularly used as an adjective, rather than as a verbal construction.

ברך means ____________ בָּרוּךְ means ____________

42.4 Translate sentence: ____________

42.5 Our imperative picture is now complete:

Cohortative	**Imperative**	**Jussive**
1st person	2nd person	3rd person
Let me/us do	*Do*	*Let him/her/them do*
usually lengthens (41.1)	may lengthen (30.1a)	may shorten (42.1)

All of these are closely related to the prefix forms. Indeed, in some cases of the cohortative and jussive, the forms themselves may be indistinguishable. Sometimes נָא will be a broad hint for you; sometimes only context will guide you in interpreting these forms.

42.6 Assignments:

A. Read and tranlate 1 Kings 17:6-10

B. Translate:

1 יַעַשׂה יהוה עִמָּכֶם חֶסֶד [יַעַשׂ as יַעַשׂה Ruth 1:8 [Read

2 וַיֹּאמֶר אֱלֹהִים יְהִי אוֹר וַיְהִי־אוֹר׃ [אוֹר *light*] Genesis 1:3

3 יהוה יִשְׁמָר־צֵאתְךָ וּבוֹאֶךָ מֵעַתָּה וְעַד עוֹלָם׃ Psalms 121:8

4 יְהִי־נָא דְבָרְיךָ כִּדְבַר אַחַד מֵהֶם (Do you see the scribal error here?)
1 Kings 22:13

5 אִם־יִשְׁמְרוּ בָנֶיךָ בְּרִיתִי Psalms 132:12

6 וְיִקְחוּ־נָא חֲמִשָּׁה מִן־הַסּוּסִים (Why doesn't וְיִקְחוּ have a dagesh forte?)
2 Kings 7:13

7 הוּא יִבְנֶה־לִּי בָּיִת 1 Chronicles 17:12

8 בָּרוּךְ יהוה אֱלֹהֵי אֲדֹנִי אַבְרָהָם Genesis 24:27

9 וַיְשַׁלְּחוּ אֹתוֹ וְאֶת־אִשְׁתּוֹ וְאֶת־כָּל־אֲשֶׁר לוֹ Genesis 12:20

10 וַיֹּאמֶר יהוה אֶל־מֹשֶׁה בְּלֶכְתְּךָ לָשׁוּב מִצְרַיְמָה רְאֵה
כָּל־הַמֹּפְתִים אֲשֶׁר־שַׂמְתִּי בְיָדֶךָ וַעֲשִׂיתָם לִפְנֵי פַרְעֹה וַאֲנִי אֲחַזֵּק
אֶת־לִבּוֹ וְלֹא יְשַׁלַּח אֶת־הָעָם׃ [מֹפְתִים *wonders*] Exodus 4:21

11 יַעֲמָד־נָא דָוִד לְפָנַי כִּי מָצָא חֵן בְּעֵינָי 1 Samuel 16:22

12 וְיוֹאָב וְכָל־הַצָּבָא אֲשֶׁר־אִתּוֹ בָּאוּ וַיַּגִּדוּ לְיוֹאָב לֵאמֹר בָּא־אַבְנֵר
בֶּן־נֵר אֶל־הַמֶּלֶךְ וַיְשַׁלְּחֵהוּ וַיֵּלֶךְ בְּשָׁלוֹם׃ 2 Samuel 3:23

13 וָאֶתְּנָה אֶת־הַלְוִיִּם נְתֻנִים לְאַהֲרֹן וּלְבָנָיו Numbers 8:19

14 בָּנֶיךָ וּבְנֹתֶיךָ נְתֻנִים לְעַם אַחֵר וְעֵינֶיךָ רֹאוֹת וְכָלוֹת אֲלֵיהֶם
כָּל־הַיּוֹם Deuteronomy 28:32

15 וָאֶקַּח אֶת־רָאשֵׁי שִׁבְטֵיכֶם אֲנָשִׁים חֲכָמִים וִידֻעִים Deuteronomy 1:15

16 וְנַעֲמָן שַׂר־צְבָא מֶלֶךְ־אֲרָם הָיָה אִישׁ גָּדוֹל לִפְנֵי אֲדֹנָיו
וּנְשֻׂא פָנִים 2 Kings 5:1

17 וַיֹּאמֶר הַמֶּלֶךְ לְהָמָן הַכֶּסֶף נָתוּן לָךְ וְהָעָם לַעֲשׂוֹת בּוֹ
כַּטּוֹב בְּעֵינֶיךָ׃ Esther 3:11

18 וַיָּקֻמוּ כָּל־הַקְּרֻאִים אֲשֶׁר לַאֲדֹנִיָּהוּ וַיֵּלְכוּ אִישׁ לְדַרְכּוֹ 1 Kings 1:49

וְהָיָה בִּקְרָב־אִישׁ לְהִשְׁתַּחֲוֹת לוֹ וְשָׁלַח אֶת־יָדוֹ וְהֶחֱזִיק לוֹ
וְנָשַׁק לוֹ׃ 2 Samuel 15:5

43.1 וְהָיָה בִּקְרָב־אִישׁ

Frequently וְהָיָה announces a future event, which is what you would expect when you see וְ followed by the affix. However, it may also be used to introduce past events which were repeated over a period of time. The feeling of future or **frequentive past** time must be ascertained from the larger context of the story. Here the latter meaning fits best. וְהָיָה itself is usually left untranslated.

בִּקְרָב is composed of how many segments? ______ What are they? ______________

____

Review 35.1c if necessary and translate the phrase בִּקְרָב־אִישׁ ______________

______________ Do you know why the infinitive is not written בְּקְרֹב (6.3b)

43.2 לְהִשְׁתַּחֲוֹת לוֹ

We have here a unique language "fossil" — a remnant of a once larger system that still survives in other Semitic languages. This word is a verb. What form? ________

______________ The stem is called **Hishtaf`el** — the letters השת were prefixed to the root. There is evidence that this stem was extensively used in Semitic languages, but only one verb has survived in Biblical Hebrew with which this stem is used (and this verb occurs in the Bible only in the Hishtaf`el). The root is חוה *prostrate oneself in worship* which you can find by taking off the stem letters השת and following the infinitive rule in which 3rd ה verbs use וֹת____ in the infinitive. [In some older lexicons the root is considered to be שחה]

The infinitive, imperative, and affix of this verb are easy to recognize by the השת combination. The 3 m. sg. prefix form is יִשְׁתַּחֲוֶה and the m. sg. participle is מִשְׁתַּחֲוֶה

Analyze לְהִשְׁתַּחֲוֹת

Root	Stem	Form	Person/Gender/Number	Special Features

43.2a Translate the phrase: ______________________________

וְהָיָה בִּקְרָב־אִישׁ לְהִשְׁתַּחֲוֹת לוֹ וְשָׁלַח אֶת־יָדוֹ וְהֶחֱזִיק לוֹ וְנָשַׁק לוֹ׃

43.3 וְשָׁלַח אֶת־יָדוֹ

The sense of frequentive past continues throughout the verse.

Translate the phrase: ______________________________

43.4 וְהֶחֱזִיק לוֹ וְנָשַׁק לוֹ

Analyze וְהֶחֱזִיק

Root	Stem	Form	Person/Gender/Number	Special Features

Note the frequentive ו in the Special Features column.

After abstracting the root, what function will you give the extra letters? ______________ ______________ Can you think of a reason why the ה is pointed with a segol ֶ ______________

The meaning of חזק in the Qal is ______________ In the Hif'il it can have several connotations, *make strong, take hold, seize.*

Review 16.4a if necessary and translate the phrase: ______________________________ ______________________________

43.5 Translate the verse: ______________________________ ______________________________

43.6 Assignments:

A. Read and translate 1 Kings 17:11-15

B. Translate:

1 וַיִּקְרָא לִשְׁלֹמֹה בְנוֹ וַיְצַוֵּהוּ לִבְנוֹת בַּיִת לַיהוה אֱלֹהֵי יִשְׂרָאֵל׃
1 Chronicles 22:6

2 הִשְׁתַּחֲווּ־לוֹ כָּל־אֱלֹהִים Psalms 97:7

3 עֲבָדֶיךָ יַעֲשׂוּ כַּאֲשֶׁר אֲדֹנִי מְצַוֶּה Numbers 32:25

4 וַיִּפֹּל עַל־פָּנָיו וַיִּשְׁתָּחוּ 2 Samuel 9:6

וְהָיָה בִּקְרָב־אִישׁ לְהִשְׁתַּחֲוֺת לוֹ וְשָׁלַח אֶת־יָדוֹ וְהֶחֱזִיק לוֹ
וְנָשַׁק לוֹ׃

---

5 לִפְנֵי הַמִּזְבֵּחַ הַזֶּה תִּשְׁתַּחֲווּ 2 Kings 18:22

6 וְהִשְׁתַּחֲוִיתָ לִפְנֵי יהוה אֱלֹהֶיךָ Deuteronomy 26:10

7 כִּי־בָרֵךְ יְבָרֶכְךָ יהוה בָּאָרֶץ Deuteronomy 15:4

8 נַפְשִׁי יָצְאָה בְדַבְּרוֹ Song of Songs 5:6

9 וַיְהִי בְּשַׁלַּח פַּרְעֹה אֶת־הָעָם Exodus 13:17

*10 וַיְכַל יַעֲקֹב לְצַוֺּת אֶת־בָּנָיו Genesis 49:33

11 וְהִשְׁתַּחֲווּ לַיהוה בְּהַר הַקֹּדֶשׁ בִּירוּשָׁלָםִ Isaiah 27:13

12 וּצְבָא הַשָּׁמַיִם לְךָ מִשְׁתַּחֲוִים Nehemiah 9:6

13 כִּי בֶאֱמֶת שְׁלָחַנִי יהוה עֲלֵיכֶם לְדַבֵּר בְּאָזְנֵיכֶם Jeremiah 26:15

אַתָּה הָרְאֵתָ לָדַעַת כִּי יהוה הוּא הָאֱלֹהִים אֵין עוֹד מִלְבַדּוֹ׃

Deuteronomy 4:35

44.1 אַתָּה הָרְאֵתָ

The pronoun here is used to ____________________ the verb. (36.7) You may easily pick out the root of the verb, since it is a common one. This in turn suggests that the ה in front of the root is ____________________________ and that the תָ at the end is ____________________ There is just one additional twist here: what vowel would you expect to see under the ה in the Hif'il affix?[1] __________ (28.5) This form is called the Hof'al rather than Hif'il. (The ָ in the verb is qamets ḥatuf, pronounced "o," just as the ָ in כָּל). The **Hof'al** is the Hif'il stem in a passive mood:

Active:	you **showed** me
Passive:	I **was shown** by you

There are not many instances of the Hof'al in the Bible in comparison to the total number of verbs. But you should be aware of its existence; when the vowels in a Hif'il type of form do not seem to fit the regular pattern, but are ָ or ֻ or וֹ where this is unexpected, you should think of the Hof'al.

Root	Stem	Form	Person/Gender/Number	Special Features

Translation of phrase: ____

44.2 Analyze לָדַעַת

Root	Stem	Form	Person/Gender/Number	Special Features

---

[1] The verb ראה is not altogether regular in the Hif'il affix. Its preformative is pointed not הִ but הֶ However, you should note that when the vowel of a preformative changes, it usually does so within its own class. (See: Vowel Points.) That means ִ would exchange with ֵ or ֶ and ַ would likely exchange with ָ This phenomenon is almost perfectly illustrated in the conjugations of hollow verbs in the Hif'il. (33.5)

44.3 כִּי יהוה הוּא הָאֱלֹהִים means ____________________

44.4 אֵין means ____________ עוֹד means ____________

44.5 מִלְּבַדּוֹ has several components, including two prepositions, a noun, and a pronoun. Can you locate these? The noun is בַּד *part, piece*, but it appears rarely in this form in the Bible. Usually it appears in the combination לְבַד meaning *alone, by itself*. Pronouns attached to such a word indicate <u>who</u> is alone. Other prepositions, such as מִן can be attached also, altering the concept. The word here will mean ____________________

44.6 The final three words of the verse form a phrase meaning ____________________
____

44.7 Sentence translation: ____________________
____

44.8 Assignments:

A. Read and translate 1 Kings 17:16-20

B. Analyze the following verbs:

הוֹדַע	דְּעוּ	יָדוּעַ
יוֹדֵעַ	לְדַעְתּוֹ	יְדַעְתִּיךְ
לְהוֹדִיעֲךָ	יוֹדִיעַ	תֵּדָעוּהָ
וְהוּבָא	מוּדַעַת	הוֹדַעְתִּיךְ
מֻכִּים	הַמּוּבָא	תְּבִיאֵם
וּמַכֵּה	וְיִתֵּן	הוּרַד
יַכֶּה	מוֹת	יוּמַת

C. Translate:

1 הוֹדַע אֵלָיו חַטָּאתוֹ Leviticus 4:23

2 וְהוּבָא אֶל־אַהֲרֹן הַכֹּהֵן אוֹ אֶל־אַחַד מִבָּנָיו הַכֹּהֲנִים׃ Leviticus 13:2

3 וְהִנֵּה עֲבָדֶיךָ מֻכִּים Exodus 5:16

4 וְיוֹסֵף הוּרַד מִצְרָיְמָה Genesis 39:1

5 יֻתַּן אֶת־הָאָרֶץ הַזֹּאת לַעֲבָדֶיךָ Numbers 32:5

6 וּמַכֵּה אָבִיו אוֹ אִמּוֹ מוֹת יוּמָת׃ Exodus 21:15

7 וְאִישׁ כִּי יַכֶּה כָּל־נֶפֶשׁ אָדָם מוֹת יוּמָת׃ Leviticus 24:17

8 יִהְיוּ־לְךָ לְבַדֶּךָ וְאֵין לְזָרִים אִתָּךְ׃ Proverbs 5:17

Lesson 45

וָאַעַשׂ בַּבֹּקֶר כַּאֲשֶׁר צֻוֵּיתִי Ezekiel 24:18

45.1 Analyze וָאַעַשׂ

Root	Stem	Form	Person/Gender/Number	Special Features

45.2 בַּבֹּקֶר means ______________________ כַּאֲשֶׁר means ____________

45.3 צֻוֵּיתִי

Here again we have a variation of a more familiar stem. Think how this word is pronounced. The ו is not a vowel but ______________________ (37.2a)

What stem does this suggest? ________________ The vowels are not the expected ones for the Pi`el affix, however.

> Qibbuts ֻ under the first root letter, plus doubling of the middle root letter, are signs of the **Pu`al**, the passive of the Pi`el system.

Root	Stem	Form	Person/Gender/Number	Special Features

If the verb צוה were active it would be translated ______________________

But the verb is passive, so the translation will be ______________________

45.4 Verse translation: ____

____

45.5 Some compounds with אֲשֶׁר are:

לַאֲשֶׁר *to him who*   עַל אֲשֶׁר *to* (the place)   בַּאֲשֶׁר *in* (the place)

אֲשֶׁר...שָׁם *where* or *whence*   כַּאֲשֶׁר *when, as*   עַד אֲשֶׁר *until*

45.6 Assignments:

A. Read and translate 1 Kings 17:21-24

B. Analyze the following verbs:

יָלַדְתִּי	יֻלַּדְתִּי	יְלוּדִים
יָלַד	יוֹלְדוֹת	יֻלְּדוּ
יָלְדָה	לֶדֶת	יֵלֵד
הַיּוּלָּד	הַמְיַלְּדוֹת	תֵּלְדִי
יְבֹרַךְ	הֻלֶּדֶת	הוֹלִיד
בּוֹרֵךְ	מְבָרֵךְ	מְבֹרָךְ
צַוּוּ	צֻוֵּיתָה	יְצֻוֶּה

C. Translate:

1 וּלְשֵׁת גַּם־הוּא יֻלַּד־בֵּן Genesis 4:26

2 אָרוּר הַיּוֹם אֲשֶׁר יֻלַּדְתִּי בּוֹ Jeremiah 20:14 [אָרוּר *cursed* adj.]

3 וְאַתָּה צֻוֵּיתָה זֹאת עֲשׂוּ Genesis 45:19

4 אֵלֶּה יֻלְּדוּ לְדָוִד בְּחֶבְרוֹן 2 Samuel 3:5

5 יהוה נָתַן וַיהוה לָקָח יְהִי שֵׁם יהוה מְבֹרָךְ Job 1:21

6 יְבֹרַךְ בֵּית־עַבְדְּךָ לְעוֹלָם 2 Samuel 7:29

7 וְדִבֶּר אֶל־בְּנֵי יִשְׂרָאֵל אֵת אֲשֶׁר יְצֻוֶּה Exodus 34:34

8 וְיָשַׁבְתָּ עִמּוֹ יָמִים אֲחָדִים עַד אֲשֶׁר־תָּשׁוּב חֲמַת אָחִיךָ׃
Genesis 27:44 [חֵמָה *fury* אֲחָדִים pl. of אֶחָד of course!]

9 וְאָמְרוּ עַל אֲשֶׁר עָזְבוּ אֶת־בְּרִית יהוה אֱלֹהֵי אֲבֹתָם אֲשֶׁר כָּרַת
עִמָּם בְּהוֹצִיאוֹ אֹתָם מֵאֶרֶץ מִצְרָיִם׃ Deuteronomy 29:24

10 אַל־תִּירְאִי כִּי־שָׁמַע אֱלֹהִים אֶל־קוֹל הַנַּעַר בַּאֲשֶׁר הוּא־שָׁם
Genesis 21:17

Deuteronomy 28:10 וְרָאוּ כָּל־עַמֵּי הָאָרֶץ כִּי שֵׁם יהוה נִקְרָא עָלֶיךָ

46.1 וְרָאוּ כָּל־עַמֵּי הָאָרֶץ

Analyze וְרָאוּ

Root	Stem	Form	Person/Gender/Number	Special Features

46.1a Translate the phrase: ______________________________

46.2 כִּי means ______________

46.3 שֵׁם יהוה means ____________________

46.4 נִקְרָא

Here you meet the last family in the stem classification. It is called **Nif'al**, and the stem indicator is a נ added in front of the root letters. Its secondary recognition sign often is ַ or ָ under the second root letter. (Hence the stem name Nif'a̲l, as in "A" class vowel.) The form here is affix — what is the PGN? __________

Root	Stem	Form	Person/Gender/Number	Special Features

The Nif'al is a passive stem. Qal is almost always active, Pi'el and Hif'il are active stems, with related passive forms; for this reason, verbs that occur in the Qal for the most part usually occur in the Nif'al also, while verbs that occur mostly in the Pi'el or Hif'il systems use the passives of those stems.

קָרָא means ______________ נִקְרָא means ______________

46.5 עָלֶיךָ means ______________

46.6 Sentence translation: ______________________________

____

46.7 The Nif`al affix is formed like the affix of most of the derived stems.

affix pronoun ⟵ root ⟵ stem preformative

תָּ ___ ___ ___ נִ

You should be able to fill in the chart, making the internal vowel adjustments where necessary. The vowel under the preformative will not change.

Nif`al Affix ברך

3 m. sg.	נִבְרַךְ	3 c. pl.	___
3 f. sg.	___		
2 m. sg.	___	2 m. pl.	___
2 f. sg.	___	2 f. pl.	___
1 c. sg.	___	1 c. pl.	___

46.7a For 1st נ verbs, there will be a dagesh forte in the second root letter to represent the assimilation of the נ of the root:

3 f. sg. Qal affix	3 f. sg. Nif`al affix
נָשְׂאָה	נִשְּׂאָה

1st י verbs have וֹ between the preformative and the root:

3 f. sg. Qal affix	3 f. sg. Nif`al affix
יָדְעָה	נוֹדְעָה

Hollow verbs (happily, rare in the Nif`al) will have נָ preformative or נְ for the longer PGNs. These latter have an extra וֹ syllable between the root and the affix pronoun:

3 f. sg. Qal affix	3 f. sg. Nif`al affix
רָמָה	נָרוֹמָה

1 c. pl. Qal affix	1 c. pl. Nif`al affix
רַמְנוּ	נְרוּמוֹנוּ

With 1st **Gutturals** the preformative is usually pointed נֶ but נַ or נִ is possible:

3 f. sg. Qal affix	3 f. sg. Nif`al affix
עָמְדָה	נֶעֶמְדָה

The נ preformative can create a common ambiguity which you may have thought of already. The 3 m. sg. Nif`al affix can be identical to the 1 c. pl. Qal prefix. This is most common with verbs which follow the regular patterns and 1st נs. In such cases, the context of the verse should indicate which stem and PGN is meant.

וְנִבְחַר מָוֶת מֵחַיִּים לְכֹל הַשְּׁאֵרִית הַנִּשְׁאָרִים Jeremiah 8:3

3 m. sg. Nif`al affix

and death shall be chosen rather than life by all the residue of those who are left

נִשָּׂא לְבָבֵנוּ אֶל־כַּפַּיִם אֶל־אֵל בַּשָּׁמָיִם Lamentations 3:41

1 c. pl. Qal affix

Let us lift up our heart with our hands to God in the heavens.

כִּי־נָגַע אֶל־הַשָּׁמַיִם מִשְׁפָּטָהּ וְנִשָּׂא עַד־שְׁחָקִים Jeremiah 51:9

3 m. sg. Nif`al affix

for her judgment reaches heaven and is lifted up to the clouds

46.8 Assignments:

A. Learn the Nif`al affix (46.7-46.7a)

B. Read and translate 1 Kings 18:20-24

C. Analyze the following verbs. If a form is ambiguous, note that:

נוֹדַע	נֵדַע	יָדוּעַ
וְנִבְנוּ	נוֹדִיעַ	וְנִבְנְתָה
נִתְּנָה	נִבְנָה	נִבְנֶה
נִתְּנוּ	נִתֵּן	נֶתְנָה
נִהְיְתָה	נִהְיָה	נוֹתֵן
הֶעֱשׂוּ	יַעֲשׂוּ	נַעֲשׂוּ
נִרְאוּ	נִרְאָה	נוֹלַד

D. Translate:

1 וְנִקְרְאָה יְרוּשָׁלַםִ עִיר־הָאֱמֶת Zechariah 8:3

2 לֹא נוֹדַע מִי הִכָּהוּ Deuteronomy 21:1

3 שִׁשָּׁה נוֹלַד־לוֹ בְחֶבְרוֹן 1 Chronicles 3:4

4 וְנוֹדַע יהוה לְמִצְרַיִם וְיָדְעוּ מִצְרַיִם אֶת־יהוה בַּיּוֹם הַהוּא Isaiah 19:21

5 וּשְׁמִי יהוה לֹא נוֹדַעְתִּי לָהֶם [English needs a preposition before שְׁמִי]
Exodus 6:3

6 וְנִבְנְתָה הָעִיר לַיהוה Jeremiah 31:38 (37)

7 בִּדְבַר יהוה שָׁמַיִם נַעֲשׂוּ Psalms 33:6 (46.7a)

8 וְנִבְנוּ בְּתוֹךְ עַמִּי Jeremiah 12:16

9 כִּי לֹא־נִבְנָה בַיִת לְשֵׁם יהוה 1 Kings 3:2

10 הַיּוֹם יהוה נִרְאָה אֲלֵיכֶם Leviticus 9:4

11 וְהָעִיר נִתְּנָה בְּיַד הַכַּשְׂדִּים Jeremiah 32:24

12 נִרְאוּ רָאשֵׁי הֶהָרִים Genesis 8:5

13 כִּי מֵאִתִּי נִהְיָה הַדָּבָר הַזֶּה 1 Kings 12:24

14 כִּי שִׁמְךָ נִקְרָא עַל־עִירְךָ וְעַל־עַמֶּךָ Daniel 9:19

15 וַאֲנִי לֹא נִקְרֵאתִי לָבוֹא אֶל־הַמֶּלֶךְ Esther 4:11

16 מָה הָרָעָה הַזֹּאת אֲשֶׁר נִהְיְתָה בָּכֶם Judges 20:12

17 נַעֲשָׂה הַפֶּסַח הַזֶּה לַיהוה בִּירוּשָׁלָםִ [פֶּסַח *passover*] 2 Kings 23:23

18 וּבְכָל־דְּגֵי הַיָּם בְּיֶדְכֶם נִתָּנוּ [דָּג *fish*] Genesis 9:2

ـ נִי is *me*

מִי is *who*

הוּא is *he*

הִיא is *she* AND

דָּג is *fish*

Genesis 35:1 וַעֲשֵׂה־שָׁם מִזְבֵּחַ לָאֵל הַנִּרְאֶה אֵלֶיךָ

47.1 וַעֲשֵׂה־שָׁם מִזְבֵּחַ

Analyze וַעֲשֵׂה

Root	Stem	Form	Person/Gender/Number	Special Features

Translate phrase: ______________________________

47.2 לָאֵל הַנִּרְאֶה

אֵל is a shorter form of אֱלֹהִים

הַנִּרְאֶה is a new verb form.

Root	Stem	Form	Person/Gender/Number	Special Features

◻הַ is the ______________________ and occurs with which verb form? ______________ With this help, you should be able to analyze the rest of the verb. The נ in front of the root indicates ______________________ (46.4) Since no special endiNGs are added the number and gender will be __________

If you compare the vowel patterns of the 3 m. sg. Nif'al affix and the m. sg. participle in the Ni'fal you will see there is not much difference. In the absence of the definite article, context is the best indication in deciding between these two. With other PGNs, of course, this is not a problem. A less than perfect guide: if the vowel under the 2nd root letter is ַ the form is affix as in נִבְרַךְ If the vowel is ָ it may be a participle as in נִבְרָךְ

> The Qal and the Nif'al are the only stems in which the participle does not have a preformative מ

Some verbs in the Nif'al have taken on specialized meanings, rather than being translated more literally. Such is the case with ראה In the Nif'al it means literally _____________ but is translated *appear* (active, not passive). Such Nif'al meanings appear in the vocabulary list for the most common verbs.

47.3 Translate sentence: ____

____

47.4 Meanings of the Nif'al stem

You have already seen the passive function of the Nif'al in נִקְרָא (Lesson 46) This Lesson shows how English sometimes imparts an active meaning to a Nif'al by using a different verb in translation. Like the other derived stems, the Nif'al can impart a variety of meanings to a root.

A. A lot of verbs have a **reflexive** meaning in the Nif'al:

Qal		Nif'al	
שָׁמַר	*be on one's guard*	נִשְׁמַר	*take heed to oneself*

B. It can be used to express **reciprocal** action:

Pi'el		Nif'al	
דִּבֶּר	*speak*	נִדְבַּר	*speak to one another*
Qal		Nif'al	
שָׁפַט	*judge*	נִשְׁפַּט	*enter into controversy with*

C. It can be the **active** + **to** or **for oneself**:

Qal		Nif'al	
שָׁאַל	*ask*	נִשְׁאַל	*ask for oneself*

D. The Nif'al is often used to express an **emotional state**:

Pi'el	Nif'al
נִחַם יהוה עַמּוֹ (Isaiah 49:13)	נִחַם יהוה עַל־זאת (Amos 7:3)
comfort (someone else)	*be sorry, console oneself*

What are the features of נחם that make the affix in this PGN of these two stems look the same?

47.5 Assignments:

A. Read and translate 1 Kings 18:25-29

B. Translate:

1 נוֹדָע בִּיהוּדָה אֱלֹהִים Psalms 76:2

2 וַיִּהְיוּ נִקְרָאִים לִפְנֵי הַמֶּלֶךְ Esther 6:1

3 הִנֵּה־בֵן נוֹלָד לְבֵית־דָּוִד 1 Kings 13:2

4 וְנִבְרְכוּ בְךָ כֹּל מִשְׁפְּחֹת הָאֲדָמָה Genesis 12:3

5 וַיֹּאמֶר מִצְרַיִם אָנוּסָה מִפְּנֵי יִשְׂרָאֵל כִּי יהוה נִלְחָם לָהֶם
בְּמִצְרָיִם Exodus 14:25

6 וּפְלִשְׁתִּים נִלְחָמִים בְּיִשְׂרָאֵל וַיָּנֻסוּ אַנְשֵׁי יִשְׂרָאֵל מִפְּנֵי
פְּלִשְׁתִּים 1 Samuel 31:1

7 וְהַקֹּל נִשְׁמַע בֵּית פַּרְעֹה לֵאמֹר בָּאוּ אֲחֵי יוֹסֵף וַיִּיטַב בְּעֵינֵי
פַּרְעֹה וּבְעֵינֵי עֲבָדָיו׃ Genesis 45:16

8 אֵין־קֹרֵא בְצֶדֶק וְאֵין נִשְׁפָּט בֶּאֱמוּנָה [אֱמוּנָה *steadfastness*] Isaiah 59:4

9 חִזְקוּ עָלַי דִּבְרֵיכֶם אָמַר יְהוָה וַאֲמַרְתֶּם מַה־נִּדְבַּרְנוּ עָלֶיךָ׃
Malachi 3:13

10 וַיִּקְרָא אַבְרָהָם אֶת־שֶׁם־בְּנוֹ הַנּוֹלַד־לוֹ אֲשֶׁר־יָלְדָה־לּוֹ שָׂרָה
יִצְחָק׃ Genesis 21:3

Isaiah 65:19 וְלֹא־יִשָּׁמַע בָּהּ עוֹד קוֹל בְּכִי

48.1 וְלֹא־יִשָּׁמַע

Analyze יִשָּׁמַע

Root	Stem	Form	Person/Gender/Number	Special Features

Do you recognize a familiar root? ______________ The stem is the only problem. This is the Nif`al prefix which has been formed in the following way:

dagesh forte ↓ ↓stem indicator

יִשָּׁמַע ⟵ יִ נְ שָׁמַע

↑prefix pronoun

That is, the נ of the Nif`al stem in the prefix form has been assimilated to the following consonantal sound. This form is usually not too difficult to recognize except when the first consonant cannot take a dagesh; in such a case there must be compensation for the missing dagesh:

no dagesh ↓

וַיֵּאָמֵר

↑ ַ lengthened to ֵ

Translate the phrase: ______________________________

48.2 בָּהּ עוֹד

בָּהּ means The antecedent for הּ ָ is *Jerusalem*, which appears earlier in the verse. Translate the phrase: ______________________

48.3 קוֹל בְּכִי

קוֹל means ______________ In the word בְּכִי the component ִי is a not a suffix; it is part of the noun בְּכִי which means *weeping*. How does this phrase relate to the verb? ____________________________

48.4 Translate the verse: ____

48.5 Fill in the chart for the regular Nif'al prefix pattern. Do not forget the dagesh forte!

Nif'al Prefix שׁמע

3 m. sg.	יִשָּׁמַע	3 m. pl.	___
3 f. sg.	___	3 f. pl.	___
2 m. sg.	___	2 m. pl.	___
2 f. sg.	___	2 f. pl.	___
1 c. sg.	___	1 c. pl.	___

48.5a Now fill in the chart for the Nif'al prefix of 1st Guttural/ר verbs.

Nif'al Prefix אמר

3 m. sg.	יֵאָמֵר	3 m. pl.	___
3 f. sg.	___	3 f. pl.	___
2 m. sg.	___	2 m. pl.	___
2 f. sg.	___	2 f. pl.	___
1 c. sg.	___	1 c. pl.	___

48.5b The Nif'al prefix patterns for weak verbs can be identified by the dagesh forte in the first root letter and ָ under it. Even 1st נs follow this pattern: תִּנָּגַע In 1st י verbs the י of the root becomes the older ו as it does in the Nif'al affix. But here, because it has a dagesh forte, it is consonantal: יִוָּשֵׁב תִּוָּלֵד etc. (Note the similarity of formation of 1st י verbs in the Nif'al and Hif'il.)

48.6 Write the 3 m. pl. Nif'al prefix for the following verbs:

ידע	מלך	זכר
עמד	רדף	נשע
יתר	אכל	נשה

48.7 Extra Grammar

You have had plenty of practice finding the roots for nouns which have more than three letters. What about nouns with three or fewer letters?

1. Nouns which end in י come from roots which end in ה

root	noun
בכה	בְּכִי

2. Some two letter nouns are found listed as two letter nouns:

דָּם   פֶּה   יָד   בֵּן

3. Most two letter nouns are listed as being from a hollow, geminate, or 3rd ה root:

root	noun
גור	גֵּר
הרר	הַר
אבה	אָב

48.8 Assignments:

A. Memorize the Nif`al prefix patterns in 48.5 and 48.5a

B. Read and translate 1 Kings 18:30-34

C. Translate

1 וְאַתֶּם כֹּהֲנֵי יהוה תִּקָּרֵאוּ Isaiah 61:6

2 יִוָּדַע הַנָּבִיא אֲשֶׁר־שְׁלָחוֹ יהוה בֶּאֱמֶת Jeremiah 28:9

3 לֹא יַעֲקֹב יֵאָמֵר עוֹד שִׁמְךָ Genesis 32:29

4 וָאֵרָא אֶל־אַבְרָהָם אֶל־יִצְחָק Exodus 6:3

5 יֵרָאֶה אֶל־אֱלֹהִים בְּצִיּוֹן Psalms 84:8

*6 לְזֹאת יִקָּרֵא אִשָּׁה כִּי מֵאִישׁ לֻקֳחָה־זֹּאת Genesis 2:23
(the verb יִקָּרֵא does not agree with its subject in what respect?)

7 אַל־יִוָּדַע כִּי־בָאָה הָאִשָּׁה Ruth 3:14

8 כִּי לֹא יֵעָשֶׂה כֵן בְּיִשְׂרָאֵל 2 Samuel 13:12

9 בְּחָכְמָה יִבָּנֶה בָּיִת Proverbs 24:3

10 בְּיַד מֶלֶךְ־בָּבֶל תִּנָּתֵן Jeremiah 37:17

11 וַיֵּרָא יהוה אֶל־אַבְרָם Genesis 12:7
(What is the difference between this verb and the one in #5?)

12 לֹא תִנָּתֵן יְרוּשָׁלַםִ בְּיַד מֶלֶךְ אַשּׁוּר 2 Kings 19:10

13 כִּי־יֶלֶד יֻלַּד־לָנוּ בֵּן נִתַּן־לָנוּ Isaiah 9:5

14 כִּי תִּמָּלֵא הָאָרֶץ לָדַעַת אֶת־כְּבוֹד יהוה כַּמַּיִם יְכַסּוּ עַל־יָם׃
Habakkuk 2:14

Ezekiel 37:9 וַיֹּאמֶר אֵלַי הִנָּבֵא אֶל־הָרוּחַ הִנָּבֵא בֶן־אָדָם

49.1 וַיֹּאמֶר אֵלַי means ______________________________

49.2 Analyze הִנָּבֵא

Root	Stem	Form	Person/Gender/Number	Special Features

Two Nif`al forms, the imperative and the infinitive, often give beginning students trouble because these forms are prefixed with the syllable ____ הִנ instead of simply ____ נ In the present example notice what happened to these Nif`al forms:

הִנְ + נָבֵא ⟵ הִנָּבֵא

The form with the assimilated נ is now the regular form for the Nif`al imperative. Note that the imperative cannot be confused with the affix in this stem, nor with the participle. You must be careful not to fall into the trap of thinking that you have a Hif`il form — remember the dagesh!

> The Nif`al imperative and the Nif`al infinitive can be recognized by the הִ◻ preformative.

נבא means *prophesy*, and is translated in the active voice even in the Nif`al.

49.3 אֶל־הָרוּחַ means ______________________________

49.4 הִנָּבֵא בֶן־אָדָם means ______________________________

49.5 Sentence translation: ______________________________

____

49.6 The sample verb in this Lesson shows how a 1st נ verb looks in the Nif`al imperative. Following the explanation in 49.2, write the m. sg. Nif`al imperative for the strong verb שׁפט ____________ The changes you saw in the Nif`al prefix for compensation in 1st Gutturals, and the change in 1st י apply also to the Nif`al imperative.

Write the m. sg. Nif`al imperative for אמר __________ and ילד __________

49·7 Assignments:

A. For Lessons 49-55 learn vocabulary words 350-415

B. Read and translate 1 Kings 18:35-40

C. Translate:

1 לֵךְ הֵרָאֵה אֶל־אַחְאָב 1 Kings 18:1

2 הִשָּׁמֶר לְךָ מִדַּבֵּר עִם־יַעֲקֹב Genesis 31:29

3 הִשָּׁמֶר מִפָּנָיו וּשְׁמַע בְּקֹלוֹ Exodus 23:21

4 וְעַתָּה הִשָּׁבְעָה לִּי בֵאלֹהִים Genesis 21:23

5 וַיַּצֵּב אַבְרָהָם אֶת־שֶׁבַע כִּבְשֹׂת הַצֹּאן לְבַדְּהֶן׃ Genesis 21:28
[נצב (Hif`il) + לבד *set apart*]

6 עַל־כֵּן קָרָא לַמָּקוֹם הַהוּא בְּאֵר שָׁבַע כִּי שָׁם נִשְׁבְּעוּ שְׁנֵיהֶם
Genesis 21:31

7 וַיֹּאמֶר יהוה הִנֵּה מָקוֹם אִתִּי וְנִצַּבְתָּ עַל־הַצּוּר׃ Exodus 33:21
[צור *rock*]

8 ויהוֹנָתָן וַאֲחִימַעַץ עֹמְדִים בְּעֵין־רֹגֵל וְהָלְכָה הַשִּׁפְחָה וְהִגִּידָה
לָהֶם וְהֵם יֵלְכוּ לַמֶּלֶךְ דָּוִד כִּי לֹא יוּכְלוּ לְהֵרָאוֹת
לָבוֹא הָעִירָה׃ 2 Samuel 17:17

1 Samuel 3:21 וַיֹּסֶף יהוה לְהֵרָאֹה בְּשִׁלֹה

50.1 וַיֹּסֶף יהוה

The first word cannot be a name because it begins with ______________________

Pay careful attention to the stem of the verb; it may look as if you have a missing letter, but it is actually a case of a camouflaged letter. The holem here is more commonly written plene וֹ and represents the first root letter, which has ________ ______________________________ (31.2)

Root	Stem	Form	Person/Gender/Number	Special Features

יסף means *add, continue, do again* and is used most often in the Hif`il stem.

Translate phrase: ______________________________

50.2 Analyze לְהֵרָאֹה

Root	Stem	Form	Person/Gender/Number	Special Features

We said in 49.2 that the imperative and the infinitive of the Nif`al are marked by the combination □הִ ⟵ הִנְ before the root. But before a letter which cannot take a dagesh the vocalization will be ________ (48.1) Here the form is ______________

You would expect this word to end in ______ This is an alternate spelling.

How can you distinguish this form from a Hif`il infinitive? What key vowel is different? ________ (31.2)

50.3 בְּשִׁלֹה involves a place name: ______________________

50.4 יסף is almost always to be translated in co-ordination with another verb, either conjugated or in infinitive form. When so used it means *do x again* or sometimes, *continue to do x.*

50.5 Translate sentence: ______________________________

50.6 Assignments:

A. Review the signs of the Nif'al, Lessons 46-50

B. Read and translate 1 Kings 18:41-46

C. Translate:

1 וַיֹּאמֶר הַמֶּלֶךְ לְהֵעָשׂוֹת כֵּן Esther 9:14

2 כִּי הִנָּתֹן יִנָּתֵן בְּיַד מֶלֶךְ־בָּבֶל Jeremiah 32:4

3 וַיֹּסֶף עוֹד לְדַבֵּר אֵלָיו וַיֹּאמַר אוּלַי יִמָּצְאוּן שָׁם Genesis 18:29
[אוּלַי *perhaps*]

4 וַיֵּלֶךְ אֵלִיָּהוּ לְהֵרָאוֹת אֶל־אַחְאָב וְהָרָעָב חָזָק בְּשֹׁמְרוֹן׃ 1 Kings 18:2

5 וְלֹא־יוֹסִפוּ לַעֲשׂוֹת כַּדָּבָר הָרָע הַזֶּה Deuteronomy 13:12

6 כֹּה יַעֲשֶׂה־לְּךָ אֱלֹהִים וְכֹה יוֹסִיף 1 Samuel 3:17

7 הָעָם הַזֶּה אָמְרוּ לֹא עֶת־בֹּא עֶת־בֵּית יהוה לְהִבָּנוֹת Haggai 1:2

Review and Drill 5

I. Nif'al Synopses

	Regular	1st Guttural	1st נ [3rd ע]
Affix	נִשְׁפַּט	נֶאֱמַר	נִטַּע
Prefix	יִשָּׁפֵט	יֵאָמֵר	יִנָּטַע
Imperative	הִשָּׁפֵט	הֵאָמֵר	הִנָּטַע
Participle	נִשְׁפָּט	נֶאֱמָר	נִטָּע
Infinitive	הִשָּׁפֵט	הֵאָמֵר	הִנָּטַע

	1st י	Hollow	3rd ה
Affix	נוֹלַד	נָבוֹן	נִבְנָה
Prefix	יִוָּלֵד	יִבּוֹן	יִבָּנֶה
Imperative	הִוָּלֵד	הִבּוֹן	הִבָּנֵה
Participle	נוֹלָד	נָבוֹן	נִבְנֶה
Infinitive	הִוָּלֵד	הִבּוֹן	הִבָּנוֹת

II. Now here is a comparison of the Qal, Nif'al, and Hif'il for 1st נ/3rd ה

	Qal	Hif'il	Nif'al
Affix	נָטָה	הִטָּה	נִטָּה
Prefix	יִטֶּה	יַטֶּה	יִנָּטֶה
Imperative	נְטֵה	הַטֵּה	הִנָּטֵה
Participle	נוֹטֶה	מַטֶּה	נִטֶּה
Infinitive	לִנְטוֹת	לְהַטּוֹת	לְהִנָּטוֹת

III. In this exercise, some ambiguous forms are presented. Each is a Qal and can also be either a Hif'il, Nif'al, or Pi'el. Give the form and PGN for the Qal and the other stem(s).

יַעֲלֶה נְבָרֵךְ נָבִין

נִלְחַם נַעֲשֶׂה נִטֶּה

IV. Give the stem: Qal, Pi'el, Hif'il, or Nif'al, and form for the following forms of זכר

נִזְכּוֹר זוֹכֵר הַזְכֹּר

בְּזַכֵּר נְזַכֵּר נַזְכִּיר

בִּזְכֹּר בְּהַזְכִּיר בְּהִזָּכֵר

תִּזְכֹּרְנָה תַּזְכֵּרְנָה הִזָּכְרוּ

הַזְכִּירוּ תִּזָּכַרְנָה תְּזַכֵּרְנָה

זִכְרוּ זַכְּרוּ הִזָּכְרוּ

מַזְכִּירָה זְכוּרוֹת מְזַכְּרִים

V. In the verbs below, identify each נ as a root letter, prefix pronoun, prefix complement, affix pronoun, stem indicator, or suffix. Assimilated נs count!

הִנָּגְעִי נַגִּיעַ נֵלֵךְ

נַבִּיט אֶנָּגַע נֶהֱלָךְ

תִּנָּתֵן נִגַּעְנוּ נוֹלִיךְ

נָח נִנּוֹחַ נְתוּנִים

נִפֹּל נֶהֶלְכוּ נוֹגֵד

מַגִּיעַ הִגַּעְתֶּן הֵנַחְנוּ

נָגַעְנוּ נֵגְעוּ נְנַגַּע

נְתוּנוֹת נַעֲמֹד נֶאֱמַן

נוֹתְרוּ נִכְתַּב וַתְּכַסֵּנִי

VI. Analyze the following verbs:

קָרְבָה	הִקְרִיב	נִקְרַבְתֶּם
וַיִּקְרַב	קְרַב	יִקָּרְבוּ
יְקָרְבוּ	יִקְרְבוּ	יַקְרִיבוּ
מְקָרֵב	מַקְרִיב	הִקָּרֵב
נוֹתָר	נוֹתִיר	הוֹתֵר
הִוָּתֵר	מְיַתֵּר	יַתֵּר
בְּהִוָּתֵר	יִתַּרְנוּ	נוֹתַרְנוּ
הוֹתַרְנוּ	מוֹתִיר	בְּהוֹתִיר
בְּיַתֵּר	מְיַתְּרִים	מוֹתִירִים
נוֹתָרִים	נֹאכַל	אוֹכֵל
נֵאָכֵל	אָכְלוּ	יֹאכַל
נֶאֱכַל	הֶאָכֵל	מַאֲכִיל
תַּאֲכֵל	נֶאֱכֶלֶת	אָכַל

VII. Write the Hebrew for the following verbs:

שמע
3 m. pl. Nif'al affix
3 m. sg. Hof'al affix
1 c. pl. Hif'il prefix

ראה
1 c. sg. Nif'al prefix
1 c. sg. Qal affix
f. pl. Qal participle

שלח
m. sg. Pi'el participle
2 m. pl. Pi'el affix
3 c. pl. Hif'il affix

בוא
3 m. pl. Qal prefix
3 f. sg. Hif'il affix
3 m. pl. Nif'il prefix

אסף
1 c. pl. Qal affix
1 c. pl. Pi'el prefix
3 m. sg. Nif'al prefix

שלח
2 m. sg. Nif'il affix
2 m. sg. Nif'al prefix
m. sg. Hof'al participle

Deuteronomy 2:1 וַנָּסָב אֶת־הַר־שֵׂעִיר יָמִים רַבִּים

51.1 Analyze וַנָּסָב

There is one type of irregular verb which has no consistent patterns which are exclusively its own, but appears with patterns characteristic of several other verb types. The verbs of this type do not even use the same pattern in a particular form. This type of verb has identical second and third root letters, and is called a **geminate** (related to "gemini" — twins). The root in this case will be ________________

Root	Stem	Form	Person/Gender/Number	Special Features

How is one to recognize such verbs?

1. You can memorize the basic patterns.
2. You can keep the possibility of a geminate in mind when you analyze a verb according to the basic rules but then cannot find it in the dictionary. Before you give up, try a geminate. **סבב** means *go around, surround.*

51.2 אֶת־הַר־שֵׂעִיר means ____________________ יָמִים means ____________

רַב is an adjective meaning ____________________

51.3 Translate the verse: ____

51.4 The chart below shows the most common Qal affix pattern for geminates. Note that the double ב is represented by a dagesh forte in many PGNS and that וֹ is inserted between the root and many of the affix pronouns.

51.4a **Qal Affix סבב**

3 m. sg.	סָבַב	3 c. pl.	סָבְבוּ
3 f. sg.	סָבְבָה		
2 m. sg.	סַבּוֹתָ	2 m. pl.	סַבּוֹתֶם
2 f. sg.	סַבּוֹת	2 f. pl.	סַבּוֹתֶן
1 c. sg.	סַבּוֹתִי	1 c. pl.	סַבּוֹנוּ

51.4b In these, the two most common Qal prefix patterns, notice that:

1. Those PGNs which have no prefix complement do not show a doubled ב (analogous to the formation of וַיֵּצְאוּ 39.1)
2. The יִסֹּב pattern shows a doubled 1st root letter, making it look like a ________ ________
3. The יָסֹב pattern has the vowel under the prefix pronoun of ________
4. Here again holem appears but its position is different from that in the Qal affix.

Qal Prefix סבב

3 m. sg.	יָסֹב	יִסֹּב	3 m. pl.	יָסֹבּוּ	יִסְּבוּ
3 f. sg.	תָּסֹב	תִּסֹּב	3 f. pl.	תְּסֻבֶּינָה	תִּסֹּבְנָה
2 m. sg.	תָּסֹב	תִּסֹּב	2 m. pl.	תָּסֹבּוּ	תִּסְּבוּ
2 f. sg.	תָּסֹבִּי	תִּסֹּבִי	2 f. pl.	תְּסֻבֶּינָה	תִּסֹּבְנָה
1 c. sg.	אָסֹב	אֶסֹּב	1 c. pl.	נָסֹב	נִסֹּב

51.4c The **Qal imperatives** of סבב follow the pattern of יָסֹב So the m. sg. imperative is סֹב Write these others: f. sg. ________ m. pl. ________

51.4d The **Qal participles** are regular. The m. sg. Qal active participle is סוֹבֵב Write the m. sg. Qal passive participle ________ (42.3)

51.4e The **Qal infinitives** of סבב are סֹב (construct) and סָבוֹב (absolute).

51.5 Geminates have two equivalents of the Pi`el. The **Pol`el** gets its name from the vowel וֹ after the first root letter: סוֹבֵב (Unfortunately this PGN looks just like the m. sg. Qal participle.) This stem is absolutely regular: you will always see the holem and all three root letters.

The **Pilp`el** is formed by doubling the two strong consonants: כִּלְכֵּל

Hollow verbs can do the same thing so one cannot tell from looking at a Pol`el or Pilp`el whether the root is geminate or hollow.

51.6 The **Hif`il** and **Nif`al** preserve the difficulties of the other stems, especially the (3) m. sg.

We will look at synopses of סבב for these two stems:

	Hifil	Nifal
3 m. sg. Affix	הֵסֵב	נָסַב
2 m. sg. Affix	הֲסִבּוֹתָ	נְסַבּוֹתָ
3 m. sg. Prefix	יָסֵב	יִסַּב
3 m. pl. Prefix	יָסֵבּוּ	יִסַּבּוּ
m sg. Imperative	הָסֵב	הִסַּב
m. pl. Imperative	הָסֵבּוּ	הִסַּבּוּ
m. sg. Participle	מֵסֵב	נָסָב
f. sg. Participle	מְסִבָּה	נְסַבָּה
Infinitive Construct	הָסֵב	הִסַּב
Infinitive Absolute	הָסֵב	הִסּוֹב

51.7 Analyze the following forms of סבב

סוֹבַבְתִּי	תְּסוֹבֵב	הֲסִבּוֹתֶם
מְסוֹבֵב	אָסֵב	נְסַבּוֹתָ
נְסַבּוֹנוּ	תָּסֹבִּי	תָּסֵבִּי
תִּסַּבִּי	סְבָבוּנִי	וַיְסִבֵּנִי
נָסֵב	נְסַבָּה	יְסֹבְבֵנִי

51.8 Geminates are not as rare as you might wish. Some you are likely to encounter are:

הלל	*praise*	פלל	*pray*	חלל	*profane*
רבב	*become great*	תמם	*be complete*	רעע	*be evil*
המם	*make a noise*	רנן	*give a ringing cry*	חנן	*show favor*
חמם	*become warm*	ארר	*curse*	שׁמם	*be desolate*
שׁדד	*lay waste*	צרר	*be hostile*	מדד	*measure*

51.9 Assignments:

A. Learn to identify geminates which follow the patterns of סבב (51.4-6)

B. Read and translate 1 Kings 19:1-5

C. Translate:

1 וְסַבֹּתֶם אֶת־הָעִיר Joshua 6:3

2 סַבּוּנִי גַם־סְבָבוּנִי בְּשֵׁם יהוה Psalms 118:11

3 סוֹבֵב סֹבֵב הוֹלֵךְ הָרוּחַ Qohelet 1:6

4 וַיִּסֹּב וַיַּעֲבֹר וַיֵּרֶד הַגִּלְגָּל 1 Samuel 15:12

5 סֹב אֶל־אַחֲרָי 2 Kings 9:18

6 וַיָּסָב אֶת־אֶרֶץ אֱדוֹם Judges 11:18

7 וַיַּסֵּבּוּ אֶת־אֲרוֹן אֱלֹהֵי יִשְׂרָאֵל 1 Samuel 5:8

8 עִבְרוּ וְסֹבּוּ אֶת־הָעִיר Joshua 6:7

9 וַיָּסֹבּוּ בְּכָל־עָרֵי יְהוּדָה וַיְלַמְּדוּ בָּעָם 2 Chronicles 17:9

10 בֵּאלֹהִים הִלַּלְנוּ כָל־הַיּוֹם Psalms 44:9

11 וַאֲסֹבְבָה אֶת־מִזְבַּחֲךָ יהוה וְשִׁמְךָ לְעוֹלָם נוֹדֶה Psalms 26:6

12 הַלְלוּ אֶת־יהוה כָּל גּוֹיִם Psalms 117:2

13 וְהֵסֵב לֵב מֶלֶךְ־אַשּׁוּר עֲלֵיהֶם Ezra 6:22

14 מְהֻלָּל אֶקְרָא יהוה 2 Samuel 22:4

15 וְהִלַּלְתֶּם אֶת־שֵׁם יהוה אֱלֹהֵיכֶם Joel 2:26

16 הַלְלוּ יָהּ הַלְלוּ אֶת־שֵׁם יהוה הַלְלוּ עַבְדֵי יהוה׃ Psalms 135:1

17 וְאַתָּה יהוה חָנֵּנִי וַהֲקִימֵנִי Psalms 41:11 [חנן *show favor*]

18 וְאַנְשֵׁי הָעִיר...נָסַבּוּ עַל־הַבַּיִת Genesis 19:4

19 וַיַּסֵּב אֱלֹהִים אֶת־הָעָם דֶּרֶךְ הַמִּדְבָּר Exodus 13:18

20 מִי יוֹדֵעַ יְחָנַּנִי יהוה וְחַי הַיָּלֶד 2 Samuel 12:22

21 שָׁדְּדָה נִינְוֵה מִי יָנוּד לָהּ מֵאַיִן אֲבַקֵּשׁ מְנַחֲמִים לָךְ Nahum 3:7
[נוד *wander* מֵאַיִן *from where*]

אֵלֶּה אֲשֶׁר שָׁלַח יהוה לְהִתְהַלֵּךְ בָּאָרֶץ Zechariah 1:10

52.1 אֵלֶּה אֲשֶׁר שָׁלַח יהוה

Note that אֲשֶׁר here stands for several words in English: *(the) ones who*

Translate phrase: ______________________________

52.2 Analyze לְהִתְהַלֵּךְ

Root	Stem	Form	Person/Gender/Number	Special Features

Can you find a familiar root in the verb? Note the dagesh in the ל It is a dagesh __________ What stem does this suggest? ______________ We have here yet another variation of the Pi`el system. This one is called **Hitpa`el**, and usually yields a reflexive/intensive or iterative meaning. Its signs are the doubling of the middle root letter and the infixed ת "Infixed" means "fixed inside the word." Note that the ה is what infixes the ת here. The infinitive, imperative, and affix infix the ת in the Hitpa`el by means of the ה So the Hitpa`el pattern is: הת ___ ּ___ ___ The stem meaning here seems to be iterative, conveying the notion of *walking about, to and fro.*

Translate the verb: ______________________

52.3 Translate sentence: ____

____

52.4 You have learned a lot of stems and verb types. Make sure you are confident of these. In this exercise, identify the stem. Possibilities are: Qal, Pi`el, Pu`al, Pol`el, Pilp`el, Hif`il, Hof`al, Nif`al, Hitpa`el, or Hishtaf`el.

גַּדְּלוּ	הִתְגַּדֵּל	גִּדֵּל
לְהִתְהַלֵּל	יְהוֹלֵל	הִגְדִּיל
הוֹלְלִים	תְּהַלְלוּ	מְהֻלָּל
יָקִים	גָּר	מִתְגּוֹרֵר

קוֹמֵם	תְּקוֹמֵם	מֵקִים
וּמְעֹלֵל	עוֹלֵל	כִּלְכֵּל
כְּהֵרָאוֹת	הֵרָאֵנִי	הִתְרָאָה
מַרְאֶה	מַרְאֶה	הֶרְאֵה
הֵרַע	וְרַבֵּה	וְהִשְׁתַּחֲוִיתָ

52.5 Assignments:

A. Read and translate 1 Kings 19:6-10

B. Translate:

1 וְהִתְקַדִּשְׁתֶּם וִהְיִיתֶם קְדֹשִׁים כִּי קָדוֹשׁ אָנִי וְלֹא תְטַמְּאוּ
אֶת־נַפְשֹׁתֵיכֶם Leviticus 11:44

2 כִּי־חַסְדְּךָ לְנֶגֶד עֵינָי וְהִתְהַלַּכְתִּי בַּאֲמִתֶּךָ׃ Psalms 26:3

3 קוּם הִתְהַלֵּךְ בָּאָרֶץ Genesis 13:17

4 וַיְהִי בְּצֵאת הַכֹּהֲנִים מִן־הַקֹּדֶשׁ כִּי כָּל־הַכֹּהֲנִים הַנִּמְצְאִים
הִתְקַדָּשׁוּ אֵין לִשְׁמוֹר לְמַחְלְקוֹת 2 Chronicles 5:11
[מַחֲלֹקֶת *division* What is the root?]

5 הִתְהַלְלוּ בְּשֵׁם קָדְשׁוֹ יִשְׂמַח לֵב מְבַקְשֵׁי יהוה׃ Psalms 105:3

6 וְשָׁבוּ אֵלֶיךָ וְהוֹדוּ אֶת־שְׁמֶךָ וְהִתְפַּלְלוּ וְהִתְחַנְּנוּ אֵלֶיךָ
בַּבַּיִת הַזֶּה 1 Kings 8:33

7 וְהִתְבָּרֵךְ בִּלְבָבוֹ לֵאמֹר שָׁלוֹם יִהְיֶה־לִּי כִּי בִּשְׁרִרוּת לִבִּי
אֵלֵךְ [שְׁרִרוּת *firmness*] Deuteronomy 29:18

8 וְהָאֲמֻצִּים יָצְאוּ וַיְבַקְשׁוּ לָלֶכֶת לְהִתְהַלֵּךְ בָּאָרֶץ וַיֹּאמֶר לְכוּ
הִתְהַלְּכוּ בָאָרֶץ וַתִּתְהַלַּכְנָה בָּאָרֶץ׃ [אֲמֻצִּים *steeds*] Zechariah 6:7

9 וַיֹּאמֶר אֵלָי יהוה אֲשֶׁר־הִתְהַלַּכְתִּי לְפָנָיו יִשְׁלַח מַלְאָכוֹ אִתָּךְ
וְהִצְלִיחַ דַּרְכֶּךָ וְלָקַחְתָּ אִשָּׁה לִבְנִי מִמִּשְׁפַּחְתִּי וּמִבֵּית אָבִי׃
Genesis 24:40 [צלח *make successful*]

Genesis 5:24 וַיִּתְהַלֵּךְ חֲנוֹךְ אֶת־הָאֱלֹהִים וְאֵינֶנּוּ כִּי־לָקַח אֹתוֹ אֱלֹהִים׃

53.1 Analyze וַיִּתְהַלֵּךְ

Root	Stem	Form	Person/Gender/Number	Special Features

Note that the prefix of the Hitpa`el infixes the ת by use of the regular prefix pronouns. The participle is even simpler: it infixes the ת by the preformative מ

53.2 וַיִּתְהַלֵּךְ חֲנוֹךְ אֶת־הָאֱלֹהִים means ______________________________
____

53.3 וְאֵינֶנּוּ

What components can you find? אַיִן means ______________________ What kind of dagesh is in the נ ____________________ This is not the 1 c. pl. suffix, as you may have expected, but a different and rarer form of the 3 m. sg. suffix. Originally נְהוּ____ in time this suffix became נּוּ ֶ Such a form (which exists for other pronouns as well) is called an **energic form**. Watch for suffixes with dagesh forte. Translate: ______________________

53.4 כִּי־לָקַח אֹתוֹ אֱלֹהִים

Notice the two different meanings of את in this verse.

Translate the phrase: ______________________________

Translate sentence: ______________________________
____

53.5 The suffixes with energic נ are object suffixes. They can be attached to verbs, most frequently in pause, and to some particles, most particularly הִנֵּה
You will also see energic נ on adverbs (which really are particles), but they are not suffixes for nouns. These nunated forms of the suffix do not exist for every PGN. And note that the 3 m. sg. and the 1 c. pl. suffix are the same **only** in the nunated form.

53.5a

Suffixes with energic נ

1 c. sg.	*me*	◌ֶנִּי	◌ַנִּי
2 m. sg.	*you*	◌ֶנְּךָ	◌ֶךָּ
3 m. sg.	*him*	◌ֶנְהוּ	◌ֶנּוּ
3 f. sg.	*her*	◌ֶנָּה	
1 c. pl.	*us*	◌ֶנּוּ	

53.5b Now we will review the various forms of the regular object suffix. The suffixes for verbs, prepositions, and other particles are virtually the same except for two differences:

1. The 1 c. sg. suffix on a preposition may be simply ◌ִי or ◌ַי
2. Prepositions may have a connecting י before the suffix.

Object Suffixes

1 c. sg.	*me*	נִי	◌ַנִי	◌ֵנִי			
2 m. sg.	*you*	ךָ	◌ְךָ	◌ָךְ	◌ֶךָ		
2 f. sg.	*you*	ךְ	◌ָךְ	◌ֵךְ	◌ֶךְ		
3 m. sg.	*him*	הוּ	ו	וֹ	◌ָהוּ	◌ֵהוּ	
3 f. sg.	*her*	הָ	◌ָהּ	◌ֶהָ			
1 c. pl.	*us*	נוּ	◌ָנוּ	◌ֵנוּ			
2 m. pl.	*you*	כֶם	◌ְכֶם				
2 f. pl.	*you*	כֶן	◌ְכֶן				
3 m. pl.	*them*	הֶם	ם	◌ָם	◌ַם	◌ֵם	◌ֶם
3 f. pl.	*them*	הֶן	ן	◌ָן			

53.5c Nouns take possessive suffixes. Review those Lessons which discuss the construct and absolute states of the noun.

	masculine noun			feminine noun
		Singular		
	a horse	סוּס	*a mare*	סוּסָה
1 c. sg.	*my horse*	סוּסִי	*my mare*	סוּסָתִי
2 m. sg.	*your horse*	סוּסְךָ	*your mare*	סוּסָתְךָ
2 f. sg.	*your horse*	סוּסֵךְ	*your mare*	סוּסָתֵךְ
3 m. sg.	*his horse*	סוּסוֹ	*his mare*	סוּסָתוֹ
3 f. sg.	*her horse*	סוּסָהּ	*her mare*	סוּסָתָהּ
1 c. pl.	*our horse*	סוּסֵנוּ	*our mare*	סוּסָתֵנוּ
2 m. pl.	*your horse*	סוּסְכֶם	*your mare*	סוּסַתְכֶם
2 f. pl.	*your horse*	סוּסְכֶן	*your mare*	סוּסַתְכֶן
3 m. pl.	*their horse*	סוּסָם	*their mare*	סוּסָתָם
3 f. pl.	*their horse*	סוּסָן	*their mare*	סוּסָתָן
		Plural		
	horses	סוּסִים	*mares*	סוּסוֹת
1 c. sg.	*my horses*	סוּסַי	*my mares*	סוּסוֹתַי
2 m. sg.	*your horses*	סוּסֶיךָ	*your mares*	סוּסוֹתֶיךָ
2 f. sg.	*your horses*	סוּסַיִךְ	*your mares*	סוּסוֹתַיִךְ
3 m. sg.	*his horses*	סוּסָיו	*his mares*	סוּסוֹתָיו
3 f. sg.	*her horses*	סוּסֶיהָ	*her mares*	סוּסוֹתֶיהָ
1 c. pl.	*our horses*	סוּסֵינוּ	*our mares*	סוּסוֹתֵינוּ
2 m. pl.	*your horses*	סוּסֵיכֶם	*your mares*	סוּסוֹתֵיכֶם
2 f. pl.	*your horses*	סוּסֵיכֶן	*your mares*	סוּסוֹתֵיכֶן
3 m. pl.	*their horses*	סוּסֵיהֶם	*their mares*	סוּסוֹתֵיהֶם
3 f. pl.	*their horses*	סוּסֵיהֶן	*their mares*	סוּסוֹתֵיהֶן

53.6 When you know what's ־ֶנּוּ__ and who owns the horse, do the following exercise. Not every word will have a suffix, although most do. Translate each word, noting whether the suffix is the energic נ form. For those pronouns which are ambiguous in English, *their* (for gender) and *your* (for gender and number), note those things.

אֵלֶיךָ	הוֹלֵךְ	אֵלַיִךְ
אִישְׁתּוֹ	אִישָׁהּ	אִשָּׁה
נְשֵׁיכֶם	אִשְׁתְּךָ	אֲנָשֶׁיהָ
אַחַי	אַחִיךָ	אַחֶיךָ
אָחִי	אָחֵיהָ	אֲחוֹתָם
אָבִיךָ	אֲבוֹתָיו	אֹהֲבִים
בָּתַּיִךְ	בְּנָהּ	בֵּיתִי
בִּתִּי	בְּנֹתֶיהָ	בִּתְּכֶם
יִשְׁמְרֶנּוּ	שָׁמְרוּ	הִשָּׁמְרִי
הִשְׁלִיךְ	שְׁלַחְתָּנִי	וַיְשַׁלְּחֵם
וַאֲרֹמְמֶנְהוּ	רֹמְמוּ	מִנִּי
מִכֶּם	מֵהֵנָּה	מִמֵּךְ
קוּמִי	תַּחְתָּיו	מִמֶּנּוּ
בְּכִי	לְמַעַנְכֶם	עוֹדֶנִּי
עָנַנִי	וַעֲנֵנִי	יִתְּנֶנָּה
תְּנוּ	יִתֶּנְךָ	יִתְּנֶנִּי
לָכֶם	לָהֶם	לְבַדְּהֶן
עָשָׂהוּ	עֲשׂתוֹ	עֹשֵׂנִי
עֹשַׂיִךְ	יְבָרֵךְ	יְבָרֶכְךָ
תְּבָרְכֵנִי	הִנְּךָ	הִנָּךְ
הִנֵּהוּ	הִנְנִי	הִנֵּנִי
הִנְנוּ	הִנֵּנוּ	הִנֶּנּוּ

53.7 Assignments:

A. Read and translate 1 Kings 19:11–15

B. Translate:

1 וָאֶתְנַפַּל לִפְנֵי יהוה Deuteronomy 9:18

2 וַיִּתְנַבֵּא גַם־הוּא לִפְנֵי שְׁמוּאֵל 1 Samuel 19:24

3 וְגַם־אִישׁ הָיָה מִתְנַבֵּא בְּשֵׁם יהוה Jeremiah 26:20

4 בַּיהוה תִּתְהַלֵּל נַפְשִׁי Psalms 34:3

5 כִּי אֵינֶנּוּ מִתְנַבֵּא עָלַי לְטוֹבָה 2 Chronicles 18:7

6 וַיִּתְקַדְּשׁוּ הַכֹּהֲנִים וְהַלְוִיִּם 1 Chronicles 15:14

7 כִּי אִם־בְּזוֹאת יִתְהַלֵּל הַמִּתְהַלֵּל Jeremiah 9:23

8 וְיִשְׁתַּחוּ וְיִתְפַּלֵּל אֵלָיו [פלל *pray*] Isaiah 44:17

9 הִנֵּה הַמֶּלֶךְ מִתְהַלֵּךְ לִפְנֵיכֶם 1 Samuel 12:2

10 וָאֶתְפַּלֵּל אֶל־יהוה וָאֹמַר Deuteronomy 9:26

11 וְהִתְבָּרְכוּ בוֹ גּוֹיִם וּבוֹ יִתְהַלָּלוּ Jeremiah 4:2

12 וְכָל־הַנְּבִיאִים מִתְנַבְּאִים לִפְנֵיהֶם 1 Kings 22:10

13 עַל־כֵּן מָצָא עַבְדְּךָ אֶת־לִבּוֹ לְהִתְפַּלֵּל אֵלֶיךָ 2 Samuel 7:27

14 הִתְפַּלֶּל־נָא בַּעֲדֵנוּ אֶל־יהוה אֱלֹהֵינוּ [בְּ + עַד ⟷ *on behalf of*] Jeremiah 37:3

15 וַיֵּצֵא יוֹאָב וַיִּתְהַלֵּךְ בְּכָל־יִשְׂרָאֵל 1 Chronicles 21:4

16 אֶתְהַלֵּךְ לִפְנֵי יְהוָה בְּאַרְצוֹת הַחַיִּים׃ Psalms 116:9

17 אֵלֶיךָ יהוה אֶקְרָא וְאֶל־אֲדוֹנָי אֶתְחַנָּן׃ Psalms 30:9

18 עַד־הַגְּבוּל שִׁלְּחוּךָ כֹּל אַנְשֵׁי בְרִיתֶךָ Obadiah 7

בִּשְׁנַת עֶשְׂרִים וָשֶׁבַע שָׁנָה לְיָרָבְעָם מֶלֶךְ יִשְׂרָאֵל מָלַךְ עֲזַרְיָה
בֶן־אֲמַצְיָה מֶלֶךְ יְהוּדָה׃ בֶּן־שֵׁשׁ עֶשְׂרֵה שָׁנָה הָיָה בְמָלְכוֹ
וַחֲמִשִּׁים וּשְׁתַּיִם שָׁנָה מָלַךְ בִּירוּשָׁלָםִ 2 Kings 15:1-2

54.1 In this very long Lesson sentence there are several numbers. The cardinals from 1-10 were presented in Lesson 41.2a. Review that section if necessary.
Note the following:

The numbers from **eleven** to **nineteen** combine the proper words for ten plus the other number between 1-10 with no "and" between the words. The smaller number precedes the ten in these combinations. שֵׁשׁ עֶשְׂרֵה is an example.

The **tens** words are plurals of the basic words. **Twenty** is עֶשְׂרִים (two 10s). The words for **thirty** to **ninety** are the plurals of 3-9.

With **numbers over ten**, the singular of the noun is most often used. That means they do not agree in number and gender with the noun they modify.

Ordinals (*first, second, third*) are forms related to the cardinals and can be recognized by finding the relevant root: שֵׁנִי שְׁלִישִׁי Ordinals are attested only for the numbers 1-10, after which the cardinal numbers must be employed with ordinal meaning (by context).

A **hundred** has the following forms:

absolute	construct	dual	plural (for 100s over 200)
מֵאָה	מְאַת	מָאתַיִם	מֵאוֹת

A **thousand** is אֶלֶף plural אֲלָפִים

Age formula: A person is *a son* (or *daughter*) *of X years* בֶּן [בַּת]...שָׁנָה

54.2 מָלַךְ as a verb means ____________________________ Here the meaning of the first occurrence verges on *began to reign.*

54.3 Translate verses: ____

בִּשְׁנַת עֶשְׂרִים וָשֶׁבַע שָׁנָה לְיָרָבְעָם מֶלֶךְ יִשְׂרָאֵל מָלַךְ עֲזַרְיָה
בֶן־אֲמַצְיָה מֶלֶךְ יְהוּדָה׃ בֶּן־שֵׁשׁ עֶשְׂרֵה שָׁנָה הָיָה בְמָלְכוֹ
וַחֲמִשִּׁים וּשְׁתַּיִם שָׁנָה מָלַךְ בִּירוּשָׁלִָם

54-4 Assignments:

A. Review all vocabulary words.

B. Read and translate 1 Kings 19:16-21

C. Translate:

1 וּלְאַחְאָב שִׁבְעִים בָּנִים בְּשֹׁמְרוֹן 2 Kings 10:1

2 הִכָּה שָׁאוּל בַּאֲלָפָיו [אֶלֶף *thousand*] 1 Samuel 18:7

3 וְאַבְרָהָם בֶּן־מְאַת שָׁנָה בְּהִוָּלֶד לוֹ אֵת יִצְחָק בְּנוֹ׃ Genesis 21:5

4 בִּשְׁנַת עֶשְׂרִים וְשָׁלֹשׁ שָׁנָה לְיוֹאָשׁ בֶּן־אֲחַזְיָהוּ מֶלֶךְ יְהוּדָה מָלַךְ
יְהוֹאָחָז בֶּן־יֵהוּא עַל־יִשְׂרָאֵל בְּשֹׁמְרוֹן שְׁבַע עֶשְׂרֵה שָׁנָה׃ 2 Kings 13:1

5 וַיְחִי־שֵׁת חָמֵשׁ שָׁנִים וּמְאַת שָׁנָה וַיּוֹלֶד אֶת־אֱנוֹשׁ׃ וַיִּהְיוּ
כָּל־יְמֵי־שֵׁת שְׁתֵּים עֶשְׂרֵה שָׁנָה וּתְשַׁע מֵאוֹת שָׁנָה וַיָּמֹת׃ Genesis 5:6, 8

6 וַיְשַׁמַּע שָׁאוּל אֶת־הָעָם וַיִּפְקְדֵם בַּטְּלָאִים מָאתַיִם אֶלֶף רַגְלִי
וַעֲשֶׂרֶת אֲלָפִים אֶת־אִישׁ יְהוּדָה׃ [טְלָאִים name of a place] 1 Samuel 15:4

7 וְאָנֹכִי הֶעֱלֵיתִי אֶתְכֶם מֵאֶרֶץ מִצְרָיִם וָאוֹלֵךְ אֶתְכֶם בַּמִּדְבָּר
אַרְבָּעִים שָׁנָה לָרֶשֶׁת אֶת־אֶרֶץ הָאֱמֹרִי Amos 2:10

As you have already seen, much Biblical Hebrew prose is written in an elevated style. Such elements as euphony, repetition of roots, inverted word order, and careful phrasing create heightened images. Sometimes these components blend so exquisitely that it is difficult not to label certain passages as poetry. But in order to study Biblical poetry as a specific literary style, we have to identify some stylistic features that are peculiar to it.

In English, we recognize traditional poetry by meter and rhyme scheme, and by the way the lines are set out on the page. Biblical poetry has no rhyme; it does have rhythm and certain structural indications. We don't know what the metrical conventions were, and so the structural indications are very important.

The basic structural characteristic of Biblical Hebrew poetry is **parallelism**. A line is paralleled by a statement that relates to the first one, and the poetry proceeds by means of couplets or less frequently triplets. This is a characteristic of all ancient Semitic poetry. If the second line echoes the thought of the first line, then the parallelism is said to be **synonymous**:

מָה־אֱנוֹשׁ כִּי־תִזְכְּרֶנּוּ
וּבֶן־אָדָם כִּי תִפְקְדֶנּוּ׃ Psalms 8:5

What is man, that you are mindful of him?
And the son of man that you think of him?

If the second line contrasts with the first, the parallelism is called **antithetic**:

בַּבֹּקֶר יָצִיץ וְחָלָף
לָעֶרֶב יְמוֹלֵל וְיָבֵשׁ׃ Psalms 90:6

In the morning it flourishes and grows up;
In the evening it is cut down and withers.

The thought may continue from line to line to build up a cumulative effect; in this case the parallelism is said to be **synthetic**:

יהוה רֹעִי לֹא אֶחְסָר׃
בִּנְאוֹת דֶּשֶׁא יַרְבִּיצֵנִי
עַל־מֵי מְנֻחוֹת יְנַהֲלֵנִי׃
נַפְשִׁי יְשׁוֹבֵב
יַנְחֵנִי בְמַעְגְּלֵי־צֶדֶק לְמַעַן שְׁמוֹ׃ Psalms 23:1-3

The Lord is my shepherd; I shall not want.
He causes me to lie down in green pastures;
He leads me beside the still waters.
He restores my soul;
He guides me in straight paths for his name's sake.

Very rarely will all the elements of one line be paralleled by the second. If they do, the parallelism is called **complete**:

d c b a
בְּטֶרֶם אֶצָּוֹרְךָ בַבֶּטֶן יְדַעְתִּיךָ
d^I c^I b^I a^I
Jeremiah 1:5 וּבְטֶרֶם תֵּצֵא מֵרֶחֶם הִקְדַּשְׁתִּיךָ

Before I formed you in the belly I knew you;
And before you came out of the womb I sanctified you.

Most parallelism is **incomplete** with more elements in the first line than in the second:

d c b a
וַתֹּאמֶר צִיּוֹן עֲזָבַנִי יְהוָה
c^I d^I
Isaiah 49:14 וַאדֹנָי שְׁכֵחָנִי׃

But Zion said, "The the Lord has forsaken me;
And my Lord has forgotten me."

Also there is incomplete parallelism with **compensation**:

c b a
אָכֵן שָׁמַע אֱלֹהִים
e d b^I
Psalms 66:19 הִקְשִׁיב בְּקוֹל תְּפִלָּתִי׃

But surely God has heard;
He has attended to the voice of my prayer.

We do not know how the lines were laid out when the poetry was first written down. In many Bibles, there is a horizontal or vertical space between the two halves of a line or **couplet**. A section of a poem, which in English is called a stanza, is usually referred to in Hebrew poetry as a **strophe**.

Some of the other features of Hebrew poetry are highly compressed expression, frequent absence of the DDO marker את absence of particles, greater variety of word order, lots of vocatives, and the occurrence of much vocabulary not seen in prose literature. Lines tend to be short and rhythmic. We will look at some of these poetic elements in **Psalms 24**.

Psalms 24 starts out with the words לְדָוִד מִזְמוֹר We simply do not know if this means that David wrote the psalm, that it was written during his period, or whether it was dedicated to him. It could mean that it is part of a collection of psalms belonging to him. *David* may refer not specifically to King David, but might refer to the House of David, i.e., a Davidic King.
We do not know whether לְדָוִד מִזְמוֹר is supposed to be a title, although when sung in a service, these words are included. This heading, with which many psalms begin, usually appears מִזְמוֹר לְדָוִד The term מִזְמוֹר is a technical term used only in regard to psalms, and occurs in the heading of fifty-seven of them. Both in Hebrew and in Greek the root-meaning is *to play instrumental music* or *to sing to musical accompaniment.*

The first line is (a) לַיהוה (b) הָאָרֶץ (c) וּמְלוֹאָהּ

The second is (b^I) תֵּבֵל (c^I) וְיֹשְׁבֵי בָהּ׃

In the word וּמְלוֹאָהּ the feminine possessive suffix is referring to הָאָרֶץ and so it means *and its fullness.* Interestingly, a contrasting thought is expressed in Psalms 115:16:

הַשָּׁמַיִם שָׁמַיִם לַיהוָה
וְהָאָרֶץ נָתַן לִבְנֵי־אָדָם׃

In the second line תֵּבֵל is a parallel for הָאָרֶץ It is a poetic term for world, but may refer specifically to the habitable parts of the earth. Like most terms for earth or world it is feminine. Poetic convention allows the definite article ה to be dropped in front of תֵּבֵל The ה of הָאָרֶץ does "double duty." Notice that the more general noun is used first and the more specific one, second.

וְיֹשְׁבֵי בָהּ These words are parallel to וּמְלוֹאָהּ and so are identified as c^I. The holem after the first root letter identifies יֹשְׁבֵי as a ______________________________
בָהּ is a separate word but its parallel lies in the suffix of וּמְלוֹאָהּ Note that both וּמְלוֹאָהּ and וְיֹשְׁבֵי בָהּ have four syllables.
The first colon maps out: a b c // b^I c^I, an example of incomplete, synonymous parallelism.

Psalms 24:2

כִּי־הוּא An emphatic use of the independent subject pronoun.

עַל־יַמִּים Do not confuse יַמִּים with יָמִים (See: The Noun H.) The word order of this couplet is: subject / adverbial phrase / verb + DO. The image here is that the earth rests upon the great cosmic ocean and is supported by pillars which are, at the same time, bases of the mountains.

יְסָדָהּ The suffix is still referring to the feminine תֵּבֵל or הָאָרֶץ If the verb did not have a suffix it would be pointed יָסַד But the suffix causes shortening of the first syllable and so the familiar landmark of the Qal affix, ______________________ is gone. We can assume it's a Qal because there is no preformative or internal doubling of a letter to indicate another stem.

וְעַל־נְהָרוֹת This begins the second half of the second couplet, and you can see that it is a parallel statement to עַל־יַמִּים There is no parallel for כִּי־הוּא the first phrase in the couplet, and so וְעַל־נְהָרוֹת is designated b^I. These נְהָרוֹת are likely the subterranean waters, and may be translated as *floodwaters*. Some interpreters take נְהָרוֹת to mean actual rivers such as the Jordan and Euphrates.

יְכוֹנְנֶהָ This verb is in the ____________ which is one of the ways to give a hollow verb Pi'el intensity. (51.5) The suffix is still the 3 f. sg. object suffix but it does not have a mappiq because ______________________ (23.2c) Text note 2^b suggests reading כּוֹנְנָהּ instead of יְכוֹנְנֶהָ so that the aspects of the two verbs in this couplet would be the same.

Psalms 24:3

מִי־יַעֲלֶה What stems are possible for the verb? ______________________ (32.3b) How will you decide? The verb עלה can be used to mean making a pilgrimage to the sanctuary.

בְּהַר־יהוה Mountains feature prominently in the imagery of Psalms. They are thought to be a link between earth and heaven. Although the imagery in this psalm can be taken in an abstract sense, it probably is referring specifically to the temple in Jerusalem and *the mountain* is most likely Mt. Zion.

קָדְשׁוֹ This is the noun קֹדֶשׁ + the 3 m. sg. possessive suffix; not the adjective קָדוֹשׁ Why then is the ק pointed קָ ______ The phrase בִּמְקוֹם קָדְשׁוֹ is an example of **hendiadys**: using two nouns in apposition rather than a noun and an adjective. (Compare with the use of קֹדֶשׁ in 39.4.) This third couplet demonstrates complete parallelism.

c b a
מִי־יַעֲלֶה בְהַר־יהוָה

cI bI aI
וּמִי־יָקוּם בִּמְקוֹם קָדְשׁוֹ׃

Psalms 24:4

נְקִי It is true that 3 f. sg. imperatives end in ִי but there is no antecedent for a f. sg. imperative here. What are two other possibilities for the ending? (8.3 and 48.7) נְקִי is functioning as a m. sg. adjective in construct, so the י is acting as the replacement for the ה of the root.

כַפַּיִם This is the dual of a vocabulary word. Why is there a dagesh in the פּ

וּבַר The syntax of the verse suggests that this is a noun.

לֵבָב Vocabulary word.

Verse 4 is a triplet and this first line contains its own internal parallelism:

bI aI b a
נְקִי כַפַּיִם וּבַר־לֵבָב

נַפְשִׁי There are two different Masoretic conventions not only for the reading of this word but also for the writing of it. Some texts have נַפְשׁוֹ If it is read נַפְשִׁי then the meaning is *who has not sworn deceitfully by my* נֶפֶשׁ (literally: *who has not lifted up my* נֶפֶשׁ *to vanity)* and נַפְשִׁי is taken to be a substitute for *my name*. This idea is expressed in the commandment לֹא תִשָּׂא אֶת־שֵׁם־יהוה אֱלֹהֶיךָ לַשָּׁוְא (Ex. 20:7).
If the word is taken to be נַפְשׁוֹ then the meaning becomes *who has not lifted up his* נֶפֶשׁ *to vanity.*

י and ו were written the same way by copyists for hundreds of years and so it is difficult to know which meaning was intended.

וְלֹא נִשְׁבַּע The word **אֲשֶׁר** introduced the previous clause and is understood in this one. It is an example of a word doing double duty, like the definite article **ה** in the word **הָאָרֶץ** (Ps. 24:1) Is the ___**נ** a preformative or the 1 c. pl. subject pronoun?

לְמִרְמָה It is difficult to abstract the root of this word. Taking off the preposition leaves **מרמה** There are many possibilities with this combination of letters; you should be able to think of about four but in order to get on with the psalm let it be known that the root is **רמה**

Psalms 24:5

יִשָּׂא בְרָכָה The use of the verb **נשׂא** is contrasted with its use in the previous verse.

מֵאֵת This is a compound preposition. What then is the function of the component **את**

יִשְׁעוֹ The fact that this word comes after a word in the construct form should tell you that you are looking at a noun. What part of it is not part of the root?
The parallelism in this couplet is incomplete with compensation. Diagram it:

יִשָּׂא בְרָכָה מֵאֵת יהוה

וּצְדָקָה מֵאֱלֹהֵי יִשְׁעוֹ׃

Psalms 24:6

זֶה דּוֹר Why can this phrase not be *this generation?* (15.2)

דֹּרְשׁוֹ Note the **כְּתִב קְרֵא** It tells us that the participle is to be read as a plural. The verb **דרשׁ** can mean seeking after, i.e., *knowing God's ways.* It is also the term used for consulting an oracle.

מְבַקְשֵׁי Analyze this word. The stem is a bit tricky. (36.3b)

יַעֲקֹב Vocative, but may be a shortened epithet for **אֱלֹהֵי יַעֲקֹב** *O God of Jacob.* It may mean *even Jacob.*

סֶלָה Nobody knows what **סֶלָה** means. It could mean "crash the cymbals here." It could represent a musical direction, or some kind of interruption or change. It is not intrinsic to the poem and is found in many psalms at the end of a strophe. It may be a word like *amen* or what David said when he broke a harpstring. Notice how it marks a break in the psalm. What follows seems to be a chorus or refrain.

This couplet is an example of synthetic parallelism. Diagram it:

זֶה דּוֹר דֹּרְשָׁו

מְבַקְשֵׁי פָנֶיךָ יַעֲקֹב סֶלָה

Psalms 24:7

שְׂאוּ שְׁעָרִים רָאשֵׁיכֶם How do the words **שְׁעָרִים רָאשֵׁיכֶם** fit with the imperative **שְׂאוּ** The word **רָאשֵׁיכֶם** is a DO and **שְׁעָרִים** is a vocative. This is the third use of **נשׂא** in the psalm. In verse 4 it was used with **לַשָּׁוְא** *who has not lifted up his soul to deceit.* In verse 5 it is used with **בְּרָכָה** *he has lifted up a blessing.* Here it is used with *gates.* Most likely this is supposed to be a physical image and not a metaphor. According to tradition, this psalm was composed to celebrate the bringing of the ark into Jerusalem. At this point in the psalm, the bearers of the ark are at the gates and the address to the gates to *lift up your heads* means to extend their height because they are too low for the king of glory to enter.

וְהִנָּשְׂאוּ Another use of the verb **נשׂא** This time the stem is ________ (49.2)

פִּתְחֵי עוֹלָם It is not known whether the image is a reference to the gates of Jerusalem or the gates of heaven since in ancient times the temple was thought to be representative of its heavenly counterpart. It may very well be a double image.

מֶלֶךְ הַכָּבוֹד This is either hendiadys (see קָדְשׁוֹ Ps. 24:3) or a construct chain. הַכָּבוֹד cannot be a simple adjective modifying מֶלֶךְ because it is definite and מֶלֶךְ is not. But then again, none of the prose conventions are solid in poetry.

The concept expressed here, of God as king, is very ancient and was never challenged by the institution of the monarchy.

Verses 7-10 are all triplets. Verses 7 and 9 make a pair; as do verses 8 and 10.

Psalms 24:8

מִי זֶה An interrogative noun sentence.

עִזּוּז וְגִבּוֹר Adjectives modifying יהוה In the word עִזּוּז what does the ו between the second and third root letters signify? (42.3)

מִלְחָמָה English needs a preposition before this word. The images of God as warrior stem from the days when the ark used to be carried into battle.

Psalms 24:9

Not an exact repetition of verse 7.

Psalms 24:10

מִי הוּא זֶה Even more emphatic than מִי זֶה in verse 8.

יהוה צְבָאוֹת A problem (for moderns) with this phrase is the meaning of צְבָאוֹת It can refer to the armies of Israel, but more likely refers to the heavenly bodies or heavenly armies.

Psalms 100:1

מִזְמוֹר לְתוֹדָה Some dictionaries list תּוֹדָה as is, but if yours doesn't, and the root is a problem, review The Noun C. This is the only one of the psalms labeled לְתוֹדָה It is thought that it was originally intended to accompany the bringing of the sacrifice. It is sung, in contemporary Jewish liturgy, on days other than the Sabbath and Festivals when that offering was not brought.

הָרִיעוּ The stem, and PGN are straightforward. Of the Hif'il forms, only three have the ה preformative. One obviously is the Hif'il affix, the others are the ____________ Which fits here? What about the root? It looks like ריע but if your dictionary doesn't list it that way remember: in the Hif'il the middle letter of hollow verbs, which may be ____ or ____ is replaced by י (29.2) Explain the vowel under the preformative. (29.5)

Psalms 100:2

Diagram these lines and tell what type of parallelism they exemplify: ____________

עִבְדוּ אֶת־יהוה בְּשִׂמְחָה

בֹּאוּ לְפָנָיו בִּרְנָנָה׃

Psalms 100:3

דְּעוּ The mood is a continuation of that expressed in the verbs in the previous verse.

יהוה הוּא אֱלֹהִים Where else have you seen this phrase (with one slight difference)?

עָשָׂנוּ If this looks like an ambiguous form STUDY 26.5 and 53.5b.

הוּא עָשָׂנוּ וְלֹא אֲנַחְנוּ There are two conventions regarding this line. One takes it the way it is written and translates it *He made us and not we ourselves.* The other, and more widely accepted tradition, claims that וְלֹא is a scribal error and it should read וְלוֹ Then the line becomes *He made us and we are his.* There is no "right" answer.

מַרְעִיתוֹ Roots that look as if they might end in י most likely end in ______ The image of God as shepherd is found frequently in Psalms.

Verse 3 is set out as a triplet. It is difficult to analyze this verse in terms of parallelism. Actually, it's a list; some would interpret that feature to be an example of synthetic parallelism. If parallelism is difficult to find, it doesn't mean that the writing isn't poetic. Parallelism is just one feature, albeit a major one, of Hebrew poetry and is particularly useful when we come upon a difficult phrase or an obscure word — then turning to what appears to be a parallel line may help decipher the problematic expression.

Psalms 100:4

שְׁעָרָיו Of the temple.

בְּתוֹדָה According to rabbinic interpretation, all forms of sacrifice and prayers of petition should become obsolete in the Messianic era with the exception of thanksgiving offerings, because even in a perfect world people should show their appreciation to God.

חֲצֵרֹתָיו The temple had outer courts where the people gathered.

בִּתְהִלָּה What kind of dagesh is in the ל The components of בִּתְהִלָּה are:
preposition ב / noun preformative ת / root הלל / and feminine endiNG הָ
This type of prayer is recited aloud as opposed to תְּפִלָּה which is usually silent prayer.

הוֹדוּ Same root as תּוֹדָה

בָּרֲכוּ The combination of three strong letters, qamets under the first root letter, and a m. pl. suffix usually suggest 3 m. pl. Qal affix. But then why is there a composite shewa under the ר A composite shewa takes the place of a vocal shewa normally under a letter which cannot take a dagesh. What would make a shewa in this position vocal, is a dagesh forte in the consonant. Since ר cannot accept a dagesh, the preceding vowel is compensating.
ָ is longer than pataḥ ַ the usual vowel in this position for this stem and form. So what stem and form have pataḥ under the first root letter and dagesh in the middle root letter? Most compensations we have seen involve hireq ִ and tsere ֵ e.g.: מִמִּצְרַיִם but מֵאָדָם However ַ lengthened to ָ is also common as demonstrated for example with הָרִיעוּ (Ps. 100:1) a hollow verb in a derived stem.

Psalms 100:5

חַסְדּוֹ | חסד is one of those untranslatable words, rendered in English as *loving kindness,* or *steadfast love,* or *mercy.*

וְעַד־דֹּר וָדֹר A frequently used expression to convey the idea of perpetuity, often translated *from generation to generation.*

אֱמוּנָתוֹ Knowing that this is a noun is the clue to abstracting the root.

Verse five is a fine example of compressed poetic expression. We usually put it into English using three sentences. But notice that in the Hebrew there is not one verb in the entire verse.

There are two ways to look at verse 5, either as a couplet or triplets. It depends on whether or not you think כִּי־טוֹב יהוה is an independent clause.

About the structure of this psalm: it has a symmetrical structure. It is composed of two strophes. The first strophe (verses 1-3) has four plural imperatives and then a כִּי clause which proclaims the omnipotence of God. The second strophe (verses 4-5) has three plural imperatives followed by a כִּי clause which proclaims God's goodness. That there are seven imperatives is significant. It is common to see groups of either five or seven verbs or names for God in a psalm.

Genesis 22:1 [Lesson 13]

וַיְהִי | וַיְהִי is a common way to begin a narrative. It is usually translated *And it happened*, or *And it came to pass.* Does it have the signs of vav conversive? (2.12) What is the root? (12.1)

אַחַר can be found in the dictionary under אָחַר

הַדְּבָרִים הָאֵלֶּה What are the gender and number of the noun דְּבָרִים (6.5a) What is the ◌ַה in front of it? (4.3)

הָאֵלֶּה is an adjective modifying הַדְּבָרִים and means *these.* An adjective which follows a noun and agrees with it in gender (masculine or feminine), number (singular or plural), and definiteness is called an **attributive adjective**. הַדְּבָרִים is masculine, plural, and definite and so its adjective הָאֵלֶּה must also be masculine, plural, and definite. Actually, the gender of הָאֵלֶּה is common; that means it is used to modify both masculine and feminine plural nouns. To review why the ה of הָאֵלֶּה is pointed with a qamets ◌ָ see 4.5b.

The attributive adjective *this*

זֶה	*this*	(m. sg.)
זוֹאת	*this*	(f. sg.)
אֵלֶּה	*these*	(c. pl.)

וְהָאֱלֹהִים It is not unusual to see the definite article prefixed to a proper name. English translation, however, does not differentiate between the name with and without the article.

נִסָּה The dagesh in the ס is a dagesh forte. (1.2, 3.3b) For one reason, it is not in one of the BeGaDKePhaT letters ב ג ד כ פ ת and so it cannot possibly be lene. That means that the ס is doubled either because it is representing an assimilated letter (7.1) or because it is being strengthened. (2.3c) Do the easy thing first: look up נסה in a dictionary. The entry indicates that this root is found in the Bible exclusively in the Pi`el stem. Although the word for God is plural, it takes a singular verb. (2.4) The usual word order in a Hebrew sentence is verb – subject. For emphasis, the subject may precede the verb as it does here.

אֶת־אַבְרָהָם Why is אַבְרָהָם preceded by אֶת (7.2)

וַיֹּאמֶר אֵלָיו אַבְרָהָם The prefix pronoun and the the fact that there is no prefix complement at the end of **וַיֹּאמֶר** tells us that the subject of the verb will be 3 m. sg. The verb by itself thus has as its subject the pronoun **י** which could be the pronoun *he.* But two words further along is the name **אַבְרָהָם** Perhaps that is the subject of **וַיֹּאמֶר** Let us suppose that it is. The phrase would read *And Abraham said to him.* Who is *him? Him* refers to the closest preceding noun, which is also **אַבְרָהָם** and would mean that Abraham is talking to himself (which he certainly may have done from time to time, but not here!) So *he* must refer to another noun. **אֱלֹהִים** was the subject of the verb in the first half of the verse and so we could assume that **אֱלֹהִים** is still the subject. (10.2c discusses the difficulties in identifying direct speech in the Hebrew Bible.)
אֵלָיו (2.9) To whom does the suffix refer?

Genesis 22:2 [Lesson 13]

קַח־נָא | **קַח** is the m. sg. imperative of the irregular verb **לקח** There is no exact equivalent in English for **נָא** It is a stylistic feature, often used with the imperative, and conveys the formality of the old fashioned phrase *I pray thee.*

אֶת־בִּנְךָ The suffix **ךָ__** is the 2 m. sg. possessive pronoun *your.* The addition of a suffix to a noun may cause shortening of the first vowel(s). (8.5)

אֶת־יְחִידְךָ This is an adjectival phrase often translated as *your only one.* This is an incorrect rendering as you will see if you examine the root. First remove the suffix **ךָ__** Four letters **י ח י ד** are left. **י ו ה** can be either consonants or vowel letters. You can tell when they are consonants because they will have a vowel with them. When they are vowel letters, they may or may not be part of the root. If there are more than three letters for the root, look to a vowel letter to remove something. The first **י** has shewa **ְ** under it and so it is a consonant. The second **י** is part of the vowel plene hireq **ִי** so it is a vowel letter. If you remove the second **י** you are left with the three letter root **יחד** which means *be united, make as one.* The phrase means, then, *the-one-with-whom-you-are-one.* English has no word for this concept. Some translations use *favored.*

אָהַבְתָּ | **תָּ__** is the 2 m. sg. affix subject pronoun. That leaves three letters for the root. Affix form usually means past tense translation, but <u>with verbs denoting affections or states of mind the affix form often requires present tense translation into English</u>.

אֶת־יִצְחָק This is the third DDO in this verse. Give the reason for the definiteness of each.

The three ways in which a noun can be definite:

1. If it has the definite article הַדְּבָרִים
2. If it is a proper noun אַבְרָהָם
3. If it has a possessive pronoun בִּנְךָ

A word about the style of this part of the verse: notice how each phrase builds upon and intensifies the one before:

אֶת־בִּנְךָ אֶת־יְחִידְךָ אֲשֶׁר־אָהַבְתָּ אֶת־יִצְחָק

These short phrases, the repetition of אֶת and the repetition of the harsh ḥ sounds, relieved by the softness of אֲשֶׁר־אָהַבְתָּ give the verse a rhythm, strength, and emotional quality not captured in translation.

וְלֶךְ־לְךָ It is common in Hebrew prose for one imperative to be followed by another. לֶךְ is another example of a Qal imperative losing a root letter. It is from the root ________ לְךָ conveys the idea of action done to or for oneself. Thus the phrase is a way of saying *pick yourself up and go!* Because we don't have this construction in English, and the literal translation *go-for-yourself* is clumsy, most translations ignore the לְךָ segment. Notice that לְךָ is constructed like the compound לוֹ (7.2c)

אֶרֶץ הַמֹּרִיָּה This is a construct chain. (5.1b) מֹרִיָּה is the name of a place.

וְהַעֲלֵהוּ There are far too many letters for a root. First take off the conjunction וְ in front. ___הוּ at the end is the 3 m. sg. object suffix *him*. It is a variation of the suffix ו or וֹ We are left with העל Looking in the dictionary, you will find that no such root exists. ל and ע in these positions are always root letters so you have to assume that the ה is not part of the root. You don't know if the missing letter is in the first, second, or third position. According to what you have learned so far, if the missing letter were in the first position it would probably be a י or a נ In the second position it would be a י or a ו and in the third position it would be a ה Among the first fifty vocabulary words is one of these combinations, עלה and it happens to be the root here. (For reasons which we will not go into here, the other possibilities would have to be discarded in this case even though a couple of them are roots.) The ה in front of the verb is a sign of the Hif'il stem. The Hif'il takes a basic root idea and makes it causative. The Hif'il of עלה is *cause to go up* (as smoke of a sacrifice), i.e., *sacrifice* or *offer up*. The form is imperative. The whole word

וְהַעֲלֵהוּ means *and sacrifice him.* This is the third time a m. sg. imperative is used in this verse.
Why could the final letter וּ___ not be the 3 m. pl. affix ending? Because verbs that end in ה always loose the ה before a subject or object pronoun is added to the verb. [The m. pl. Hif'il imperative would be הַעֲלוּ]

לְעֹלָה Taking off the preposition ל reveals a repetition of the root עלה In this case the word is the noun *sacrifice.*

אַחַד הֶהָרִים | אַחַד means *one.* ___הֶ is another possible pointing for the definite article in front of a guttural. After taking off the definite article and the masculine plural noun endiNG, you are left with הַר *mountain.* This phrase is a construct chain. Is it definite or indefinite? (5.2)

אֹמַר The holem ___ after what appears to be the first root letter is usually the sign of the Qal participle pattern. (9.3a) However, this is an irregular verb. The root is indeed אמר and the stem is Qal but the form is prefix. The א is the 1 c. sg. prefix pronoun. We would expect to see אמר|א

root ↑ prefix pronoun

But the א of the root has elided. That means it isn't heard or seen, nor does it leave a remnant in the form of a dagesh as does an assimilated נ (7.1a)
אֹמַר may be translated *I will say* or *I am about to say.*

Synopsis of אמר

Verb	PGN/Form	Special Feature	Usual Translation
אָמַר	3 m. sg. affix	-------	past
אֹמֵר	m. sg. participle	-------	depends on context
אֹמַר	1 c. sg. prefix	-------	future or present
וְאָמַר	3 m. sg. affix	vav reversive	future
יֹאמַר	3 m. sg. prefix	-------	future or present
וַיֹּאמֶר	3 m. sg. prefix	vav conversive	past

אֵלֶיךָ The suffix ךָ___ has appeared three times already in this verse and it was the possessive pronoun *your.* It is still 2 m. sg. but is now the object pronoun *you.* It is the object of the preposition אֶל (2.9a) Several prepositions may take a connecting י before a suffix is added. Four frequently seen are: אֶל עַל תַּחַת אַחַר

Genesis 22:3 [Lesson 14]

וַיַּשְׁכֵּם | **שׁכם** means *get up early.* This verb appears only in the Hif`il (even though its causativeness or transitiveness is not apparent). Here it is the 3 m. sg. prefix form with vav conversive. The Hif`il prefix does not have a preformative ה but it does have two distinguishing characteristics:

1. The vowel pataḥ ַ under the prefix pronoun.
2. A "dot vowel" ִ ֵ or ֶ under the second root letter.

Note: the marks of vav conversive □וַ are the same regardless of the stem of the verb.

בַּבֹּקֶר | **בֹּקֶר** means *morning.* בְּ is a prefixed preposition. To say *in the morning,* you need בְּ+הַ□ before the noun. Since that sound combination is hard to maintain, the ה elided (dropped out) but left its vowel pataḥ ַ behind with the בּ Both בs of בַּבֹּקֶר have a dagesh; what is the reason for each? (3.3b)

וַיַּחֲבשׁ The root is ________ The form is Qal prefix. The vowel under the prefix pronoun looks like that of the Hif`il prefix (see וַיַּשְׁכֵּם just above) but there is no "dot vowel" between the second and third root letters to confirm a Hif`il prefix form. It is the guttural ח which creates the change in vowel pattern.

חֲמֹרוֹ The root is ________ The suffix should be familiar.

וַיִּקַּח This is another form of the irregular verb לקח seen in קַח־נָא (Gen. 22:2) It acts like נתן (7.1a) and נפל (12.3) except that its assimilated root letter is ל

שְׁנֵי The number *two.* Notice the m. pl. construct endiNG. (6.5a)

נְעָרָיו | **נַעַר** means ________ The suffix ָיו is the 3 m. sg. possessive suffix on a plural noun. The י is the remnant of the masculine plural noun endiNG. It is not functioning as the connecting י we spoke about in the discussion of אֵלֶיךָ (Gen.22.2)

Synopsis of נַעַר

נַעַר	*servant*	נְעָרִים	*servants*
נַעֲרוֹ	*his servant*	נְעָרָיו	*his servants*

אִתּוֹ | אֵת looks like the DDO marker, but with the "accompanying" dagesh and a pronominal suffix, it means *with*. את by itself can be either the sign of the DDO or the preposition *with*.

<u>Synopsis of</u> אֵת

אֶת־הַבֵּן	*the son* (DDO) <u>or</u> *with the son*
אֵת הַבֵּן	*the son* (DDO) <u>or</u> *with the son*
אֹתוֹ	*him* (DDO)
אִתּוֹ	*with him*

וַיְבַקַּע Note the stem. (2.3c) The root is ________

עֲצֵי עֹלָה | עֵץ means *tree, wood, timber.* For help with the construction see 6.5a. The noun עֹלָה appears in Gen. 22:2 as part of the the phrase לְעֹלָה

וַיָּקָם See 6.1a for help determining the root.

הַמָּקוֹם | מָקוֹם is the noun *place.* As with וַיָּקָם just above, the root is also קוּם

Genesis 22:4 [Lesson 14]

בַּיּוֹם הַשְּׁלִישִׁי | בַּיּוֹם is constructed like בַּבֹּקֶר (Gen. 22:3) Note how the same preposition in Hebrew may be translated by different prepositions in idiomatic English. שְׁלִישִׁי means *third.* It is another example of an attributive adjective because it follows the noun and agrees with it in gender, number and definiteness. (See הַדְּבָרִים הָאֵלֶּה Gen. 22:1.)

וַיִּשָּׂא For help determining the root see 7.1a and again 12.3. The root sounds like נסה (Gen. 22:1) but their meanings are, of course, entirely different.

אֶת־עֵינָיו The root of עֵינָיו is ________ (vocabulary word). The suffix is discussed in the word נְעָרָיו (Gen. 22:3)

וַיַּרְא 12.1 discusses the root.

מֵרָחֹק | רָחֹק is a noun. מֵרָחֹק is constructed like מִשָּׁם (3.4b) But since ר can't take a dagesh, the vowel under the מ is lengthened in compensation. We can say that the dagesh that couldn't stand in the ר went under the מ turning the hireq ◌ִ into tsere ◌ֵ We call this "The case of the **travelling dagesh.**"

Genesis 22:5 [Lesson 14]

שְׁבוּ־לָכֶם | שְׁבוּ is a m. pl. Qal imperative from the verb ישׁב and ו___ is the m. pl. imperative ending. לָכֶם is like לְךָ (Gen. 22:2) but כֶם__ is the m. pl. suffix *you.* After all there are two נְעָרִים A literal translation might be *sit yourselves* or *stay* (on *behalf of) yourselves*, or perhaps לָכֶם adds emphasis to the imperative.

<u>Synopsis of imperatives</u>

All the imperatives you have seen in this reading come from verbs with a weak root letter or verbs which act as if they have a weak root letter. That letter is lost in the imperative form.

(Gen. 22:2)	קַח	from	לקח
	לֶךְ־לְךָ	from	הלך
	וְהַעֲלֵהוּ	from	עלה
(Gen. 22:5)	שְׁבוּ־לָכֶם	from	ישׁב

פֹּה The adverb *here.*

וַאֲנִי The guttural letter א is causing the change in pointing of the conjunction ו

וְהַנַּעַר This word has one connotation here and another earlier in this verse.

נֵלְכָה This is a new form of an irregular verb, but it's a verb you've seen twice so far in this story. The two consonants לכ should remind you of the root ________ (11.2a) The נ is a prefix pronoun (14.5) and the ◌ֵ under it reinforces the fact that this is a verb missing its first root letter. (3.1) Following the prefix pronoun and the root is a special ending ◌ָה

This triple combination:
1. first person prefix pronoun
2. verb root
3. special ending ◌ָה [in some cases the ending may be ◌ָה]

means the form is cohortative and is translated (in the plural) *let us,* or *that we may.*

כֹּה The adverb *thus, thither*

וְנִשְׁתַּחֲוֶה Like imperatives, cohortatives often come in clusters. You just saw a cohortative and so you might expect others to follow and they do. Take off the conjunction ו and remove indicators of the cohortative. You are left with שתחו The root of this verb is disputed and so is the name of its stem, but it will be discussed later in the course. When you see this four letter cluster it means *prostrate oneself in worship.* There are about 170 occurrences of this verb in the Hebrew Bible, always in this stem, so be on the lookout for it.

וְנָשׁוּבָה This is a new verb but perhaps you can get some clues about it from the features it has in common with the verbs preceding it. All three are prefixed with נ and end with ָה or ֶה Why is the prefix pronoun pointed with qamets ָ (6.1a)

אֲלֵיכֶם is the plural of אֵלֶיךָ (Gen. 22:2) You saw the suffix כֶם____ earlier in this verse in the expression שְׁבוּ-לָכֶם

Genesis 22:6 [Lesson 15]

וַיִּקַּח See Gen. 22:3 same word.

אֶת־עֲצֵי הָעֹלָה Compare with עֲצֵי עֹלָה (Gen. 22:3) Can you explain the differences?

וַיָּשֶׂם What does the vowel under the prefix pronoun tell you? (6.1a)

בְּיָדוֹ is made up of how many parts?

אֵשׁ is the noun *fire.*

הַמַּאֲכֶלֶת Is this word a noun or a verb? There is a feature which should tell you: the DDO sign אֶת in front of it. To find the root you must take off the definite article ☐הַ A מ in front of a verb root can make it into a noun. ת at the end indicates the noun is feminine. You are left with the root אכל which means __________ The noun מַאֲכֶלֶת is *knife.* [You were expecting *food!* Not to worry; it also is built from the root אכל]

שְׁנֵיהֶם The suffix is discussed in 12.4. שְׁנֵי appears in Gen. 22:3.

יַחְדָּו *together.* It comes from the same root as יְחִידְךָ (Gen. 22:2) It means physical proximity and often also includes connotations of *being of like mind* or *together in purpose.*

Genesis 22:7 [Lesson 15]

וַיֹּאמֶר יִצְחָק Watch for direct speech in this verse; there are several changes of speakers.

אָבִיו...אָבִי 10.1b and 10.2b discuss these words.

וְהָעֵצִים This word is made up of four components; can you identify them? The mid-portion is seen in the phrase עֲצֵי עֹלָה (Gen. 22:3)

וְאַיֵּה הַשֶּׂה A literal translation would be *and where the sheep?* This is another type of noun sentence (2.10b) and smooth English requires the addition of a form of *to be.*

Genesis 22:8 [Lesson 15]

יִרְאֶה־לוֹ | יִרְאֶה is the same verb, stem, form, and PGN as וַיַּרְא (12.1 and above in verse 4) but without vav conversive. Some verbs may have a shortened prefix form with vav conversive; that is what וַיַּרְא is.

Remember that the suffix וֹ___ can be translated *it* as well as *him. It* is the object pronoun referring to the masculine noun שֶׂה

Genesis 22:9 [Lesson 16]

וַיִּבֶן 12.1 tells how to find the root.

אֶת־הַמִּזְבֵּחַ After taking off the definite article and the noun indicator (see הַמַּאֲכֶלֶת Gen. 22:6) you are left with the root זבח meaning *sacrifice.* Upon what did the ancients sacrifice?

וַיַּעֲרֹךְ The root is ________

וַיַּעֲקֹד The root is ________

וַיָּשֶׂם Gen. 22:6 same word.

אֹתוֹ Holem is the vocalization that goes with the DDO marker את when an object pronoun is added. Compare אתו with אִתּוֹ (Gen. 22:3)

מִמַּעַל A combination of the prepositions מִן and עַל

Genesis 22:10 [Lesson 16]

וַיִּשְׁלַח The root is ________

לִשְׁחֹט The preposition ל in front of a verb is usually a sign of ________ (11.2b)

Genesis 22:11 [Lesson 16]

מַלְאַךְ This is a noun; is it definite or indefinite? Which consonant is most likely to be extraneous to the root? (See הַמַּאֲכֶלֶת Gen 22:6.)

הַשָּׁמַיִם | שָׁמַיִם means *heaven(s).* It never appears in the singular. שָׁמַיִם may possibly be a compound of the words אֵשׁ *fire* and מַיִם *water.*

Genesis 22:12 [Lesson 17]

אַל־תִּשְׁלַח The root שלח appears in Gen. 22:10. The prefix pronoun ת can be either 3 f. sg. or 2 m. sg. (14.5); context will tell you which is meant. אַל + the prefix form of the verb expresses a negative command.

וְאַל־תַּעַשׂ   Another negative command. That means that the form of the verb is __________ The תּ then is the prefix pronoun and not part of the root. 12.1 gives help finding the root which is among the "first fifty."

מְאוּמָה   means *anything.*

כִּי | כִּי   and אֲשֶׁר are the two most common words which introduce clauses.

עַתָּה   Do not confuse this adverb with the independent subject pronoun אַתָּה

יָדַעְתִּי   This verb, like אָהַבְתָּ (Gen. 22:2), uses the affix form although present tense may give a better English translation.

יְרֵא   From the root ירא It is an adjective in the construct form and means *fearing, reverencing.* Because it is masculine and singular, it can imply *one who fears* or *a fearer.*

מִמֶּנִּי   When the preposition מִן appears with a suffix it takes this lengthened form. ___נִי is the 1 c. sg. object suffix. (10.3b)

Genesis 22:13 [Lesson 17]

וַיִּשָּׂא...וַיַּרְא   A repetition of Gen. 22:4a. "a" is the part of the verse up to the atnaḥ ֑

אַיִל   May be listed under איל or אול

אַחַר   This can be the preposition *after, behind* as in Gen. 22:1 or the adverb *hind part, back part.*

נֶאֱחַז   The root אחז means *seize, grasp.* A נ in front of a root can be one of two things:

1. The first person plural prefix pronoun. (14.5)
2. The sign of some Nif`al forms.

Since the first person wouldn't make sense here, try the Nif`al. נֶאֱחַז is the 3 m. sg. Nif`al affix. The Nif`al usually imparts passive meaning.

בַּסְּבַךְ | סְבַךְ   is a noun. בַּ ⟵ הַ□ + בְּ (See בַּבֹּקֶר Gen. 22:3.)

בְּקַרְנָיו This word is composed of a preposition + noun + suffix. (If you need help with the suffix, see נְעָרָיו Gen. 22:3.) One of the functions of the preposition בְּ is to express *means* or *instrument*, so here it would mean *by*.

Some uses of the preposition בּ

Gen. 22:3	בַּבֹּקֶר
Gen. 22:4	בַּיּוֹם הַשְּׁלִישִׁי
Gen. 22:6	בְּיָדוֹ
Gen. 22:13	בְּקַרְנָיו

וַיַּעֲלֵהוּ In Gen. 22:2 you saw וְהַעֲלֵהוּ a Hif'il imperative. Here you have a Hif'il prefix with vav conversive. What happened to the characteristic ה in front of the root marking the Hif'il? (See וַיַּשְׁכֵּם Gen. 22.3.)

תַּחַת The adverb and preposition *under, beneath, in place of.*

Genesis 22:14 [Lesson 17]

שֵׁם־הַמָּקוֹם הַהוּא The noun שֵׁם is a vocabulary word; מָקוֹם appears in Gen. 22:3; and for a refresher on the uses of הוּא see 6.6. הַהוּא is functioning as an attributive adjective modifying הַמָּקוֹם and because they are both definite, they cause שֵׁם to be definite. Why is there no dagesh after the הַ of הַהוּא

יהוה יִרְאֶה These words make perfect sense translated literally but many translators treat the whole phrase יהוה יִרְאֶה as the name of the place and simply transliterate it: *Adonaijireh.*

אֲשֶׁר In 5.3a אֲשֶׁר was introduced as the relative pronoun *which* or *who*. It can also open a dependent clause, as it does here, and mean *that, when, because, where, as.*

יֵאָמֵר The root and prefix pronoun are familiar but the pointing is new. This is the 3 m. sg. Nif'al prefix form. The Nif'al affix form is distinctive because it has a preformative נ

as the name Nif`al suggests. But the Nif`al prefix does not begin with a preformative נ
It is recognized by a characteristic vowel pattern:

Nif`al prefix vowel pattern	
For roots beginning with a guttural	◌ֵ | ◌ָ ◌ֵ ◌
For other roots	◌ִ | ◌ָּ ◌ֵ ◌

הַיּוֹם Literally, *the day*, often translated idiomatically *today* and in some translations even more freely *until this day*. The third rendition seems to be taking great liberty with the text because the phrase עַד הַיּוֹם הַזֶּה appears frequently in Biblical literature. It is hard to know exactly what time frame is meant by הַיּוֹם here.

בְּהַר יהוה יֵרָאֶה There is more than one way to translate the last three words in this verse and we will consider three possibilities.

First let us assume that בְּהַר יהוה is a construct chain. Would the phrase be definite? (5.2a) Why does הַר have בְּ in front of it and not בַּ
יֵרָאֶה is another 3 m. sg. Nif`al prefix like יֵאָמֵר earlier in the verse. The subject of the verb is the pronoun *he* and we could translate יֵרָאֶה *is seen, will be seen, appears* or *will appear.*

Now let us assume that the phrase בְּהַר יהוה is not a construct chain. In that case בְּהַר is no longer definite and יהוה becomes the subject of the verb.

A third approach is taken by some scholars who believe that יֵרָאֶה is a scribal error and that the word should really read יִרְאֶה making it the Qal prefix and so putting the verb in the active voice: *he will see.* Notice that the difference is only one of pointing, not of consonants and that עד היום הזה *to this day* Torah scrolls are unpointed. Well, no matter what you do with this clause, it's tricky. But before deciding that an error has been made in the Masoretic text, you should have a strong argument. A difficult text is not necessarily an incorrect text. Is Biblical Hebrew often like this? Yes!

Genesis 28:10 [Lesson 18]

מִבְּאֵר שָׁ֑בַע | בְּאֵר שָׁבַע is the name of a place. בְּאֵר means *well.* שׁבע is the root for *swear* and is the number *seven.* Read Gen. 21:24-34 to see the connection made between these meanings of the root.

חָרָֽנָה The name of a place plus ה- directive. (11.3)

Genesis 28:11 [Lesson 18]

וַיִּפְגַּע What kind of dagesh is in the ג (3.3) What is the stem?

וַיָּ֤לֶן If you are having trouble determining the root, refer to 6.1a.

כִּי־בָא הַשֶּׁ֔מֶשׁ What are the two possible forms for בָּא (9.5a) Do you think it is possible that either verb form could be used here? After looking up the words you might think that this clause means *because the sun was rising.* But no! בּוֹא הַשֶּׁמֶשׁ is an idiom referring to the setting of the sun.

וַיִּקַּח Hebrew does not require an explicit DO here although one is needed in English.

מֵאַבְנֵי The root is ________ The preposition is pointed מֵ instead of מִ⊡ because ____________ (See מֵרָחֹק Gen. 22:4.) מִן is being used in the partitive sense, to mean *some of.*

וַיָּ֖שֶׂם As with וַיִּקַּח just above, English needs a DO.

מְרַאֲשֹׁתָ֑יו If your dictionary does not list this under מְרַאֲשֹׁת it can be found under its root ________ (vocabulary word). This noun appears rarely, but always in the plural and with a suffix. It is usually taken to mean *at his head place.* In the four Biblical passages in which this noun appears, someone is asleep or is going to sleep, and something unusual happens. Here, the placement of the stones מְרַאֲשֹׁתָיו may mean something more significant than is apparent on the surface.
Notice throughout the reading how variously אֶבֶן is used.

Genesis 28:12 [Lesson 18]

סֻלָּם This word is most often translated *ladder.* However, this is the only time the word appears in the Hebrew Bible and its root is somewhat obscure. It is probably from the root סלל which means *lift up* or *cast up.* So even if *ladder* is not precise, we can assume from associated words and the context that some sort of thing-which-goes-up is meant.

מֻצָּב Can this be מִן + צָב Although there is a dagesh in the צ which could represent the assimilated ן of the preposition, the מ of מִן never has qibbuts ֻ under it, so we can exclude the possibility of that compound. That still leaves four strong letters from which we must abstract a root. We could approach the problem of finding the root the way we did with נִסָּה (Gen. 22:1) There we found that נסה was a root, and that the dagesh represented strengthening indicating the Pi`el stem. Here we find that מצב is not a root and therefore the dagesh must represent an assimilated letter, most likely נ There is a root נצב so that takes care of the dagesh. Now what about the מ A preformative מ can be an indication of a noun; it can also be the sign of a participle in stems other than Qal and Nif`al. A participle in the Hof`al is characterized by qamets ḥatuf ָ or qibbuts ֻ under a preformative מ (It is not among the top ten forms but you will come across it from time to time.) It so happens that מֻצָּב can be found listed as a noun meaning *palisade,* but that does not fit the context here; or perhaps it does at least to the extent that it enhances the image of the verb.

אַ֫רְצָה The ending ָה looks just the same as the ה- directive (11.3) but this is where it's <u>at</u> and is called the **locative** - ה There are grammarians who consider ה- directive and locative - ה the same construction; others think they are completely different. The important thing to remember is that both *place to which* and *place at which* or *on which* can be expressed by ָה

וְרֹאשׁוֹ To what does the suffix refer?

מַגִּיעַ Again you have to dig for a root. When there are too many letters for a root, a vowel letter is a good one to delete. (See יְחִידְךָ Gen. 22:2) That leaves מ ג ע Proceed the same way as with מֻצָּב earlier in the verse to find the root and form. However, the pointing is different here, which means the stem is different. Just as the Hif`il prefix form has pataḥ ַ under its prefix pronoun (see וַיַּשְׁכֵּם Gen. 22:3) so the Hif`il participle has ַ under its preformative מ The "dot vowel" ִי between the second and third root letters which we cast aside earlier can be brought back as further support for a Hif`il form.

הַשָּׁמָ֫יְמָה If you are up-to-date learning your vocabulary words, you will know this one. This time is the ָה directive or locative?

מַלְאֲכֵי The construct plural of מַלְאָךְ (Gen. 22:11)

עֹלִים The holem ֹ after the first root letter identifies the form as a ____________ (9.3a) The endiNG is ________ (6.5a) That leaves two letters for the root. If you can't figure out the root re-read the comments about וְהַעֲלֵהוּ (Gen. 22:2) and study your vocabulary.

בּוֹ preposition + suffix.

Genesis 28:13 [Lesson 19]

נִצָּב The same root as מֻצָּב (Gen. 28:12) but what is the stem? If it were Qal, the pointing would be ________ (4.2a) If it were a Pi`el, it would be pointed ________ (15.4) It is a Nif`al participle. Remember: all participles except Qal and Nif`al have a preformative מ (See מֻצָּב Gen. 28:12.) Again הִנֵּה was the clue to watch for a participle. The נ you see is the preformative נ stem indicator of some Nif`al forms. The dagesh represents the assimilated נ of the root. (16.1a)

ננצב

נ of the root ↑↑ נ preformative of the Nif`al affix and participle

עָלָיו Constructed like אֵלֶיךָ (Gen. 22:2) עַל can mean, among other things, *on* or *near*. The suffix could refer to the ladder or to Jacob.

וַיֹּאמַר Starting in Gen. 28:12 there has been a series of constructions made up of הִנֵּה followed by a participle. The reappearance of a finite verb means that the main narrative has resumed. (13.2) (The מ is pointed with pataḥ ַ because of the accent.)

יִצְחָק There is a major break in the sense of the verse after the atnaḥ ֑

הָאָרֶץ אֲשֶׁר אַתָּה שֹׁכֵב עָלֶיהָ This is a complicated phrase syntactically. It is best to translate it literally and then turn it into idiomatic English. שֹׁכֵב is pointed for a ____________ עָלֶיהָ is the feminine counterpart of עָלָיו It is referring to ____________

Why does the ה of עָלֶיהָ not have a mappiq? (14.3) Because the ה has its own vowel which gives it consonantal value and so does not need a mappiq to perform that function.

לְךָ means the same as אֵלֶיךָ (Gen. 22:2)

אֶתְּנֶנָּה A first person prefix pronoun + ָה ending are the signs of the cohortative. (See נֵלְכָה Gen. 22:5.) From the consonants that are left, you should be able to abstract a familiar root if, of course, you remember to account for the dagesh in the תּ (If not, consult 16.6.) But you still have to account for the ֶנּ There is a set of endings in Hebrew which we will call nunated forms[1] because they have an extra accented נ syllable. This syllable has no grammatical function which we can discern, but it is thought to add strength to the suffix. The conventional singular cohortative would be אֶתְּנָה If perhaps you were thinking that the ָה at the end of אֶתְּנֶנָּה might be the feminine singular DO, remember, in that case, the ה would need a mappiq. (14.3)

וּלְזַרְעֶךָ | וּ is the same conjunction as וְ but it will appear this way before the letters ב מ פ (affectionately known as the **BuMP** letters) and before other letters when they are pointed with a shewa ְ as is the case here. In English four words are needed for this one in Hebrew. Look at its components: conjunction + preposition + root + suffix.

The second half or "b" part of this verse is long and complicated. First there is a noun הָאָרֶץ which is actually the DDO of the verb אֶתְּנֶנָּה but it does not have the DDO marker את in front of it. Furthermore it is far in front of the verb and has a descriptive clause following it. After this clause [which is introduced by אֲשֶׁר] comes an indirect object, לְךָ then the main verb, אֶתְּנֶנָּה and then another indirect object, וּלְזַרְעֶךָ What is the purpose of this convoluted word order? Emphasis. הָאָרֶץ standing at the front, is emphasized and לְךָ preceding the verb is also emphasized.

Genesis 28:14 [Lesson 19]

כַּעֲפַר Here כַּ is not analogous to בַּ in בַּבֹּקֶר (Gen. 22:3) כַּעֲפַר is in construct and so it cannot have the definite article. It is pointed כַּעֲפַר instead of כְּעֲפַר because of the guttural ע which follows the preposition.

---

[1] The name most commonly used for this ending is *nun energicum* or *energic nun*.

וּפָרַצְתָּ Is this an affix form with vav reversive?

יָמָּה וָקֵדְמָה וְצָפֹנָה וָנֶגְבָּה Four nice examples of ה- directive. These words are the names of the four directions. Imagine yourself standing in Israel facing North:

יָם	*West* ⟷	*sea*
קֶדֶם	*East* ⟷	*sunrise place*
צָפֹן	*North* ⟷	*hide (beyond the mountains)*
נֶגֶב	*South* ⟷	*be dry*

וְנִבְרְכוּ Remove the conjunction and the 3 m. pl. affix pronoun to get closer to the root. Which of the remaining letters do you think is "extra?" Root letters are found together in a cluster. [There is no reason to discard the כ because if it were part of a suffix it would come after everything else and would be in its final form ך] That leaves נ which can be either the 1 c. pl. prefix pronoun or the sign of the Nif`al. If it were the 1 c. pl. prefix pronoun, what would וּ be doing at the end of the word? That leaves us with a Nif`al preformative. The form is affix + vav reversive and the PGN is ______

מִשְׁפְּחֹת This is a noun formed the same way as מַאֲכֶלֶת (Gen. 22:6) but the endiNG ֹת of מִשְׁפְּחֹת is feminine plural.

וּבְזַרְעֶךָ This word is made up of four components. It is almost a repetition of the last word in Gen. 28:13. Incidentally, in both cases the vowel under the ע is a segol ֶ Normally it would be a shewa ְ but in these places the syllable is in pause. That is, it receives the accent or tone at a major breaking point, which often causes a change in vocalization.

Genesis 28:15 [Lesson 19]

אָנֹכִי Another form of אֲנִי

עִמָּךְ This word usually appears pointed עִמְּךָ But here it is in pause. (19.4b) Why is there a dagesh in the מ "Short" two letter words followed by a suffix often take a dagesh forte in the second letter. We will call this dagesh the **Napoleonic dagesh**. Note that יָמָּה (in Gen. 28:14) has a dagesh for the same reason.

וְשָׁמַרְתִּיךָ This word has four components. Verbs which are inflected (built up) this way may lose some of their identifying characteristics. For example, although this verb is a Qal affix it does not have qamets ָ under the first root letter. The suffix, because it lengthens the word, causes a shortening of the vowels at the beginning of the word. But you can deduce that this isn't one of the derived stems because there is no stem preformative or dagesh forte in the middle root letter.

וַהֲשִׁבֹתִיךָ The initial וַ is a vav reversive. It is pointed with a pataḥ ַ instead of the expected shewa ְ because the following letter ה is a guttural. It cannot be a sign of the vav conversive because it is not followed by a prefix pronoun+ dagesh forte. Moving in from the end of the word, you can remove the object suffix and the affix subject pronoun. That leaves השב but that is not a root. The preformative ה is a Hif`il indicator and the root is the hollow verb שׁוּב Hollow verbs can also lose their middle root letter in stems other than the Qal. The Hif`il of שׁוּב is *cause to return* or *bring back.*

כִּי The translation you give the conjunction can have a big effect on the meaning of the verse.

אֶעֱזָבְךָ The components are slightly different from those in the verbs immediately preceding because a switch has been made from affix form to prefix form. The vocalization is unfamiliar, though. Not only does א as a prefix pronoun cause a change in pointing, so does the following letter ע But as with וְשָׁמַרְתִּיךָ earlier in the verse, there is no augment (dagesh or preformative letter, for example) to the root to suggest a stem other than Qal, and Qal it is!

עַד אֲשֶׁר אִם These three words can be translated together as *until.*

עָשִׂיתִי You can take off the תִי____ as an affix subject pronoun but the root cannot be עשי because no root ends in י The root is עשה Verb roots that end in ה drop the ה before a subject pronoun is added. (Discussed with וְהַעֲלֵהוּ Gen. 22:2.) Some PGNs of 3rd ה verbs take a connecting י between the second root letter and the subject pronoun.

אֵת אֲשֶׁר | **אֲשֶׁר** is the DDO.

דִּבַּרְתִּי If this poses a problem do not party Saturday night. Do not pass *Go.* Do not collect $200.00.

לָךְ 19.4b.

Genesis 28:16 [Lesson 20]

וַיִּיקַץ 17.2 discusses this type of verb.

מִשְּׁנָתוֹ | שֵׁנָה is the noun *sleep.* All feminine nouns in the singular construct end in ת and a noun usually takes the construct form before a suffix is added.

אָכֵן An adverb.

יֵשׁ *There is*, a predicator of existence like הִנֵּה

יָדָעְתִּי What "tense" do you think fits best here? (See יָדַעְתִּי Gen. 22:12.) This is a case where the fluidity of Hebrew time concepts embraces a dimension not available with the English tense system.

Genesis 28:17 [Lesson 20]

מַה־נּוֹרָא | מָה is the interrogative pronoun *what? which?* It is also an exclamation *how! what!* נוֹרָא is the m. sg. Nif`al participle of ירא In 1st י verbs you will often see a ו in the י position, in stems other than Qal, after a preformative letter or prefix pronoun. נוֹרָא means literally *awed, reverenced, being feared.* English needs to twist this to come up with a smooth phrase.

אֵין | אֵין is the negative of יֵשׁ (Gen. 28:16) יֵשׁ is what it is. אֵין is what it ain't!

כִּי אִם A compound preposition meaning *but, but indeed, certainly.*

וְזֶה שַׁעַר Why does the adjective precede the noun? (15.2)

Three uses for an adjective

1. Attributive: Modifies a noun. It follows the noun and must agree with it in gender, number, and definiteness: הָאֲדָמָה הַזֹּאת (Gen. 28: 15) סֻלָּם מֻצָּב (Gen. 28:12)
2. Predicate: It functions as the predicate of a noun sentence: וְהָאֶבֶן גְּדֹלָה (Gen. 29:2)
3. Substantive: Makes a noun out of an adjective: יְרֵא אֱלֹהִים (Gen. 22:12)

Genesis 28:18 [Lesson 20]

וַיַּשְׁכֵּם For a discussion of the stem, see Gen. 22:3 same word.

מְרַאֲשֹׁתָיו Gen. 28:11 same word.

אֹתָהּ When את is followed by an object pronoun, the pointing changes to holem. You will see it both plene אוֹתָהּ and defectiva as it is here.

מַצֵּבָה A noun from the root נצב seen earlier in מֻצָּב (Gen. 28:12) and in נִצָּב (Gen. 28:13) It means *pillar* — the type used in worship. This is what the Israelites were told not to do in later times. How does this word fit in with the phrase immediately preceding? — either by our assuming a comma after אֹתָהּ or adding a link such as *as a.*

וַיִּצֹק According to the missing letter rules, this looks like it should be missing its third root letter, (12.1) but it isn't. This is a highly irregular spelling. It is a 1st י verb masquerading as a 1st נ But even worse, the י has not even left a footprint dagesh; it has elided (dropped out altogether). This problem is touched on in 17.6a-c.

עַל־רֹאשָׁהּ Whose head gets the oil?

Genesis 28:19 [Lesson 21]

אוּלָם *But*

לוּז שֵׁם־הָעִיר A noun sentence + a construct chain. (2.10b and 5.1b)

לָרִאשֹׁנָה An adverb meaning *at first, formerly.* Can you determine the root?

Genesis 28:20 [Lesson 21]

וַיִּדַּר. . .נֶדֶר It is common Hebrew style to use the same root in different ways close together. It strengthens the idea, and is euphonic.

לֵאמֹר A preposition in front of a verb root almost certainly signals an infinitive. (The tsere ֵ under the ל is not regular pointing for infinitive forms.) In Hebrew, an infinitive is not always translated "to + verb." It can be "verb + ing." It gives the idea of the verb in the abstract sense. Both infinitives and participles have verb and noun-like qualities but there is a distinction between the two:

The **participle** stresses the doer of the action.

The **infinitive** focuses on the action itself.

אִם introduces a string of clauses. You can consider the preposition to be repeated before each one.

עִמָּדִי A lengthened form of **עִם** with the 1 c. sg. object suffix.

וּשְׁמָרַנִי | **ַנִי____** is another form of the 1 c. sg. object suffix. (10.3b) **שְׁמָרַנִי** is a potentially ambiguous form. You learned in 18.1a that often the Qal singular imperative can be recognized by the shewa ְ under the first root letter and here there is no affix or prefix pronoun to identify a PGN as in **וּשְׁמַרְתִּיךָ** (Gen. 28:15) But context tells us that an imperative does not fit here. The subject of this verb is the same as for the previous verb, **יִהְיֶה** This is another Qal affix whose landmark vowel has been shortened from qamets ָ to shewa ְ because of the addition of a suffix. For those who are curious, the m. sg. Qal imperative with a 1 c. sg. object suffix is **שָׁמְרֵנִי** In unpointed text both forms would look the same.

הוֹלֵךְ Notice the plene spelling.

לֶאֱכֹל This is composed of a preposition + a verb root, and so the form is most likely ____________ **לֶאֱכֹל** is pointed differently from **לֵאמֹר** because there are different patterns for 1st **א** verbs.

וּבֶגֶד | **בֶּגֶד** is a noun from the root **בגד**

לִלְבֹּשׁ There have been three Qal infinitives in this verse, all pointed somewhat differently; yet each is recognizable because of the attached preposition.

Genesis 28:21 [Lesson 21]

וְשַׁבְתִּי After removing the conjunction and affix pronoun you are left with two letters for the root. In the Qal affix, 3rd ה and hollow verbs may show only two root letters. But only hollow verbs can have the vowel pataḥ ַ (instead of qamets ָ) under the first root letter. Thus the root here is ________
Some translators believe that this verse is a continuation of verse 20 and that the conditional אִם still applies. Others feel that the new verse ends the condition and translate the conjunction ו *then.*

בְּשָׁלוֹם When you are looking for a root, remember that a plene spelling does not introduce a new consonant.

וְהָיָה יהוה לִי לֵאלֹהִים There are two prepositional phrases here and each is introduced by ל (17.1) Translate literally and then smooth out the English.

Genesis 28:22 [Lesson 21]

The syntax of the first part of verse is:

1. וְהָאֶבֶן הַזֹּאת subject: noun + attributive adjective
2. אֲשֶׁר introduces a clause modifying the subject
3. יִהְיֶה verb
4. בֵּית אֱלֹהִים predicate

תִּתֶּן־לִי 16.6 concentrates on this verb. The second vowel has been shortened from tsere ֵ to segol ֶ because the verb is followed by a maqqef. Most frequently, shortening of a vowel for this reason is seen with nouns in construct chains.

עַשֵּׂר אֲעַשְּׂרֶנּוּ Notice that the consonants ע שׂ ר are common to both words. First look at אֲעַשְּׂרֶנּוּ An א in front of a root can be only a prefix pronoun. That means that נּוּ___ at the end cannot be an affix subject pronoun; it must have some other function. It can be the 3 m. sg. or 1 c. pl. object suffix, nunated form. (See אֶתְּנֶנָּה Gen. 28:13.) Context will determine which it is. It serves the same function as הוּ___ in וְהַעֲלֵהוּ (Gen. 22:2) What are the root and stem?

Now look at the word עַשֵּׂר Hebrew has two infinitives. You have already seen the infinitive construct. As its name implies, you can build with it: prepositions on the front, suffixes at the end. עַשֵּׂר is an example of the other infinitive, the infinitive absolute. It serves to intensify the idea of the root. It most commonly stands right before the conjugated verb in the same stem. English has no corresponding construction which uses the verb twice. We use the verb and an adverb such as *surely* or *indeed* to try to capture the intensification in translation.

Genesis 29:1 [Lesson 22]

רַגְלָיו Constructed like נְעָרָיו (Gen. 22:3)

בְנֵי־קֶדֶם | בְּנֵי in front of a name is one of the ways of referring to a people. The most common example is בְּנֵי־יִשְׂרָאֵל which can be translated *the sons of Israel, the children of Israel, the people of Israel,* or *Israelites*. The gentilic ending presented in 22.5 is another way of expressing nationhood.

Genesis 29:2 [Lesson 22]

שְׁלֹשָׁה עֶדְרֵי־צֹאן What you are seeing is not a feminine adjective modifying a m. pl. noun and what would be even more irregular, preceding the noun! Numbers in Hebrew have a complicated and varied syntax. Here the number שְׁלֹשָׁה is being used as a substantive: *a triad, flocks of sheep.*

עָלֶיהָ Gen. 28:13 same word. What is the antecedent?

הַהִוא This word is really הַהִיא When a word in the Hebrew Bible is spelled "incorrectly," the consonants are not changed but the correct spelling is noted in the margin. The word is to be pronounced not the way it is written but according to the marginal notation. This system is called כְּתִב (written) קְרֵא (read). Some words are so commonly spelled "incorrectly" that the error is not noted for each instance. Such is the case for הִוא which appears as it does here all but twelve times in the Bible. It is interesting to bear in mind that י and ו were not consistently differentiated by scribes until about the time of the Common Era so that what is being notated here is not so much a mistake as a change in the written language over time.

יַשְׁקוּ Why is this not a 3 m. pl. Qal affix? It is the 3 m. pl. Hif`il prefix of שקה *cause to drink (water)* or *give to drink.* 3rd ה verbs lose the ה of the root before subject pronouns are added, or in the case of the prefix form, before the prefix complement. The Hif`il prefix is distinctive because of the pataḥ ַ under the prefix pronoun. (See וַיַּשְׁכֵּם Gen. 22:3.)

וְהָאֶבֶן גְּדֹלָה The conjunction וְ can mean *but.* The adjective follows the noun, but is it an attributive adjective? (14.2c and 15.2)

פִּי is the construct form of פֶּה

Genesis 29:3 [Lesson 22]

וְנֶאֶסְפוּ Like וְנִבְרְכוּ (Gen. 28:14) but the guttural א causes a change in pointing. All the verbs in this verse are affix forms + vav reversive, but they are not translated in the future. (As you read on you will see why.) This may be a specialized use of the vav reversive for actions which have been completed but were repeated over a period of time.

שָׁמָּה For the dagesh see עִמָּךְ (Gen. 28:15) For the ָה ending see אַרְצָה (Gen. 28:12)

וְגָלְלוּ A root cannot begin with the same two letters but the second and third root letters can twin. Such roots are called **geminates**, and as you will discover, they can cause no end of trouble. Here, fortunately, the components are straightforward.

מֵעַל A compound preposition. For the vowel under the מ see מֵרָחֹק (Gen. 22:4)

וְהִשְׁקוּ Hif`il affix of שקה with vav reversive.

וְהֵשִׁיבוּ The Hif`il affix of שׁוּב The preformative ה and a "dot vowel" between the second and third root letters (in the case of hollow verbs, the "dot vowel" takes the place of the middle root letter) are the stem indicators.

לִמְקֹמָהּ Components: preposition + noun + suffix. The ָהּ cannot be the ה- directive because:

1. It has a mappiq which is always the sign of ______________ (14.3)
2. The preposition לְ gives the meaning of direction toward.

Would you have recognized the noun more easily if it had been written מָקוֹם Defectiva and plene spellings, and final forms of letters can change the appearance of a word from the way you may be accustomed to seeing it.

Genesis 29:4 [Lesson 23]

וַיֹּאמֶר לָהֶם יַעֲקֹב Compare this to וַיֹּאמֶר אֵלָיו אַבְרָהָם (Gen. 22:1) The components are the same in both cases but are these two segments translated the same way? In a case like this, it is context rather than rigid rules of word order which must be considered.

אַחַי This word is in the vocative. (18.2) As was the case in that Lesson sentence, there are no guidelines here, other than context, to identify that part of speech. About the suffix: you have already seen that ִי is the sign of the 1 c. sg. possessive suffix.

If the noun is singular, you will see ִי as in אָחִי *my brother.*

If the noun is plural you will see ַי as in אַחַי *my brothers.*

<u>Two common but irregular nouns</u> אָב <u>and</u> אָח

אָבִי	*my father*	אָחִי	*my brother*
אֲבִי	*father of*	אֲחִי	*brother of*
אֲבוֹתַי	*my fathers*	אַחַי	*my brothers*
אֲבוֹתֵי	*fathers of*	אֲחֵי	*brothers of*

מֵאַיִן A compound preposition *from where.* What are the two components?

אַתֶּם Plural of אַתָּה

אֲנַחְנוּ Plural of אֲנִי

Genesis 29:5 [Lesson 23]

הַיְדַעְתֶּם The PGN is The form is The root is ________

That leaves the ה unaccounted for. Is it the sign of the Hif'il? Not here. In 1st י verbs, the addition of a stem preformative causes the י of the root to appear as a ו so the 2 m. pl. Hif'il

affix of ידע for example, is הוֹדַעְתֶּם A ה in front of a verb or noun can be the interrogative particle. When this interrogative ה is used, it will be appended to a word at the beginning of a verse or clause. Usually the interrogative ה is pointed הֲ but it may be pointed הַ or rarely הֶ
Context would indicate present tense translation even though הַיְדַעְתֶּם is an affix form. This is discussed with the phrase כִּי עַתָּה יָדַעְתִּי (Gen. 22:12)

לָבָן בֶּן־נָחוֹר This is how a person's full name is expressed in Hebrew: *so-and-so* בֶּן or בַּת *so-and-so.*

יָדָעְנוּ What about the נוּ___ Is it the 1 c. pl. affix pronoun, (13.5) or the 1 c. pl. suffix *us?* (18.3b) Which makes more sense? (It cannot be the 3 m. sg. suffix as in אֲעַשְּׂרֶנּוּ (Gen. 28:22) because the only time נוּ___ can be a 3 m. sg. suffix is when it is in the nunated form ֶנּוּ
Note that although English would use an object pronoun here, Hebrew doesn't require one.

Genesis 29:6 [Lesson 23]

הֲשָׁלוֹם The noun שָׁלוֹם is in Gen. 28:21. It is a word with a broad range of meanings. In Hebrew שָׁלוֹם carries the ideas of *peace, welfare, well being, completeness, wholeness.* What about the ה in front? You have seen a preformative ה as a sign of the Hif`il, as the definite article and as an interrogative particle. You should be able to come up with reasons to eliminate two of these possibilities here. ("Context" doesn't count as a sufficient reason this time.) The phrase הֲשָׁלוֹם לוֹ should be treated as a noun sentence.

בִּתּוֹ | בַּת is an irregular noun and בִּתּוֹ shows the change in vocalization when a suffix is added. Why the dagesh forte? (See עִמְּךָ Gen. 28:15.)

בָּאָה The 3 m. sg. Qal affix and the m. sg. Qal participle of a hollow verb look the same. (9.5a) This is true also for the 3 f. sg. Qal affix and the f. sg. Qal participle. Which is the intended form here? Well, הִנֵּה introduces the clause which points to its being a participle. Also the accent can be a clue. If it is placed with the first syllable, the form is probably affix. So here, the accent is supporting the participial form, and in this context a participle makes more sense.

Genesis 29:7 [Lesson 23]

הֵן A shortened form of הִנֵּה

הַיּוֹם גָּדוֹל What kind of adjective is גָּדוֹל here? Compare with וְהָאֶבֶן גְּדֹלָה (Gen. 29:2)

עֵת *time*

הֵאָסֵף What will you take off to find the root? This is a use of a preformative ה you have not seen yet. It is the indicator of two Nif`al (yes, Nif`al) forms: the imperative and the infinitive. Context should tell you which form הֵאָסֵף is. The vowel pattern ◌ִ | ◌ָ ◌ֵ ◌ or ◌ֵ | ◌ָ ◌ֵ ◌ [before a guttural or ר] may be the signpost of this sometimes difficult stem. (See יֵאָמֵר Gen. 22:14 for an example of the Nif`al prefix.)

הַמִּקְנֶה The dagesh in the מ should alert you to the function of the first ה What is the function of the מ (See הַמַּאֲכֶלֶת Gen. 22:6.) The atnaḥ ◌֑ marks a significant break in thought here.

הַשְׁקוּ This is the third occurrence of שקה in this chapter. A preformative ה or ◌ַ under a prefix pronoun has been a consistent identifier:

(Gen. 29:2)	יַשְׁקוּ	3 m. pl. Hif`il prefix
(Gen. 29:3)	וְהִשְׁקוּ	3 m. pl. Hif`il affix
(Gen. 29:7)	הַשְׁקוּ	m. pl. Hif`il imperative

וּלְכוּ The consonant cluster לכ should signal the root.

רְעוּ The PGN is ________ That leaves ______ for root letters. 20.3 indicates that in an imperative form missing a root letter, that missing letter can be in the first, second, or third position. In the case of this word, there is a root for all those possibilities. As a reward for so much hard work so far, here's a suggestion: try the third position first.

Genesis 29:8 [Lesson 24]

נוּכַל The root of נוּכַל is יכל *be able* (an irregular verb). Grammarians argue as to whether the stem here is an old Qal passive or a Hof`al (passive of Hif`il) but neither the passiveness or causativeness is transmitted into English. This word is another illustration of ו appearing in the position of a 1st י But here the ו appears after a prefix pronoun rather than after a stem preformative as in נוֹרָא (Gen. 28:17) נוּכַל

נ sign of Nif'al ↑ ↑ נ 1 c. pl. prefix pronoun

עַד אֲשֶׁר This compound preposition, meaning *until,* introduces a string of clauses just as אִם does in Gen. 28:20.

יֵאָֽסְפוּ This is the third occurrence in this chapter of the verb אסף

(Gen. 29:3)	נֶאֶסְפוּ	3 m. pl. Nif'al affix
(Gen. 29:7)	הֵאָסֵף	Nif'al infinitive
(Gen. 29:8)	יֵאָֽסְפוּ	3 m. pl. Nif'al prefix

You saw the same stem and form in יֵאָמֵר and יֵרָאֶה (Gen. 22:14). The reason that יֵאָֽסְפוּ has a shewa ְ under the ס rather than a tsere ֵ is that the length of the word has caused this syllable to shorten. Note the meteg after the vowel qamets אָֽ It is there to make sure you separate the syllables and sound the shewa, and indicates the vowel is not a qamets ḥatuf. You should hear four syllables in this word.

וְגָֽלֲלוּ Gen. 29:3 same word.

וְהִשְׁקִ֫ינוּ Glance back to הַשְׁקוּ (Gen. 29.7) The summary there should be of value in determining the stem and form of this verb. י appears between the two strong letters and affix pronoun in some PGNs of 3rd ה verbs. The atnaḥ ֑ just before וְהִשְׁקִינוּ is a signal that the conditional עַד אֲשֶׁר no longer applies, and so we introduce this verb by saying *that we may.*

הַצֹּאן This is a DDO not preceded by את

Genesis 29:9 [Lesson 24]

עוֹדֶ֫נּוּ | עוֹד + suffix. Put together it becomes *while he was still. . .* How do we know that the suffix is 3 m. sg. and not 1 c. pl.? It could be either, but 90% of the time it's 3 m. sg. and that PGN fits the context better. The construction of עוֹדֶ֫נּוּ is like that in מִמֶּ֫נִּי (Gen. 22:12) אֶתְּנֶ֫נָּה (Gen. 28:13) and אֲעַשְּׂרֶ֫נּוּ (Gen. 28:22).

מְדַבֵּר All participles except those in the Qal and Nif'al begin with מ The dagesh in the middle root letter and the shewa ְ under the preformative are indicators of the stem here. That there is no extra endiNG is the sign of what gender and number?

עִמָּם Constructed like עִמָּךְ (Gen. 28:15) Some prepositions take הֶם____ as the 3 m. pl. suffix as in אֲלֵהֶם and some, like this one, take only ם____

וְרָחֵל The conjunction acts as a connecting link to the preceding clause, introducing the action that was going on עוֹדֶנּוּ מְדַבֵּר עִמָּם

בָּאָה For help with the form, see בָּאָה (Gen. 29:6)

לְאָבִיהָ For help with the suffix, see עָלֶיהָ (Gen. 28:13)

רֹעָה 3rd ה participles do not show the ה of the root. The f. sg. endiNG is ָה as in רֹעָה The m. sg. endiNG is ֶה as in רֹעֶה Review the functions of participles. (9.3b)

הִוא For the spelling see Gen. 29:2 same word and for use of independent subject pronouns see 6.6.

Genesis 29:10 [Lesson 24]

וַיְהִי כַּאֲשֶׁר This combination: וַיְהִי כַּאֲשֶׁר + the affix form of the verb means *when so-and-so did....* After the atnaḥ ֑ the second part, *then such-and-such...* will begin.

אֲחִי See אַחַי (Gen. 29:4)

אִמּוֹ There is a conjunction אִם and there is a noun אֵם From which do you think אִמּוֹ is built?

<u>Synopsis</u>

אִם	*if*
עִם	*with*
עַם	*people*
אֵם	*mother*
אִמּוֹ	*his mother*

וַיִּגַּשׁ Featured in 16.5b.

וַיָּגֶל This verb appears in the Qal affix form וְגָלֲלוּ in Gen. 29:3 and 8. Here it is a Qal prefix. The qamets under the prefix pronoun makes it look like a hollow verb (6.1a), and in some forms geminates often masquerade as hollow verbs. Why is the second ל missing? Geminates do not always show the doubled root letter.

וַיַּשְׁקְ See יַשְׁקוּ (Gen. 29:2) for the stem. There the third root letter ה is missing because of the prefix complement. Here it is missing because this is shortened form with vav conversive. The 3 m. sg. Hif`il prefix form without vav conversive is יַשְׁקֶה

Genesis 29:11 [Lesson 24]

וַיִּשַּׁק Look carefully. Where is the missing root letter? This is not a form of שקה If you mix up these two verbs you will have Jacob watering Rachel and kissing the sheep.

קֹלוֹ defectiva spelling.

וַיֵּבְךְּ 16.3a discusses this verb. The sound of ךְּ is a hard, catch-in-the-throat "k" sound. (4.4a)

Exodus 3:1 [Lesson 25]

וּמֹשֶׁה It is a common stylistic device to use the conjunction ו to connect a new narrative to the previous one, and that is its function here.

הָיָה רֹעֶה The combination of the verb היה in the affix form + a participle gives emphasis to action in the past. רֹעֶה being a participle, can be translated verbally, *was shepherding* or as the noun *shepherd*. Here the verbal form fits better because there is a DDO coming up as you can tell by the word אֶת which follows. If you said *And Moses was a shepherd*, what would you do with אֶת־צֹאן
Compare the translation of the participle here with כִּי רֹעָה הִוא (Gen 29:9)

אֶת־צֹאן This is a DDO but there is no definite article. You would expect to see אֶת־הַצֹּאן But looking ahead to the next few words, you can see that צֹאן is the first part of a construct chain and the definiteness of the word(s) in the absolute makes the whole chain definite. (5.2) Where do you think the chain ends?

חֹתְנוֹ The root is ___________

אֶת־הַצֹּאן Notice that here the definite article is used because there is no other element to make the noun definite.

וַיִּנְהַג When a clause with the verb הָיָה is followed by a clause with a vav conversive, as is the case in this verse, it means that the two actions are going on at the same time. The second verb introduces the main action.

אַחַר הַמִּדְבָּר We generally translate מִדְבָּר as *wilderness*. But it is a word which has shades of meaning peculiar to the geography and topography of Israel and its environs. It most often refers to large tracts of sparsely inhabited land used for pasturage. Some areas of מִדְבָּר actually supported cities; some were desolate. But the term is not meant to give an image of uninhabitable desert; there are other words for that.
אַחַר הַמִּדְבָּר emphasizes the isolation of Moses.

אֶל־הַר הָאֱלֹהִים חֹרֵבָה | **חֹרֵב** is a proper noun. Notice that two different ways of expressing "direction toward" are used in this segment of the verse. The best way to put together the elements of אֶל־הַר הָאֱלֹהִים חֹרֵבָה is to think of there being a comma between הָאֱלֹהִים and חֹרֵבָה

Text Criticism

↓

Note the small superscript "a" after [a]הָאֱלֹהִים It refers to text note "a" for this verse, found at the bottom of the page. (This assumes you are using *Biblia Hebraica.*)

Cp 3, 1[a]	is what to look for first.
||	is the division mark between text notes.
Cp	Chapter
3,1	Chapter and verse are divided by a comma. The chapter number is given only for the first note in the chapter. After that, only the verse numbers are given.
a	the first note for this verse.

Before interpreting this particular note, there is another matter to be considered. There are many more textual variants that could be listed, many more observations from the ancient versions which could be noted, than could possibly be included in a volume this size. So we begin with the presumption that the editors were selective, not haphazard, in deciding which to print and which to omit. Presumably these notes are here to aid the reader in some way, to help with a difficulty, whether it be grammatical, lexical, stylistic, theological, or whatever. It is a good habit to cultivate when looking at textual notes, to begin by asking yourself what the editors are trying to fix. Sometimes the difficulty is plain; sometimes it is esoteric. At other times you may even be reminded of that great maxim, "If it ain't broke, don't fix it." Students and scholars alike approach these text critical notes with varying degrees of skepticism or enthusiasm. Whether or not the notes sway us to consider an alternate reading, they are nonetheless valuable as an insight into other text traditions.

The notes are given in a very compressed, sometimes even cryptic, form. The note we are considering, 3[a], consists of three symbols:

> G*

Consulting the key at the front of BHS, you can "translate" the note to read, literally, "not in / Septuagint / original" or "not in the original Septuagint."

Some questions to ponder and perhaps discuss:

1. What is the difficulty with הָאֱלֹהִים in this context? In other words, why do you think the editor selected this word for comment? Do you think his concern is grammatical, stylistic, or theological?
2. What is the Septuagint [LXX]?
3. What is the "original" LXX?
4. Where is the "original" LXX today?
5. How could the determination be made that something was not in the "original" LXX? (Remember that the language of the LXX is Greek, not Hebrew.)
6. Are there any other extant sources which seem to find this phrase a problem?
7. If all you had was your Hebrew text, could you make sense out of this passage as it stands?

Exodus 3:2 [Lesson 25]

וַיֵּרָא According to the missing letter rule in Lesson 3.1 this verb looks as if it should be a 1st י The "rules" are valuable and they work most of the time but not here. וַיֵּרָא is the 3 m. sg. Nif'al of ראה with vav conversive. We encountered this verb, stem, and form but without vav conversive in Gen. 22:14 יֵרָאֶה and discussed the Nif'al prefix vowel pattern in that same chapter and verse with the verb יֵאָמֵר But with vav conversive, there is often a shortened form for verbs with weak letters, and so all that is left of the characteristic Nif'al prefix vowel pattern for a 3rd ה verb is ◌ ◌ִ | ◌ֵ

בְּלַבַּת Here is a case where the text critical note (2a) may help to identify the root. The Samaritan Pentateuch has בלהבת at this point, indicating that the dagesh forte represents an assimilated ה something rarely seen. Another provocative thought is that the root is לבב (Our thanks to George Landes for this latter suggestion.)

מִתּוֹךְ What two elements make up this word?

וַיַּ֫רְא Be sure you can distinguish this confidently from וַיֵּרָא at the beginning of the verse.

אֵינֶ֫נּוּ | אֵין is the construct form of אַיִן (vocabulary word not to be confused with עַיִן and see Gen. 28:17). The suffix is discussed in אֲעַשְּׂרֶ֫נּוּ (Gen. 28:22)

אֻכָּל The first thing to determine is whether the dagesh represents an assimilated letter or strengthening of the middle root letter. Or to ask the question another way, is the א part of the root or a prefix pronoun? There are roots for both possibilities, but would a 1 c. sg. subject make sense here? So the root is ________

There are few verbs in the Pu'al stem in the Hebrew Bible. Qibbuts ◌ֻ under the first root letter and the dagesh forte in the middle root letter are sure signs of that stem. אֻכָּל may be an irregular spelling of the Pu'al participle which should read מְאֻכָּל Another way of reading the form is as an archaic 3 m. sg. Qal passive affix form.

Exodus 3:3 [Lesson 25]

אָסֻרָה־נָּא One clue to this verb form is נָּא at the end of the phrase. It is seen with imperatives as in קַח־נָא (Gen. 22:2) and imperative-like forms. In the word אָסֻרָה the prefix pronoun א and the ending ה ָ reinforce the cohortative pattern. (See נֵלְכָה Gen. 22:5.) Removing those two letters leaves only two letters for the root. The vowel under the prefix pronoun is the indicator of the missing root letter. (6.1a) In hollow verbs the vowel between the two strong letters indicates the missing root letter. Qibbuts ֻ becomes וּ in the middle position. Of course א and ה can be root letters, but when you see the possibility of a first person prefix pronoun, ה ָ at the end of a verb and נָא immediately following, you should be thinking "cohortative."

וְאֶרְאֶה אֶת־הַמַּרְאֶה If you look closely you will see that the consonants ר א ה are common to both words, which means that וְאֶרְאֶה and הַמַּרְאֶה probably come from the same root. First look at the verb. It is a safe assumption that it is a cohortative because of the link with the verb before it, although you don't see an additional ה at the end: 3rd ה verbs don't add an extra ה in the cohortative.

What about the conjunction וְ Can it be vav conversive? (14.5a) Can it be vav reversive? With a cohortative the conjunction וְ often serves to express intention, *that I may...*

A word about הַמַּרְאֶה Nouns which end in ה need another component to make them feminine. (14.2b) Does this one have it? (See also The Noun A.)

מַדּוּעַ Some dictionaries list the word just this way. If your dictionary doesn't, look under the root ידע

יִבְעַר Although we usually translate prefix forms in the future, there are other possibilities. In this case the present is better. We must not forget that prefix form expresses <u>incomplete action</u>, not a specific tense.

Exodus 3:4 [Lesson 26]

סָר One way to determine the root is to recognize that this verb appears in Ex. 3:3 in the phrase אָסֻרָה־נָּא Another is to know that when you see two strong letter and qamets ָ or pataḥ ַ under the first one, you most likely have a 3 m. sg. Qal affix of a hollow verb. A pluperfect translation would be appropriate here. Notice how often the subject switches in this verse.

לִרְאוֹת 25.3b discusses this very word.

Exodus 3:5 [Lesson 26]

אַל־תִּקְרַב | אַל in front of a prefix form of a verb is the sign of the negative imperative. It is the only circumstance in which אַל is used with a verb.

הֲלֹם An adverb.

שַׁל is a verb. How can you tell? You just saw a negative imperative in direct speech and there are likely to be other verbs as the speech continues. שַׁל looks as if it could be a 3 m. sg. Qal affix of a hollow verb according to what we just said about סָר (Ex. 3:4) but there is no root שׁיל or שׁול An alternative is the imperative, because they often appear in clusters, especially in direct speech. Verbs whose first root letter is weak may lose that weak letter in the imperative. (20.6a) Of the two most likely possibilities, which shows the vocalization of שַׁל in the imperative? (16.2)

נְעָלֶיךָ. . .רַגְלֶיךָ What are the state, gender, and number of these nouns? Look at text note 5[a]. This note may be not so much the editor's solution to a problem as giving us an interesting bit of information. Again, using the key, we can "translate" the note: "many / manuscripts / Samaritan Pentateuch / Septuagint / Vulgate / נַעַלְךָ"

1. How many manuscripts are represented by "many"?
2. Could the LXX or the Vulgate really say נַעַלְךָ
3. How might this change, from plural to singular, have come about?
4. 5[b] seems to support 5[a] for a change to the singular but strangely cites different sources: adds one, subtracts 2, and keeps one the same.

כִּי is introducing a clause just as it did in Ex. 3:4 but we would use a different conjunction here in English.

אֲשֶׁר אַתָּה עוֹמֵד עָלָיו This type of construction is discussed in 22.8a.

אַדְמַת־קֹדֶשׁ This is a construct chain. The first link is the feminine noun אֲדָמָה undergoing the regular change for the construct form. (22.4) קֹדֶשׁ is a masculine noun. Using two nouns together rather than a noun and an adjective, as we might in English, is regular syntax in Hebrew.

Exodus 3:6 [Lesson 26]

אָבִ֫יךָ As you go on to read the verse you will see that a plural noun seems to make more sense here. Note 6[a] cites some sources where a plural does in fact appear, but these are minor citations. Also, a difficult reading is not necessarily an incorrect reading.

וַיַּסְתֵּר Is this a Pi'el? Don't let the dagesh in the ת sway you too quickly; wait at least until you check the vowel before it. Also check the vowel under the prefix pronoun. (15.5) This is a Hif'il prefix. Two distinguishing characteristics of this stem and form are discussed with וַיַּשְׁכֵּם (Gen. 22:3)

פָּנָיו | פָּנָיו is a DDO but it is not preceded by את The omission of the DDO marker is something you will see from time to time, although more frequently in poetry than in prose.

יָרֵא 17.7 discusses the pointing for this form.

מֵהַבִּיט Abstracting the root from this word is a real challenge. The מ looks like either a noun indicator, participial preformative, or the attached preposition מִן The ה looks like either the sign of the definite article, a Hif'il preformative, or a root letter. The dagesh in the בּ looks like either the footprint of an assimilated letter, confirmation of the definite article, or the sign of the Pi'el. The י is a vowel letter (it has no vowel of its own) and so is not a serious contender for a root letter. Since root letters come in a cluster, let's try הבט It isn't a root, which means that מ here cannot be a participial preformative or a noun indicator. Therefore, it is ________________ That הבט is not a root also means ה is not a root letter, and so the dagesh cannot be the sign of the Pi'el. Because a noun can't be derived from בט the הַ is not the definite article; that leaves it with its being the sign of the Hif'il. So, the dagesh must be __________________ and the root is __________ The prefixed preposition strongly suggests infinitive form. You have seen the following <u>verb</u> patterns:

1. Preformative ה | וַהֲשִׁבֹתִיךָ (Gen. 28:15); וְהֵשִׁיבוּ (Gen. 29:3); וְהִשְׁקוּ (Gen. 29:3)
2. Prefix pronoun or other preformative + pataḥ _ and a dot vowel between the second and third root letter: וַיַּשְׁכֵּם (Gen. 22:3) וַיַּעֲלֵהוּ (Gen. 22:13) מַגִּיעַ (Gen. 28:12). 93% of the time these patterns will yield a Hif'il. Where are the other 7%? See הֲיְדַעְתֶּם (Gen. 29:5) and הֵאָסֵף (Gen. 29:7)

Another problem here is how to translate the preposition מִן Although it is awkward English to say *from looking,* do you think *to look* means the same thing?

Exodus 3:7 [Lesson 27]

רָאֹה רָאִיתִי See עַשֵּׂר אֲעַשְּׂרֶנּוּ (Gen. 28:22) for a discussion of this construction and 26.5 for a discussion of the conjugated form of the verb.

עֳנִי This sounds like, but is not, the first person independent pronoun אֲנִי It looks as if it might be a two letter noun with the 1 c. sg. possessive suffix. However, two letter words almost always have a dagesh in the second letter when a suffix is added. (See עִמְּךָ Gen. 28:15.) So perhaps this word is not made up of these two elements. Roots do not end in י When there is a word, like this one, whose third letter is י and the י is not the 1 c. sg. possessive suffix, it is likely that the root from which the noun is derived is composed of the first two letters of the word + ה

עַמִּי You can see how the composition of this word differs from עֳנִי

צַעֲקָתָם Remember, a noun most usually takes the construct form when a suffix is added. (The Noun G) Why can this not be a 2 m. pl. Qal affix?

נֹגְשָׂיו Be careful not to confuse the root here with the more common נגשׁ You may have noticed that this is a plural noun with a singular suffix and that just before was צַעֲקָתָם a singular noun with a plural suffix. Both of these words refer to the collective עַם Switching from singular to plural and vice versa is common Biblical Hebrew style. There is another frequently used stylistic device in this verse, **chiasm**, in which the words are arranged:

verb — direct object
direct object — verb

יָדַעְתִּי For a discussion of the translation of the affix form of ידע see Gen. 22:12.

אֶת־מַכְאֹבָיו Although this word is made up of several elements, it should not be too difficult to break down. אֵת in front indicates that the word functions as a __________ Root letters come in a cluster. The rest should be smooth sailing.

Exodus 3:8 [Lesson 27]

וָאֵרֵד 14.5 discusses the unusual pointing of the conjunction. Look at text note 8[a]. Can you see the different nuance the alternate reading would impart?

לְהַצִּילוֹ This word is constructed like מֵהַבִּיט (Ex. 3:6) with two differences. Here the first letter is unambiguously a preposition, and there is a suffix to cope with. The antecedent for the suffix is in Ex. 3:7a.

מִצְרַיִם The name of the country is also used for the name of the people.

וּלְהַעֲלֹתוֹ After removing the conjunction, preposition, and suffix, you are still faced with too many letters for a root. Consider the function of the ה It is not part of the root because there is no root העל It is unlikely to be the definite article because the ה of the definite article would normally elide after a preposition. An interrogative ה would not appear in this position in a verse. (See הַיְדַעְתֶּם Gen. 29:5.) That leaves us with a Hif'il indicator. Any further problems? See 25.3b.

הַהִוא See Gen. 29.2 same word.

זָבַת Here are three strong letters but a search through the dictionary has, no doubt, revealed that they do not compose a root. זָבַת is a f. sg. participle in the construct. It is from the hollow verb זוּב Hollow verbs have an irregular participial form in the Qal. (9.5a) The f. sg. Qal participle in the absolute is זָבָה and so, remembering the endiNG that f. sg. nouns have in the construct (22.4a), it follows that זָבַת is precisely that, even though it certainly is not immediately apparent. Usually we use *of* to link the construct with the absolute, but here *with* works better.

הַכְּנַעֲנִי 22.5 discusses the gentilic ending.

Exodus 3:9 [Lesson 27]

בָּאָה The form is discussed in Gen. 29:9 same word. The subject is ____________

רָאִיתִי Learn the chart in 26.5 if you had to refer to it.

לֹחֲצִים The ל is not a preposition here. Although prefixed prepositions take different vowels, they are never pointed with holem. The vowel pattern and endiNG indicate that לֹחֲצִים is a ____________ What is its subject?

אֹתָם 23.2b discusses the vocalization.

Exodus 3:10 [Lesson 28]

לְכָה | לְכָה is a lengthened form of the m. sg. imperative לֵךְ The ה ָ ending is analogous to the cohortative ending. (See אָסֻרָה Ex. 3:3.) It is not unusual to see it on an imperative. It may be there for no other reason than that it sounds better.

וְאֶשְׁלָחֲךָ This word may be harder to pronounce than to break down. What is the function of the ו Is it possible for it to be vav reversive or vav conversive? (See וְאֶרְאֶה Ex.3:3.)

וְהוֹצֵא Remove the conjunction. Set aside the vowel letter ו (See יְחִידְךָ Gen 22: 2.) That leaves the combination ה צ א which is not a root. A final א and a middle צ will always be root letters but ה in the first position may function as something other than a root letter. A familiar root using צא is יצא and that is the root here. What about the function of the ה It is not pointed for the definite article or the interrogative ה and so Hif`il indicator seems to be the best choice. Back to the vowel letter ו Why could it not have been considered for a root letter? Because no root starts with vav. Whenever there is a stem indicator or a prefix pronoun followed by a וֹ you have a 1st י verb. To confirm the Hif`il, note the "dot vowel" tsere ֵ between the second and third root letters. הוֹצֵא is a m. sg. Hif`il imperative. יצא is *go out* so the Hif`il is *cause to go out*, in other words *bring out.*

Exodus 3:11 [Lesson 28]

מִי The interrogative pronoun *who?*

כִּי אֵלֵךְ | כִּי followed by the prefix form often expresses purpose *that I should...*

אוֹצִיא Review the remarks about וְהוֹצֵא (Ex. 3:10) The form here is ____________

Exodus 3:12 [Lesson 28]

כִּי־אֶהְיֶה | כִּי can have many meanings. In this context it is expressing absolute certainty. Notice how different the sense seems here from that in the phrase כִּי אֵלֵךְ

(Ex. 3:11) Part of the difference lies in their syntactical settings: כִּי־אֶהְיֶה is the main clause of a statement and כִּי אֵלֵךְ is the subordinate clause of a question.

עִמָּךְ You would expect to see this phrase pointed עִמְּךָ Once again the change in pointing is due to the accent.

וְזֶה־לְּךָ These elements, when translated into English require a verb to link them together. What tense will you give the needed verb?

הָאוֹת The pattern ___וֹת looks like a 3rd ה infinitive. (25.3b) It also looks like a f. pl. noun. (22.4) But there is no root האה And a fortunate thing too. Can you imagine conjugating a triply rebellious, doubly weak, first guttural, 3rd ה verb? The ה is none other than the definite article and אוֹת is a noun. Why is it not preceded by את

כִּי The translation of the conjunction will affect the meaning of the rest of the verse.

אָנֹכִי What do you think is the purpose of the independent subject pronoun here?

שְׁלַחְתִּיךָ The components are straightforward but the landmark vowel of the Qal affix has been shortened because of the addition of a suffix.

בְּהוֹצִיאֲךָ Remove the preposition and the suffix. That leaves הוציא This consonant cluster appears in Ex. 3:10 with one difference. There it has a defectiva spelling and here we see a plene spelling. But again it is a Hif'il form of יצא The preposition in front of the root indicates that the form is most likely ___________ בְּ often means *in* but it can also have a temporal meaning when used with an infinitive. The PGN of the suffix is ________ The literal translation of this whole combination is *in-your-causing-to-go-out.* More colloquially we can say *when you bring out.*

תַּעַבְדוּן The paragogic or emphatic ן is an optional ending for a prefix form that ends in a vowel. There are a lot of these endings in Deuteronomy.

Exodus 3:13 [Lesson 28]

הִנֵּה אָנֹכִי בָא How many reasons can you give to support your choice of meaning for the ambiguous verb form? (9.3b) The sense is of imminent action *about to.*

אֲבוֹתֵיכֶם Compare **אֲבוֹתֵיכֶם** with **אָבִיךָ** (Ex. 3:6)

שְׁלָחַנִי First remove the suffix. What is left is a potentially ambiguous form. The shewa under the first root letter looks like the sign of a m. sg. Qal imperative. (18.1a) But look at **שְׁלַחְתִּיךָ** (Ex. 3:12) What happened there to the qamets ָ under the **שׁ** **שְׁלָחַנִי** is the same combination of parts, but its PGN does not have additional consonants. If this were an unpointed text, the 3 m. sg. Qal affix + suffix **שְׁלָחַנִי** and the m. sg. Qal imperative + suffix **שְׁלָחֵנִי** would look identical.

שְׁמוֹ *Name* is often a synonym for power. **מַה־שְּׁמוֹ** implies the question, *What are his great deeds? What is his power?* as well as *What is his name/identity?*

אֹמַר This verb form appears in Gen. 22:2. There are only five first **א** verbs in which the **א** of the root regularly elides in the first person singular prefix form. They are:

אמר *say* **אבה** *be willing* **אכל** *eat* **אפה** *bake* **אבד** *perish*

They can be remembered by this little ditty:

The bride **said** to the bridegroom, "I am **willing** to **eat** what you **bake** though I **perish**."

Review of terms

Elide: A letter disappears without a trace: **אֹמַר** for **אאמר**

Assimilate: A letter disappears but leaves a footprint dagesh: **וַיִּתֵּן** for **וינתן**

Quiesce: A letter loses its vowel and its own sound. Though it can still be seen in the word, it cannot be heard: the **א** in **וַיֹּאמֶר**

Quiesce, Elide, and Assimilate
Went out for a stroll about half past eight.
Quiesce was seen, but never heard.
Elide disappeared without a word.
Whatever happened to assimilate?
A footprint dagesh points to its fate.

Exodus 3:14 [Lesson 29]

אֶהְיֶה אֲשֶׁר אֶהְיֶה "Incomplete action" expressed in the prefix form can imply endless time. Present and/or future tense severely limits the sense of timelessness implied here. אֲשֶׁר can mean *who, what,* or *which.* אֶהְיֶה may be a word play on יהוה perhaps stressing that aspect of God which causes to be. (Reading אהיה unpointed tempts us to entertain the possibility of a Hif'il.) In any case, this is a mysterious and elusive answer, stressing God's essence and eternity. It might be best to leave this phrase untranslated.

אֶהְיֶה שְׁלָחַנִי אֲלֵיכֶם A literal translation of אֶהְיֶה is never used here.

Exodus 3:15 [Lesson 29]

לְדֹר דֹּר Two words repeated can convey continuity. Here idiomatic use of prepositions has to be supplied in translation to get the meaning across.

Exodus 3:16 [Lesson 29]

לֵךְ וְאָסַפְתָּ...וְאָמַרְתָּ An imperative followed by an affix form gives the affix imperative force, so it is as if there were a string of commands even though not every verb is in the imperative form. Text note 16[a] could lead to an interesting "political" discussion!

נִרְאָה presents a few possibilities: נ in this position can be a root letter, the 1 c. pl. prefix pronoun or it can be a Nif'al preformative. The first choice doesn't lead to an extant root; the second doesn't fit the context. נִרְאָה is a Nif'al affix. Because there is no additional affix pronoun the PGN is __________ In Gen. 22:14 God also "appears." There the verb is יֵרָאֶה the 3 m. sg. Nif'al prefix of ראה

פָּקֹד פָּקַדְתִּי There is a discussion of this construction with the phrase עַשֵּׂר אֲעַשְּׂרֶנּוּ (Gen. 28:22)

הֶעָשׂוּי Look at the chart of 3rd ה verbs (26.5) and notice that a י stands in for the ה in some cases when a subject pronoun is added. Well, here is a case of a 3rd ה verb undergoing a different change which also causes the י to appear. הֶעָשׂוּי is a m. sg. Qal passive participle: *that which is done.* (Remember, a participle is the one verb form which can take the definite article.) The Qal passive participle is formed by inserting ו between the second and third root letters, e.g.: בָּרוּךְ אַתָּה *blessed are you.* In a 3rd ה passive participle, the ו is between the second root letter and the substitute for the third root letter.

Exodus 3:17 [Lesson 29]

וָאֹמַר The conjunction is pointed as in וָאֵרֵד (Ex. 3:8) Text note 17[a] points out that the Septuagint has a 3 m. sg. subject pronoun here.

אַעֲלֶה Pataḥ ַ under the prefix pronoun is a sign of the Hif`il prefix and the dot vowel, a segol ֶ in this case, confirms it. The Qal prefix of many 1st guttural verbs mimics the Hif`il prefix. (17.3a) But in the Qal, the 1 c. sg. prefix pronoun usually takes segol before a guttural. So with the verb עלה for example, the 1 c. sg. Qal prefix form is אֶעֱלֶה

מֵעֳנִי See עֳנִי (Ex. 3:7)

זָבַת See Ex. 3:8 same word.

Genesis 37:1 [Lesson 30]

וַיֵּשֶׁב You have seen many shortened forms of the prefix with vav conversive. Below is a sample of such forms seen in the readings so far. Identify the root in each.

________	וַיֵּלֶךְ	(Gen. 28:10)	________	וַיְהִי	(Gen. 22:1)
________	וַיֵּגֶל	(Gen. 29:11)	________	וַיָּקָם	(Gen. 22:3)
________	וַיַּשְׁק	(Gen. 29:10)	________	וַיַּרְא	(Gen. 22.4)
________	וַיֵּבְךְּ	(Gen. 29:11)	________	וַיָּשֶׂם	(Gen. 22:6)
________	וַיֵּרָא	(Ex. 3:2)	________	וַיִּבֶן	(Gen. 22.9)

בְּאֶרֶץ Is this word definite or indefinite?

מְגוּרֵי The endiNG reveals that you are looking at what form of the word? If your dictionary does not list this word under מ where would you look next?

Genesis 37:2 [Lesson 30]

אֵלֶּה תֹּלְדוֹת | תֹּלְדוֹת is from the root ילד The whole phrase is often used when a report of a genealogy is about to begin. But as you read on you will see that doesn't happen here. How is אֵלֶּה related to תֹּלְדוֹת (15.2)

בֶּן־שְׁבַע־עֶשְׂרֵה שָׁנָה The idiom for telling someone's age is *a son (or daughter) of so-and-so-many-a-year.* The number is composed much the same way as we compound it in English.

הָיָה רֹעֶה אֶת־אֶחָיו The construction looks the same as הָיָה רֹעֶה אֶת־צֹאן in Ex. 3:1, but is it?

אֶחָיו An unscientific but practical way to tell the singular from the plural of אָח with a 3 m. sg. endiNG is: אָחִיו אֶחָיו

one dot one brother ↑ ↑ more than one dot, more than one brother

בַּצֹּאן The individual words from **רֹעֶה** to here are not difficult but you may be having trouble making sense out of them. **רֹעֶה בַּצֹּאן** constitutes an idiom meaning *herdsman,* and if you put mental commas around **אֶת־אֶחָיו** it will all fall into place.

וְהוּא נַעַר Another parenthetical remark in the form of a noun sentence.

אֶת־בְּנֵי Again think of the two possibilities for **אֶת**

נְשֵׁי This is the construct of an irregular noun. (See: The Noun H.) Notice particularly the m. pl. endiNG on a feminine noun.
Are there any other **בָּנִים** or other **נָשִׁים** you would expect to see mentioned here?

וַיָּבֵא You have seen **וַיָּבֹא** and this form looks as if it comes from the same the same root. It does indeed! It is the 3 m. sg. Hif'il prefix with vav conversive. The familiar pataḥ _ is not under the prefix pronoun (see **וַיַּשְׁכֵּם** Gen. 22:3) because the missing letter convention takes precedence over the pataḥ rule. Notice that a "dot vowel" is taking the place of the middle root letter. (29.2)

דִּבָּתָם The root of **דִּבָּתָם** is the geminate **דבב** If you have difficulty finding the form in the dictionary review 22.4a.

רָעָה This word certainly looks like it might be related to **רֹעֶה** further back in the verse, but in this context, it isn't. It is an adjective from the root **רעע** You should be able to see three features that **דִּבָּתָם** and **רָעָה** have in common.

Genesis 37:3 [Lesson 30]

וְיִשְׂרָאֵל אָהַב אֶת־יוֹסֵף מִכָּל־בָּנָיו After translating this clause, you may decide to use a comparative adverb for **מִכָּל** even though that does not match a more literal translation.

זְקֻנִים The root is ______ A noun in the plural may be used to express an abstract idea.

לוֹ Which use of **לוֹ** is this? (7.5)

וְעָשָׂה לוֹ To treat the verb as an affix plus vav reversive doesn't work. This may be a special use of the vav reversive which we saw in Gen. 29:3. An affix followed by an affix plus vav reversive may refer to an action which has been completed but has been done more than one time. You can see from text note 3[a] that the difficulty of this construction has not gone unnoticed.

כְּתֹנֶת פַּסִּים This phrase occurs five times in the Bible: three times in the Joseph story (Gen. 37:3, 23 and 32) and twice in the story of Tamar (2 Samuel 13:18 and 19). What is fascinating is that traditionally the tunic is called, in English translation, *a coat of many colors* when Joseph's coat is being referred to, but Tamar's garment is called a *long robe with sleeves.* The noun **פַּס** means *flat of hand or foot.* So maybe this was a garment which reached to the palms and to the soles. There is no etymological evidence that this was a coat of many colors. Where does the famous image come from? It is as old as some of the earliest translations. Ancient Egyptian tomb paintings show that there was indeed a striped garment worn by Hebrew dignitaries. Later evidence from Middle Eastern countries shows that coats into which colored threads were woven were worn by young boys of rank.
It is possible that the idea of a *coat of many colors* came from sociological assumption rather than from an attempt at literal translation accuracy. In any case the robe must have had some special significance.

Genesis 37:4 [Lesson 30]

וַיִּרְאוּ According to the missing letter rules (3.1; 6.1a; 12.1) what should the root be? ______ Is it? ______ (17.5) If this were being recited, do you think the listener might think the root is something else? Do you think it possible that some ambiguity is intended?

אֹתוֹ Notice the emphatic position of **אֹתוֹ** in this part of the verse. It is placed before the verb rather than the more usual place following both the verb and subject.

יָכְלוּ Of the consonants in this word, it is sure that the cluster **כל** is part of the root. ו_ _ _ indicates what PGN? The potentially ambiguous component is the initial **יָ**. It could be part of the root of a Qal affix. (4.2 and 8.1) But perhaps you are thinking, "hollow verb in the Qal prefix." (6.1) It may help to remember that in a hollow verb, Qal prefix (<u>without</u> vav conversive), the middle root letter will appear.

_ י _	_ ו _	_ ו _
יָשִׂימוּ	יָבוֹאוּ	יָכוּלוּ

דַּבְּרוֹ The root, stem, and suffix are familiar. What vowel would you expect under the first root letter if this were a Pi`el affix? (15.4) There are two Pi`el forms which take pataḥ under the first root letter. One is the ______________ (19.2a) The other is the Pi`el infinitive. Which form makes more sense here? Note 4[b] is a nice help.

לְשָׁלֹם This is an example of yet another use of the preposition **לְ** in front of a noun. Some English translations have it give the noun an adverbial sense.

Genesis 37:5 [Lesson 31]

וַיַּחֲלֹם If the pointing looks ambiguous check the vowel between the second and third root letters and then 17.3a if you are still stumped.

חֲלוֹם You can see that the DO and the verb are built from the same root. Why is this DO not preceded by **אֶת**

וַיַּגֵּד When you are looking for a missing root letter what do you do first? (The answer is not *cry!*) Look for a footprint dagesh. Only if that doesn't work do you try the missing letter rules. (16.1b) The next question is why is pataḥ ַ under the prefix pronoun? There are two verb stems which may take that pointing in the prefix, one of which you have already learned. (12.3) The other you have seen in the readings [**וַיַּשְׁכֵּם** Gen 22:3 for example]. Here the pointing is characteristic of the Hif`il prefix and of course we look for a dot vowel under the second root letter to confirm that stem. This particular verb, which is quite common, occurs almost exclusively in the Hif`il.

לְאֶחָיו See **אֶחָיו** Gen. 37:2. Note that sometimes English wants a pronominal direct object *he made it known to his brothers*, although Hebrew does not need one.

וַיּוֹסִפוּ | **וֹ** between the prefix pronoun and the root means the missing root letter is ____ (31.2) So the root is __________ (Does this root not evoke the name of the leading persona in this drama?) Look at the vowel under the second root letter. What stem most often has this type of vowel in this position in the prefix form?

שְׂנֹא 25.4 discusses the pointing of this form.

Now look at the whole phrase **וַיּוֹסִפוּ עוֹד שְׂנֹא אֹתוֹ** The words make sense individually but it doesn't seem to flow very well in English. Although **יסף** means *increase* or *add*, it is very often used, as it is here, to mean *to do something more strongly*. Thus there are two strengthenings (expressed in the verb and the adverb) to the basic idea **שָׂנְאוּ אֹתוֹ**

Genesis 37:6 [Lesson 31]

שִׁמְעוּ־נָא For help with the form see 20.6a.

הַחֲלוֹם 21.3a explains the pointing of the definite article before a guttural. **ח** is a "strong" guttural and often does not cause compensation in the preceding vowel for an inadmissible dagesh. This happens whether it is the part of a noun or a verb that needs a dagesh (if it is the middle root letter of a Pi`el for example). We are supposed to assume that the necessary doubling is "implied."

Genesis 37:7 [Lesson 31]

מְאַלְּמִים The root is ________ What choices of form does the endiNG provide? What can the preformative **מ** be? What stem would you deduce this word to be from?

אֲלֻמִּים This word is a sibling of the word just before it.

קָמָה If the root cannot be **קמה** is there a consonant you can remove? What possibilities are there for a missing letter? Which one gives you a familiar root? Reread Genesis 29:6 **וְהִנֵּה רָחֵל בִּתּוֹ בָּאָה** for a refresher on this form.

אֲלֻמָּתִי Does seeing **תִי**____ at the end of the word cause the reflex response, "1 c. sg. affix pronoun?" Why could it not be here? What else could these components be?

נִצָּבָה Perhaps this word looks familiar. The root appears in **מֻצָּב** (Gen. 28:12) in **נִצָּב** (Gen. 28:13) and in **מַצֵּבָה** (Gen 28:18)

תְּסֻבֶּינָה A prefix pronoun pointed with shewa ְ and a dagesh forte in the second root letter should signal "Pi`el," in which case the third root letter would be ____ However, there is no such root. The root is סבב a geminate verb, so you can see that the dagesh is representing the doubled ב of the root. The י is a connecting letter in this case. Incidentally, תְּסֻבֶּינָה does read exactly like a 3rd ה Pi`el. Geminates are the **great masqueraders**, taking on the characteristics of other verb types. Bear in mind that when all else fails to yield a root, think of the possibility of a geminate.

וַתִּשְׁתַּחֲוֶיןָ The root and stem were discussed with וְנִשְׁתַּחֲוֶה (Gen. 22:5) The endiNG you see here ןָ is a variant of the more usual f. pl. prefix complement נָה____ What element constitutes the prefix pronoun? What is the subject of this verb?

לַאֲלֻמָּתִי The root of this word appears five times in this verse. Look especially at the phrase מְאַלְּמִים אֲלֻמִּים and then at אֲלֻמֹּתֵיכֶם Do you see anything unusual about the gender?

Genesis 37:8 [Lesson 31]

אֶחָיו How does this word relate to וַיֹּאמְרוּ

הֲמָלֹךְ The root is __________ What is the function of the הֲ Choices to consider: definite article, Hif`il preformative, root letter, interrogative ה

תִּמְלֹךְ What are the stem, form, and PGN of this verb form? For a review of the whole construction הֲמָלֹךְ תִּמְלֹךְ see עַשֵּׂר אֲעַשְּׂרֶנּוּ (Gen. 28:22)

עָלֵינוּ What is the function of the י (See אֵלֶיךָ Gen. 22.2.)

אִם Although used most frequently to mean *if,* אִם can have other meanings. *Or* seems to work here.

מָשׁוֹל תִּמְשֹׁל A repetition of the same construction seen earlier in the verse with the root מלך The interrogative mood carries through this phrase. Notice the plene spelling of מָשׁוֹל

The force of these infinitive absolute phrases is far stronger, more impressive and euphonic than anything we can do with them in English.

בָּנוּ Choices: a 3 c. pl. Qal affix of a 3rd ה or a preposition + DO. Luckily, context can resolve the dilemma.

וַיּוֹסִפוּ עוֹד שְׂנֹא אֹתוֹ An exact repetition of the phrase in Gen. 37:5.

עַל־חֲלֹמֹתָיו | עַל here gives the sense of *because of*, or *on account of.* Can you identify the components of **חֲלֹמֹתָיו** Pay particular attention to the gender and number of the segments.

Genesis 37:9 [Lesson 32]

אַחֵר Not the same as **אַחַר**

אֹתוֹ To what is the suffix referring?

לְאֶחָיו See Gen. 37:2 same word.

וְאַחַד עָשָׂר Add these two numbers together.

מִשְׁתַּחֲוִים The root and stem are discussed with **וְנִשְׁתַּחֲוֶה** (Gen. 22:5) The preformative **מ** may indicate ______________ and the endiNG is ________

Genesis 37:10 [Lesson 32]

וַיִּגְעַר־בּוֹ 16.7a discusses the combination: verb + preposition + DO.

הֲבוֹא נָבוֹא Like **הֲמָלֹךְ תִּמְלֹךְ** (Gen. 37:8) What is the PGN of **נָבוֹא**

וְאִמְּךָ Why is there a dagesh in the **מ** (See **עִמָּךְ** Gen. 28:14.) If the rest of the word is a problem, refer to the synopsis in Gen. 29:10.

לְהִשְׁתַּחֲוֹת | וֹת___ can be the f. pl. noun endiNG or the sign of a 3rd ה infinitive. Which fits the context?

אַרְצָה Need a reminder about the ending? See comments in Gen 28:12, same word.

Genesis 37:11 [Lesson 32]

וַיְקַנְאוּ The difficulty with this word is the identity of its stem. Shewa ְ under the prefix pronoun indicates ______________ (15.5) But there is no dagesh in the middle root letter. The combination dagesh forte + shewa ְּ may cause disappearance of the dagesh ְ a convention which is echoed elsewhere in this word.

וְאָבִיו | ו need not be translated as *and*. It is the "all purpose conjunction" so pick the conjunction you think best links this phrase with the one before it.

הַדָּבָר Suggestions for meanings of this noun occupy four columns in a major dictionary.

Genesis 37:12 [Lesson 32]

לִרְעוֹת That לרע is not a root should cut down your choices in determining the root and form.

Genesis 37:13 [Lesson 33]

הֲלוֹא | לוֹא is the plene spelling for לֹא

לְכָה See Ex. 3:10 same word or 30.1a.

וְאֶשְׁלָחֲךָ Identify the four components of this word.

Genesis 37:14 [Lesson 33]

רְאֵה The context itself is the biggest clue to the form.

וַהֲשִׁבֵנִי That this word begins with a conjunction and ends with a suffix is fairly obvious. The consonants ה ש ב are left. They do not make a root. The one to set aside then is ____ Two familiar roots containing שב are ישב and שוב If the root here were ישב with a ה preformative, then what would have happened to the י of the root? (31.2) The root then is ________

Lesson 29.2 discusses the Hif`il affix of hollow verbs and 30.1 goes on to discuss Hif`il imperatives. But part of the difficulty in identifying these features in וַהֲשִׁבֵנִי is caused by the addition of the suffix, which reduces the vowel under the preformative; also, the word has defectiva spelling. It would be valuable to remember the features of this verb in the Hif`il; it occurs frequently.

וַיִּשְׁלָחֵהוּ   Same root, same form, same components as וְאֶשְׁלָחֲךָ Different PGN and suffix.

Genesis 37:15 [Lesson 33]

וַיִּמְצָאֵהוּ   Another highly inflected verb, but containing no surprises. What is the subject of this verb? How do you know it cannot be Joseph?

תֹעֶה   Pointed like a 3rd ה m. sg. participle, and that is what it is.

וַיִּשְׁאָלֵהוּ הָאִישׁ   The elements of the verb are just like those of וַיִּמְצָאֵהוּ Again it's a matter of sorting out who is the subject and who is the direct object.

Genesis 37:16 [Lesson 33]

וַיֹּאמֶר אֶת־אַחַי   We are not witnessing the phenomenon of an intransitive verb suddenly taking a direct object? This verse, like many others in the chapter, uses inverted word order for emphasis.

מְבַקֵּשׁ   The stem and form are discussed in 31.1.

הַגִּידָה־נָּא   Featured in 30.1.

אֵיפֹה   Which consonant will you leave out to find the three letter root necessary to locate this word in the dictionary?

Genesis 37:17 [Lesson 34]

מִזֶּה | זֶה is functioning as a substantive meaning *this place.*

שָׁמַ֫עְתִּי Text note 17[a] cites sources which read שְׁמַעְתִּים here. Do you think the addition of the suffix alters the sense?

נֵלְכָה Gen. 22.5 same word.

אַחַר אֶחָיו | אַחַר has appeared in different contexts in the readings:

אַחַר הַדְּבָרִים הָאֵלֶּה (Gen. 22:1)

וְהִנֵּה־אַיִל אַחַר (Gen. 22:13)

וַיִּנְהַג אֶת־הַצֹּאן אַחַר הַמִּדְבָּר (Ex. 3:1)

Genesis 37:18 [Lesson 34]

וַיִּרְאוּ Is the root more likely to be ירא or ראה (17.5)

וּבְטֶרֶם A temporal adverb meaning *before.* It appears as בְּטֶרֶם or טֶרֶם without the initial ב

וַיִּתְנַכְּלוּ The stem of this verb is the Hitpa`el. It can be recognized in the prefix form by the prefix pronoun followed by ת and in every form it has a doubled middle root letter. Like all the derived stems it can have many shades of meaning. It is often intensive and usually either reflexive and/or interactive. Here *they planned deceitfully among themselves* seems to make the point.

לַהֲמִיתוֹ The attached preposition should help with the form, and the suffix is familiar. הֲ cannot be interrogative ה because of its position in the word; the clue to its function lies in the suffix which demands a transitive form of the verb. (See 29.1 for help with the root.)

Genesis 37:19 [Lesson 34]

וַיֹּאמְרוּ אִישׁ אֶל־אָחִיו This is an interesting bit of phraseology. We have seen a collective noun taking a singular verb. Now we have just the opposite: a plural verb and what seems to be a singular subject. But אִישׁ meaning *a man* can imply *each man* so *They said each to his brother* would smooth out the English without distorting the meaning of the text.

בַּעַל הַחֲלֹמוֹת הַלָּזֶה This phrase is a complicated construction. First look at הַלָּזֶה It is considered to be an old form of זֶה The adjective הַלָּזֶה modifies בַּעַל though it lies outside the construct chain. Yet it could not be within the construct chain because theoretically, nothing should come between the word in the construct and the word in the absolute. We should think of הַלָּזֶה parenthetically, much like וְהוּא נַעַר (Gen. 37:2) This phrase injects a heavy note of sarcasm.

בָּא Will you treat this as a participle or an affix form?

Genesis 37:20 [Lesson 34]

לְכוּ וְנַהַרְגֵהוּ וְנַשְׁלִכֵהוּ Do you notice that the subject of all these verbs is not the same? This is a feature of Hebrew which is seen quite often. It is not the mark of poor prose; but rather a stylistic device.

הַבֹּרוֹת This is a very difficult word to look up in the dictionary. When faced with six letters, it's time to do surgery. First to be excised from the contenders for consideration as a root letter is the vowel letter וֹ Then there is ◌ַה in front of the word, so it can be assumed that the word is preceded by the definite article. Left are one ב and ר which definitely are root letters and a final ת Well, unfortunately ברת is not a root. It seems logical then to consider וֹת___ a feminine plural noun endiNG. That leaves only two letters for the root, so where is the missing letter? Suppose we try a 3rd ה There is a root ברה In fact there is more than one. There just isn't one that makes any sense here. We have to try for another missing letter. What about trying בור That may work but you will find that the entry may send you to באר [although, some dictionaries do list the root as בור] which is the singular absolute of בֹּרוֹת The א has elided or so the logic of it would go. בְּאֵר appears in Gen. 29:2, 3, and 10 causing no trouble because in those places it is spelled with its three dictionary root letters. One more possibility: בּוֹר and בְּאֵר are not variations in spelling but rather two distinct words. That thought offers little comfort when one has to do battle with a dictionary which lists both under the same root.

חַיָּה רָעָה Is חַיָּה a 3 m. sg. Qal affix? Check the vowel under the first root letter. Would a Qal affix have a dagesh forte in the middle root letter? The root is חיה [not היה] and חַיָּה is a noun.
Now take a look at רָעָה In this chapter we have seen רֹעֶה and רָעָה (verse 2), לִרְעוֹת (verse 12), and רֹעִים (verse 13). The root in these words is either רעע or רעה Which root fits here? Imagine listening to this phrase recited. Do you think a double entendre is intended?

אֲכָלַתְהוּ Remove the suffix. Of the consonants left, one group is not a root and the other composes a root which you have seen: הַמַּאֲכֶלֶת (Gen. 22:6), לֶאֱכֹל (Gen. 28:20), and אֻכָּל (Ex. 3:2). What about the PGN? This verb seems to be pointed for a second person feminine singular subject; but considering the gender and number of the immediately preceding noun and adjective (which are the subject for this verb), you would expect a third person feminine singular affix pronoun. What is going on here? Well, the 3 f. sg. affix pronoun is ה ָ which, due to the characteristics of ה in such a position, cannot be followed by a suffix. So the ת is a euphonic substitute. One has to depend on context for such a form to be relieved of its ambiguity.

וְנִרְאֶה It is a reasonable possibility that ראה is the root. The functions of the conjunction and the נ become the issues to consider. The נ could be the 1 c. pl. subject pronoun. That would give the verb prefix form and the conjunction could be a simple vav ו Perhaps the form is cohortative. In that case the conjunction would express purpose. (See וְאֶרְאֶה Ex.3:3.) Could you make a case for a Nif`al here?

יִהְיוּ What is the subject of this verb? Indeed, what is the verb? For the dagesh see 17.3b.

חֲלֹמֹתָיו | חֲלוֹם does not have the plural endiNG you would expect on a masculine noun.

Genesis 37:21 [Lesson 35]

רְאוּבֵן Text note 21[a] proposes יהודה in place of רְאוּבֵן so that the text would harmonize with verse 26. There is no textual support for the suggestion but it is provocative. Later on in the story, in Genesis 44:18, it is יהודה who speaks on behalf of the brothers.

וַיַּצִּלֵהוּ Take care of the dagesh forte to get the root, then go to the stem signs and suffix.

מִיָּדָם Hmmm, יָד is a two letter noun that does not take a Napoleonic dagesh.

נַכֶּנּוּ On a scale of 1-10 this is about a 9 in degree of difficulty! See 34.1 for help with the root. The subject is ______ The suffix is a nunated form; what are its components?________

נָפֶשׁ This word seems to have no syntactical place. Set it off parenthetically; it is qualifying the DO which is the suffix of the verb. Its pointing is due to its being in pause.

Genesis 37:22 [Lesson 35]

אַל־תִּשְׁפְּכוּ | אַל + the prefix form ⟶ negative imperative.

הַשְׁלִיכוּ 30.1 discusses the form.

וְיָד אַל־תִּשְׁלְחוּ־בוֹ The verb שלח is not the same as that just previous שלך The word order is tricky here. The subject precedes the verb. Compare this phrase with אַל־תִּשְׁלַח יָדְךָ (Gen. 22:12)

לְמַעַן הַצִּיל Although a preposition is often an attached particle, it needn't be.

לַהֲשִׁיבוֹ Same characteristics as לַהֲמִיתוֹ (Gen. 37.18)

Genesis 37:23 [Lesson 35]

וַיְהִי כַּאֲשֶׁר This combination gives a temporal sense *And it happened when...*

אֶת־יוֹסֵף אֶת־כֻּתָּנְתּוֹ אֶת־כְּתֹנֶת הַפַּסִּים How many DOs are there here? Are they definite or indefinite? Review 5.2a if you cannot come up with a different reason for the definiteness of each one. Text note 23[a] cites two sources, the Septuagint and the Syriac versions of the text, which omit the segment אֶת־כֻּתָּנְתּוֹ How unfortunate! It is an essential part of the crescendo. This same intensive style is used in Gen. 22:2:

קַח־נָא אֶת־בִּנְךָ אֶת־יְחִידְךָ אֲשֶׁר־אָהַבְתָּ אֶת־יִצְחָק

אֲשֶׁר עָלָיו   is a noun sentence.

Genesis 37:24 [Lesson 35]

וַיִּקָּחֻהוּ   Defectiva spelling.

וַיַּשְׁלִכוּ   Compare with וְנַשְׁלִכֵהוּ (Gen. 37:20) and הַשְׁלִיכוּ (Gen. 37:22)

הַבֹּרָה   What economical use of language!

רֵק   Where do you find the third letter? If you look under these two letters and your dictionary doesn't give you the meaning, you will be referred to ריק or רקק Hint: try the first suggestion! רֵק is an adjective describing בּוֹר In some dictionaries בְּאֵר is listed as a feminine noun and בּוֹר as a masculine noun.

בּוֹ   The antecedent is ________

Deuteronomy 6:1 [Lesson 36]

וְזֹאת הַמִּצְוָה This construction is called ______________________ **מִצְוָה** is usually interpreted as *commandment, precept*, or *religious duty.* It refers to all the commandments, both positive and negative, of the Torah. It is in the singular because it is referring to the whole body of law. The term **מִצְוָה** has also come to mean *good deed* but that interpretation is from a later time.

הַחֻקִּים וְהַמִּשְׁפָּטִים You have to decide whether this phrase is qualifying and is parenthetic to **וְזֹאת הַמִּצְוָה** or whether three different things are meant here.

The root **חקק** means *inscribe* or *engrave* and so probably refers to enactments passed by an authoritative body and engraved on a tablet. There is the masculine noun **חֹק** from this root and also a feminine noun **חֻקָּה** They have such possible meanings as: prescribed portion (Gen. 47:22), an offering due to the priests (Lv. 16:11), a specific decree (Gen. 47:26), law in general (Ps. 94:20). According to traditional thinking **חֻקִּים** also include precepts, the reason for the observance of which we do not know, such as which foods may not be eaten (Lv. 11).

מִשְׁפָּט deals with matters pertaining to the relationship between person and person, i.e., civil and criminal law, and not to precepts governing the relationship between oneself and God, i.e., the laws of Passover.

For purposes of consistency, we will use the following terms:

מִצְוָה	*commandment*
חֹק	*statute*
מִשְׁפָּט	*judgment*

לַעֲשׂוֹת Check 14.3a if you are unsure about the root.

אַתֶּם עֹבְרִים שָׁמָּה The question here is what tense to give the participle. The sense is of the imminent future *about to.* Also notice that **ה**- directive can be attached to an adverb.

לְרִשְׁתָּהּ The suffix is __________ (14.3) The fact that neither **לרש** nor **רשת** is a root reveals that neither **ל** nor **ת** is a root letter and so each must have some other function. The **ל** is a ______________ It wouldn't be giving away a secret to say that at this point in the verse, an infinitive would suit the syntactical design. Two categories of weak verbs end in ת___ in their infinitive forms. One is 3rd ה but its infinitive ends in וֹת___ The other is ______ (25.2) So the root is __________ (and it is a vocabulary word).

Deuteronomy 6:2 [Lesson 36]

לְמַעַן Vocabulary word. Although the verb form which often follows a preposition is the infinitive, it is not unusual for an independent preposition to introduce a prefix form.

תִּירָא The verb form is discussed in 17.2. Deuteronomy is written in the style of a sermon and so you will want to consider that feature in your translation. Here, from the fact that the verb is preceded by לְמַעַן one infers that the mood conveyed is of strong obligation. An interesting feature of Deuteronomy is the frequent switching between second person singular and plural: *you* the individual as in תִּירָא as opposed to *you* the group as in אַתֶּם עֹבְרִים (Dt. 6:1)

אֶת־כָּל־חֻקֹּתָיו The noun here is what gender? Compare this to חֻקִּים (Dt. 6:1)

וּמִצְוֹתָיו There are three vavs ו in this word. How many have consonantal value? If you don't know it's O.K. - this is covered in the next Lesson.

מְצַוֶּךָ 31.1 discusses the stem and form.

חַיֶּיךָ The masculine plural of an adjective is often used to create an abstract noun.

יַאֲרִכֻן The root is __________ What about the stem of this verb? Pataḥ ַ under the prefix pronoun may be an ambiguous indicator when the first root letter is a guttural (17.3a) so check the vowel between the second and third root letters. (32.1) Qibbuts ֻ is the defectiva spelling of shureq וּ so the PGN of the verb is ________ The ending ן___ in יַאֲרִכֻן is called paragogic nun and is a favorite in Deuteronomic style. (See תַּעַבְדוּן Ex. 3:12.)

יָמֶ֫יךָ An irregular noun (see: The Noun H) with a possessive suffix. Could this be confused with the plural of יָם *sea*? No, because there would always be a "fish" in the sea יַמִּים represented by the aquarium dagesh (subgroup of the Napoleonic).
What is the relationship of יָמֶיךָ to the verb יַאֲרִכֻן which comes just before it?

Deuteronomy 6:3 [Lesson 36]

וְשָׁמַעְתָּ יִשְׂרָאֵל What is the relationship between these two words? (18.2) The verbs in this part of the verse have imperative force: *and you will...*

וְשָׁמַרְתָּ לַעֲשׂוֹת This combination of verbs is troublesome to translate because English doesn't say *guard to do*, and yet we have nothing as emphatic. *Observe to do*, or *take care to do* is seen in some translations.

יִיטַב 17.2 discusses this type of first י verb. Can אֲשֶׁר be the subject? That seems to work until you get further into the verse. Because of the ordered, oratorical style of this passage it seems unlikely that the syntactical function of אֲשֶׁר would change in two adjacent, parallel clauses. Look at text note 3[a] to see what a Qumran scroll has here; that may affect your decision. The subject may be *it* understood.

תִּרְבּוּן | ן ____ is? (Dt. 6:2) The root is ____ (26.5) Why is there a dagesh in the ב

לָךְ English seems to want a verb before לָךְ Text note 3[d] appreciates this need.

אֶרֶץ זָבַת חָלָב וּדְבָשׁ In which other passage did you read this description?

Deuteronomy 6:4 [Lesson 36]

Lesson 18 is devoted to the grammar of this verse. Note that in the text, the ע of שְׁמַע and the ד of אֶחָד are written in large script. Jewish commentary explains that the large ד is to distinguish clearly the word אחד *one* from אחר another. (Look also at Ex. 34:14.) The reason for the large ע is not so clear. It may have been done to avoid ambiguity with שֶׁמָּא a Mishnaic word which means *perhaps*. Commentators point out that the enlarged letters ע and ד form the word עֵד which means *testimony* or *witness*.

Deuteronomy 6:5 [Lesson 36]

וְאָהַבְתָּ An imperative followed by the affix + vav reversive gives the affix imperative force: *you* <u>*will*</u> ... In this case the imperative שְׁמַע is in the previous verse, but the verse breaks are not indigenous to the text and a sequence can cross the sof passuq ׃ In fact, the imperative mood continues through verse 9.

בְּכָל־לְבָבְךָ וּבְכָל־נַפְשְׁךָ וּבְכָל־מְאֹדֶךָ | לֵבָב נֶפֶשׁ and מְאֹד are difficult words to put into English.

לֵבָב refers to the inner person. Rabbinic commentary interprets the word to mean *all desires.* BDB interprets the word to mean *knowledge, thought, purpose, mind, will.* A blending of both of these probably gives the sense. In English "figurative physiology" the heart is the seat of the emotions, the feeling organ. לֵבָב on the other hand, is the decision-making part of the body, the seat of the will. Many cross cultural mixups, good natured and otherwise, can result from the different interpretations peoples put on different body parts.

נֶפֶשׁ is a person's very life force, the self, the soul, the inner being, akin to the Greek *anima.*

מְאֹד is *vitality, force, might.* This is the same word that appears in the phrase תִּרְבּוּן מְאֹד (Dt. 6:3) where we use it as an adverb in translation. You can see that what is conveyed by the noun is stronger than the meaning the English adverb carries.

Deuteronomy 6:6 [Lesson 37]

וְהָיוּ 26:5 deals with the root, and 37.2 handles it specifically.

הַדְּבָרִים הָאֵלֶּה Referring to the words in Dt. 6:4 and 5.

הַיּוֹם In addition to its literal translation, הַיּוֹם can be an idiom meaning *to-day.* Compare with אֲשֶׁר יֵאָמֵר הַיּוֹם (Gen. 22:14)

Deuteronomy 6:7 [Lesson 37]

וְשִׁנַּנְתָּם How many נs are in this word? The root is geminate. The stem is ______ The subject is ______ If this were the 2 m. pl. affix form, the subject pronoun would be

תֶּם___ It is true that the addition of a suffix could cause a change in pointing but **תֶּם___** at the end of a verb will always be 2 m. sg. affix subject + 3 m. pl. object pronoun. The combination affix form + object suffix will be seen many times in this section. There really isn't an English word that captures the essence of **שׁנן** but *inculcate* approaches it. *Incise* is more precise because **שׁנן** means *sharpen* and the noun **שֵׁן** means *tooth.*

לְבָנֶיךָ Is the noun singular or plural? Compare with **וּבִנְךָ** (Dt. 6:2)

וְדִבַּרְתָּ בָּם It is hard to tell whether this is a slightly different use of a verb followed by preposition + suffix as discussed in Lesson 16.7 a-b or whether the difference is due to English translation. In any event, the preposition **בְּ** is sometimes used with verbs of speaking or mentioning to mean *about* or *of.*

בְּשִׁבְתְּךָ Refer to 35.1 and **בְּהוֹצִיאֲךָ** (Ex. 3:12b) for a discussion of the syntax; see 25.2 for the spelling of the form. In Lesson 35 the subject of the infinitive is a separate word. Here that function is taken up by the pronominal suffix **ךָ___** Another difference from the similar construction in Lesson 35 is the tense that would make the most sense in English. Obviously a past tense does not work here.
The verbs in Dt. 6:7b constitute two sets of polarities. This is a literary device to mean not only those actions but also everything between them.

וּבְלֶכְתְּךָ This is a repetition of the construction just above. You can start from the inside, with a familiar consonant cluster and work out, or you can go from the ends to the middle. In either case, you should end up with four components.

Deuteronomy 6:8 [Lesson 37]

וּקְשַׁרְתָּם The components are like those in **וְשִׁנַּנְתָּם** (Dt. 6:7)

לְאוֹת Could **אות** be the plene spelling of the DDO marker as in **אוֹתִי** No. The DDO marker takes that form only when a suffix is added and it never takes an attached preposition. **אות** is a noun from the root **אוה** *describe with a mark.* (Notice that the vocalic **ו** of the root becomes a vowel letter in the noun.) 3rd **ה** roots frequently create nouns ending in **ת___**

עַל־יָדֶךָ What is the usual pointing of **יָדֶךָ** (19.5)

לְטֹטָפֹת There are very few Hebrew words which appear to have the same first two root letters. This is one and יַיִן is another. To avoid the embarrassment of accounting for such anomalies, some etymological purists term them "loan words." The origin and derivation of טטפת are uncertain. Possibilities include *tatapu* from the Assyrian word for *encircle* and the Arabic word *toof* meaning *go around.* The word might best be left untranslated although *frontlets* is common English translation. The big question is whether or not these were to be physical signs or whether this is a figure of speech. Most researchers agree that a physical token was implied.

Deuteronomy 6:9 [Lesson 37]

מְזוּזֹת Generally this word is transliterated or else is given the English term *doorpost.* It is another word whose origin is not certain. There is a root זוז which means *move* or *rise* and so it is possible that the mezzuzah was originally part of a tent.

בֵּיתֶ֫ךָ is in pause. The usual spelling of this word is בֵּיתְךָ The plural would be בָּתֶּיךָ Plural nouns <u>always</u> have a י before a suffix.

Synopsis of בַּיִת and בַּת

בַּיִת	sg. absolute	בַּת
בֵּית	sg. construct	בַּת
בֵּיתְךָ	sg. with suffix	בִּתְּךָ
בֵּיתֶךָ	sg. with suffix, in pause	בִּתֶּךָ
בָּתִּים	pl. absolute	בָּנוֹת
בָּתֶּיךָ	pl. with suffix	בְּנֹתֶיךָ

וּבִשְׁעָרֶ֫יךָ Presumably of cities.

Deuteronomy 6:10 [Lesson 37]

יְבִיאֲךָ This verb form looks as if it is sending a mixed message. On the one hand it has shewa ְ under the prefix pronoun, which usually indicates __________ stem. (15.5) But there is no other sign of that stem. It is the suffix which is causing the vowel under the prefix pronoun to shorten from qamets ָ the usual vowel for the prefix pronoun for this kind of verb in this stem, to shewa ְ Lesson 29:1 discusses the mid portion of the form.

נִשְׁבַּע The נ here looks as if it could be the 1 c. pl. prefix pronoun or a Nif`al preformative. When you look up this verb you will see that it occurs primarily in one stem.

לָתֶת 25.7. But wait, you should know what irregular verb could present with a double ת

לָךְ 19.5 remarks on the pointing.

עָרִים גְּדֹלֹת וְטֹבֹת At first glance it looks as if the adjectives do not agree with the noun but עָרִים is irregular. (See: The Noun A.) It is interesting that there are some masculine nouns with f. pl. endiNGs such as אָב and feminine nouns with m. pl. endiNGs such as עִיר

לֹא־בָנִיתָ 26.5 but by now you shouldn't have to look.

Deuteronomy 6:11 [Lesson 38]

וּבָתִּים מְלֵאִים Is בָּתִּים a m. pl. noun or a 1 c. sg. Qal affix + suffix? Context can answer that. מָלֵא is a stative or "A" class verb. (17.7) A characteristic of statives is that adjectives can be formed from the 3 m. sg. Qal affix. The phrase וּבָתִּים מְלֵאִים looks as if it could be a noun sentence or a noun and an attributive adjective. You have to go further into the verse to see which works out better.

טוּב The root טוב yields three nouns: טֹוב and טוּב (m.) and טוֹבָה (f.)

מִלֵּאתָ Here's a perfect illustration of a verb which is intransitive in the Qal and transitive in the ____________

וּבֹרֹת The root of this noun appears variously as באר (Gen. 29:2) and בור (Gen. 37:20 where it is discussed). Here again is a masculine noun with a feminine endiNG in the plural.

חֲצוּבִים The root will be readily apparent if you read ahead just two words. The stem and form of the verb here are Qal passive participle. You saw one of these before in הֶעָשׂוּי

(Ex. 3:16) The indicator is again ו between the second and third root letters.

וְאָכַלְתָּ Is the א part of the root or a prefix pronoun?

וְשָׂבָעְתָּ Does this word contain the same root as נִשְׁבַּע (Dt. 6:10)

Deuteronomy 6:12 [Lesson 38]

הִשָּׁמֵר This is a Nif'al imperative. It is believed that in the early stages of the language the preformative of the Nif'al was ___ הִן This syllable is still seen in the imperative and infinitive forms but with the נ assimilated. That is why there is a dagesh forte (footprint dagesh) in the first root letter of these two forms. Although many Hif'il forms have a ה preformative they do not have a dagesh forte in their first root letter. The other distinctive characteristic of some Nif'al forms is their vowel pattern. (See יֵאָמֵר Gen. 22:14.)

A Synopsis of some forms of the Strong Verb

Prefix		Imperative		Infinitive Construct	
3 m. sg. Qal	יִפְקֹד	m. sg. Qal	פְּקֹד	Qal	פְּקֹד
3 m. sg. Hif'il	יַפְקִיד	m. sg. Hif'il	הַפְקֵד	Hif'il	הַפְקִיד
3 m. sg. Nif'al	יִפָּקֵד	m. sg. Nif'al	הִפָּקֵד	Nif'al	הִפָּקֵד

הִשָּׁמֶר לְךָ | לְךָ is the same syntactical construction as לֶךְ־לְךָ (Gen 22:2) but הִשָּׁמֶר לְךָ is stronger because it is doubly reflexive; once in the stem and then in the suffix. Notice the abrupt change in the tone of the passage that occurs with this phrase.

תִּשְׁכַּח Is this a Pi'el?

אֲשֶׁר הוֹצִיאֲךָ After אֲשֶׁר you usually see a finite (affix or prefix) form of the verb. The subject is ___________ The stem is ___________ What is the function of the suffix?

עֲבָדִים Another case of a masculine plural noun being used to represent an abstract idea. In Gen. 37:3 זְקֻנִים functions similarly.

Deuteronomy 6:13 [Lesson 38]

אֶת־יהוה אֱלֹהֶיךָ תִּירָא Notice the word order: DDO followed by verb. The same inverted word order is used for emphasis in **כִּי־אֹתוֹ אָהַב אֲבִיהֶם** (Gen. 37:4)

וְאֹתוֹ תַעֲבֹד A continuation of the emphatic construction. The pointing of **אֹתוֹ** is discussed in 23.2b. Why is there a pataḥ ◌ַ under the prefix pronoun of **תַעֲבֹד** (17.3a)

וּבִשְׁמוֹ The style of the verse should be your clue that this phrase is related to the verb which follows it in a way similar to the patterns (DO followed by verb) which precede it.

תִּשָּׁבֵעַ The root of this verb appears in **נִשְׁבַּע** (Dt. 6:10) and you probably discovered at that point that this verb occurs almost exclusively in the Nif`al. Note again the dagesh forte in the first root letter (representing the assimilated **נ** of the stem preformative) and the vowel pattern __ ◌ֵ ◌ָּ | ◌ִ The pataḥ ◌ַ with the **ע** is ________________ (5.4)

Deuteronomy 6:14 [Lesson 38]

תֵּלְכוּן Another paragogic **ן** (See **יַאֲרִכֻן** Dt. 6:2.) Notice that this passage started with its address in the 2 m. pl., switched to the 2 m. sg., and now is back to the 2 m. pl.

אַחֲרֵי אֱלֹהִים אֲחֵרִים Both the preposition **אַחֲרֵי** and the adjective **אֲחֵרִים** come from the same root.

מֵאֱלֹהֵי Here the preposition **מִן** means *from among* just as in **מֵאַבְנֵי** (Gen. 28:11)

סְבִיבוֹתֵיכֶם This word (in its m. sg. absolute form) is a vocabulary word from way back! Its root is **סבב** The form here is the f. pl. construct and it is most often seen this way, with a suffix, to mean *surrounding.*

Deuteronomy 6:15 [Lesson 38]

אֵל One of the titles used for God.

קַנָּא As an adjective, this word is used with reference to God only. It is another one of those words almost impossible to translate into English. Two frequently used terms are *jealous* or *zealous.*

יֶחֱרֶה אַף First the verb: the usual pointing for this verb in the 3 m. sg. Qal prefix is יִחַר The form here, which occurs only three times in the Bible, is a lengthened form of the prefix. (30.3) אַף can be a conjunction or a noun. As a noun it means *nose.* יֶחֱרֶה אַף is an anthropomorphic image of a nose breathing fire but it is tamed in translation to give a picture of burning anger.

בָּךְ One of the many uses suggested for the preposition בְּ is adversative, i.e., *against.* However, it might be possible that a more literal meaning *in you* captures another aspect of feeling.

וְהִשְׁמִידְךָ This is a Hif`il whose causative sense is not apparent in English.

Deuteronomy 6:16 [Lesson 39]

תְנַסּוּ Spelled out, this would read תְּנַסְּסוּ Is נסס a root? Yes it is. Could the root be anything else? What are the stem indicators? Read on in the verse and you will see the same root used again, but in the affix form. In fact the root is used three times in this verse. The reference is to Exodus 17:7.

Deuteronomy 6:17 [Lesson 39]

שָׁמוֹר תִּשְׁמְרוּן See עַשֵּׂר אֲעַשְּׂרֶנּוּ (Gen. 28:22) for a discussion of the construction.

וְעֵדֹתָיו Here is another word for a kind of law, עֵדוּת or עֵדֶת It is from the root עוד *bear witness* or *testify.* It is a testimony of divine will on matters of moral and religious duties, as in the דְּבָרִים on the tablets.

צִוָּךְ The stem of צִוָּךְ is __________ Do you understand the pointing of the suffix? (19.5) The verb root has appeared several times in this reading:

Verse 1	הַמִּצְוָה	Verse 2	וּמִצְוֹתָיו
	צִוָּה		מְצַוֶּךָּ
Verse 6	מְצַוְּךָ	Verse 17	מִצְוֹת

Deuteronomy 6:18 [Lesson 39]

הַיָּשָׁר וְהַטּוֹב | טוֹב and יָשָׁר are substantive adjectives. What is the function of the □הַ in front of these two words? There is a problem getting smooth English out of this Hebrew construction. We have to turn it into a clause introduced by something like *what is....*

יִיטַב Used as in Dt. 6:3.

נִשְׁבַּע The same word appears in Dt. 6:10.

Deuteronomy 6:19 [Lesson 39]

אֹיְבֶיךָ Holem after the first root letter indicates what stem and form? (9.3a) Colloquial English often prefers a noun rather than the more verb-like force of a participle. The definition of a participle "someone doing something" still holds: *those-who-are-being hostile-to-you* translate as *your enemies.*

Deuteronomy 6:20 [Lesson 39]

כִּי Text note 20[a] may be of some help in choosing an appropriate translation for this conjunction.

יִשְׁאָלְךָ בִנְךָ Observe that one ךָ___ is an object suffix and the other is a possessive suffix. Do you know why?

מָחָר The vowel under the second root letter indicates that this is <u>not</u> a 3 m. sg. Qal affix. מָחָר can be specific or refer to time in the future in a general sense.

מָה הָעֵדֹת וְהַחֻקִּים וְהַמִּשְׁפָּטִים אֲשֶׁר צִוָּה יהוה אֱלֹהֵינוּ אֶתְכֶם

This section is analogous to Exodus 13:15. At the Passover seder these questions are asked. The answers, which consist mainly of passages from Exodus and Deuteronomy, with midrashic interpretation, deal with the deliverance from Egypt.

Deuteronomy 6:21 [Lesson 40]

עֲבָדִים הָיִינוּ Notice the word order. עֲבָדִים is being used as a m. pl. noun here but it was used in an abstract sense in Dt. 6:12. If הָיִינוּ is a problem see 37.2.

וַיּוֹצִיאֵנוּ 33.1 deals with the stem. נוּ___ cannot be the subject because that function is taken up by the prefix pronoun. Then נוּ___ must be a ___________ Can it be 3 m. sg. or 1 c. pl.? No. That ambiguity exists only if the suffix is in the nunated form: ֶנּוּ

בְּיָד חֲזָקָה This is a frequently used anthropomorphic image.

Deuteronomy 6:22 [Lesson 40]

אוֹתֹת See לְאוֹת (Dt. 6:8) The gender and number of אוֹתֹת are ___________

וּמֹפְתִים If your dictionary is kind to you, it will have a listing for מוֹפֵת If you are working with an unrelenting three-root-letter variety, you will most likely find this noun listed under אפת certainly not the first place one would expect it to be.

גְּדֹלִים וְרָעִים The consonant cluster רע leads one to think of a couple of possible roots. (See Gen. 37:2a and b for example.) But only one of those roots has an adjective pointed like this one, and context will support one meaning over the other. רָעִים and גְּדֹלִים refer to מֹפְתִים and אוֹתֹת Although אוֹתֹת has a f. pl. endiNG, it functions as either a masculine or feminine noun. Furthermore, a masculine noun and a feminine noun in combination would have masculine modifiers.

בְּמִצְרַיִם בְּפַרְעֹה וּבְכָל־בֵּיתוֹ לְעֵינֵינוּ Here the prepositions בְּ and לְ require some thought — as is often the case.

Deuteronomy 6:23 [Lesson 40]

וְאוֹתָנוּ Is אוֹתָנוּ the noun אוֹת (Dt. 6:8 and 22) with a suffix, or the plene spelling of the DDO marker with suffix? (23.2b)

הֵבִיא The preformative is the stem indicator. The form is ambiguous. What makes syntactical sense?

לָתֶת Dt. 6:10 same word.

נִשְׁבַּע Dt. 6:10 same word. Who is the subject?

Deuteronomy 6:24 [Lesson 40]

וַיְצַוֵּנוּ In the discussion of צִוְּךָ (Dt. 6:17) there is a collection of forms of צוה from this reading. Here is yet another.

לְיִרְאָה Context and the attached preposition ל suggest an infinitive. Is the root ירא or ראה If it is ירא what is the ה doing on the end? If the root is ראה what is the י doing in front? Well ה has turned up before to be something extra on the end of a word but a י in front of a root can function only as a prefix pronoun. So logic points to the root being ירא The infinitive construct of ירא takes several forms. Without an attached preposition or suffix it is usually יְרֹא With a prefixed ל it is לְיִרְאָה Almost every occurrence of לְיִרְאָה is followed by את and so it is possible that the ה was added to the infinitive so that two אs would not be next to each other.

לְטוֹב This is not an infinitive form. יטב is a first י verb which never loses its י in any Qal form. לְטוֹב is a noun + a preposition.

לְחַיֹּתֵנוּ This is a difficult word because it looks as if it could be a verb with an attached preposition and a suffix, or a noun with those additions. It is commonly taken to be a verb (but that does not mean that you couldn't argue for something else). Assuming it is a verb what is the stem? (15.4) What is the root? (14.3a) The factitive function of the Pi`el (15.6) is demonstrated here, which means that an adjective complement is needed to complete the verb, *keep alive.*

כְּהַיּוֹם If you are wondering why the ה has not elided to give כַּיּוֹם you are very astute. It is not usual.

Deuteronomy 6:25 [Lesson 40]

וּצְדָקָה Although this word has come to mean *charity*, its primary meaning is *righteousness.*

נִשְׁמֹר לַעֲשׂוֹת This combination of verbs is seen in Dt. 6:3.

הַמִּצְוָה הַזֹּאת As in Dt. 6:1 the sense of a body of law is implied.

1 Kings 17:1 [Lesson 41]

אֵלִיָּהוּ "Translate" the components of this name.

הַתִּשְׁבִּי One way to read this word is as a gentilic. (22.5) In the apocryphal literature there is reference to a place, Tishbe, in Northern Galilee. (Tobit 1:2) The *Oxford Bible Atlas* puts Tishbe on the brook of **כְּרִית** (very near Jabesh Gilead) the place where **אֵלִיָּהוּ** is told to go. (1 Ki. 17:2) Some commentators say there was no such place, which of course destroys the gentilic notion. Another way to read **תִּשְׁבִּי** is as a variant of the noun **תּוֹשָׁב** *sojourner* under the root **ישׁב** Text note 17[a] offers yet another approach by pointing out that some versions of the Septuagint have the word for **הַנָּבִיא** *prophet* instead of **הַתִּשְׁבִּי** Obviously this word has been problematic for many readers.

מִתֹּשָׁבֵי גִלְעָד The problem of how to read the word **הַתִּשְׁבִּי** continues into this phrase. Text note 17[b] suggests changing the vocalization to read **מִתִּשְׁבֵּי** *from Tishbe [of Gilead].* Part of the difficulty of the words lies in the interpretation of □מִ Of course it can be the preposition *from,* but it can also function as the partitive as in **מֵאַבְנֵי** (Gen. 28:11) These first phrases about the vagueness of Elijah's origins immediately imbue him with a sense of mystery.

חַי־יהוה | חַי is a vocabulary word from the root __________ The phrase **חַי־יהוה** introduces an **oath formula**. The formula consists of three parts:

1. The deity by whom the person is swearing, which here is **יהוה אֱלֹהֵי יִשְׂרָאֵל**
2. Then a clause will be introduced by **אִם** which is understood as a negative, even though a negative particle as such doesn't appear: i.e., that such-and-such-won't-happen.
3. **כִּי אִם** begins the third clause and is translated as *but, except,* or *unless.*

An oath formula can consist of only the first two components but usually you will see all three. It exists mostly in 1 Kings. Here we have a particularly full and complete example:

1. **חַי־יהוה אֱלֹהֵי יִשְׂרָאֵל אֲשֶׁר עָמַדְתִּי לְפָנָיו**
2. **אִם־יִהְיֶה הַשָּׁנִים הָאֵלֶּה טַל וּמָטָר**
3. **כִּי אִם־לְפִי דְבָרִי**

עָמַדְתִּי In direct speech, the affix form of the verb is sometimes used even though the action is taking place in the present.

אִם־יִהְיֶה This introduces the second part of the oath.

הַשָּׁנִים הָאֵלֶּה There are several seemingly unrelated meanings for the word שׁנה One theory is that they developed from entirely different roots. Context will tell you which root to use.

טַל can be found under the root טלל Two letter nouns are usually formed from geminate or hollow roots.

וּמָטָר The מ is not a preformative here. It is actually part of the root! Hebrew has many words for rain, each having to do with the season in which it falls and the type of rain that it is. מָטָר is the most general term for rain. טַל is a very fine rain, like a mist or dew. גֶּשֶׁם is heavy rain. The early, light rain is יוֹרֶה and the later, heavier rain is מַלְקוֹשׁ

כִּי אִם This introduces the third part of the oath.

לְפִי Three letters and only one is part of the root! What root letter have you seen which falls off before a suffix can be added? (See וְהַעֲלֵהוּ Gen. 22:2.) That happens with nouns as well as verbs. The root here can be found in the dictionary as a two letter word. But even easier than that, it is a vocabulary word.

דְבָרִי Why is there a shewa ְ under the ד Is this word singular or plural?

1 Kings 17:2 [Lesson 41]

דְּבַר־יהוה אֵלָיו Such a phrase is often seen in Prophets. It can be read as a noun sentence but the verb *came* is often used instead of *was* to make it flow better in English. It is grammatically possible that וַיְהִי is the verb for this phrase, but stylistically unlikely.

1 Kings 17:3 [Lesson 41]

לֵךְ...וּפָנִיתָ לְּךָ The sequence here: imperative followed by affix + vav reversive gives the affix form imperative force. (See שְׁמַע יִשְׂרָאֵל...וְאָהַבְתָּ Dt. 6:4-5.) לֵךְ used precisely this way appears in לֶךְ־לְךָ (Gen. 22:2)

מִזֶּה | זֶה is being used as a substantive adjective.

וְנִסְתַּרְתָּ The consonant cluster סתר can be extracted from this word to supply the root; that leaves three other elements. וְ is ________________ Now you have תָּ___ ___ ___נִ Which of these consonants must be the subject pronoun? What will the other one be? ______________ This verb is still part of the sequence imperative + affix.

בְּנַחַל The word נַחַל is a segolate noun (see: The Noun F) but it is pointed with pataḥ ַ instead of segol ֶ because of the middle guttural. Gutturals have a propensity for the vowel ַ under them, before them, and even after them.

1 Kings 17:4 [Lesson 41]

תִּשְׁתֶּה What will you take off to find the root? Does either dagesh represent doubling?

הָעֹרְבִים The root here like שׁנה has a number of different basic meanings. One of these roots means *to become dark,* which is where the translation *raven* comes from. There are other roots that don't make sense here and some that you might find possible. For example, one of them is treated to mean *arid.* Nouns from that root are *steppe dweller, merchant,* and *Arab.*

לְכַלְכֶּלְךָ Remove the preposition and the suffix. You are left with the two letters כל which are repeated. Doubling of the two strong consonants is one way that a hollow verb can be intensified because the middle letter, being a vowel letter, cannot be doubled.[1] This stem is called the Pilp`el and is a variant of Pi`el.

1 Kings 17:5 [Lesson 41]

וַיֵּלֶךְ וַיַּעַשׂ...וַיֵּלֶךְ וַיֵּשֶׁב You can translate these verbs literally. Some translators consider הָלַךְ in front of another verb to be idiomatic, being used to convey a sequence of actions, and they leave it out of the translation. We just don't know whether הלך used this way is emphatic, stylistic, idiomatic, or colloquial.

[1] This statement is not quite true but a hollow verb in the Pi`el is a rare find.

1 Kings 17:6 [Lesson 42]

מְבִיאִים This word has the same endiNG as the word וְהָעֹרְבִים just before it and so the two words are probably connected in some way. If מְבִיאִים were a noun, it would need a conjunction to link it to וְהָעֹרְבִים If it were an attributive adjective, it would be definite. There is one verb form which has a מ preformative in most stems and takes adjective endiNGs. The vowel under the preformative seems to indicate Pi`el. (31.1) BUT there is no doubled middle root letter. What is the middle root letter? (This is a very familiar root. Check 35.3 if necessary.) What is the stem?

Remember: 1. Hollow verbs do not go into the Pi`el.

2. The addition of a suffix to a form can cause vowel shortening at the front of the word.

Review question: How would the m. sg. of this word be pointed? (33.5)

בָּעֶרֶב The root ערב is being used to mean something different from that at the beginning of the verse.

יִשְׁתֶּה A good example of the prefix form being used to show action over a period of time.

1 Kings 17:7 [Lesson 42]

מִקֵּץ The first thing to figure out is what the dagesh is for. Well, מקץ is not a root so the dagesh most likely represents the letter ______ Is נקץ a root? The assimilated letter, then, has what function? That leaves only two visible root letters. The root is a geminate and so the third root letter is ______

מִקֵּץ יָמִים The preposition מִן occasionally gives a temporal sense. יָמִים is the plural of an irregular noun. (See יָמֶיךָ Dt. 6:2.) The phrase will not go into English exactly as it stands but the idiom is fairly clear.

הַנָּחַל How is this word related to וַיִּיבַשׁ

לֹא־הָיָה What tense choices are possible in English? (Review: The Verb.)

1 Kings 17:9 [Lesson 42]

קוּם לֵךְ The form of these words is ____________

צָרְפַ֫תָה The root reveals something about the industry of the place.

וְיָשַׁבְתָּ Is this a prefix or an affix form? Is the י a root letter or a prefix pronoun?

צִוִּיתִי What are the root, stem, form, and PGN of this verb? How is the ו in this word different from the ו in כּוּל (1 Ki. 17:4)

אִשָּׁה אַלְמָנָה Why isn't את in front of this phrase? אִשָּׁה אַלְמָנָה is an example of pleonastic (overly full) language. We already know from the word אַלְמָנָה that the person must be a woman so the word אִשָּׁה is not necessary to make the point. Pleonastic is merely a descriptive term and does not mean that the writing is redundant. Colloquial English does exactly the same thing in the phrase *widow woman.*

לְכַלְכְּלֵךְ (See לְכַלְכֶּלְךָ 1 Ki. 17:4.) These words differ slightly in pointing because of the accent each receives.

1 Kings 17:10 [Lesson 42]

אֶל־פֶּ֫תַח הָעִיר This description reveals that צָרְפַת was most likely a walled, that is, a fortified city.

מְקֹשֶׁשֶׁת There are two possibilities for the root of this word. One is that it is hollow, the other is that it is a geminate. (The dictionary most likely has it as a geminate.) How does the hollow verb possibility come up — because there are two ways to intensify a hollow verb. One is to repeat the two strong letter cluster as in לְכַלְכֶּלְךָ (1 Ki. 17:4) The other is to double the second strong letter. Shewa ְ under the preformative מ holem ֹ after the first root letter, and doubling of the second strong radical (root letter) mean that this verb is in the Pol`el (a variation of the Pi`el), a stem saved for troublesome verb types such as hollows and geminates. You should be able to identify the form and PGN of מְקֹשֶׁשֶׁת

Warning: The introduction of a female character means that you should be on the lookout for feminine singular verb forms and suffixes.

אֵלֶ֫יהָ What is the suffix and why is it written this way? (23.2c)

קְחִי־נָא If the form of the verb is not obvious review 21.7c.

בִּכְלִי | בכל is not a root and so although ִי looks like the 1 c. sg. possessive pronoun, it isn't here. Like עֳנִי (Ex. 3:7) כְּלִי is a noun (and a vocabulary word) which can be found in the dictionary under the three letter root כלה

וְאֶשְׁתֶּה In 3rd ה verbs the prefix form and the cohortative (41.1b) look the same. (See וְנִרְאֶה Gen. 37:20.)

Review

Imperative + affix + vav rev.: affix has imperative force: לֵךְ מִזֶּה וּפָנִיתָ לְּךָ קֵדְמָה

Imperative + prefix: prefix expresses purpose: קְחִי־נָא לִי מְעַט־מַיִם. . .וְאֶשְׁתֶּה

1 Kings 17:11 [Lesson 43]

לָקַ֫חַת 25.7 discusses the form. English requires the addition of the implied object.

וַיֹּאמַר | וַיֹּאמֶר in pause.

לִקְחִי This is an irregular imperative. קְחִי in the previous verse is the regular form. The Masoretic note cites this as the sole occurrence of such a spelling. Text note 11[b], seeking to account for this unusual spelling, suggests it may be meant to be read לָהּ קְחִי *[And he said] to her, "Take..."* There are a number of unusual forms in this chapter; perhaps they preserve the flavor of northern dialect.

פַּת To find the root see comment on טַל (1 Ki. 17:1)

בְּיָדֵךְ | ֵךְ is the f. sg. possessive suffix.

1 Kings 17:12 [Lesson 43]

חַי־יהוה See the discussion about the oath formula. (1 Ki. 17:1)

אִם־יֶשׁ־לִי This begins the second part of the oath. You see יֶשׁ instead of יֵשׁ in this phrase because of the maqqef.

אֱלֹהֶיךָ It was considered proper etiquette to swear by the deity of the person in whose company the speaker was. So although the widow was a Phoenician and presumably therefore a worshiper of Ba`al, she swears by the God of Elijah.

מָעוֹג A noun from the root עוג Unfortunately we cannot know exactly what a מָעוֹג was. The word occurs infrequently in Biblical literature. The identification of utensils and foods is problematic. Text note 12[a] tells us that the Syriac and Targum(s) read a completely different word here, מְאוּמָה as in: וְאַל־תַּעַשׂ לוֹ מְאוּמָה (Gen. 22:12)

כִּי אִם Introduces the third part of the oath.

מְלֹא Can be found as a noun under מלא

כַּף Those up to date with vocabulary will now be rewarded.

בַּכַּד To break down this word, figure out the function of each dagesh and then if necessary refer to טַל (1 Ki. 17:1)

שְׁנַיִם This word is from a root of שנה different from that of הַשָּׁנִים (1 Ki. 17:1) Literally how many sticks is this? Rather than referring to a precise number it may be like the English expression *a couple of.*

וּבָאתִי There are four verbs from here until the end of the verse; all of them are affix forms with vav reversive. Not one of the conjunctions is pointed with a shewa either because of the first root letter or in the case of וָמָתְנוּ because of the tone.

וַעֲשִׂיתִיהוּ The suffix is referring to ________ Analyze this verb.

וְלִבְנִי Five letters comprising four components.

וַאֲכַלְנֻהוּ When you see qibbuts ֻ in a verb form, think shureq וּ to help you analyze it.

וָמָתְנוּ This last word in the verse is jarring. How you translate the conjunction greatly affects the meaning of the passage.

1 Kings 17:13 [Lesson 43]

אַל־תִּירְאִי 39.3b

בֹּאִי עֲשִׂי 20.6a

כִּדְבָרֵךְ The suffix appears in בְּיָדֵךְ (1 Ki. 17:11)

אַךְ An adverb found under אַךְ In spite of the three-letter-root theory, some words are found under a two letter listing.

בָרִאשֹׁנָה The adjective is רִאשׁוֹן The ending ָה on an adjective may give it adverbial meaning.

וְהוֹצֵאתְ The root and stem are the topic of 31.3 but by this time you should be dreaming about such forms as הוֹצִיא מוֹצִיא and יוֹצִיא We expect a DO to follow because of the transitive meaning of the verb, but it doesn't; it must be supplied for smoother English.

וְלָךְ Here the conjunction conveys sequence. We have seen לָךְ many times before but always as the m. sg. form of לֵךְ in pause. Here it is the regular combination of the preposition ל with the 2 f. sg. object suffix ָךְ or ֵךְ Text note 13[c] tells us that two other extant Hebrew manuscripts understood it differently. Can you see how the other reading is possible?

בָּאַחֲרֹנָה Approach this the same way as בָרִאשֹׁנָה earlier in the verse.

1 Kings 17:14 [Lesson 43]

תִכְלָה Is this ָה + תכל or כלה + ת What is the subject?

תֶחְסָר | חסר is an "E" class verb (17.7) and segol ֶ under the prefix pronoun is usual for these 1st gutturals in the Qal prefix. What is the usual vowel under the prefix pronoun of a Qal prefix for a 1st guttural?

תֵּתֶן The Masoretic note cites this as כְּתִב קְרֵא (See הַהִוא Gen. 29.2.) and tells us that it should be read תֵּת The infinitive is being used as an abstract noun *[the] giving.*

1 Kings 17:15 [Lesson 43]

וַתַּעֲשֶׂה This is a 1st guttural in which the Qal and Hif`il prefix look identical in this PGN.

וַתֹּאכַל Often when there are a lot of subjects, as there are here, the verb agrees with the first one. So far the subject has been 3 f. sg. but after וַתֹּאכַל another subject is introduced.

הִוא־וָהִיא Another כְּתִב קְרֵא supported by text note 15[b]. There is a dagesh in the י to stand for וּ Read this as הִיא וָהוּא The verb is 3 f. sg. and so we can assume that הִיא comes first. Here both the Masoretic notation and text note are commenting on and saying the same thing. They frequently attend to completely different matters.

וּבֵיתָהּ The widow's household has not been mentioned before and this did not escape the eye of the BHS editor who proposes וּבְנָהּ in place of וּבֵיתָהּ

יָמִים An idiomatic use; we need to supply a preposition in English.

1 Kings 17:16 [Lesson 44]

כָלָתָה Compare this to תִכְלָה (1 Ki. 17:14)

חָסֵר This verb, in the Qal prefix, appears in 1 Ki. 17:14.

דִּבֶּר בְּיַד | יַד has a lot of figurative meanings. Here it implies agency.

1 Kings 17:17 [Lesson 44]

וַיְהִי אַחַר הַדְּבָרִים הָאֵלֶּה This expression is the sign of a new story. Genesis 22 starts the same way. The 3 m. sg. Qal prefix of וַיְהִי is ________________

בַּעֲלַת הַבָּיִת This phrase is qualifying הָאִשָּׁה Remember that the construct of a feminine noun ends in ת____ though the absolute may end in ______
The ב in בַּעֲלַת is part of the noun, not the sign of a preposition + definite article.

חֳלְיוֹ This is a noun (with a suffix) formed like **כְּלִי** (1 Ki. 17:10) The root occurs earlier in the verse.

עַד אֲשֶׁר A compound preposition which is translated as the conjunction *until.*

נוֹתְרָה The two indisputable root letters are ______ If you can figure out the function of the **ו** you will have the root. The subject is at the end of the verse.

בּוֹ The pronoun **וֹ** is referring to __________

נְשָׁמָה is close in meaning to **נֶפֶשׁ** (Dt. 6:5) but **נְשָׁמָה** is one's actual breath.

1 Kings 17: 18 [Lesson 44]

מַה־לִּי וָלָךְ Literally *What [is it] to me and to you?* An idiom meaning *What is there between you and me?*

אִישׁ הָאֱלֹהִים Same syntactical function as **יִשְׂרָאֵל** in Dt. 6:4: **שְׁמַע יִשְׂרָאֵל**

אֵלַי means the same as **לִי**

לְהַזְכִּיר Do not panic. There are three strong letters here from which to abstract the root. The text is not explicit as to just who is doing the remembering.

עֲוֹנִי The root is **עוה** The number is ______ Hebrew has many words for sin. Some are:

- **עוה** which means *err* and is most frequently seen as the noun **עָוֹן**
- **חטא** usually means *miss the mark, err, offend.*
- **רשע** connotes *acting wickedly, gross crass wickedness.*
- **פשע** is *rebel, revolt*

Trivia question: when does **ו** represent a defectiva holem? (Answer at the bottom of page.)

וּלְהָמִית The form is ____________ The stem is ______________ The root, which you may recall, appears in 1 Ki. 17:12.

Answer to trivia question: in **עָוֹן**

1 Kings 17:19 [Lesson 44]

תְּנִי 20.6a

בְּנֵךְ For the suffix see בְּיָדֵךְ (1 Ki. 17:11)

וַיִּקָּחֵהוּ The root is ________ (21.1) The suffix is ______

<u>Synopsis of common 3 m. sg. suffixes</u>

___וֹ ___וֹ 3 m. sg. possessive suffix on a noun

חָלְיוֹ <u>his</u> *sickness* (1 Ki. 17:17) נְעָרָיו <u>his</u> *youths* (Gen. 22:3)

___וֹ ___וֹ 3 m. sg. object suffix on a preposition

וַיִּגְעַר־בּוֹ *and he rebuked* <u>*him*</u> (Gen. 37:10) אֵלָיו *to* <u>*him*</u> (Gen. 22:1)

___וֹ ___הוּ ֶ֫נּוּ 3 m. sg. object suffix on a verb

לַהֲמִיתוֹ *to kill* <u>*him*</u> (Gen. 37:18) לֹא נַכֶּנּוּ *let us not kill* <u>*him*</u> (Gen. 37:2

וַיִּקָּחֵהוּ *and he took* <u>*him*</u> (1 Ki. 17:19)

מֵחֵיקָהּ Hollow roots often have biforms. This root may be listed חיק or חוק

וַיַּעֲלֵהוּ What stem(s) could וַיַּעֲלֵהוּ be? (32.3b) The suffix is the determining feature.

הָעֲלִיָּה The same root as in וַיַּעֲלֵהוּ Review question: why is the first ה pointed הָ (4.5b)

אֲשֶׁר־הוּא יֹשֵׁב שָׁם Syntax: see 22.8

וַיַּשְׁכִּבֵהוּ Pay particular attention to stem indicators.

מִטָּתוֹ The reason for the dagesh is very interesting. The מ is not the remnant of the preposition מִן because you would not see עַל־מִן The מ is part of the noun מִטָּה which comes from the root נטה *stretch out, extend, incline* and so the dagesh is the footprint of the נ of the root.

1 Kings 17:20 [Lesson 44]

וַיֹּאמַר What is the subject of the verb? The fact that the atnaḥ comes here suggests that what comes next starts a new thought.

אֱלֹהָי The usual pointing would be אֱלֹהַי but the accent over this word (the two dots) sometimes causes the word to be in pause and so may cause lengthening of the vowel.

הֲגַם Can the הֲ here be the sign of the Hif`il or the definite article? If not, why not? What else could it be? (28.6) There is a long אֲשֶׁר clause (22.8) before the main verb.

מִתְגּוֹרֵר The Hitpa`el participle can be recognized by the ____מִתְ preformative. The Hitpa`el, like the Pi`el, requires a doubling of the middle root letter which, as we have seen, is a problem with hollow verbs. The root here is גור and the intensification is achieved by doubling the third root letter. To be technically correct, we have to call this the Hitpol`el rather than the Hitpa`el because of the pointing. (See לְכַלְכֶּלְךָ 1 Ki. 17:4 for another solution to the same problem.)

הֲרֵעוֹתָ Finally the main verb! This time הֲ cannot be the interrogative ה because
1. there already is an interrogative in this sentence and
2. it is not at the beginning of a phrase or clause.
So הֲ is probably a sign of __________ The PGN is ________ That leaves רעו Like י a ו cannot be a third root letter. The root is the geminate רעע Geminates can have two spellings in the Qal and the Hif`il. One of those inserts holem ו before the affix pronoun in some PGNs. The Qal of רעע is *be evil;* the Hif`il is ____________

1 Kings 17:21 [Lesson 45]

וַיִּתְמֹדֵד The Hitpol`el prefix form. The root looks like a geminate or hollow (See מִתְגּוֹרֵר 1 Ki. 17:20.) As opposed to its handling of מְקֹשֶׁשֶׁת (1 Ki. 17:10) the dictionary assigns this a hollow root but cites a geminate root as a secondary form. Note the reflexive character of וַיִּתְמֹדֵד

וַיֹּאמַר Although the words following are masculine and singular do you think they are functioning as the subject of וַיֹּאמַר The same syntax is used in 1 Ki. 17:20.

תָּשָׁב נָא What is the root of the verb? (6.1a) The form of the verb is ________ The PGN could be either ______ or ______ Read on further into the verse before deciding what the subject is. What is the syntactical function of the verb form in this clause? (42.1)

נֶפֶשׁ Interesting that in 1 Ki. 17:17 the term נְשָׁמָה is used.

עַל־קִרְבּוֹ The prepositions אֶל and עַל seem to interchange in later writings. One theory is that ע and א had come to sound alike and when the material was dictated the letters were sometimes confused. Another possibility is that we don't understand the whole meaning of the words. Prepositions tend to be highly idiomatic, each having a multitude of nuances related to the context. English has not escaped this problem. Look at a sampling of the preposition *in:* To come in a rage, in a car, in a door, in a minute, in a suit, in a hurry, in spite of it all!
There are two roots listed for קרב One means *come near, approach;* the other means *inward part* or *midst*. Notice the pointing because of the suffix.

1 Kings 17:22 [Lesson 45]

וַיִּשְׁמַע יהוה בְּקוֹל אֵלִיָּהוּ 16.7b discusses the use of a preposition before a DO.

וַיֶּחִי The vowel under the prefix pronoun is not what you would expect to see but, as in וַיֹּאמַר (1 Ki. 17:21) the word is in pause. Segol ֶ often exchanges with qamets ָ or pataḥ ַ in pause. What is the root? (12.1)

1 Kings 17:23 [Lesson 45]

וַיֹּרִדֵהוּ This is a defectiva spelling, so you can assume ו between the prefix pronoun and the root. The suffix tells us that the verb must be transitive. In the Qal this verb means ________

הַבַּיְתָה What is the ending הָ here?

וַיִּתְּנֵהוּ See also וַיִּקָּחֵהוּ (1 Ki. 17:19)

לְאִמּוֹ Why is there a dagesh in the מ (See עִמָּךְ Gen. 28:14.)

רְאִי 20.6a. What familiar weak root would fit the context here?

חַי Is this a verb? The same word appears in 1 Ki. 17:1.

1 Kings 17:24 [Lesson 45]

אִישׁ אֱלֹהִים If we must follow the "rules" of grammar, then this must be <u>the</u> *man of God.* (5.2a) There is a similar translation problem with מַלְאַךְ יהוה (Gen. 22:11) The philosophical and theological question is, "Can there be only one angel or one prophet at a time?"

בְּפִיךָ A suffix is attached to the __________ form of a noun.

1 Kings 18:20 [Lesson 46]

וַיִּשְׁלַח אַחְאָב Is אַחְאָב the subject or the object of the verb?

הַנְּבִיאִים Text note 20b tells us that a few texts insert כָּל before הַנְּבִיאִים. Because כָּל precedes בְּנֵי יִשְׂרָאֵל earlier in the verse, its presence before הַנְּבִיאִים would make the verse more balanced. One of the things the editor looks for is stylistic consistency and you will see many notes like this one in this chapter.

1 Kings 18:21 [Lesson 46]

עַד־מָתַי In spite of all the previous discussion about words which seem to end in י the interrogative adverb מָתַי is listed precisely this way in the dictionary.

אַתֶּם What purpose is this pronoun serving?

פֹּסְחִים Whether פסח has two different roots is a point of controversy. Do you think the choices given are so different as to be incompatible with one root meaning?

עַל־שְׁתֵּי | שְׁתֵּי is from the root of שׁנה meaning *repeat, do again.* שְׁתֵּי is the feminine construct form of the number *two.* Numbers are introduced in Lesson 41.

אִם...אִם *Either...or*

יהוה הָאֱלֹהִים What is this construction called?

אַחֲרָיו What is the function of the י (See אֵלֶיךָ Gen. 22:2.)

וְלֹא־עָנוּ הָעָם What is the root of עָנוּ In Deuteronomy 6 there was a lot of switching between 2 m. sg. and 2 m. pl. In this reading the switch between singular and plural is with עַם and consequently third person verbs.

אתו דָּבָר The את identifies the suffix ו as the DDO. Where then does דָּבָר fit into the phrase? It is also a DO. It is possible in Hebrew to have two direct objects: *answer him* (DDO) *a word* (DO). In English grammar, *him* would be called the indirect object.

1 Kings 18:22 [Lesson 46]

אֲנִי Is this pronoun serving the same function as **אַתֶּם** in 1 Ki. 18:21?

נוֹתַרְתִּי If you have trouble with the root or stem see 1 Ki. 17:17 **נוֹתְרָה** This is another example of the affix form used in direct speech to convey present time as in **עָמַדְתִּי** (1 Ki. 17:1) and **יָדַעְתִּי** (1 Ki. 17:24)

לְבַדִּי On the vocabulary sheet, **לבד** is listed as a word. In the dictionary, however if not listed that way, it will be found under the geminate root **בדד** *be separate.* The noun is sub-listed as **בד** But for all practical purposes, it is always found with a prefixed **ל** to mean *alone* and often with a suffix to express the idea of by oneself, e.g.: **לְבַדּוֹ** *by himself.*

אַרְבַּע־מֵאוֹת וַחֲמִשִּׁים Vocabulary words or derivatives all.

אִישׁ Compare the use of **אִישׁ** here with **וַיֹּאמְרוּ אִישׁ אֶל־אָחִיו** (Gen. 37:19)

1 Kings 18:23 [Lesson 46]

וְיִתְּנוּ־לָנוּ Jussive mood works best here (42.1) and can be applied to all the verbs in the verse. What kind of a **ו** is this? It serves to express purpose as in **וְאֶרְאֶה** (Ex. 3:3) This verse is long and complicated. Use each **ו** as a division marker.
Notice that both words in this phrase end in **נו**____ However, in **וְיִתְּנוּ** the **נ** is part of the root but in **לָנוּ** it is part of the suffix. Can the suffix be ambiguous? (See **וַיּוֹצִיאֵנוּ** Dt. 6:21.)

שְׁנַיִם פָּרִים For translation purposes it may not be critical whether we think of **שְׁנַיִם** as an adjective or a noun, but for the sake of syntactical awareness, how is it being used? About **פָּרִים** The roots of two letter nouns are usually ____________ or ____________ (See **טַל** 1 Ki. 17:1.)

לָהֶם The suffix has a reflexive meaning here.

הַפָּר הָאֶחָד At last, a number used adjectivally!

וַיְנַתְּחֻהוּ There is no vowel under the י because ______________________ (23.2a) Shureq ֻ is a defectiva ______ Analyze this verb.

וַיָּשִׂימוּ The pronominal DO הוּ ____ which is part of the previous verb, and understood here, has to be supplied in English.

וְאֵשׁ Remember that *and* is not the only meaning for the conjunction ו How does this word relate to the verb יָשִׂימוּ which follows?

1 Kings 18:24 [Lesson 46]

בְּשֵׁם־יהוה Text note 24[a] notes that the Septuagint, Syriac, and Vulgate add the equivalent of *my God* after יהוה perhaps to balance the verse.

יַעֲנֶה What about the stem? The prefix pronoun is pointed for ______ or ______

בָאֵשׁ The preposition is being used as it is in בְּקַרְנָיו (Gen. 22:13)

הוּא הָאֱלֹהִים It is more than awkward to have to choose a tense.

וַיַּעַן כָּל־הָעָם This time עַם is taking a singular verb. (See וְלֹא־עָנוּ הָעָם 1 Ki. 18:21.) But go one word further וַיֹּאמְרוּ and the verb becomes plural.

טוֹב הַדָּבָר When an adjective precedes the noun it is functioning as ______________ (15.2) דָּבָר has many meanings but even so, the idea is so compressed in Hebrew, it will be difficult to find something that goes smoothly into English.

1 Kings 18:25 [Lesson 47]

בַּחֲרוּ If the form is giving you trouble, read through the rest of the verse; that may help reveal the mood. The pointing could be either Qal or Pi`el.

לָכֶם is functioning like לָהֶם (1 Ki. 18:23)

וַעֲשׂוּ What is the usual vowel under the first root letter in this stem and form? Why is there a composite shewa ֲ in that position? The ו has a pataḥ ַ under it to harmonize with the vowel next to it.

רִאשֹׁנָה Discussed in 1 Ki. 17:13 same word.

1 Kings 18:26 [Lesson 47]

אֲשֶׁר־נָתַן An affix form in a subordinate clause is often referring to an action which was done before the main action of the sentence and so we would use the pluperfect in English.

הַבַּעַל It is common to see ה◻ in front of a proper name, although we don't acknowledge it in English translation. Some occurrences of this convention are: הָאֱלֹהִים (Gen. 22:1) and הַמֹּרִיָּה (Gen. 22:2)

עֲנֵנוּ If the root is not apparent, review your vocabulary; and if this section of the translation is difficult, study Lessons 18 and 20.
Valuable hint: when you see ֵנוּ at the end of a verb (realizing, of course, that the accented tsere ֵ syllable is a critical component of this segment), then the נוּ____ will always be the 1 c. pl. object suffix.

וַיְפַסְּחוּ You saw this verb in another stem and form in 1 Ki. 18:21.

אֲשֶׁר עָשָׂה The tense relationships in this clause parallel אֲשֶׁר נָתַן at the beginning of the verse. (There are some tense relationships in the story, too.)

1 Kings 18:27 [Lesson 47]

כִּי שִׂיחַ The conjunction, which is repeated in the following phrases, conveys the idea of *perhaps.*

לוֹ וְכִי־שִׂיג לוֹ וְכִי־דֶרֶךְ לוֹ | **לוֹ** here is either a specific colloquialism, or it is being used in apposition to the verb like לְךָ as in לֶךְ־לְךָ (Gen. 22:2)

אוּלַי Listed precisely this way in the dictionary.

יָשֵׁן Do you recognize this verb type? (17.7)

וְיִקָץ A root you have seen which uses the two strong letters here is קצץ (1 Ki. 17:7) but וְיִקָץ is not pointed for a Qal prefix of a geminate verb. יקץ is a 1st י verb like ירא which retains the י of the root in most forms. Here, unfortunately, the י of the root has elided and so the root's identifying characteristic is lost. (In Gen. 28:16 this verb appears in the Qal prefix with vav conversive and is written וַיִּיקַץ the way one would expect to see it.) Quiz: Is the וְ a vav reversive? What is the form of the verb?

1 Kings 18:28 [Lesson 47]

וַיִּתְגֹּדְדוּ Another Hitpol`el of a geminate verb like וַיִּתְמֹדֵד (1 Ki. 17:21) Both reflexive and interactive meanings might be appropriate here.

כְּמִשְׁפָּטָם Although *judgment* is the primary meaning of מִשְׁפָּט *custom* or *fashion* are also possibilities.

בַּחֲרָבוֹת The preposition is functioning like that in בָּאֵשׁ (1 Ki. 18:24) What is וֹת____ here?

עַד־שְׁפָךְ־דָּם This clause is similar syntactically to בִּהְיוֹת שָׁאוּל (35.1) except the conjunction here is not attached to the verb. What is the form of the verb?

1 Kings 18:29 [Lesson 47]

כַּעֲבֹר הַצָּהֳרַיִם This phrase is constructed like עַד־שְׁפָךְ־דָּם In both cases there is a preposition + infinitive + subject.

וַיִּתְנַבְּאוּ The root should be familiar. Some scholars believe that one of the meanings of the Hitpa`el is to feign something, like *to play the prophet.* But it is a major interpretation difference to say *they prophesied* or *they feigned prophesy.* Other possibilities could be *they prophesied to each other, they prophesied to themselves* (a bit far out perhaps but "correct"), *they prophesied over and over.*

לַעֲלוֹת הַמִּנְחָה   Analyze לַעֲלוֹת The verb עלה is intransitive in the Qal and so הַמִּנְחָה cannot be the DO. Besides, if it were, it would probably have את in front of it. עלה in the Qal can mean *be offered* and הַמִּנְחָה is the subject of the infinitive. The מִנְחָה was probably an offering that was given late in the afternoon because it fits the context, and later in Judaism it became the term for the late afternoon service. Because the verb עלה is used, it seems likely that this was a burnt offering although some interpreters think the term applies to any offering made to God.

וְאֵין   Note the repetition and extension of the וְאֵין clauses here and also in 1 Ki. 18:26.

1 Kings 18:30 [Lesson 48]

גְּשׁוּ   If you don't recognize the root, read a little further into the verse and it may become apparent.

הֶהָרוּס   42.3 discusses the form. The word is in this position because it is modifying מִזְבַּח which is the first word in a construct chain. Because nothing comes between the construct and the absolute, a modifier of the construct must come after the whole chain. You saw this arrangement in בַּעַל הַחֲלֹמוֹת הַלָּזֶה (Gen. 37:19)

1 Kings 18:31 [Lesson 48]

שְׁתֵּים עֶשְׂרֵה   The compound שְׁתֵּים עֶשְׂרֵה is feminine but the noun אֲבָנִים is masculine. This is like the construction שְׁלֹשָׁה עֶדְרֵי־צֹאן (Gen. 29:2) The complications in expressing numbers are touched on in Lesson 41.

כְּמִסְפַּר שִׁבְטֵי בְנֵי־יַעֲקֹב   This is a phrase with three words in the construct. Separate out the component parts of כְּמִסְפַּר

אֲשֶׁר הָיָה דְבַר־יהוה אֵלָיו   The syntactical expression in Hebrew is so different from English that some liberty must be taken in translation. First of all, you should recognize that this is the type of clause that was discussed in 22.8c, so for our purposes in English אֲשֶׁר can combine with אֵלָיו to create *to whom*.

1 Kings 18:32 [Lesson 48]

אֶת־הָאֲבָנִים מִזְבֵּחַ Hebrew handles this as a double DO or what we might call a DO and an object complement. English needs something like *into an* between the two nouns.

תְּעָלָה A noun.

כְּבֵית | בית is not translated *house* here but rather *recepticle.*

סָאתַיִם is the dual of סְאָה and because we don't know what size this measure represented, we simply transliterate it as *two seahs.*

זֶרַע is the last part of a construct chain which began with כְּבֵית

1 Kings 18:33 [Lesson 48]

וַיַּעֲרֹךְ אֶת־הָעֵצִים Compare this section with Genesis 22:9.

וַיְנַתַּח The stem is ________ The guttural causes a change in the pointing.

וַיָּשֶׂם If you need help, glance back at the chart in Gen. 37:1. This is yet another case where English needs an expressed DO.

1 Kings 18:34 [Lesson 48]

מִלְאוּ Qal imperative of an "E" class verb. This is a place where a verb which is usually intransitive in the Qal certainly seems to be transitive here.

כַדִּים Can't find the root? See בַּכַּד (1 Ki. 17:12)

וְיִצְקוּ You saw this verb before in the phrase וַיִּצֹק שֶׁמֶן עַל־רֹאשָׁהּ (Gen. 28:18) It is interesting that יצק and יקץ (1 Ki. 18:27), whose letters are metathetic, are both irregularly spelled 1st י verbs.

As has been the case earlier in the narrative, the word *it* has to be supplied in English.

וַיֹּאמֶר שְׁנוּ וַיִּשְׁנוּ וַיֹּאמֶר שַׁלֵּשׁוּ וַיְשַׁלֵּשׁוּ This is a magnificent example of compressed Hebrew expression. We have seen this type of thing all along, particularly in the readings in Kings but these phrases top them all. Notice also that the first set of verbs is in the Qal but the second set, being an intensification, is in the Pi`el.

1 Kings 18:35 [Lesson 49]

וַיֵּלְכוּ הַמַּיִם | מַיִם is always used in the plural (dual?) and always takes a plural verb. What is the subject of this phrase?

מִלֵּא־מָיִם Can מַיִם be the subject of the verb? What is the stem of the verb? What is the DO of the part of the verse after the atnaḥ ֑ So what happens with מַיִם The comment with אֶת־הָאֲבָנִים מִזְבֵּחַ (1 Ki. 18:32) might help.

1 Kings 18:36 [Lesson 49]

בַּעֲלוֹת הַמִּנְחָה Is this phrase analogous to בַּעֲלַת הַבָּיִת (1 Ki. 17:17) or perhaps to לַעֲלוֹת הַמִּנְחָה (1 Ki. 18:29)

אֵלִיָּהוּ הַנָּבִיא This is the only time in the three chapters which comprise this narrative that Elijah is referred to as הַנָּבִיא

יִוָּדַע A ו between the prefix pronoun and the verb means the first root letter is ______ The stem is more difficult. What does the dagesh forte in the ו represent? (48.5b) Only part of the characteristic Nif`al vowel pattern is seen because of the guttural ע Jussive mood best fits the sense here with an impersonal *it* as the subject.

וּבִדְבָרֶיךָ A כְּתִב קְרֵא See the marginal notation and text note 36[f]. The large number of text critical notes for this verse indicates that the editor is concerned with the stylistic inconsistencies in the Masoretic version. For example the evocation of יהוה אֱלֹהֵי אַבְרָהָם יִצְחָק וְיִשְׂרָאֵל is not the usual formulaic expression.

1 Kings 18:37 [Lesson 49]

עֲנֵנִי See עֲנֵנוּ (1 Ki.* 18:26)

הֲסִבֹּתָ The form and PGN are straightforward but the rest is not quite so obvious. The dagesh gives us הסבב and so a root you have seen before is exposed. (See סְבִיבוֹתֵיכֶם Dt. 6:14.) The preformative ה is ________ The vowel under it ֲ is seen with geminates, sometimes with hollow verbs, and with other verbs if they have four syllables (causing the vowels in front to shorten).

לִבָּם Compare with לְבָבְךָ (Dt. 6:5)

אֲחֹרַנִּית This is an adverb whose root you have seen many times before. The meaning of the last half of this verse is puzzling and certainly has intrigued the commentators.

1 Kings 18:38 [Lesson 49]

וַתִּפֹּל Is there a noun subject to clear up the ambiguous prefix pronoun?

אֵשׁ־יהוה Do you think the variation put forth in text note 38[a] changes the image?

לִחֵכָה Both חכה and לחך are roots. So you have to figure out whether the ל or the ה is extraneous to the root. Here is a case where the pointing helps define the stem and form. Take into account that there is a guttural in this word. This verb is sort of an add-on. What is its subject?

1 Kings 18:39 [Lesson 49]

וַיַּרְא Is the root ירא or ראה

וַיֹּאמְרוּ Note 39[c] tells us that the Septuagint inserts the equivalent of אָמֵן here.

יהוה הוּא הָאֱלֹהִים The use of the independent pronoun and the repetition of the entire phrase create the highest degree of emphasis.

1 Kings 18:40 [Lesson 49]

תִּפְשׂוּ Decision: this word is constructed תפשׂ + ו or ת + פשׂ + ו in which case there is a missing root letter.

אִישׁ Used as in Gen. 37:19.

אַל־יִמָּלֵט For אַל + the prefix form of the verb, see 39.3b. The stem and form are presented in the previous Lesson. The root מלט is not found in the Qal in the Bible.

וַיִּתְפְּשׂוּם At first glance this looks as if it might be a Hitpa`el prefix form, (see וַיִּתְנַבְּאוּ 1 Ki. 18:29) but it is missing one key ingredient: a dagesh forte in the second root letter. The root appears in another form earlier in the verse.

וַיּוֹרִדֵם Difficult, but not impossible. 1. ו between a prefix pronoun and the root means ________ 2. The root is ________ 3. A dot vowel between the 2nd and 3rd root letter means ________ 4. This verb is a) transitive b) intransitive c) both a and b d) neither a nor b 5. ם___ is one spelling of the object suffix for which PGN ________

Notice that even though וַיִּתְפְּשׂוּם and וַיּוֹרִדֵם are joined by a conjunction, they do not have the same subject.

1 Kings 18:41 [Lesson 50]

עֲלֵה אֱכֹל וּשְׁתֵה These three verbs have the same form but each has different pointing because of the characteristic of its first root letter.

כִּי־קוֹל הֲמוֹן הַגָּשֶׁם This is a clause because it is introduced by כִּי Where is the verb? קוֹל is a ________ Now look at הֲמוֹן The ה can't be the interrogative ה because it is not at the beginning of a phrase. It can't be the sign of the Hif`il because the rest of the pointing does not support a Hif`il pattern. הֲמוֹן is a noun in construct, listed as being from the root המה *murmur, growl, roar,* even though there is a root המן meaning *rage, be turbulent.* The word הַגָּשֶׁם is in pause. If pointed regularly, it would read הַגֶּשֶׁם in which case, of course, you would immediately recognize it as a segolate noun.

This whole clause is a noun sentence and so a form of the verb *to be* has to be inserted in the translation. Usually the verb is put between two nouns, but here an impersonal *there is* can function as the verb if inserted after כִּי Other creative solutions are possible.

1 Kings 18:42 [Lesson 50]

וַיַּעֲלֶה Taking this verb out of context gives two choices for the form. Putting it in context solves the problem.

לֶאֱכֹל Remember 1st א verbs have more than one pattern.

וְלִשְׁתּוֹת What is the root? (14.3a)

בִּרְכָּו The Masoretic note and text note 42[b] agree that this spelling represents a scribal error (although it may just represent a pre-exilic spelling). Without consulting the notes, can you identify the problem?

1 Kings 18:43 [Lesson 50]

הַבֵּט What kind of dagesh is in the בּ __________ You have to discern its function. As always, it is best to do the easiest thing first. See if הבט is a root. If the dagesh is the footprint of an assimilated letter, what letter is it most likely to be? Under that root, you will see that this verb occurs almost always in one stem. The form is __________

דֶּרֶךְ־יָם A literal translation gets the idea across. It may be referring to the major road along the coast which later became known as the Via Maris.

מְאוּמָה Some identify the root as אום This would allow the assumption that the מ is a noun identifier and the ָה the endiNG. Others identify the root as מאם which is where you will probably find it in the dictionary. (This word occurs also in Gen. 22:12.)

שָׁב Remember that ָ is a defectiva ________

1 Kings 18:44 [Lesson 50]

בַּשְּׁבִעִית The ordinal form of שֶׁבַע plus a preposition.

וַיֹּאמֶר The usual introductory *and, then,* or *but* for a vav conversive doesn't sound right here. *That* may be better.

עָב Note: this is not אָב

כְּכַף־אִישׁ A phrase further modifying עָב קְטַנָּה

מַיִם Not to be confused with מַיִם

וָרֵד Context should reveal the form. What kind of ו is this?

יַעַצָרְכָה Obviously too many letters for a root, but three can be nothing else. The ending כָה__ is a rare emphatic form. Notice the PGN of this verb; it is not the same as that of the two previous verbs.

הַגָּשֶׁם Can this be the DDO of יַעַצָרְכָה How else might it be related to the verb?

1 Kings 18:45 [Lesson 50]

עַד־כֹּה וְעַד כֹּה The expression עַד־כֹּה appears in Gen. 22:5 meaning *hither.* Here it also is functioning as an adverb but has a temporal sense and means *now...until, then,* or *meanwhile.*

הִתְקַדְּרוּ The ____הִתְ preformative and the doubled middle root letter identify this stem. (See: The Verb.)

עָבִים Hebrew doesn't need a preposition before this word; English does.

וַיְהִי גֶּשֶׁם גָּדוֹל For a parallel, including locale, read the story of Deborah and Barak, Judges 4:4 - 5:28, especially 5:21.

1 Kings 18:46 [Lesson 50]

אֶל־אֵלִיָּהוּ For discussion of the preposition see עַל־קִרְבּוֹ (1 Ki. 17:21)

עַד־בֹּאֲכָה The difficulty with בֹּאֲכָה is the ה on the end. Without it, it reads like an infinitive with a possessive pronoun acting as the subject. (35.1) The ה could be thought of as a variant spelling or perhaps a ה- directive. The phrase is given several different translations: *as far as, to the entrance of, until coming to* are some samples.

1 Kings 19:1 [Lesson 51]

וַיַּגֵּד The root and stem signs are classic. (32.1) This is a verb you are likely to encounter in the Hof`al. So in future readings watch for forms such as הֻגַּד and וַיֻּגַּד

אֵת כָּל־אֲשֶׁר עָשָׂה In 1 Ki. 18:26 there is a discussion of אֲשֶׁר followed by the affix form of the verb.

וְאֵת כָּל־אֲשֶׁר הָרַג This clause parallels the one just before it.

אֶת־כָּל־הַנְּבִיאִים qualifies the previous אֲשֶׁר

בֶּחָרֶב For this use of the preposition see בָּאֵשׁ (1 Ki. 18:24) The pointing is altered because בֶּחָרֶב is in pause.

The structure of this verse is an elaboration of the style of Gen. 22:2 and Gen. 37:23b, where the DDO is extended and heightened by the repetition of את phrases.

1 Kings 19:2 [Lesson 51]

מַלְאָךְ *Angel* is not the only meaning of this word. The root is ________________

כֹּה־יַעֲשׂוּן אֱלֹהִים This is a variation of the oath formula we saw before in 1 Ki. 17:1 and 1 Ki. 17:12, where it is introduced by חַי־יהוה Notice that אֱלֹהִים has a plural verb. Jezebel, a Phoenician, is swearing by her gods. (She may be seen as a foil for the widow woman 1 Ki. 17.) The final ן in יַעֲשׂוּן is ________________ (See יַאֲרִכֻן Dt. 6:2.) Jussive mood is likely to be intended in direct speech and *So may...* can be a way of expressing the mood.

וְכֹה יוֹסִפוּן A literal translation of וְכֹה יוֹסִפוּן would certainly not be wrong but it may be rendered idiomatically. See 50.4 or refer to וַיּוֹסִפוּ עוֹד שְׂנֹא אֹתוֹ (Gen. 37:5) In this verse oratorical impact is achieved by balanced phrasing and repetition of the paragogic ן_____ in adjacent phrases.

כִּי־כָעֵת The second part of the oath is introduced by כִּי rather than אִם (1 Ki. 17:1) כָעֵת is a compound word and is used idiomatically to mean *at about this time.* Note: this vow has only two clauses.

מֵהֶם See מֵהֶם (1 Ki. 18:40) The reference is to the massacre of the 450 prophets of Ba`al in the previous chapter.

1 Kings 19:3 [Lesson 51]

וַיַּרְא Look at text note 3[a]. It cites sources which read this word וַיִּרָא [an alternate spelling of וַיִּירָא] You can see (pun intended) what a change in pointing does to the meaning of the text.

אֶל־נַפְשׁוֹ Even if we are dealing with an אֶל/עַל ambiguity, as suggested by note 3[b], we are still left with an idiom which means something like *for his life.*

וַיַּנַּח If this doesn't look like anything you have ever seen before, it's because it isn't. You may recall the discussion in Lesson 17.6 about roots with weak letters having more than one form. Well, this is such an example. The usual form is וַיָּנַח or without vav conversive יָנִיחַ Sometimes, in later Biblical Hebrew, hollow verbs and geminates in the Hif`il with vav conversive follow the form of וַיַּנַּח That is, they have a short vowel under the prefix pronoun and dagesh forte in the following consonant. Now you have to figure out if the root is נחח נוח or ניח (Hint: it's the one that is a vocabulary word.)

אֶת־נַעֲרוֹ There is an interesting parallel here to Gen. 22:5.
Trivia question: How many נְעָרִים did Abraham and Elijah each have?

1 Kings 19:4 [Lesson 51]

וְהוּא־הָלַךְ This is an emphatic use of the personal pronoun inserted to emphasize Elijah's being alone, something which was already implied in the previous verse.

דֶּרֶךְ יוֹם Different from דֶּרֶךְ־יָם (1 Ki. 18:43) The translation difficulty is due to the fact that Hebrew doesn't need articles or prepositions here. Put a mental comma after בַּמִּדְבָּר Treat this phrase as a construct chain and note that the word in the absolute is indefinite.

וַיֵּשֶׁב Make sure you are straight on וַיֵּשֶׁב and וַיָּשָׁב

רֹתֶם It is often a problem to identify vegetation. This is translated *juniper, broom tree,* or left transliterated as *rotem.*

אֶחָת Look at the Masoretic marginal note, text note 4^a, and this word in the next verse.

וַיִּשְׁאַל אֶת־נַפְשׁוֹ לָמוּת Yet another instance in which it is difficult to move the Hebrew into English and maintain the flavor of the expression. It is simply too pedestrian to say *that I may die.* In 1 Ki. 19:3 אֵלִיָּהוּ fled to save his נֶפֶשׁ Here he is entreating that his נֶפֶשׁ (a synecdoche for himself) die.

רַב There is a double difficulty here: the root and the part of speech. Do you think יהוה is the subject? It works grammatically but it wouldn't make sense. Don't forget the possibility of using an impersonal pronoun as a subject.

יהוה If not the subject of רַב what other syntactical function might it have?

כִּי־לֹא־טוֹב אָנֹכִי מֵאֲבֹתָי The elements in this clause are a little bit different from those in the preceding one. Both רַב and טוֹב are predicate adjectives but אָנֹכִי is not a parallel to יהוה It is an independent subject pronoun.
The comparative is expressed in Hebrew by an adjective + מִן attached to the noun being compared.

1 Kings 19:5 [Lesson 51]

תַּחַת רֹתֶם אֶחָד Note 5^a finds this phrase redundant, and would prefer us to read שָׁם instead. Such an objection to the text without major citation is more a reflection of the editor's literary taste than anything else.

וְהִנֵּה־זֶה מַלְאָךְ When an adjective precedes a noun it functions as __________ (15.2)

נֹגֵעַ בּוֹ What form is נֹגֵעַ For help with verb + preposition + DO see 16.7b.

אֱכוֹל This word occurs in 1 Ki. 18:41 but with defectiva spelling.

1 Kings 19:6 [Lesson 52]

וַיַּבֵּט This verb appears in another form, הַבֵּט (1 Ki. 18:43)

מְרַאֲשֹׁתָיו Discussed in Gen. 28:11, same word.

עֻגַת רְצָפִים A construct chain which is much too compressed for English; something like *baked on* has to be inserted between these two words. עֻגָה is a variation, perhaps, of מָעוֹג (1 Ki. 17:12)

וַיֵּשְׁתְּ A 3rd ה disguised as a 1st י (16.3a)

וַיָּשָׁב Just as יסף can be used to convey doing something more intensely, so שׁוּב can be used to convey doing something again.

1 Kings 19:7 [Lesson 52]

רַב מִמְּךָ Like טוֹב...מֵאֲבֹתָי (1 Ki. 19:4) The formation of the preposition מִן + an object pronoun is discussed with מִמֶּנִּי (Gen. 22:12)

1 Kings 19:8 [Lesson 52]

וַיִּשְׁתֶּה This is the way we would expect to find the 3 m. sg. Qal prefix of שׁתה Compare with וַיֵּשְׁתְּ (1 Ki. 19:6)

בְּכֹחַ You have to determine whether בּ here is a root letter or a preposition.

הָאֲכִילָה The root appears earlier in this verse. מַאֲכֶלֶת (Gen. 22:6) is another noun you have seen from the same root.

הַהִיא How does this word relate to the word before it?

אַרְבָּעִים יוֹם Why is יוֹם singular? Peek ahead to Lesson 54.

עַד הַר הָאֱלֹהִים חֹרֵב Text note 8a is reminiscent of Exodus 3:1 text note 1a.

1 Kings 19:9 [Lesson 52]

הַמְּעָרָה From a geminate or hollow root — depending on your dictionary.

מַה־לְּךָ פֹּה Another expression which cannot go easily into English. Translate the words literally as if they form a noun sentence (albeit an interrogative sentence) and then find an English expression which seems to make the point.

1 Kings 19:10 [Lesson 52]

קַנֹּא קִנֵּאתִי 40.2 presents the construction. What is the stem of these verbs? קנא used as a verb is not restricted to God. See comments about קַנָּא (Dt. 6:15)

עָזְבוּ Look for a 3 m. pl. noun subject. The word order patterns are not consistent in this verse.

בְּרִיתְךָ This word (minus the suffix) is on the vocabulary list. But if you look at it as an exercise in root identification, where would you find it in the dictionary?

מִזְבְּחֹתֶיךָ Can you analyze this word?

וָאִוָּתֵר אֲנִי לְבַדִּי About וָאִוָּתֵר First remove the conjunction. What is its function? (14.5a) The vowel pattern of the rest of the word should ring a bell. If you need help with the root see 48.5b. לְבַדִּי is discussed in 1 Ki. 18:22. The three words here constitute a highly emphatic construction. The first person is expressed in the prefix pronoun of the verb, then repeated by the independent subject pronoun and again in the suffix of לבד

וַיְבַקְשׁוּ If you can identify the stem you are ready for intermediate Biblical Hebrew.

לְקַחְתָּהּ Is the ל functioning as a root letter here or a preposition? What is the role of the ת And one more question: to what is the suffix referring?

1 Kings 19:11 [Lesson 53]

צֵא 20.6a

וְהִנֵּה יהוה עֹבֵר There is heavy use of participles in this verse. Sometimes a participle is used instead of a finite form of the verb when the verb is expressing a single continuous event. The tense must be inferred from the context.

וְרוּחַ גְּדוֹלָה וְחָזָק This is a curious combination of a noun which is usually feminine but may at times be masculine, taking one feminine and one masculine adjective. What is it about the pointing of **וְחָזָק** that precludes its being a verb?

מְפָרֵק The vowel under the preformative **מ** is the stem identifier. (31.1) This stem usually has another indicator. Why is it missing here? Incidentally, although many nouns begin with **מ** it is unusual for them to begin with **מְ**

לִפְנֵי יהוה This phrase is part of the preceding thought and translation would be easier if the following word **לֹא** read **וְלֹא** The main syntactical difficulty of this whole chapter has been the paucity of words Hebrew needs to express concepts compared with the much larger number of words English uses. This feature contributes a highly poetic quality to the Hebrew in these verses.

לֹא בָרוּחַ יהוה English handles the phrases from here until the end of verse 12 as a string of noun sentences.

1 Kings 19:12 [Lesson 53]

קוֹל דְּמָמָה דַקָּה Traditionally **דְּמָמָה** and **דַקָּה** are translated as adjectives describing **קוֹל** but do they agree in gender? This is an example of hendiadys: two nouns used in apposition e.g. **אַדְמַת־קֹדֶשׁ** *ground of holiness* (Ex. 3:5) instead of a noun and an adjective **וְגוֹי קָדוֹשׁ** *and a holy nation.* (Ex. 19:6)

1 Kings 19:13 [Lesson 53]

כִּשְׁמֹעַ אֵלִיָּהוּ is the same type of construction as **בִּהְיוֹת שָׁאוּל** (36.1)

הַמְּעָרָה This word appears in 1 Ki. 19:9. It violates the observation made with מְפָרֵק (1 Ki. 19:12) that most nouns constructed with preformative מ do not begin with מְ

אֵלָיו קוֹל The word order is not what we are used to seeing. As in the phrase דְבַר־יהוה אֵלָיו this phrase needs a verb in English.

וַיֹּאמֶר מַה־לְּךָ פֹה אֵלִיָּהוּ This segment through verse 14 repeats 1 Ki. 19:9b-10.

1 Kings 19:15 [Lesson 53]

אֶת־חֲזָאֵל לְמֶלֶךְ One of the functions English assigns to the preposition ל is to specify something, so here לְמֶלֶךְ would mean *as king*.

1 Kings 19:16 [Lesson 54]

יֵהוּא There are two reasons why this word must be a noun. It comes after את and following it is the phrase בֶּן־נִמְשִׁי which means it must be the first part of a name.

מֵאָבֵל מְחוֹלָה Where אֱלִישָׁע is from.

תַּחְתֶּיךָ Clue: one of the components of this word is a preposition.

1 Kings 19:17 [Lesson 54]

הַנִּמְלָט 47.2 discusses the stem and form. Why is there a dagesh in the נ This verb appears in the prefix form 1 Ki. 18:40.

יָמִית Stem? (29.2) Qal prefix would be ____________

יֵהוּא Is this the subject or the object of יָמִית

1 Kings 19:18 [Lesson 54]

שִׁבְעַת אֲלָפִים How fortunate that the vagaries about numbers above ten happen to be presented in the Lesson for this reading.

כָּל־הַבִּרְכַּיִם This phrase is connected to the last one as if there were a comma between the two and it is the subject of the following אֲשֶׁר clause.

וְכָל־הַפֶּה A repetition of the previous syntactical pattern.

לֹא־נָשַׁק לוֹ This is clear visually but is a great aural pun.

1 Kings 19:19 [Lesson 54]

חֹרֵשׁ There are two ways to proceed after this participle: tie it to the next phrase with a preposition:. *with*, or consider the next part of the verse a separate thought:. *there were.*

שְׁנֵים־עָשָׂר צְמָדִים Like שְׁתֵּים עֶשְׂרֵה אֲבָנִים (1 Ki. 18:31) only here the number is masculine.

וְהוּא בִּשְׁנֵים הֶעָשָׂר Knowing how the number is constructed is one thing; being able to make sense out of it is another.

וַיַּשְׁלֵךְ Stem?

אַדַּרְתּוֹ The meanings of this word create a rich image.

אֵלָיו Look at text note 19[b]. Does the other preposition affect the meaning?

1 Kings 19:20 [Lesson 54]

אֶשְּׁקָה־נָּה Why is there a dagesh in the שׁ What is the mood of the verb? (41.1)

וְאֵלְכָה Notice how differently this cohortative might be translated compared with **אֶשְׁקָה־נָּא** which comes just before. The first one is an independent main verb and has the sense of *let me...* Whereas **וְאֵלְכָה** is a subordinate verb with a conjunction attached and seems to mean *that I may...*

לֵךְ שׁוּב Whereas the meanings of the word **אַדַּרְתּוֹ** heighten the image, here the ambiguity in the word **שׁוּב** is confusing. Does it mean *go back* **לְאָבִי וּלְאִמִּי** or *return* to Elijah? The next clause does not solve the problem because it, too, can be read in more than one way.

כִּי מֶה־עָשִׂיתִי לָךְ We don't know whether a statement or a question is implied here. If a statement, it refers to what was said in 1 Ki. 19:15 and 18. If it is a question, as Rashi interprets it, then Elijah's casting his mantle over Elisha was meant to be a test to see whether Elisha meant to follow him wholeheartedly. Elijah is still giving him the opportunity to go back. The events in 1 Kings 17:8-24 are echoed in 2 Kings 4 and demonstrate quite eloquently the relationship that developed between Elijah and Elisha.

1 Kings 19:21 [Lesson 54]

וַיָּשָׁב מֵאַחֲרָיו This is not so much a problem to translate; it's a problem to know what it means.

אֶת־צֶמֶד הַבָּקָר Notice that only the word in the absolute has the definite article.

וַיִּזְבָּחֵהוּ The pair of oxen is treated as a collective as reflected in the use of the object pronoun.

וּבִכְלִי Analyze this word. Hint: it appears in 1 Ki. 17:10 but the meaning is different here. How will you treat **ב** here?

בִּשְּׁלָם הַבָּשָׂר First a word about **בִּשְּׁלָם** The consonant which is not part of the root is either the first or the last. (Remember: root letters come in a cluster.) If **ב** is not part of the root, then what is the dagesh doing in the **שׁ** If **ב** is part of the root, what is the dagesh doing in the **שׁ** What then is the function of the **ם**____ To what is it referring? There is no m. pl. antecedent. There are two arguments. 1. Treat the **ם**____ as an indirect object: *[he cooked] for them* and the following word **הַבָּשָׂר** becomes the direct object (a DDO not preceded by את though not usual in prose is possible.) 2. The ם___ refers to the yoke of oxen, which, granted, received a singular suffix in וַיִּזְבָּחֵהוּ but we have seen many times that switching between singular and plural is not uncommon style. If we go with the second possibility, then the following הַבָּשָׂר further qualifies the oxen: *he cooked them, the meat.*

וַיֹּאכֵלוּ Analyze this form.

וַיְשָׁרְתֵהוּ Stem?

a and b

That part of a verse in the Hebrew Bible up to and including the word with the the **atnaḥ** is designated **a**; the portion following is **b**.

Deuteronomy 6:4 | יהוה אֱלֹהֵינוּ יהוה אֶחָד׃ | שְׁמַע יִשְׂרָאֵל |

b a

Absolute

The plain, independent form of a noun; the form that is the last word of a construct chain. A noun is listed in its absolute form in the dictionary, although you may have to look it up under its three root letters. (5.2)

noun		root		noun
מַאֲכֶלֶת	←	אכל	→	אָכְלָה
knife		*eat*		*meal*

Accentual System

The non-vowel marks over and under the letters make up the accentual system. These marks, usually placed just to the left of the accented syllable, serve to break up each verse into small syntactical segments. The accentual markings are used to chant the Torah, Prophets, and some of the Writings.

Active Voice

That state of the verb in which the subject of the verb is doing the action.
(See also: **Passive Voice**)

1 Kings 18:39 וַיַּרְא כָּל־הָעָם

subject active verb

and all the people *<u>saw</u>*

Adjective

An adjective describes or otherwise modifies a noun or a pronoun. Adjectives are either descriptive: טוֹב גְּדוֹלָה etc., or demonstrative: זֶה הוּא

The function of an adjective is either attributive, predicate, or substantive.

attributive adjective (14.2c)

Exodus 3:8 אֶל־אֶרֶץ | טוֹבָה |

attributive descriptive

to a good land

Adjective (continued)

predicate adjective (15.2)

Deuteronomy 1:14 טוֹב־הַדָּבָר אֲשֶׁר־דִּבַּרְתָּ

predicate descriptive

the thing which you have spoken is good

substantive adjective (38.2c)

Deuteronomy 6:18 וְעָשִׂיתָ הַיָּשָׁר וְהַטּוֹב

substantive descriptive

and you will do what is upright and good

Adjective Clause

A relative clause which describes or otherwise modifies a noun or pronoun.

Genesis 28:13 הָאָרֶץ אֲשֶׁר אַתָּה שֹׁכֵב עָלֶיהָ

adjective clause noun

the land on which you are sleeping

Adjective Phrase

A phrase which describes or otherwise modifies a noun or pronoun.

Genesis 37:2 יוֹסֵף בֶּן־שְׁבַע־עֶשְׂרֵה שָׁנָה

phrase describing יוֹסֵף

Joseph (a son of) seventeen year(s)

Adverb

An adverb describes or otherwise modifies a verb, adjective, or another adverb. It may tell where, when, how, or why.

where

1 Samuel 19:23 וַיֵּלֶךְ שָׁם

and he went there

when

Genesis 30:30 וְעַתָּה מָתַי אֶעֱשֶׂה גַם־אָנֹכִי לְבֵיתִי

And now when shall I provide for my house also?

how

Psalms 92:6 מְאֹד עָמְקוּ מַחְשְׁבֹתֶיךָ

your thoughts are exceedingly deep

Adverb (continued)

why — Exodus 3:3 מַדּוּעַ לֹא־יִבְעַר הַסְּנֶה

why the bush is not burnt

modifying a verb — I Samuel 19:23 וַיֵּלֶךְ שָׁם

verb adverb

and he went there

modifying an adjective — I Kings 1:15 וְהַמֶּלֶךְ זָקֵן מְאֹד

noun adjective adverb

and the king was very old

modifying an adverb — Genesis 7:19 וְהַמַּיִם גָּבְרוּ מְאֹד מְאֹד עַל־הָאָרֶץ

adverb adverb

and the water(s) prevailed so mightily upon the earth

Adverb Clause

A clause which describes or otherwise modifies a verb.

why — Exodus 3:6 וַיַּסְתֵּר מֹשֶׁה פָּנָיו כִּי יָרֵא מֵהַבִּיט אֶל־הָאֱלֹהִים

and Moses hid his face because he was afraid to look at God

when — Genesis 29:9 עוֹדֶנּוּ מְדַבֵּר עִמָּם

while he was speaking with them

result — Deuteronomy 6:18 וְעָשִׂיתָ הַיָּשָׁר וְהַטּוֹב בְּעֵינֵי יהוה לְמַעַן יִיטַב לָךְ

and you will do what is upright and good in the eyes of the LORD in order that it should be good for you

Adverb Phrase

A phrase, usually prepositional, which describes or otherwise modifies a verb, adjective, or other adverb. The phrase itself need not contain an adverb.

where — Genesis 22:2 וְלֶךְ־לְךָ אֶל־אֶרֶץ הַמֹּרִיָּה

and go to the land of Moriah

when — Genesis 22:4 בַּיּוֹם הַשְּׁלִישִׁי

on the third day

Adverb Phrase (continued)

how Deuteronomy 7:22 וְנָשַׁל...מִפָּנֶיךָ מְעַט מְעָט

and he will drive out...from before you little by little

***Affix Form**

The affix is the Hebrew verb form in which the subject pronoun is "affixed" to the end of the root. For example, the 2 m. sg. Qal affix of שׁמר → שָׁמַרְתָּ and the 2 m. sg. Hif'il affix is הִשְׁמַרְתָּ Some textbooks refer to this form as the perfect because affix form usually implies past tense translation. However, verbs of feeling and knowing may use the affix form even though these are most often translated using the present tense in English.

Antecedent

The word, phrase, or clause to which a pronoun refers or for which it has been substituted.

כִּי הַמָּקוֹם אֲשֶׁר אַתָּה עוֹמֵד עָלָיו Exodus 3:6

↑ pronoun *it* antecedent *place*

the place which you are standing on it (on which you are standing)

Apocope

A form which is shortened from the end. Weak verbs in the prefix with vav conversive and jussives are apocopated in some PGNs. (32.3a and 42.1a)

יִהְיֶה ← וַיְהִי ← יְהִי

prefix prefix/vav conv. jussive

Aspect

Hebrew does not employ a tense system comparable to the tenses in English and most other Indo-European languages. Rather the verbs refer to completed action (affix) or incomplete action (prefix). (See: **Mood** and the excursus on The Verb)

Assimilation

The adaptation of two adjacent sounds so that one consonant has come to sound like its neighbor. In such a case we say that the original letter has assimilated. It does not disappear completely; it leaves a footprint in the form of a dagesh.

יִנְשָׂא ← יִשְׂשָׂא ← יִשָּׂא

The נ is assimilating to the שׂ

Atnaḥ

In all except very short Hebrew prose verses, this caret shaped sign ֑ marks the main syntactical division of a verse.

Genesis 37:1 וַיֵּשֶׁב יַעֲקֹב בְּאֶרֶץ מְגוּרֵי אָבִ֑יו בְּאֶרֶץ כְּנָעַן׃

And Jacob dwelled in the land of his father's sojournings, in the land of Canaan.

Attributive Adjective

This type of adjective follows the noun it modifies and must agree with it in gender, number, and definiteness. (14.2c)

Genesis 21:26 מִי עָשָׂה אֶת־הַדָּבָר **[הַזֶּה]**

m. sg. definite adjective הַדָּבָר m. sg. definite noun

Who did this thing?

Exodus 3:8 אֶל־אֶרֶץ **[טוֹבָה וּרְחָבָה]**

f. sg. indefinite adjectives אֶרֶץ f. sg. indefinite noun

to a good and big land

BeGaDKePHaT Letters

A mnemonic device to rememeber the six letters בּ גּ דּ כּ פּ תּ which may contain a dagesh lene. Speakers of Modern Hebrew distinguish the sounds of only three of these letters בּ כּ פּ with and without dagesh, but some readers of Biblical Hebrew still differentiate the pronunciation of plain and dageshed גּ דּ תּ as well. (See: Vocalization p. 4)

Bible

In this textbook, Bible refers to the Hebrew Bible which consists of the five books of the Torah, Prophets, and Writings.

Bicolon

The two parallel segments of a line of Biblical Hebrew poetry.

The ox knows its owner, and the ass its master's crib.

BuMP Letter

A mnemonic device to remind us of the letters פ מ ב before which the conjunction וְ is pointed וּ

Genesis 28:14 וּבְזַרְעֲךָ — pointing of ו for word beginning with ב ↑

Genesis 28:14 וְנִבְרְכוּ — regular pointing ↑ for conjunction

Chiasm

A literary, stylistic device in which the syntactical elements of two expressions "cross." The chiastic effect in Hebrew poetry may be lost in English translation.

subject [DO +verb]

וַתֹּאמֶר צִיּוֹן עֲזָבַנִי יהוה

Isaiah 49:14 וַאדֹנָי שְׁכֵחָנִי

[DO +verb] subject

But Zion has said, the L*ORD has forsaken me,*
And my L*ORD has forgotten me.*

Clause

A sentence or part of a sentence which contains both subject and predicate. "Clause" is often used in describing Hebrew grammar and syntax in place of "sentence," because there is no clear definition of the sentence in Hebrew as there is in English. כִּי and אֲשֶׁר frequently introduce clauses. (See: **Adjective Clause** and **Adverb Clause**)

Cognate

Words in different languages which are derived from a common original are cognates.

Hebrew	אָב	Aramaic	אַבָּא	French	*abbe*
Phoenician	אב	Greek	*αββα*	Assyrian	*abu*
Sabean	אב	Old English	*abbod*		

Cognate Accusative

A direct object (noun) built from the same root as the verb.

Genesis 37:5 וַיַּחֲלֹם יוֹסֵף חֲלוֹם

cognate accusative (חֲלוֹם) — verb (וַיַּחֲלֹם)

and Joseph dreamed a dream

Cognate Language

Cognate languages are related through the same origin. Hebrew is related to the other Semitic languages: Arabic, Ugaritic, Aramaic, etc. The more closely related languages are, the more cognate words they will share. Hebrew and Aramaic have a multitude of cognates; Hebrew and English virtually none. (Words in English such as *Amen* and *Hallelujah* are more properly termed loan-words.)

Cohortative

A lengthened form of the prefix, the cohortative is used only in the first person and has a distinctive ending ָה (appears ֶה in 3rd ה verbs). The cohortative is a strong future and/or a mood of encouragement. It is sometimes referred to as the "first person imperative." It can be translated as a regular, but emphatic future, *I will go*. It can have a wishful sense, *that I might go*, or be frankly encouraging, *let us go!* (41)

Genesis 22:5 וַאֲנִי וְהַנַּעַר נֵלְכָה עַד־כֹּה וְנִשְׁתַּחֲוֶה וְנָשׁוּבָה אֲלֵיכֶם

There are several ways you could translate this passage, have it be grammatically correct, and yet have different shades of meaning.

Collective Noun

A collective noun is singular in form although it refers to more than one individual. In Hebrew it may take either singular or plural modifiers and either a singular or plural verb.

1 Kings 18:39 וַיַּרְא כָּל־הָעָם

collective subject singular verb

and all the people saw

Though the subject of the sentence *all the people* refers to many individuals, it designates the group as a unit and so the verb is singular. It is of course possible to have a plural verb with כָּל־הָעָם but in that case the emphasis is on each individual within the group.

Exodus 19:8 וַיַּעֲנוּ כָל־הָעָם יַחְדָּו וַיֹּאמְרוּ

plural verb collective subject plural verb

and all the people (they) answered as one and (they) said

Common [Gender]

Common is not the distinction between us and royalty but rather is the gender designation that includes both masculine and feminine. This can be seen in some verb and adjective forms. So, for example, the third person plural in the affix form of the verb פָּקְדוּ *they*

Common [Gender] (continued)

visited, the subject could be *they* the women, *they* the men, or *they* both men and women. The prefix form, however, has both a 3 m. pl. יִפְקְדוּ and a 3 f. pl. תִּפְקֹדְנָה Mixed groups are usually represented by masculine verbs. In English all pronouns are common except the third person singular, where a choice must be made – *he, she*, or *it*.
The one common adjective in Hebrew is the plural demonstrative adjective אֵלֶּה *these.*

Comparative Degree

The comparative degree implies *more than* as in *prettier than, faster than, taller than*.
In Hebrew this sense of comparison may be expressed by using the particle מִן in front of a noun or adjective.

Genesis 37:4 וַיִּרְאוּ אֶחָיו כִּי־אֹתוֹ אָהַב אֲבִיהֶם מִכָּל־אֶחָיו
and his brothers saw that their father loved him more than all his brothers

Compensatory Lengthening

When a letter cannot accept a needed dagesh forte the vowel before it is often lengthened to make up or compensate for the lack of the doubled consonant. (4.5b, 15.4a, 15.5a)

3 m. sg. Pi`el prefix

יְדַבֵּר — regular vowel ↑

יְבָרֵךְ — ↑ lengthened vowel

Composite Shewa

A vowel composed of a shewa ְ and either pataḥ ַ qamets ָ or segol ֶ to give the half vowels ֲ ֳ ֱ A composite shewa (called compound shewa by some) is used instead of a vocal shewa usually under a guttural letter. It is pronounced like the corresponding full vowel only shorter.

Compound Preposition

Two prepositions combining to form a new preposition.

מִן + אֵת ⟷ מֵאֵת *from (being) with*
מִן + עַל ⟷ מֵעַל *over*

Compound Subject

Two or more elements composing the subject of a sentence. They usually take a plural verb:

Genesis 22:5 וַאֲנִי וְהַנַּעַר נֵלְכָה

pl. verb compound subject

and I and the youth will go

Then again, they may take a singular verb:

Genesis 17:9 אֶת־בְּרִיתִי תִשְׁמֹר אַתָּה וְזַרְעֲךָ

compound subject 2 m. sg. verb

my covenant you will keep, you and your seed

Concordance

A reference book in which the principal words, and sometimes phrases, of the Biblical text are given in alphabetical order with a listing of the passages in which they occur. Such a book, especially in Hebrew, makes a great graduation gift.

Conjugate/conjugation

The methodical presentation of the inflected forms of a verb according to person, gender, and number. In Hebrew, the only forms of the verb which are fully conjugated are the prefix and affix. By convention the conjugation in Hebrew has the order 3 m., 3 f., 2 m., 2 f., 1 c. in the singular and then in the plural. This is because all PGNs are built on the 3 m. sg., which is the base form. Parsing,although related to conjugating, is not the same thing. When you are given the verb form, and then must tell what it is, you are parsing.

Conjunction

A conjunction connects words, phrases, clauses, or sentences and expresses the relation between the two. The most common conjunction in Biblical Hebrew is ו Other common conjunctions are כִּי *that, because, for,* and פֶּן *lest.* When a preposition and a conjunction join, the two are considered a single conjunction כְּ + אֲשֶׁר ⟶ כַּאֲשֶׁר

Connector

Some words — nouns and prepositions — may take a connecting letter, most frequently י before a suffix is added. This is different from י being used to designate the plural.

אָבִיךָ	אֵלֶיךָ	אֲבוֹתֶיךָ	דְּבָרִים
connector ↑	connector ↑	connector ↑	sign of plural ↑

Consonant

In Hebrew when we speak of the consonants we are referring to the letters of the alphabet. This is a characteristic of all Semitic alphabets. The Greeks, who took their alphabet from the Phoenicians (about the eighth or ninth century BCE), used those letters which they did not need for sounds in their language, to represent vowels.

Construct

A word(s) which depends on the following word(s), the **absolute**, for both meaning and definiteness. Many nouns have a shortened form for the construct. The construct is also that form of the word to which suffixes are usually appended. (5.1)

Genesis 37:2 אֶת־בְּנֵי בִלְהָה וְאֶת־בְּנֵי זִלְפָּה נְשֵׁי אָבִיו

vowels in construct shortened

Genesis 37:2 אֵלֶּה תֹּלְדוֹת יַעֲקֹב

vowel in construct not shortened

Genesis 37:4 כִּי־אֹתוֹ אָהַב אֲבִיהֶם

construct form of noun + suffix הֶם__

Construct Chain

A grammatical construction in which the word(s) in the construct is in close relationship with and dependent on the word(s) in the absolute. In translation the most common, but not the only, way to link the construct to the absolute is by inserting *of* between the elements. In terms of English grammar, a construct chain represents a genitive relationship. It is sometimes best rendered by a possessive. (5.1b - 5.2)

Deuteronomy 6:3 אֱלֹהֵי אֲבֹתֶיךָ

absolute construct

definite → definite

the God of your fathers

Context

The framework within which something exists.

Genesis 18:33 וְאַבְרָהָם שָׁב לִמְקֹמוֹ

ambiguous form

שָׁב can be read as a participle or an affix form depending on the context.

Copula

A linking word, usually between the subject and the predicate. The copula in Hebrew, unlike English, needn't be a verb; a pronoun often fulfills this function.

Pronoun being used as a copula:

1 Kings 18:39 יהוה הוּא הָאֱלֹהִים

noun copula noun

In many cases a form of היה serves as a copula:

Exodus 3:1 וּמֹשֶׁה הָיָה רֹעֶה אֶת־צֹאן

copula

In a Hebrew noun sentence, the copula needn't be present at all:

1 Kings 19:9 וְהִנֵּה דְבַר־יהוה אֵלָיו

Dagesh

A dot inside a letter. However a dot inside a final ה is called a **mappiq**.

1 Kings 19:10 לְקַחְתָּהּ

mappiq ↑ ↑ dagesh

Dagesh Forte

A dagesh which has grammatical significance, doubling the consonant in which it appears. It may represent an assimilated letter. It must be preceded by a full vowel. (1.2 and 3.3b)

Leviticus 27:9 כֹּל אֲשֶׁר יִתֵּן מִמֶּנּוּ לַיהוה

strengthened נ ↑ ↑——↑ assimilated נs

Dagesh Lene

A dagesh which has no apparent grammatical significance but indicates a difference in pronunciation. It can be found only in the six BeGaDKePHaT letters: ב ג ד כ פ ת

Note carefully: a dagesh in one of these letters may be a dagesh forte. (3.3a - 3.3b)

1 Kings 21:8 וַתִּכְתֹּב סְפָרִים בְּשֵׁם אַחְאָב

lene ↑ lene ↑ ↑ forte

DDO

See: **Definite Direct Object**

Defectiva

Sometimes a word can be spelled either with a vowel letter or without. The shorter spelling is termed, from the Latin, *defectiva*. The Hebrew term is כְּתִב חָסֵר *writing in want of.* It is unfortunate that the English "defective" carries the connotation of wrong, broken, or incorrect because its grammatical opposite isn't *right*, but **plene** meaning *full* or *complete.* The terminology is part of our legacy from European grammarians of several centuries ago who gave Latin names to Hebrew constructions. (What can you do?) Sometimes the difference in spelling is used for approximate dating of material because plene spellings were used more frequently in later Biblical times.

יָלֶדֶת הוֹלַדְתְּ

defectiva spelling no vowel letter ↑ ↑ plene spelling vowel letter

Definite Article

In English *the*; in Hebrew הַ attached to the front of a noun with a dagesh forte in the next letter: ⊡הַ Of course if the letter following the definite article cannot take a dagesh then the vowel under the ה may be lengthened in compensation. The only verb form which can take the definite article is a participle. (4.3, 4.5b, 21.3a)

Genesis 1:7 וַיַּבְדֵּל בֵּין הַמַּיִם

dagesh forte ↑↑ definite article

Isaiah 40:13 הָאֹמֵר לְךָ אַל־תִּירָא

guttural can't take dagesh ↑ ↑ compensatory lengthening

Definite Direct Object (DDO)

The direct object of a verb can be definite or indefinite. (See: **Definite Noun** and **Direct Object**) When it is definite it is usually designated by אֶת/אֵת in front of it. The sign of the DDO itself is not translated. It is possible to have a DDO without את preceding it; that is seen more frequently in Biblical Hebrew poetry than in prose.

Exodus 34:1 פְּסָל־לְךָ שְׁנֵי־לֻחֹת...וְכָתַבְתִּי עַל־הַלֻּחֹת אֶת־הַדְּבָרִים

DDO sign of DDO indefinite DO

hew for yourself two tablets . . .and I will write upon the tablets the words

Definite Direct Object (continued)

1 Kings 16:25 וַיַּעֲשֶׂה עָמְרִי הָרַע בְּעֵינֵי יהוה

DDO in prose without אֶת

and Omri did <u>what was evil</u> in the eyes of the LORD

Definite Noun

A noun is definite if has the definite article ☐ + הַ in front of it, if it has a possessive pronoun attached to it, or if it is a proper noun. A noun in the construct state will be definite if the absolute is definite, although a construct noun never has in itself the marks of definiteness. In English, *the* is usually the sign of the definite noun. (5.2a)

Joshua 1:2 אֶל־הָאָרֶץ

definite article: *to <u>the land</u>*

Joshua 1:3 כַּף־רַגְלְכֶם

noun in construct governed by noun in absolute which has a possessive pronoun

<u>the sole</u> of your foot

Joshua 1:1 בִּן־נוּן

noun in construct governed by noun in absolute which is a proper noun

<u>the son</u> of Nun

Demonstrative Adjective

An adjective which points out or specifies: *this* or *that*. It may be used as an attributive or a predicate adjective. In the latter use it often functions as a pronoun and is sometimes referred to as a demonstrative pronoun. (See: **Adjective** and 38.2c)

this	זֹאת	f. sg.	זֶה	m. sg.	*that*	הִיא	f. sg.	הוּא m. sg.
these	אֵלֶּה	c. pl.			*those*	הֵנָּה	f. pl.	הֵם m. pl.

Genesis 22:1 אַחַר הַדְּבָרִים הָאֵלֶּה

demonstrative adjective used as an attributive adjective

after <u>these</u> words

Exodus 19:6 אֵלֶּה הַדְּבָרִים אֲשֶׁר תְּדַבֵּר

demonstrative adjective used as a pronoun and functioning as a predicate adjective

<u>these are</u> the words which you will speak

Denominative

Formed from a noun. The verb סִפֵּר *recount, relate* is thought to be derived from the noun סֵפֶר *document, book.* It's a question of which came first, the verb or the noun.

Direct Object (DO)

That which receives the action of a transitive verb. It may be either definite or indefinite.

Genesis 1:26 וַיֹּאמֶר אֱלֹהִים נַעֲשֶׂה אָדָם בְּצַלְמֵנוּ

indefinite DO verb

and God said, "Let us make אדם *in our image"*

Genesis 1:27 וַיִּבְרָא אֱלֹהִים אֶת־הָאָדָם בְּצַלְמוֹ

DDO verb

and God created the אדם *in his image*

A verb may have more than one direct object. If they are definite, את is usually repeated:

Genesis 1:1 בָּרָא אֱלֹהִים אֵת הַשָּׁמַיִם וְאֵת הָאָרֶץ

DDO DDO

God created the heaven and the earth

The direct object may be an entire phrase or clause:

Genesis 1:25 וַיַּעַשׂ אֱלֹהִים אֶת־חַיַּת הָאָרֶץ

DDO phrase

and God made the beasts of the earth

Genesis 1:31 וַיַּרְא אֱלֹהִים אֶת־כָּל־אֲשֶׁר עָשָׂה

DDO clause

and God saw everything which he had made

The same DO may be expressed twice: as an object suffix on the verb, and by the specific object or objects being named:

Psalms 89:13 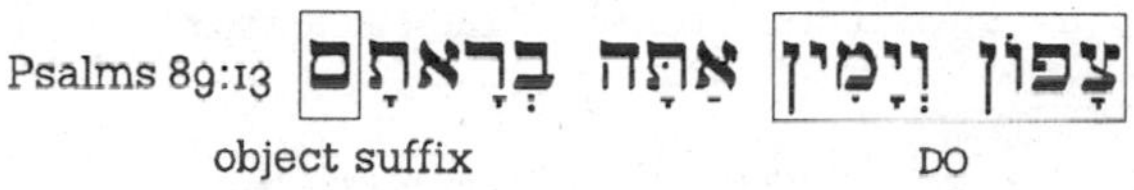

object suffix DO

the north and the south, you have created them

Direct Speech

The exact words of a speaker which are reported directly. It usually appears in a narrative and is frequently introduced by וַיֹּאמֶר or לֵאמֹר It may be difficult to recognize direct speech in Biblical Hebrew because the spoken words are not set off by any special punctuation marks.

Genesis 22:1 וַיֹּאמֶר אֵלָיו אַבְרָהָם וַיֹּאמֶר הִנֵּנִי

direct speech　　direct speech

and he said to him, "Abraham," and he said, "Here I am"

***Dot Vowel**

This term is being used specifically to remember the vowels ִ ֵ and ֶ which are characteristically found between the second and third root letters of many Hif`il forms.

Judges 6:8 אָנֹכִי הֶעֱלֵיתִי אֶת־יִשְׂרָאֵל מִמִּצְרַיִם

dot vowel ↑ sign of Hif`il

I brought up Israel from Egypt

Dual

Hebrew has a special ending ַיִם for things that come in pairs: יָדַיִם *hands* רַגְלַיִם *feet*, etc., or to denote two of something. יוֹם for example has some occurrences of יוֹמַיִם Note that the dual ending is the same for masculine and feminine nouns.

Exodus 21:21 אַךְ אִם־יוֹם אוֹ יוֹמַיִם יַעֲמֹד

dual　　singular

but if he continues a day or two (days)

Elide

When a letter falls out of a word and leaves no trace in the form of a dagesh forte (footprint dagesh) it is said to have elided. The most common letters to elide are א ה ו י

אֵצֵא

1 c. sg. Qal prefix of יצא the י of the root has elided

לְ + הַבֹּקֶר ⟶ לַבֹּקֶר

the ה of the definite article has elided

Emphatic Construction

Some of the devices used in Biblical Hebrew prose to achieve emphasis are:

A change in the normal word order:

Genesis 37:4 כִּי־אֹתוֹ אָהַב אֲבִיהֶם

DO before verb

because him their father loved

The use of an independent pronoun when it is not necessary to avoid ambiguity:

I Kings 18:39 יהוה הוּא הָאֱלֹהִים

independent pronoun

the LORD (he) is God

Repetition of a word or phrase:

Genesis 7:19 וְהַמַּיִם גָּבְרוּ מְאֹד מְאֹד עַל הָאָרֶץ

repetition of adverb

and the water prevailed mightily, mightily upon the earth

I Kings18:39 יהוה הוּא הָאֱלֹהִים יהוה הוּא הָאֱלֹהִים

repetition of entire clause

Using a verb and noun from the same root (cognate accusative):

Genesis:37:5 וַיַּחֲלֹם יוֹסֵף חֲלוֹם

root of noun and verb is חלם

and Joseph dreamed a dream

Using two verbs from the same root:

Genesis 37:8 הֲמָלֹךְ תִּמְלֹךְ עָלֵינוּ אִם־מָשׁוֹל תִּמְשֹׁל בָּנוּ

repeated construction of infinitive absolute + conjugated verb

Do you mean to be king (be king?!) over us and even to have dominion (dominion?!) over us?

***EndiNG**

This type of ending is specific because it gives **N**umber and **G**ender information about nouns, adjectives, and participles. An endiNG comes between the root and a suffix, if present.

EndiNG (continued)

Genesis 29:2 עֶדְרֵי־צֹאן

construct endiNG ֵי_ indicates the noun עדר is m. pl.

Genesis 41:2 עֹלֹת שֶׁבַע פָּרוֹת יְפוֹת

participle, noun, and adjective have f. pl. endiNG וֹת_

Deuteronomy 6:13 אֶת־יהוה אֱלֹהֶיךָ

m. pl. noun endiNG before 2 m. sg. suffix

***Ending, Special**

We are using this term to refer to a letter or letters at the end of a word which add either special information or emphasis to the word: cohortative ה emphatic ה locative ה ה- directive, gentilic ending ִי_ dual ending ַיִם_ paragogic ן

Energic נ

There is a special set of suffixes with an accented ֶנ_ syllable as their first component. This syllable is thought to add emphasis to the suffix. (53.3 and 53.5) Various names given to this nunated suffix include: nun energicum, energetic nun, nun demonstrativum, nun epentheticum or epenthetic nun. This brings us to our first principle of terminology, "The more names something has the less well it is understood."

Genesis 28:22 עַשֵּׂר אֲעַשְּׂרֶנּוּ

m. sg. object suffix with energic נ on a verb

Genesis 29:9 עוֹדֶנּוּ מְדַבֵּר עִמָּם

suffix with energic נ on an adverb

Ethical Dative

Used with verbs, most often imperatives, in order to give emphasis to the one to or for whom the action is done. It is expressed in Hebrew by the preposition ל and a possessive suffix. English translations usually ignore the phrase since English does not have an equivalent construction. This is unfortunate because the ethical dative implies a degree of interest or sympathetic concern which, consequently, is lost in translation. לֵךְ is simply not quite the same as לֶךְ־לְךָ (Genesis 22:2)

Etymology

Etymologists study the origin and derivation of words, tracing a word back as far as possible, generally by the methods of comparative linguistics. (Entomologists study insects.)

Factitive

The addition of an adjective to a verb to designate its meaning. This use of an adjective complement applies only to the English; Hebrew conveys this notion by using the Pi`el. The use of an entirely different verb in English may mask the factitive quality.

Exodus 23:7 כִּי לֹא־אַצְדִּיק רָשָׁע

DO verb root and adjective complement

for I will not declare innocent (acquit) the guilty

Exodus 1:16 וַיֹּאמֶר בְּיַלֶּדְכֶן

verb root ילד in Pi`el meaning *help bear*

and he said, "When you do the office of midwife"

Feminine

A grammatical distinction is made between masculine and feminine with nouns, pronouns, adjectives, and 2nd and 3rd person verbs. For some things — words for *girl* and *queen* for example, the feminine designation is obvious. For others — *city* or *year* there doesn't seem to be any reason. But since Hebrew has no grammatical neuter, all objects must be assigned a gender. If a group is mixed, then the masculine form is used. (See: The Noun B)

Esther 2:4 וְהַנַּעֲרָה...תִּמְלֹךְ תַּחַת וַשְׁתִּי

3 f. sg. prefix pronoun ↑ ָה f. sg. noun endiNG

and let the girl...be queen instead of Vashti

Joshua 6:2 נָתַתִּי בְיָדְךָ אֶת־יְרִיחוֹ וְאֶת־מַלְכָּהּ

f. sg. possessive pronoun ↑ feminine noun

I have given into your hand Jericho and its (her) king

***Feminine Period**

Because the mappiq in a final ה is always the sign of a feminine singular suffix, we call it the "feminine period" as a reminder of both its use and its position in a word.

Genesis 2:15 וַיַּנִּחֵהוּ בְגַן־עֵדֶן לְעָבְדָהּ וּלְשָׁמְרָהּ

↑ 3 f. sg. object ↑ suffix feminine noun

and he set him to rest in the Garden of Eden to till it (her) and to keep it (her)

Finite Verb

In Hebrew grammar, this term refers to the prefix and affix forms of the verb.

וַיַּחֲלֹם וְהִנֵּה סֻלָּם מֻצָּב אַרְצָה Genesis 28:12

מֻצָּב Hof'al participle, ≠ finite verb form   3 m. sg. Qal prefix, finite verb

and he dreamed and behold, (there was) a ladder set up on the earth

***Form**

There are five verb forms in Hebrew: affix, prefix, imperative, participle, infinitive. (Jussive and cohortative are considered to be subgroups of the imperative.) These forms are traditionally referred to as "the principal parts of the verb."

***Form Indicator**

Any consonant and/or vowel which is a sign of a certain verb form.

כִּי שָׁמַרְתִּי דַּרְכֵי יהוה Psalms 18:22

subject pronoun at the end of a verb root → sign of affix form

for I have kept the ways of the LORD

מְשַׁמְּרִים הַבְלֵי־שָׁוְא Jonah 2:9

preformative מ and noun ending ִים → signs of participle

they that guard lying vanities

Formulaic Language

Phrases which occur in different passages according to a fixed pattern such as:

אֱלֹהֵי אַבְרָהָם אֱלֹהֵי יִצְחָק וֵאלֹהֵי יַעֲקֹב Exodus 3:6, 15; 4:5, etc.

Full Vowel

Any of the vowels except shewa and the composite shewa vowels.

אֱלֹהִים

ִ and ֹ full vowels ↑ half vowel

Furtive Pataḥ

A pataḥ ַ under a ח or ע when one of those consonants is the last letter of a word and is

Furtive Pataḥ (continued)

immediately preceded by a long vowel. The pataḥ (which may be written slightly to the right of its normal position) in such a case is actually pronounced before the ע or ח The pronunciation difference is particularly noticeable with ח

Genesis 27:46 לוֹקֵחַ — pronunciation of furtive patah under חַ aḥ

Ezekiel 22:12 לָקַחַתְּ — usual pronunciation of חַ ḥa

Geminate Verb

A verb whose root has the same second and third root letters: גלל סבב רעע (51)

Gender

Hebrew uses two genders, masculine and feminine. There is no neuter *it*. All nouns, pronouns and adjectives have gender; particles, prepositions, conjunctions, and infinitives do not. Gender determination for nouns is discussed in The Noun sections A and B. A few nouns in Hebrew are masculine in some occurances and feminine in others. For example Genesis 1:1 reads וְרוּחַ אֱלֹהִים מְרַחֶפֶת There the noun רוּחַ is feminine as shown by the endiNG on the participle. 1 Kings 19:11 reads רוּחַ...מְפָרֵק which shows the same noun using a masculine participle. Those verb forms which do not have separate masculine and feminine designators are called **common**.

Geniza

A geniza is a storage room, attached to a synagogue, for sacred writings and objects which have become damaged. The most famous geniza, discovered in 1896, is in Cairo, where fragments of documents dating from 750 CE were found preserved. This affords us the opportunity to compare fragments of ancient Biblical texts with the Masoretic Text and other recensions of the Bible.

Gentilic

A classification which refers to members of the same class, usually in terms of nationhood. One way of expressing nationality in Hebrew is by the use of a special gentilic ending ִי It is interesting that some peoples are referred to this way with the ִי ending and some, such as the Egyptians, מִצְרַיִם usually are not.

Exodus 34:11 הִנְנִי גֹרֵשׁ מִפָּנֶיךָ אֶת־הָאֱמֹרִי וְהַכְּנַעֲנִי וְהַחִתִּי

behold, I am driving out before you the Amorite(s) and the Canaanite(s), and the Hittite(s)

Guttural Letter

ע ח ה א are the gutturals, even though in modern Hebrew the throat sound is not heard in all of them. These letters are "rebellious" because often they don't follow the rules. But worse than that, they don't necessarily behave like each other, and they cause different changes depending on their position in a word. But the gutturals do have a few things in common — they cannot accept a dagesh forte. (The dot sometimes seen in a final ה [וְעַמָּהּ Isaiah 65:18] is not a dagesh but a mappiq.) When a dagesh is needed, in the middle root letter of a Pi`el, or the first root letter of a Nif`al prefix for example, it is often forced by the guttural to become a "travelling dagesh."

Genesis 29:26 יֵעָשֶׂה
3 m. sg. Nif al prefix
ִ lengthened to ֵ because dagesh needed in ע

I Samuel 3:7 יִגָּלֶה
3 m. sg. Nif`al prefix
ִ under prefix pronoun regular pointing

A guttural takes a composite shewa instead of a simple shewa when that syllable is to be pronounced:

Isaiah 66:3 בָּחֲרוּ
composite shewa ↑

Genesis 14:24 הָלְכוּ
vocal shewa ↑

Gutturals have a propensity for pataḥ ַ before, under, and sometimes even after them:

Jeremiah 25:30 יַעֲנֶה
3 m. sg. Qal prefix of a first guttural has ַ under prefix pronoun

I Samuel 20:2 יִגְלֶה
ִ usual vowel for Qal prefix pronoun

The letter ר is not classified as a guttural although it shares some of their peculiarities, such as not being able to take a dagesh.

Half Vowel

A vocal shewa and the composite shewas are considered to be half vowels. (Vocalization p. 4)

Deuteronomy 5:8 לֹא-תַעֲשֶׂה-לְךָ
half vowels ↑ ↑

Hapax Legomenon

The single occurrence of a word in the entire Hebrew Bible. Most people refer to this term affectionately as a hapax. It is a Greek term, as you can see, meaning something said only once. Examples from the readings are סֻלָּם (Genesis 28:11) and טֹטָפֹת (Deuteronomy 6:7)

ה- Directive

A הָ on the end of a noun indicating direction toward a place, never toward a person. The construction אֶל + place name can also carry this meaning.

Genesis 28:14 וּפָרַצְתָּ יָמָּה וָקֵדְמָה וְצָפֹנָה וָנֶגְבָּה

four examples of ה-directive

and you will spread abroad to the west, and to the east, to the north, and to the south

2 Samuel 24:7 וַיֵּצְאוּ אֶל־נֶגֶב יְהוּדָה בְּאֵר שָׁבַע

אֶל־נֶגֶב used to express direction toward

and they went out to the south of Judah (which is) Be'er-Sheva

Heavy Ending

Accented endings which are at least two syllables distant from the beginning of the word cause the vowel(s) at the front of the word to shorten. The endings are called "heavy" because they weight the word at the end.

Ezekiel 16:47 וְלֹא בְדַרְכֵיהֶן הָלַכְתְּ

heavy ending; vowels under ד and ר reduced from ָ

Hif'il

The stem which, primarily, takes the basic root meaning (Qal) and makes it causative. Verbs which are intransitive in the Qal may take on a transitive force in the Hif'il: צעק (Qal) *cry* → Hif'il *call together* or *assemble.* (28-33)

1 Kings 18:45 וַיִּרְכַּב אַחְאָב וַיֵּלֶךְ יִזְרְעֶאלָה

Qal Qal

and Ahab rode and he went to Yizre'el

1 Kings 1:38 וַיַּרְכִּבוּ אֶת־שְׁלֹמֹה עַל־פִּרְדַּת הַמֶּלֶךְ דָּוִד

Hif'il

and they caused (Solomon) to ride on King David's mule

Hishtaf'el

A stem characterized by having the preformative [ה]שת___ It is found in the Hebrew Bible applied only to the root חוה giving that root an intensive, reflexive meaning *prostrate oneself in worship.* (43.2)

Hishtaf`el (continued)

Genesis 22:5 וְנִשְׁתַּחֲוֶה וְנָשׁוּבָה אֲלֵיכֶם

שׁת sign of the Hishtaf`el

and <u>we will prostrate ourselves in worship</u> and we will return to you

Hitpa`el

This stem is related to the Pi`el because its middle root letter is doubled, so some sort of intensification of the root is implied. The preformative ___הת imparts a reflexive and/or reciprocal meaning to the root. (52, 53)

Ezekiel 38:23 וְהִתְגַּדִּלְתִּי וְהִתְקַדִּשְׁתִּי

↑ dagesh forte ↑ + preformative

and I will magnify myself and I will sanctify myself

Hof`al

The Hof`al functions as the passive of the Hif`il. It is one of the more difficult stems to recognize, but then again it is not seen very often. Its distinguishing feature is the vowel qamets ḥatuf ָ or sometimes qibbuts ֻ under the preformative consonant. (44)

I Kings 13:24 וַתְּהִי נִבְלָתוֹ מֻשְׁלֶכֶת בַּדֶּרֶךְ

Hof`al participle with ֻ under preformative מ

and its carcass <u>was thrown down</u> in the road

Psalms 22:11 עָלֶיךָ הָשְׁלַכְתִּי מֵרָחֶם

Hof`al 1 c. sg. affix with ָ under preformative ה

<u>I was cast</u> upon you from the womb

Hollow Verb

When ו or י appears as the middle root letter of a verb and does not have consonantal value, as in שׁוּב בּוֹא and שִׂים it functions as a weak letter. That is, it may fall out in some forms and so the verb appears to be hollow in the middle. Roots such as חָיָה and צָוָה are not hollow because there ו and י do have consonantal value.

Proverbs 18:3 בְּבוֹא־רָשָׁע בָּא גַם־בּוּז

weak letter not part of the form — weak letter part of the form

when wickedness comes, contempt comes also

Idiom

An expression which is peculiar to a language and whose meaning doesn't necessarily follow the grammatical rules, so there is special difficulty translating it. (12.6, 16.7, 39.6)

Imperative

The verb form used to express commands. It applies only to the second person. Other ways of expressing imperative force are by using an infinitive or the sequence: imperative + affix with vav reversive.

Exodus 19:24 לֶךְ־רֵד וְעָלִיתָ

affix with vav reversive   m. sg. imperatives

go, (get yourself) down and (you will) come up

Exodus 20:8 זָכוֹר אֶת־יוֹם הַשַּׁבָּת

infinitive used to convey imperative

remember the Shabbat day

Imperfect

A term used by many grammarians to refer to the **prefix** form.

Indefinite

Not specifying or limiting. *A* and *an* are indefinite articles. Hebrew does not have a designator for indefinite articles or pronouns. You can assume indefiniteness if there are no signs of the definite article, or anything else such as a possessive pronoun that makes a word definite.

Exodus 3:2 וַיֵּרָא מַלְאַךְ יהוה אֵלָיו בְּלַבַּת־אֵשׁ מִתּוֹךְ הַסְּנֶה

definite   indefinite   definite in construct with a proper noun

and the angel of the LORD appeared to him in a flame of fire from the midst of the bush

Independent Pronoun

A word used as a substitute for a noun and which can also stand alone.

Exodus 33:12 וְאַתָּה אָמַרְתָּ

subject pronoun affixed to verb: not independent ↑   independent subject pronoun

Indirect Object

The person or thing to which something is given, shown, or told or for whom something is

Indirect Object (continued)

done. In Hebrew the preposition אֶל or לְ in front of a noun or pronoun is often a sign of the indirect object.

Exodus 34:1 וַיֹּאמֶר יהוה אֶל-[מֹשֶׁה] פְּסָל-לְ[ךָ]

2 m. sg. pronoun as indirect object — noun as indirect object

and God said <u>to Moses</u>, 'Make <u>for yourself</u>. . .'

Infinitive

The form of the verb which expresses the action or state of the verb without any indication of person, gender, or number. In English an infinitive is a verb always preceded by *to*, as in *to go* or *to do*. Not necessarily so in Hebrew. To know more, read the next two entries.

Infinitive Absolute

The infinitive absolute rarely has anything added to it. (40.2) Some of its common uses are:

To emphasize the idea of a verb in the abstract:

Jeremiah 10:5 אַל-תִּֽירְאוּ מֵהֶם כִּי-לֹא יָרֵעוּ וְגַם-[הֵיטֵיב] אֵין אוֹתָם

Hif'il infinitive absolute

do not fear them because they will not do evil, nor is it in them <u>to do good</u>

To intensify another form of the verb:

Deuteronomy 6:17 [שָׁמוֹר] תִּשְׁמְרוּן אֶת-מִצְוֹת

infinitive absolute, intensifying the verb following

you will <u>diligently keep</u> the commandments

To represent the imperative:

Deuteronomy 5:12 [שָׁמוֹר] אֶת-יוֹם הַשַּׁבָּת

infinitive absolute expressing imperative idea

<u>keep</u> the Shabbat day

Infinitive Construct

Of the two infinitives, the infinitive construct is the more common and flexible. Most often it appears with a preposition, which may be attached or unattached, and it may have a suffix. (25) Like the infinitive absolute, it can express the abstract and noun-like quality of a verb:

Isaiah 11:9 [דֵּעָה] יהוה

Note: this is an alternate form of the infinitive construct (25.2)

to know the LORD ⟶ *knowledge of the* LORD

Infinitive Construct (continued)

It can serve as the main verbal idea in a temporal clause:

Deuteronomy 6:7 בְּשִׁבְתְּךָ בְּבֵיתֶךָ

preposition + infinitive construct + 2 m. sg. suffix

when you sit in your house

It can express purpose:

Deuteronomy 13:13 אֲשֶׁר יהוה אֱלֹהֶיךָ נֹתֵן לְךָ לָשֶׁבֶת שָׁם

which the LORD your God is giving you to dwell there

Interrogative

Asking a question. There is no question mark in Hebrew, and so sometimes interrogative mood is inferred from the context. There are some interrogative indicators, however, such as interrogative ה and words such as מִי *who* מֵאַיִן *from where* מַדּוּעַ *why*

Genesis 27:24 אַתָּה זֶה בְּנִי עֵשָׂו

interrogative inferred from context

Is this you? my son? Esau?

Genesis 29:5 הַיְדַעְתֶּם אֶת־לָבָן בֶּן־נָחוֹר

interrogative ה

Do you know Laban, the son of Naḥor?

Genesis 29:4 וַיֹּאמֶר לָהֶם יַעֲקֹב אַחַי מֵאַיִן אַתֶּם

interrogative adverb

And Jacob said to them, 'My brothers, from where are you?'

Intransitive

A verb which cannot take a direct object to complete its meaning.

Genesis 29:1 וַיִּשָּׂא יַעֲקֹב רַגְלָיו וַיֵּלֶךְ אַרְצָה בְנֵי־קֶדֶם

intransitive verb DO transitive verb

and Jacob went on his journey (picked up his feet) and he went to the land of the children of the east

***Irregular Verb**

Some classifiers would call any verb irregular which does not follow exactly the pattern of

Irregular Verb (continued)

the strong verb. And that's fine. We are reserving the term to capture those verbs which do not fit into any of the strong or weak patterns.

Genesis 28:18 וַיִּצֹק שֶׁמֶן

a 1st י verb acting like a 1st נ but with no footprint dagesh in the second root letter. That is irregular.

Iterative

Done frequently or repeatedly. The infinitive absolute can impart this meaning to a verb, as can using either of the intensive stems: the Pi`el or Hitpa`el.

2 Samuel 18:25 וַיֵּלֶךְ הָלוֹךְ וְקָרֵב

infinitive absolute giving the sense of keeping on walking

and he kept on walking and drew near

1 Samuel 12:2 וַאֲנִי הִתְהַלַּכְתִּי לִפְנֵיכֶם מִנְּעֻרַי

Hitpa`el giving iterative meaning

and I have walked before you since my childhood

Jussive

A verb form expressing a command in the third person: *let him do... that they may do...* It may look no different from the imperfect (which means that its use may be an interpretation of the translator) or it may be a shortened form of the imperfect as in 3rd ה verbs for example. (42)

1 Kings 1:51 יִשָּׁבַע־לִי כַיּוֹם הַמֶּלֶךְ שְׁלֹמֹה

jussive looking the same as Nif`al 3 m. sg. prefix form

let king Solomon swear to me today

Genesis 1:3 וַיֹּאמֶר אֱלֹהִים יְהִי אוֹר

shortened form of Qal prefix יִהְיֶה

and God said, "Let there be light"

K'tiv-Q're כתב קרא

There are places in the Biblical text where there is a scribal error, or variant traditions which the Masoretes wished to preserve. In these cases, the desired pronunciation is noted in the margin or in a footnote. This is known as כְּתִב *it is written* קְרֵא *to be read.*

K'tiv Q're קרא כתב (continued)

In the phrase רֹתֶם אֶחָת (1 Kings 19:4) the word אֶחָת [כְּתִב] is referenced to a note which tells us to read אֶחָד [קְרֵא] The "error" there is that the vowels ֶ ָ ְ are for the masculine form of the word but the ending ת___ is for the feminine form. When a scribal "error" occurs frequently it may not be noted as in the words יְרוּשָׁלַםִ and הִוא This is called Q're Perpetuum.

Lexicon

The same thing as a dictionary but often used to refer to a dictionary of ancient languages. These languages were first translated into Greek and so it seems perfectly sensible that we should use the Greek word for dictionary to celebrate that happening.

Locative ה

This can mean the same as ה- directive (place to which), or it can have a narrower meaning and refer only to place in or on which.

Genesis 28:12 וַיַּחֲלֹם וְהִנֵּה סֻלָּם מֻצָּב אַרְצָה

↑ locative ה

and he dreamed and behold, a ladder set up <u>*on the earth*</u>

Major Disjunctive Accent

Silluq at the end of a verse and **atnaḥ** which marks the major break within the verse are the two most important major disjunctive accents. (We are not discussing the whole accentual system in this course.) There may be a change in pointing at these accent points where the word is said to be in **pause**.

Numbers 9:5 יַעֲשׂוּ אֶת־הַפֶּסַח

regular pointing for פֶּסַח

Numbers 9:4 וַיְדַבֵּר מֹשֶׁה אֶל־בְּנֵי יִשְׂרָאֵל לַעֲשֹׂת הַפָּסַח׃

ֶ becomes ָ because of the silluq. פָּסַח is in pause

Mappiq

A mappiq, like a dagesh, is a dot within a consonant. It is a sign that the letter is to be regarded as a full consonant and not a vowel letter. Most usually it is seen in a ה at the end of a word where it identifies the 3 f. sg. possessive or object suffix. (See: **Feminine Period**)

Mappiq (continued)

I Kings 10:13 אֶת־כָּל־חֶפְצָהּ אֲשֶׁר שָׁאָלָה

vowel letter ↑ mappiq ↑ dagesh ↑

all her desire which she asked

Maqqef

The mark which looks like a hyphen and joins two or more words together into a single accentual unit. The vowels in the first word(s) of the unit may be shortened. (2.5)

Exodus 29:12 וְאֶת־כָּל־הַדָּם

A phrase with two maqqefs: כָּל shortened from כֹּל and אֶת shortened from אֵת

Masculine

Of the two genders in Hebrew it is considered to be the prior gender. This means that if a group is composed of masculine and feminine nouns, masculine verb forms are used. Likewise, a group of masculine and feminine nouns will be referred to by a masculine pronoun. Occasionally even a feminine plural subject will take a masculine verb. (See: **Common**, **Feminine**, and **Gender**)

Genesis 18:11 אַבְרָהָם וְשָׂרָה זְקֵנִים

m. pl. adjective f. noun m. noun

Abraham and Sarah were old

Genesis 1:27 זָכָר וּנְקֵבָה בָּרָא אֹתָם

3 m. pl. object pronoun f. noun m. noun

male and female he created them

I Kings 11:3 וַיַּטּוּ נָשָׁיו אֶת־לִבּוֹ

f. pl. subj. 3 m. pl. Hif'il prefix of נטה

and his wives turned away his heart

Masora

In its fullest sense, this term is indefinable because it refers first to an oral tradition concerning the transmission of the Bible as it developed through the ages. Later, the term came to refer to the total orthography of the Hebrew Bible. It includes such issues as writing materials, sizes and shapes of the letters, length of lines, spaces between words, and proper pronunciation. In the narrow sense, Masora refers to everything that is written outside the Biblical text but accompanies it. The common technical division is between the **Masora Magna** and **Masora Parva**.

Masora Magna

A detailed explanation of the Masora Parva including some additional notes. These notes were written at the top and bottom of each page and if there was not enough room, the scribes would continue their notation at the end of the book. The purpose of these meticulously detailed notes was to guard the text from scribal errors.

Masora Parva

These brief and often abbreviated notes are found in the margins of the text. There may be a small circle over a word in the text to which the note of the Masora is directed. These notes catalogue such things as corrected pronunciations, unusual spellings, rare usages of words, the number of occurrences of a particular form, and the number of words in a book.

Masoretes

The Masoretes were those scholars who were responsible for the creation of the entire Masora. Their activities date from the fourth century CE, but are based on an oral tradition which goes back centuries earlier. Most of the Masoretes are anonymous; among the few known to us, perhaps the most prominent, were the ben Asher family.

Masoretic Text

This is the Biblical Hebrew text accepted by both Jews and Christians. The only complete extant manuscript available is the Leningrad Codex (1008 CE), which was written by Aaron ben Moses ben Asher. This codex arose from earlier traditions of the Masoretic Text.

Matres Lectionis

Mothers of reading. Before the dot-dash vowel system was developed, the letters ה ו י and rarely א were the only vowel indicators in Hebrew. This is still the case for Torah scrolls used in worship services.

י stands for hireq ◌ִ tsere ◌ֵ and segol ◌ֶ

ו for holem וֹ shureq וּ and qibbuts ◌ֻ

ה for qamets ◌ָ patah ◌ַ segol ◌ֶ at the end of a word.

א in the midddle, or at the end of a word, can stand for qamets ◌ָ

Spellings with vowel letters are called scriptio plene or כְּתָב מָלֵא (full writing): קוֹל

The omission of vowel letters is scriptio defectiva or כְּתָב חָסֵר (writing in want of): קֹל

Remember, vowel letters also function as full consonants, which was, of course, their original use. In יִהְיֶה the final ה is a vowel letter; the three other letters are consonants.

Metathesis

The transposition of letters. So you might see כֶּשֶׂב instead of כֶּבֶשׂ or שִׂלְמָה instead of שִׂמְלָה The one verb stem in which metathesis is most likely to occur is the Hitpa`el, so you will see הִשְׁתַּמֵּר instead of הִתְשַׁמֵּר

Meteg

A small vertical stroke to the left of a vowel. Its purpose is to make sure that the vowel is separated syllabically from the following vowel (often a shewa). Sometimes it gives a clue to the form. In the word כָֽבְדָה the meteg identifies the 3 f. sg. affix. כָּבְדָה without the meteg means that this is a f. sg. adjective. The meteg, in this example, is allowing us to distinguish qamets from qamets ḥatuf.

*Missing Letter Rule

An aid to help identify a missing root letter in a verb. It is usually the identification of a particular vowel under the prefix pronoun or, in the affix, under the first root letter. These "rules" are definitely worth memorizing. They can be found in 3.1, 6.1a, and 12.1.

Mood

That state of a verb which has to do with the speaker's attitude toward the action or state expressed: indicative → statement; interrogative → question; imperative → command. In English some moods, such as the subjunctive, may be expressed by using an auxiliary verb such as *might, may, should*. In Hebrew, mood may be expressed by the form but most often is inferred from the context.

1 Kings 17:10 וַיֹּאמַר קְחִי־נָא לִי מְעַט־מַיִם בַּכְּלִי וְאֶשְׁתֶּה

cohortative — imperative — indicative

and he said, "Bring me, pray, a little water in the vessel that I may drink"

Nif`al

The Nif`al is often considered to be the passive of the Qal, but like the other derived stems it has a variety of functions. It may express reflexive action: נִסְתַּר *hide oneself;* reciprocal or mutual action: נִלְחַם *engage in warfare.* Its forms are characterized by a נ or ה⊡ preformative. Fortunately, in pointed texts, the distinctive vowel patterns of this stem often help reduce seeming ambiguity: הִזָּכֶרְכֶם (Nif`al infinitive with suffix) הַזְכַּרְכֶם (Hif`il infinitive with suffix). (46-49 and Review and Drill 5)

Noun

A word used to denote a person, place, or thing. A proper noun is the name of a place or a person. In Hebrew, nouns are either masculine or feminine; singular or plural. They can occur in the absolute or construct states. Nouns can have prepositions and suffixes attached to them.

Genesis 37:1 וַיֵּשֶׁב יַעֲקֹב בְּאֶרֶץ מְגוּרֵי אָבִיו בְּאֶרֶץ כְּנָעַן

יַעֲקֹב	m. sg. proper noun
בְּאֶרֶץ	f. sg. noun in construct with a preposition attached
מְגוּרֵי	m. pl. noun in construct
אָבִיו	m. sg. noun with m. sg. suffix
כְּנָעַן	m. sg. proper noun

Noun Sentence

Two nouns, a noun and a pronoun, or a noun and an adjective. In English a verb, most often a form of *to be*, is needed between the elements to make a grammatically correct sentence.

Deuteronomy 14:1 בָּנִים אַתֶּם לַיהוה

pronoun noun

you are children of the LORD

Deuteronomy 14:4 זֹאת הַבְּהֵמָה אֲשֶׁר תֹּאכֵלוּ

demonstrative pronoun as predicate adjective+noun

this is the animal (life) which you may eat

Deuteronomy 16:8 וּבַיּוֹם הַשְּׁבִיעִי עֲצֶרֶת לַיהוה אֱלֹהֶיךָ

noun (adjective) noun

on the seventh day shall be a solemn assembly to the LORD your God

Number

Refers to singular, plural, or dual. Nouns, pronouns, adjectives, and most verb forms have number. Adverbs, infinitives, prepositions, conjunctions, and particles do not. (Numbers as in 1, 2, 3 are discussed in Lessons 41.2 and 54.)

Genesis 22:6 וַיִּקַּח בְּיָדוֹ אֶת־הָאֵשׁ

(f.) sg. noun with (m.) sg. suffix

and he took the fire in his hand

Number (continued)

f. noun + dual ending

therefore, every <u>*(pair of) hands*</u> *will be weak*

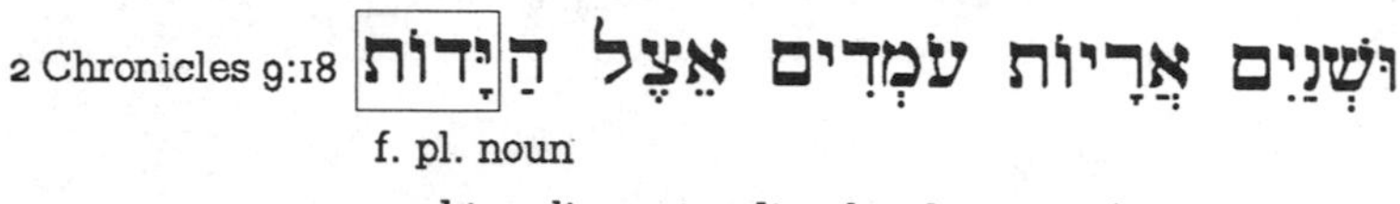

f. pl. noun

and two lions standing by the <u>*arms*</u> *(hands)*

Nunated Form

See **Energic נ**

Object of Preposition

The noun or pronoun which follows a preposition. This is not the same as a **direct object**.

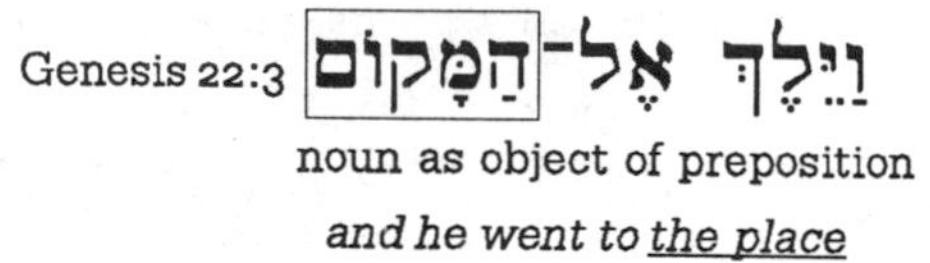

noun as object of preposition

and he went to <u>*the place*</u>

וַיִּקַּח אֶת־שְׁנֵי נְעָרָיו אִתּוֹ Genesis 22:3

pronoun ו object of preposition את

and he took two of his youths with <u>*him*</u>

Object Pronoun

A suffixed pronoun which receives the action of a verb or follows a preposition. Object pronouns have person, gender, and number. **Independent pronouns** cannot be object pronouns.

וְעָשָׂה לוֹ כְּתֹנֶת פַּסִּים Genesis 37:3

וֹ__ 3 m. sg. object pronoun; ל preposition

and he made for <u>*him*</u> *a* כְּתֹנֶת פַּסִּים

פֶּן־תֹּאמַר עָצְבִּי עָשָׂם Isaiah 48:5

ם__ 3 m. pl. object pronoun of verb עָשָׂה

lest you should say, "My idol has done <u>*them*</u>*"*

Paradigm

An example of a conjugation or a declension giving all the forms of a verb, noun, or pronoun. The paradigmatic strong verb for this course is פָּקַד

Parse

See: **Conjugate**

Participle

The verb form between the noun and the conjugated verb which emphasizes the agent of the action. Participles are declined like adjectives. They have number and gender which is displayed in their **endiNGs**. In all stems except the Qal and Nif`al, participles have a preformative מְ In the Qal, the identifying feature is holem וֹ after the first root letter. In the Nif`al there is a preformative נ and usually qamets ָ under the 2nd root letter. (9.5)

I Samuel 12:2 הִנֵּה הַמֶּלֶךְ מִתְהַלֵּךְ לִפְנֵיכֶם

m. sg. Hitpa`el participle

behold, the king is walking before you

I Kings 3:23 זֹאת אֹמֶרֶת זֶה־בְּנִי הַחַי

f. sg. Qal participle

and this one is saying, "This is my son, the living one"

Exodus 6:27 הֵם הַמְדַבְּרִים אֶל־פַּרְעֹה

m. pl. Pi`el participle

it was they who spoke to Pharaoh

Particle

A short and indeclinable part of speech such as the definite article הַ interjection הוֹי preposition בְּ בְּ לְ מִן etc., conjunction וְ כִּי לָכֵן predicator of existence יֵשׁ אֵין הִנֵּה

Passive

That state of the verb in which the subject is the recipient of the action rather than the agent. The stems in Hebrew which communicate passive action are the Pu`al, and Hof`al, and often the Nif`al. The Qal has a passive participle, which can be recognized by the shureq וּ

Passive (continued)

between the 2nd and 3rd root letters.

Genesis 6:21 וְאַתָּה קַח־לְךָ מִכָּל־מַאֲכָל אֲשֶׁר יֵאָכֵל וְאָסַפְתָּ אֵלֶיךָ

3 m. sg. Nif'al prefix

take for yourself of all the food that may be eaten and gather it to yourself

Ezekiel 2:9 וְהִנֵּה־יָד שְׁלוּחָה אֵלָי

f. sg. Qal passive participle

behold a hand was sent to me

Pause

The stress laid on the word at a **Major Disjunctive Accent**. There may be a change of vowel and even of accent position at these points.

Malachai 3:23 הִנֵּה אָנֹכִי שֹׁלֵחַ לָכֶם

אָנֹכִי not in pause, accented on last syllable

Jeremiah 1:6 כִּי־נַעַר אָנֹֽכִי

אָנֹכִי in pause, accent on נֹ rather than on כִי

Jeremiah 22:29 אֶרֶץ אֶרֶץ אָרֶץ שִׁמְעִי דְּבַר־יהוה

vowel change due to pause

Pentateuch

The Greek word, still commonly used, for the first five books of the Bible (The Torah).

Perfect

The term some grammarians use for the **affix** form.

Person

There are three grammatical "persons." 1st person refers to the speaker or speakers and is demonstrated by such pronouns as *I, we, my, mine*, and *our*. 2nd person refers to the person spoken to, designated by *you* or *your*. 3rd person refers to the person or thing spoken about. Some third person pronouns are *he, she, them, their*. All nouns use 3rd person signification. In Hebrew person is designated by affix pronouns, prefix pronouns and complements, by the use of independent pronouns, and by possessive and object suffixes.

Person (continued)

זאת הַמִּצְוָה הַחֻקִּים וְהַמִּשְׁפָּטִים אֲשֶׁר צִוָּה יהוה אֱלֹהֵיכֶם לְלַמֵּד

2 m. pl. possessive suffix 3 m. sg. verb

Deuteronomy 6:1 אֶתְכֶם לַעֲשׂוֹת בָּאָרֶץ אֲשֶׁר אַתֶּם עֹבְרִים שָׁמָּה לְרִשְׁתָּהּ

3 f. sg. object suffix 2 m. pl. independent subject pronoun 2 m. pl. object suffix

PGN (Person, Gender, Number)

Person is 1st, 2nd, or 3rd. **G**ender is masculine or feminine. **N**umber is singular or plural. Verbs, pronouns, and suffixes have PGN. Nouns, adjectives, and participles have only gender and number. Infinitives, particles, prepositions, and conjunctions have no PGN.

1 Kings 18:24 וַיַּעַן כָּל־הָעָם וַיֹּאמְרוּ טוֹב הַדָּבָר

m. sg. predicate adjective and m. sg. noun 3 m. pl. verb 3 m. sg. verb

Phrase

In English, a phrase is a group of two or more words, forming a separate part of a sentence but not containing both a subject and a verb. In Hebrew a phrase such as וּבְכָל־מְאֹדֶךָ *and with all your might* coincides with this definition. But because of the way Hebrew is built, a phrase which may need several words in English translation may be expressed by a single Hebrew word: וּבִשְׁעָרֶיךָ *and within your gates.*

Pi`el

One of the verb stems in Hebrew characterized by the strengthening of the middle root letter by means of a **dagesh forte**. The basic meaning of the stem is intensified; שׁבר *break* in the Qal becomes *smash* in the Pi`el. בחר *choose* becomes *prefer.* The Pi`el may give a transitive meaning to many verbs which are intransitive in the Qal. מלא *be full* means *fill* in the Pi`el. ישׁב *sit* or *dwell*, in the Pi`el means *colonize.* (15.4 15.7a)

Pilp`el

The Pilp`el refers to the strengthening of the two strong root letters of hollow verbs and geminates to give them the intensity of the Pi`el. גָּלַל *roll* would become גִּלְגֵּל

Plene

The spelling of a word which includes the vowel letter ו ה י plus the dot or dash vowel. הַגָּדוֹל as opposed to **defectiva** spelling הַגָּדֹל The Hebrew term for this fuller spelling is כְּתִב מָלֵא *full writing.* Some scholars believe that text heavily sprinkled with plene spellings is indicative of late composition.

Pleonastic

Literally *overly full* and refers to an expression which has more words than necessary to get an idea across. Such an expression may intensify or emphasize a thought.

1 Kings 17:10 וְהִנֵּה־שָׁם אִשָּׁה אַלְמָנָה

and behold, there was a widow woman

In this verse we know that אַלְמָנָה has to be a woman, so the word אִשָּׁה makes the phrase pleonastic.

Pluperfect

This tense can also be referred to as the past perfect. It refers to actions which have taken place before the main action of the verse. In English it is recognized by the auxiliary verb *had* plus a past tense. In Hebrew, the pluperfect is rendered by the affix form and must be inferred from the context, but often אֲשֶׁר followed by the affix is an indication of pluperfect time.

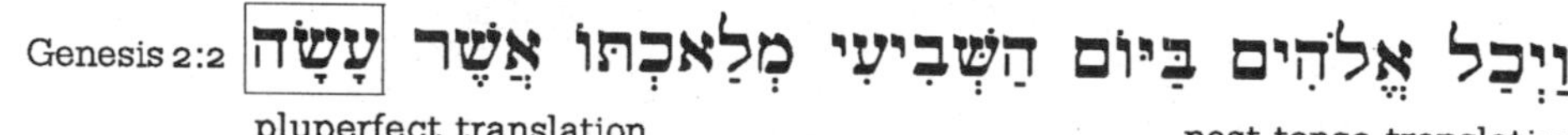

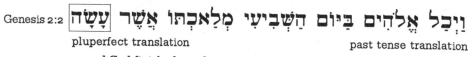

Genesis 2:2 וַיְכַל אֱלֹהִים בַּיּוֹם הַשְּׁבִיעִי מְלַאכְתּוֹ אֲשֶׁר עָשָׂה

pluperfect translation — past tense translation

and God finished, on the seventh day, his work which he had made

Pointing/points

The vowels that were inserted into the consonantal text can also be called points. Such a text is vocalized or pointed. Vocalization also refers to the other marks such as dagesh, meteg, sof passuq, and of course all the other accents. This system was developed after everyday usage of the language had died out and there was danger that correct pronunciation might be lost. Most of this work was done in the sixth and seventh centuries CE by Masoretic scholars. The insertion of the dot-dash vowel system is in itself an interpretation of the text. If you look at a sample of unvocalized text (next page), you can see that for many words there is more than one way to point the text.

Pointing (continued)

ויקרא אברהם שם המקום ההוא יהוה יראה אשר יאמר
היום בהר יהוה יראה Genesis 22:14

וַיִּקְרָא אַבְרָהָם שֵׁם־הַמָּקוֹם הַהוּא יהוה יִרְאֶה אֲשֶׁר יֵאָמֵר
הַיּוֹם בְּהַר יהוה יֵרָאֶה׃ Genesis 22:14

If you compare the unpointed text with the pointed Masoretic version, you can see that different pointing would change the meaning. With some words the difference might be slight, but with others, quite marked. Torah scrolls are not pointed.

Possessive Pronoun

A suffixed pronoun used to show ownership: *my, mine, your, yours*, etc. In Hebrew, possessive pronouns can be attached to nouns, and sometimes to infinitives. They have person, gender, and number. The other types of pronouns are **independent pronouns** (which are often **subject pronouns**) and **object pronouns**.

תִּירָא אֶת־יהוה אֱלֹהֶיךָ לִשְׁמֹר אֶת־כָּל־חֻקֹּתָיו וּמִצְוֹתָיו Deuteronomy 6:2

3 m. sg. possessive pronoun — 2 m. sg. possessive pronoun

you will fear the LORD *your God to keep all his statutes and his commandments*

Predicate

The predicate may be simply a verb, or the term may refer to everything in a sentence other than the subject and its modifiers.

וַתָּבֹא יְרוּשָׁלַ͏ְמָה בְּחַיִל כָּבֵד מְאֹד גְּמַלִּים נֹשְׂאִים בְּשָׂמִים 1 Kings 10:2

and she came to Jerusalem with a very great retinue, with camels that bore spices

The predicate could be וַתָּבֹא or וַתָּבֹא and all the phrases following. Well, that is not quite accurate because in Hebrew the subject is included in the verb form, but you should get the idea.

Predicate Adjective

This is another way of referring to an adjective which is part of a **noun sentence**. A predicate adjective often precedes the noun (or pronoun) it modifies. (15.2)

Predicate Adjective (continued)

I Kings 19:4 כִּי־לֹא־טוֹב אָנֹכִי מֵאֲבֹתָי

pronoun predicate adjective

because I am no better than my fathers

Predicator of Existence

An indeclinable word which indicates the being of something, יֵשׁ or הִנֵּה for example, or it can imply nonexistence אֵין These words may have a suffix attached.

Genesis 37:24 וְהַבּוֹר רֵק אֵין בּוֹ מָיִם

predicator of nonexistence

but the well was empty; there was no water in it

Genesis 37:13 וַיֹּאמֶר לוֹ הִנֵּנִי

predicator of exisence with 1 c. sg. suffix attached

and he said to him, "Here I am"

***Prefix Form**

The prefix is the Hebrew verb form in which the subject pronoun is "prefixed" to the front of the root. Part of the subject pronoun may also follow the root; it is called the prefix complement.

Hif'il prefix

3 m. pl. יַמְלִיכוּ — prefix complement ↑ ↑ prefix pronoun

3 m. sg. יַמְלִיךְ — ↑ prefix pronoun

The prefix form is called the imperfect by many grammarians because it refers to incomplete action. It is usually given a future or present tense translation. The prefix form may carry the notion of *could, should, would,* or *might.*

Deuteronomy 6:2 לְמַעַן תִּירָא אֶת־יהוה אֱלֹהֶיךָ

prefix form, many possibilities for "correct" translation

Preposition

An indeclinable word that introduces a phrase or clause. A preposition can be an independent word: אֶל or it can be attached to another word: לְבֵן

It may join with another preposition to create a new preposition: מִן + עַל ⟷ מֵעַל

Preposition (continued)

It may be combined with a conjunction, in which case the two words together create a single conjunction: עַל אֲשֶׁר ⟷ *because.*

Prepositions are among the most difficult elements one has to cope with in trying to get the feel of a foreign language. Example: עַל fills 13 plus columns in a standard dictionary, לְ 16.

Prepositional Phrase

In English a prepositional phrase would consist of at least two words but that is not necessarily the case in Hebrew because the preposition may be attached to its object. (See: **Adjective Phrase** and **Phrase**)

Genesis 22:3 וַיָּקָם וַיֵּלֶךְ אֶל־הַמָּקוֹם אֲשֶׁר־אָמַר־לוֹ הָאֱלֹהִים

attached preposition + pronoun — independent preposition + noun

and he arose and he went to the place which God had said to him

Pronoun

A word used in place of a noun. The adjective for pronoun is pronominal, as in the question, "In the example below, how many pronominal suffixes are there?"

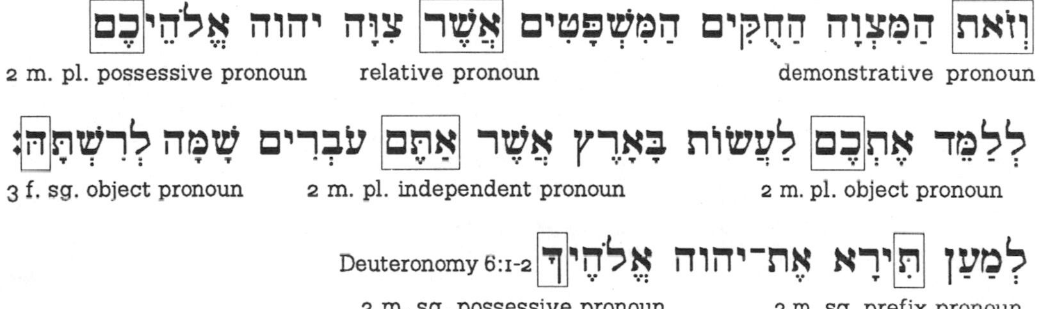

Proper Noun

Proper nouns are the names of particular people or places. It's easy to recognize them in English because they begin with a capital letter, but in Hebrew only the meaning or context will identify proper nouns.

דִּבְרֵי יִרְמְיָהוּ בֶּן־חִלְקִיָּהוּ מִן־הַכֹּהֲנִים אֲשֶׁר בַּעֲנָתוֹת בְּאֶרֶץ בִּנְיָמִן

Jeremiah 1:1 ← four proper nouns →

the words of Jeremiah, son of Hilkijahu, of the kohanim, who were in Anatoth, in the land of Benjamin

Pu`al

The Pu`al stem is the passive of the **Pi`el**. Like the Pi`el, the middle root letter is doubled by means of a dagesh forte, and the preformatives have shewa ְ under them. It also makes similar adjustments to those of the Pi`el for things such as middle guttural. The Pu`al is recognized by the vowel qibbuts ֻ under the first root letter. (45.3)

Numbers 3:16 וַיִּפְקֹד אֹתָם מֹשֶׁה עַל־פִּי יהוה כַּאֲשֶׁר **צֻוָּה**

Pu`al 3 m. sg. affix form

And Moses numbered them according to the word of the Lord, as he had been commanded.

Exodus 34:34 וְדִבֶּר אֶל־בְּנֵי יִשְׂרָאֵל אֵת אֲשֶׁר **יְצֻוֶּה**

Pu`al 3 m. sg. prefix form

and he spoke to the children of Israel that which he was commanded

Qal

The Qal is the basic stem of the verb, sometimes called the ground-form. The root Qal קלל means *light.* The derived stems are called כְּבֵדִים *heavy* because they have additions, either in terms of preformatives or strengthening, to the basic stem.

Genesis 12:10 כִּי־**כָבֵד** הָרָעָב בָּאָרֶץ

3 m. sg. Qal affix

because the famine was heavy (severe) in the land

Exodus 20:12 **כַּבֵּד** אֶת־אָבִיךָ וְאֶת־אִמֶּךָ

3 m. sg. Pi`el affix, middle root letter strengthened

honor your father and your mother

Quiescent

A letter which is seen but not heard. This most often occurs with the vowel letters ה ו י and the letters א and ע when they are at the end of a syllable and have no vowel.

יָדַע	קָרָא	הָיָה
quiescent ע ↑	quiescent א ↑	quiescent ה ↑ ↑ vocal ה

Examples of quiescent letters in English are the t in *often* and the g in *paradigm.*

Radical

Another term for root letter. In אמר א would be the first radical, מ the second, and ר the third. "The three radicals" refer then to the three root letters, not to a singing group.

Reflexive

An action which is turned back upon the subject of the verb. In Hebrew the Nif`al and Hitpa`el are the verb stems which may most commonly impart a reflexive meaning to an action. Pronouns can also fulfill this function.

Deuteronomy 8:11 הִשָּׁמֶר לְךָ פֶּן־תִּשְׁכַּח אֶת־יהוה אֱלֹהֶיךָ

reflexive use of pronoun and of Nif`al imperative

take heed (upon yourself) lest you forget the LORD your God

Ezekiel 38:23 וְהִתְגַּדִּלְתִּי וְהִתְקַדִּשְׁתִּי וְנוֹדַעְתִּי לְעֵינֵי גּוֹיִם רַבִּים

reflexive meanings of Nif`al and Hitpa`el affix

and I will magnify myself and sanctify myself and I will make myself known in the eyes of many nations

Regular Verb

See: **Strong Verb**

Relative Clause

A clause often introduced by a relative particle such as אֲשֶׁר or כִּי Sometimes in Hebrew, the relative pronoun is not used; for example, a relative clause can be introduced by means of the article before a participle.

Psalms 1:1 אַשְׁרֵי הָאִישׁ אֲשֶׁר לֹא הָלַךְ בַּעֲצַת רְשָׁעִים

relative clause introduced by אֲשֶׁר

happy is the man who does not walk in the council of the wicked

Psalms 118:26 בָּרוּךְ הַבָּא בְּשֵׁם יהוה

relative clause introduced by הַ in front of a participle

blessed is he who comes in the name of the LORD

Relative Pronoun

A word which introduces a clause and refers to an antecedent. In Hebrew this function is

Relative Pronoun (continued)

absorbed by the all-purpose relative pronoun אֲשֶׁר

Genesis 22:2 קַח־נָא אֶת־בִּנְךָ אֶת־יְחִידְךָ אֲשֶׁר־אָהַבְתָּ אֶת־יִצְחָק

relative pronoun referring to בִּנְךָ and יְחִידְךָ

whom you love

Root

A three letter consonant cluster which represents the base from which verbs and nouns develop. So for example מלך would represent the concept of ruling. From this root come the verb מָלַךְ *rule*, and such nouns as מֶלֶךְ *king* and מַלְכוּת *royalty*. There are those who do not agree entirely with this concept but reason instead that some roots are originally from a two letter or a four letter base. They believe such a hypothesis better explains such phenomena as hollow and geminate verbs. This is the stuff of advanced **etymology**.

Segolate Noun

A two syllable noun, having the emphasis on the first syllable. Its vowels are most often segol ֶ מֶ֫לֶךְ בֹּ֫קֶר אֶ֫רֶץ If the middle letter of a segolate noun is a guttural, then the vowels change to pataḥ ַ נַ֫עַר

Semitic Language

A major group of languages of southwestern Asia and northern Africa. The subgroups are East Semitic (Akkadian), Northwest Semitic (Phoenician, Punic, Aramaic, Hebrew), and Southwest Semitic (Arabic, Ethiopic, Amharic).

Septuagint

A Greek translation of the Hebrew Bible so called because it was said to be the work of seventy-two Palestinian Jews who completed the work in seventy days in the third century BCE. Contrary to this lovely legend, the actual work was done by many people over a long period of time. The original document does not exist. The reason for the translation was that the Jews were moving into Greek speaking areas, adopting that language as the vernacular, and wanted to be able to read the Bible in that tongue.

Silluq

A small vertical line ֽ (it looks just like a meteg) near the end of a verse to mark where the tone or accent is. It is one of the major disjunctive accents.

לֹא תִּרְצָח׃ וְלֹא תִּנְאָף׃ וְלֹא תִּגְנֹב׃ Deuteronomy 5:17-19

Simple Vav

The conjunction vav ו usually pointed with a shewa וְ which is seen often with nouns, adjectives, and particles, less often attached to a prefix form of the verb, and rarely on an affix form. This conjunction has a wide range of meanings some of which are *and, then, but, both. . .and.* (See also **Vav Conversive** and **Vav Reversive**)

וְהָיָה מֵהַנַּחַל תִּשְׁתֶּה וְאֶת־הָעֹרְבִים צִוִּיתִי לְכַלְכֶּלְךָ שָׁם I Kings 17:4

simple vav ↑ vav reversive ↑

And it shall be that you will drink of the wadi and the ravens I have commanded to feed you there.

Sof Passuq

The sign ׃ which marks the end of a verse. Like the vowels, it is not indigenous to the text but was added when the text (for use outside of the synagogue) began to be written with vocalization markings.

***Special Ending**

See: **Ending, Special**

Stative

Stative verbs denote the state of the subject rather than describe an action. In English, this state is usually expressed by using a form of *to be* with a predicate adjective such as *old, afraid, heavy.* Many of the statives in Hebrew have tsere ֵ (an "E" vowel) or holem וֹ (an "O" vowel) as their second vowel in the Qal and only a few are transitive. (17.7)

וְהַמֶּלֶךְ דָּוִד זָקֵן I Kings 1:1

stative verb

and King David was old

וַיִּשְׂנְאוּ אֹתוֹ Genesis 37:4

stative verb taking a DO

and they hated him

Stem

The seven major patterns of the verb. The stems other than Qal are called derived stems and are formed either by internal intensification of the root or by the addition of preformatives. Most verbs do not exist in all stems.

Qal — basic stem פָּקַד *attend, visit, muster, appoint*

Nif'al — passive or reflexive נִפְקַד *be visited (upon), be appointed*

Pi'el — intensive פִּקֵּד *muster (a host)*

Pu'al — passive of Pi'el פֻּקַּד *be passed in review*

Hif'il — causative הִפְקִיד *make overseer*

Hof'al — passive of Hif'il הָפְקַד *be made overseer*

Hitpa'el — intensive reflexive הִתְפַּקֵּד *be mustered*

Stem Indicator

A distinctive preformative, vowel, or dagesh that helps to identify the stem of a verb. So for example in the 3 m. sg. Pi'el affix form פִּקֵּד the dagesh forte in the middle root letter is a stem indicator. In the Hif'il הִפְקִיד the preformative ה and the hireq ִ under the middle root letter are stem indicators.

Strong Verb

Some classify as a strong verb one whose root is made up of three consonants which follow the paradigm exactly such as קטל and פקד We find it difficult to give a definition of the strong or regular verb. (These words are used interchangeably in this course.) So rather than define we will advise: learn the paradigms and be prepared for heated semantic arguments on this topic.

Subject

The noun or pronoun which does the action of the verb or about which something is said. In Hebrew, the subject may be indicated within the verb form and/or it may be a separate word.

וַיֵּלֶךְ וַיַּעַשׂ כִּדְבַר יהוה 1 Kings 17:5

two 3 m. sg. Qal prefix verbs: the subject is indicated by the prefix י

and he went and he did according to the word of the LORD

וַתִּשְׁלַח אִיזֶבֶל מַלְאָךְ אֶל־אֵלִיָּהוּ 1 Kings 19:2

subject a proper noun, and also indicated by prefix pronoun תּ

and Jezebel (she) sent a messenger to Elijah

Subject Pronoun

The pronoun (I, they, you, etc.) which does the action of the verb. In the affix and prefix forms, the subject pronoun is carried by the verb; in the imperative, it is understood to be 2nd person; with a participle, it is indicated by another word, either a noun or an independent subject pronoun; and if an infinitive has a subject pronoun, it will be a possessive suffix or an independent noun (most likely a proper noun). Independent subject pronouns are often used for emphasis.

Deuteronomy 9:1 שְׁמַע יִשְׂרָאֵל אַתָּה עֹבֵר הַיּוֹם אֶת־הַיַּרְדֵּן

Qal m. sg. imperative שְׁמַע subject pronoun implied

m. sg. participle עֹבֵר subject indicated by independent subject pronoun אַתָּה

(you) hear, O Israel: you are about to pass over the Jordan this day

Genesis 22:14 אֲשֶׁר יֵאָמֵר הַיּוֹם

3 m. sg. Nif'al prefix. Subject pronoun *it* indicated by prefix pronoun

it is said. . .

Subordinate Clause

See: **Adjective Clause** and **Adverb Clause**

Substantive

A word, usually an adjective or a participle, which is used for the equivalent of a noun.

Exodus 20:6 וְעֹשֶׂה חֶסֶד לַאֲלָפִים לְאֹהֲבַי וּלְשֹׁמְרֵי מִצְוֹתָי

three participles being used as substantives

but showing mercy to thousands (of generations) of those that love me and keep my commamdments

***Suffix**

We are reserving this term to refer specifically to object and possessive pronouns which are attached to verbs, nouns, and prepositions. Suffixes have person, gender, and number.

Deuteronomy 6:10 וְהָיָה כִּי יְבִיאֲךָ יהוה אֱלֹהֶיךָ אֶל־הָאָרֶץ

2 m. sg. possessive suffix attached to noun

2 m. sg. object suffix attached to a verb

and it will be that the Lord your God will bring you to the land

Syllable

A unit of pronunciation. In Hebrew a syllable starts with a consonant [except when a word starts with the conjunction vocalized as וּ]. If it ends in a consonant it is a closed syllable and if it ends in a vowel, it is an open syllable.

זאת	וּ בָ הָר
monosyllabic word of one closed syllable	trisyllabic word: closed open open

Syntax

The branch of grammar which deals with the arrangement of words and how the arrangement and the meaning conveyed are related. Syntax addresses such issues as the construction and placement of phrases, clauses, direct speech, agreement of nouns and adjectives, and use of tenses.

Text Criticism

Full text criticism would be an examination of all extant manuscripts to try to determine the best text. It is a concern of text criticism to try to explain how existing variants may have arisen. There is a modest discussion of this topic in the notes to Exodus 3:1.

Tone

Tone is another term for the accented syllable in a word.

Torah

The books Genesis, Exodus, Leviticus, Numbers, and Deuteronomy make up the Torah. In Hebrew these names are בְּרֵאשִׁית שְׁמוֹת וַיִּקְרָא בְּמִדְבַּר דְּבָרִים You can see that except for *Genesis* the English names have no relationship the Hebrew. The Hebrew titles are taken from the first distinctive word in each book. The word *Torah* is derived from the root ירה which, in the Hif`il, means *instruct, point out, show.* It is <u>not</u> synonymous with *law* as in *legislate.*

Transitive

A verb which takes a **direct object** (DO) to complete its meaning.

Genesis 37:18 וַיַּשְׁכֵּם יַעֲקֹב בַּבֹּקֶר [וַיִּקַּח] אֶת־הָאֶבֶן

DDO — transitive verb — intransitive verb

and Jacob got up early in the morning and <u>he took</u> the stone

Triliteral

"Three letters." A term used to describe the Hebrew hypothetical three letter root. Most dictionaries are organized around this concept. There are grammarians who believe that there were biliteral and also quadraliteral roots. (See: **Root**)

Trope

The musical symbols used to chant the Torah, Prophets, and some of the Writings. The sound patterns are indicated by the accent marks, over and under the words, which are not vowels.

Ultima

The last syllable in a word. It generally receives the accent or tone.

Genesis 1:1 בְּרֵאשִׁית בָּרָא אֱלֹהִים אֵת הַשָּׁמַיִם וְאֵת הָאָרֶץ׃

In this verse all the words except for הָאָרֶץ and הַשָּׁמַיִם are accented on the ultima.

Vav Consecutive

What we are calling the **vav conversive**. Each term takes into account one use of this construction. Consecutive implies "This happened and then that..." and so describes its narrative function. Conversive is descriptive of the tense being converted, in translation, from future or present to past.

***Vav Conversive**

A construction which can be recognized by a vav-pataḥ-dagesh forte ◌ּוַ in front of the prefix form of the verb: וַתְּדַבֵּר When the pronoun is יְ the dagesh is usually omitted: וַיְדַבֵּר Some 1st י verbs, hollow verbs, 3rd ה and Hif'ils have a shortened form in the vav conversive for some PGNs:

יַרְכִּיב ← וַיַּרְכֵּב	יִרְאֶה ← וַיַּרְא	יָקוּם ← וַיָּקָם	יֵשֵׁב ← וַיֵּשֶׁב
Hif'il	3rd ה	Hollow	1st י

It is a stylistic device of Biblical Hebrew when narrating a series of past events to begin the narration with an affix form of the verb and to continue it with a series of verbs in the prefix form with vav conversive.

Vav Conversive (continued)

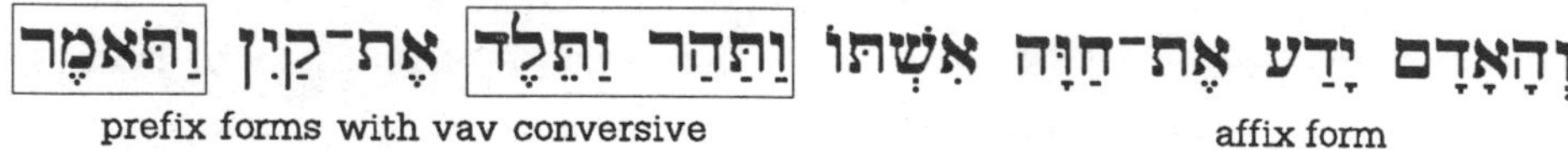
וְהָאָדָם יָדַע אֶת־חַוָּה אִשְׁתּוֹ וַתַּהַר וַתֵּלֶד אֶת־קַיִן וַתֹּאמֶר

prefix forms with vav conversive — affix form

Genesis 4:1 קָנִיתִי אִישׁ אֶת־יהוה׃

direct speech so affix form

And אָדָם *knew* חַוָּה *his wife and (then) she conceived and (then) she bore* קַיִן *and (then) she said,*
"I have acquired a man (child) with (the help of) the Lord."

A new section of a narrative often is introduced by a vav conversive:

Genesis 6:5 וַיַּרְא יהוה כִּי רַבָּה רָעַת הָאָדָם בָּאָרֶץ

and (then) the L*ORD* *saw that the wickedness of man was great on the earth*

***Vav Reversive**

When a vav ו is attached to the front of an affix form of the verb, it usually serves to give it a future tense translation. Hence the vav "reverses" the tense. The name vav reversive is an analogic extension of vav conversive for the affix. In the narration of future events, the first verb will often be a prefix form and the following ones will be affix form plus vav reversive. There are instances of the vavs not changing the tense from past to future; in that case the ו is called a **simple vav**. Such occurrences are mostly in the later books.

Deuteronomy 2:28 אֹכֶל בַּכֶּסֶף תַּשְׁבִּרֵנִי וְאָכַלְתִּי

affix form + vav reversive prefix form

you will sell me food for money that I may eat (and I will eat)

Ezekiel 37:8 וְרָאִיתִי וְהִנֵּה־עֲלֵיהֶם גִּדִים וּבָשָׂר עָלָה

simple vav

and as I beheld, lo, the sinews and the flesh came upon them

Verb

A word or words which expresses action, existence, or occurrence. In Hebrew, the verb has five **forms**: affix, prefix, participle, imperative, and infinitive. It has seven **stems**: Qal, Nif`al, Pi`el, Pu`al, Hif`il, Hof`al, and Hitpa`el. Because Biblical Hebrew uses so few adjectives and adverbs, the impact and color of the language are conveyed particularly through the verb. The fact that the verb can be built up in front with preformatives, strengthened in the middle by a dagesh, or infix, and lengthened by the addition of pronominal suffixes enhances its conspicuousness. The verbs in Dt. 6:7 are a representative example of the

Verb (continued)

strength of highly inflected verbs. Notice how English needs about four times as many words to get across the ideas which, in Hebrew, are carried on the verb.

וְשִׁנַּנְתָּם לְבָנֶיךָ וְדִבַּרְתָּ בָּם בְּשִׁבְתְּךָ בְּבֵיתֶךָ וּבְלֶכְתְּךָ בַדֶּרֶךְ
וּבְשָׁכְבְּךָ וּבְקוּמֶךָ׃ Deuteronomy 6:7

And you will inculcate them to your children, and you will speak about them when you sit in your house, when you walk by the way, when you lie down, and when you rise up.

Vocalization

See: **Pointing**

Vocative

The direct address of a person or thing.

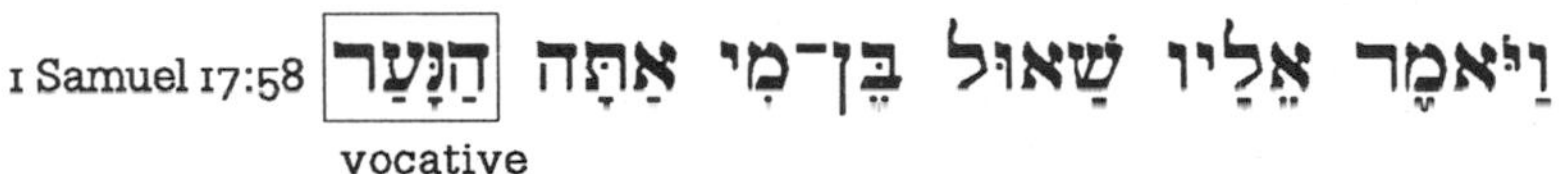

and Saul said to him, 'Whose son are you, youth?'

sing, O heavens; and be joyful, O earth

Voice

See: **Active** and **Passive**

Vowel Class

There are three classes of vowels in Hebrew: "A" "E/I" and "O/U" Most often a vowel will exchange with another of its own class for purposes of lengthening or shortening. The one vowel which conspicuously crosses class is segol. Although it is an "E/I" vowel, it exchanges with "A" vowels in pause.

יָד←יַד־ בֵּן←בֶּן־ כּוֹל←כָּל־ שֶׁמֶן←שָׁמֶן׃

qamets ḥatuf ↑

Vowel Letter

The letters א ה ו י (See: **Matres Lectionis**)

Vulgate

The Latin translation of the Hebrew Bible plus the Apocrypha and New Testament prepared primarily by St. Jerome in the fourth century CE. This translation enjoyed wide acceptance in Western Christendom during the Middle Ages, and thus became known as the *Vulgata Versio* ("common version.") Until recently it was the only authorized version of the Bible for the Roman Catholic Church.

***Weak Verb**

A verb with a root letter which may not appear in all forms. 1st י 1st נ 3rd ה hollow verbs, and geminates fall into this category. Some grammars include in this group verbs which contain a guttural letter. In the following Qal prefix forms of weak verbs note the missing root letter: (17.6)

תֵּצֵא	תִּתֵּן	וַתָּקָם	וַתֵּרָא	תֵּרַע
1st י missing	1st נ assimilated	middle ו missing	final ה missing	final ע missing

Word Order

The usual word order of a Biblical verse is: verb followed by its subject (if there is an independent subject), then the indirect object followed by the direct object. Other features such as adjectives and adverbs, which may be single words, phrases or clauses, are fitted in of course. Word order is often varied for emphasis or euphony.

וְיִשְׂרָאֵל אָהַב אֶת־יוֹסֵף מִכָּל־בָּנָיו כִּי־בֶן־זְקֻנִים הוּא לוֹ

placement of הוא לו emphatic — note: subject יִשְׂרָאֵל precedes verb אָהַב

וְעָשָׂה לוֹ כְּתֹנֶת פַּסִּים׃ וַיִּרְאוּ אֶחָיו כִּי־אֹתוֹ אָהַב אֲבִיהֶם

placement of DO אֹתוֹ before the verb is emphatic — usual word order

מִכָּל־אֶחָיו וַיִּשְׂנְאוּ אֹתוֹ Genesis 37:3 and 4a

usual word order

Zeugma

Ellipsis of a verb from one of two or more usually parallel clauses. This is a figure of speech seen often in Biblical Hebrew poetry but is usually referred to as incomplete parallelism. (55)

זָכַרְתִּי לָךְ חֶסֶד נְעוּרַיִךְ אַהֲבַת כְּלוּלֹתָיִךְ Jeremiah 2:2
לֶכְתֵּךְ אַחֲרַי בַּמִּדְבָּר בְּאֶרֶץ לֹא זְרוּעָה׃

I remember the devotion of your youth, [I remember] the love of your bridehood
[I remember] your following after me in the wilderness, in a land not sown.

Verb Charts

About these charts:

Prefix form/vav conversive is included for those verbs which are apocopated with vav conversive. For the other verbs, the prefix/vav conversive is formed by adding ◌ַו to the prefix form.

In some places you will see a second "spelling" of a form. This is because these verbs developed biforms. Most notable in this respect is the **Hof'al**. Bear in mind, even if not noted in every chart, that its preformative vowel can be ◌ָ or ◌ֻ

You will notice that in some of the charts, the **f. pl. participle** is missing. This is because of a spacing problem which forced us to remove one line of text. Because f. pl. participles are rare, that form was selected for this ignominious honor. Those who can figure out the reason why on some charts there is room for everything, but on others a line had to be omitted can have their copy of the book autographed by one of the authors.

A word about the **Pi'el middle guttural**: the representative verb is ברך which technically is not a middle guttural but fits into the category because ר does not take dagesh. It is the most common Pi'el of this type and so that is why it was selected for the paradigm. You will notice that a composite shewa appears under the ר in some PGNs. In some Biblical texts the verb appears this way; in others a simple shewa is used. In other words you will see בֵּרֲכוּ in some Bibles; בֵּרְכוּ in others.

Two inclusions require explanations. In the 1st Guttural chart חזק is listed as an alternate 1st ח pattern. In fact, it is "alternate" because it is stative, but it is an "A" class stative which brings us to the problem of terminology discussed in Lesson 17.7. It is only this type of 1st ח verb which takes such pointing.

The other entry which needs comment is ירא It may be the only 1st י "E" class of its type, but because of its frequency of occurrence, a listing of its extant PGNs in the Qal has been included.

Spaces which are blank are so because there are no extant examples of such forms in the Bible. For example, there simply are no Pu'al or Hof'al imperatives.

			Qal "A" regular	Qal "E"	Qal "O"	Nif'al
Affix	Sg.	3 m.	פָּקַד	כָּבֵד	קָטֹן	נִפְקַד
		3 f.	פָּֽקְדָה	כָּֽבְדָה	קָֽטְנָה	נִפְקְדָה
		2 m.	פָּקַדְתָּ	כָּבַדְתָּ	קָטֹנְתָּ	נִפְקַדְתָּ
		2 f.	פָּקַדְתְּ	כָּבַדְתְּ	קָטֹנְתְּ	נִפְקַדְתְּ
		1 c.	פָּקַדְתִּי	כָּבַדְתִּי	קָטֹנְתִּי	נִפְקַדְתִּי
	Pl.	3 c.	פָּֽקְדוּ	כָּֽבְדוּ	קָֽטְנוּ	נִפְקְדוּ
		2 m.	פְּקַדְתֶּם	כְּבַדְתֶּם	קְטָנְתֶּם	נִפְקַדְתֶּם
		2 f.	פְּקַדְתֶּן	כְּבַדְתֶּן	קְטָנְתֶּן	נִפְקַדְתֶּן
		1 c.	פָּקַדְנוּ	כָּבַדְנוּ	קָטֹנּוּ	נִפְקַדְנוּ
Prefix	Sg.	3 m.	יִפְקֹד	יִכְבַּד	יִקְטַן	יִפָּקֵד
		3 f.	תִּפְקֹד	תִּכְבַּד	like	תִּפָּקֵד
		2 m.	תִּפְקֹד	תִּכְבַּד	יִכְבַּד	תִּפָּקֵד
		2 f.	תִּפְקְדִי	תִּכְבְּדִי		תִּפָּקְדִי
		1 c.	אֶפְקֹד	אֶכְבַּד		אֶפָּקֵד
	Pl.	3 m.	יִפְקְדוּ	יִכְבְּדוּ		יִפָּקְדוּ
		3 f.	תִּפְקֹדְנָה	תִּכְבַּדְנָה		תִּפָּקַדְנָה
		2 m.	תִּפְקְדוּ	תִּכְבְּדוּ		תִּפָּקְדוּ
		2 f.	תִּפְקֹדְנָה	תִּכְבַּדְנָה		תִּפָּקַדְנָה
		1 c.	נִפְקֹד	נִכְבַּד		נִפָּקֵד
Imperative	Sg.	2 m.	פְּקֹד	כְּבַד		הִפָּקֵד
		2 f.	פִּקְדִי	כִּבְדִי		הִפָּקְדִי
	Pl.	2 m.	פִּקְדוּ	כִּבְדוּ		הִפָּקְדוּ
		2 f.	פְּקֹדְנָה	כְּבַדְנָה		הִפָּקַדְנָה
Participle	Sg.	m.	פֹּקֵד	כָּבֵד	קָטֹן	נִפְקָד
		f.	פֹּקְדָה	כְּבֵדָה	קְטַנָּה	נִפְקָדָה
	Pl.	m.	פֹּקְדִים	כְּבֵדִים	קְטַנִּים	נִפְקָדִים
		f.	פֹּקְדוֹת	כְּבֵדוֹת	קְטַנּוֹת	נִפְקָדוֹת
Infinitive	Construct		פְּקֹד	כְּבֹד		הִפָּקֵד
Infinitive	Absolute		פָּקוֹד	כָּבֹד		הִפָּקֵד נִפְקֹד

Prefix/vav conversive

Pi'el	Pu'al	Hif'il	Hof'al
פִּקֵּד פִּקַּד	פֻּקַּד	הִפְקִיד	הָפְקַד הֻפְקַד
פִּקְּדָה	פֻּקְּדָה	הִפְקִידָה	הָפְקְדָה
פִּקַּדְתָּ	פֻּקַּדְתָּ	הִפְקַדְתָּ	הָפְקַדְתָּ
פִּקַּדְתְּ	פֻּקַּדְתְּ	הִפְקַדְתְּ	הָפְקַדְתְּ
פִּקַּדְתִּי	פֻּקַּדְתִּי	הִפְקַדְתִּי	הָפְקַדְתִּי
פִּקְּדוּ	פֻּקְּדוּ	הִפְקִידוּ	הָפְקְדוּ
פִּקַּדְתֶּם	פֻּקַּדְתֶּם	הִפְקַדְתֶּם	הָפְקַדְתֶּם
פִּקַּדְתֶּן	פֻּקַּדְתֶּן	הִפְקַדְתֶּן	הָפְקַדְתֶּן
פִּקַּדְנוּ	פֻּקַּדְנוּ	הִפְקַדְנוּ	הָפְקַדְנוּ
יְפַקֵּד	יְפֻקַּד	יַפְקִיד	יָפְקַד יֻפְקַד
תְּפַקֵּד	תְּפֻקַּד	תַּפְקִיד	תָּפְקַד
תְּפַקֵּד	תְּפֻקַּד	תַּפְקִיד	תָּפְקַד
תְּפַקְּדִי	תְּפֻקְּדִי	תַּפְקִידִי	תָּפְקְדִי
אֲפַקֵּד	אֲפֻקַּד	אַפְקִיד	אָפְקַד
יְפַקְּדוּ	יְפֻקְּדוּ	יַפְקִידוּ	יָפְקְדוּ
תְּפַקֵּדְנָה	תְּפֻקַּדְנָה	תַּפְקֵדְנָה	תָּפְקַדְנָה
תְּפַקְּדוּ	תְּפֻקְּדוּ	תַּפְקִידוּ	תָּפְקְדוּ
תְּפַקֵּדְנָה	תְּפֻקַּדְנָה	תַּפְקֵדְנָה	תָּפְקַדְנָה
נְפַקֵּד	נְפֻקַּד	נַפְקִיד	נָפְקַד
פַּקֵּד		הַפְקֵד	
פַּקְּדִי		הַפְקִידִי	
פַּקְּדוּ		הַפְקִידוּ	
פַּקֵּדְנָה		הַפְקֵדְנָה	
מְפַקֵּד	מְפֻקָּד	מַפְקִיד	מָפְקָד מֻפְקָד
מְפַקְּדָה	מְפֻקָּדָה	מַפְקִידָה	מָפְקָדָה
מְפַקְּדִים	מְפֻקָּדִים	מַפְקִידִים	מָפְקָדִים
מְפַקְּדוֹת	מְפֻקָּדוֹת	מַפְקִידוֹת	מָפְקָדוֹת
פַּקֵּד		הַפְקִיד	
פַּקֵּד פַּקֹּד	פֻּקֹּד	הַפְקֵד	הָפְקֵד הֻפְקֵד
		וַיַּפְקֵד	

			Qal		Nif'al	Hif'il	Hof'al
Affix	Sg.	3 m.	עָמַד		נֶעֱמַד	הֶעֱמִיד	הָעֳמַד
		3 f.	עָמְדָה		נֶעֶמְדָה	הֶעֱמִידָה	הָעָמְדָה
		2 m.	עָמַדְתָּ		נֶעֱמַדְתָּ	הֶעֱמַדְתָּ	הָעֳמַדְתָּ
		2 f.	עָמַדְתְּ		נֶעֱמַדְתְּ	הֶעֱמַדְתְּ	הָעֳמַדְתְּ
		1 c.	עָמַדְתִּי		נֶעֱמַדְתִּי	הֶעֱמַדְתִּי	הָעֳמַדְתִּי
	Pl.	3 c.	עָמְדוּ		נֶעֶמְדוּ	הֶעֱמִידוּ	הָעָמְדוּ
		2 m.	עֲמַדְתֶּם		נֶעֱמַדְתֶּם	הֶעֱמַדְתֶּם	הָעֳמַדְתֶּם
		2 f.	עֲמַדְתֶּן		נֶעֱמַדְתֶּן	הֶעֱמַדְתֶּן	הָעֳמַדְתֶּן
		1 c.	עָמַדְנוּ		נֶעֱמַדְנוּ	הֶעֱמַדְנוּ	הָעֳמַדְנוּ
Prefix	Sg.	3 m.	יַעֲמֹד	יֶחֱזַק	יֵעָמֵד	יַעֲמִיד	יָעֳמַד
		3 f.	תַּעֲמֹד	תֶּחֱזַק	תֵּעָמֵד	תַּעֲמִיד	תָּעֳמַד
		2 m.	תַּעֲמֹד	etc.	תֵּעָמֵד	תַּעֲמִיד	תָּעֳמַד
		2 f.	תַּעַמְדִי	can be	תֵּעָמְדִי	תַּעֲמִידִי	תָּעָמְדִי
		1 c.	אֶעֱמֹד	a pattern	אֵעָמֵד	אַעֲמִיד	אָעֳמַד
	Pl.	3 m.	יַעַמְדוּ	for 1st ח	יֵעָמְדוּ	יַעֲמִידוּ	יָעָמְדוּ
		3 f.	תַּעֲמֹדְנָה	verbs	תֵּעָמַדְנָה	תַּעֲמֵדְנָה	תָּעֳמַדְנָה
		2 m.	תַּעַמְדוּ		תֵּעָמְדוּ	תַּעֲמִידוּ	תָּעָמְדוּ
		2 f.	תַּעֲמֹדְנָה		תֵּעָמַדְנָה	תַּעֲמֵדְנָה	תָּעֳמַדְנָה
		1 c.	נַעֲמֹד		נֵעָמֵד	נַעֲמִיד	נָעֳמַד
Imperative	Sg.	2 m.	עֲמֹד	חֲזַק	הֵעָמֵד	הַעֲמֵד	
		2 f.	עִמְדִי	חִזְקִי	הֵעָמְדִי	הַעֲמִידִי	
	Pl.	2 m.	עִמְדוּ	חִזְקוּ	הֵעָמְדוּ	הַעֲמִידוּ	
		2 f.	עֲמֹדְנָה	חֲזַקְנָה	הֵעָמַדְנָה	הַעֲמֵדְנָה	
Participle	Sg.	m.	עֹמֵד	חָזָק	נֶעֱמָד	מַעֲמִיד	מָעֳמָד
		f.	עֹמְדָה	חֲזָקָה	נֶעֱמָדָה	מַעֲמִידָה	מָעֳמָדָה
	Pl.	m.	עֹמְדִים	חֲזָקִים	נֶעֱמָדִים	מַעֲמִידִים	מָעֳמָדִים
		f.	עֹמְדוֹת	חֲזָקוֹת	נֶעֱמָדוֹת	מַעֲמִידוֹת	מָעֳמָדוֹת
Infinitive	Construct		עֲמֹד		הֵעָמֵד	הַעֲמִיד	
Infinitive	Absolute		עָמוֹד		נַעֲמוֹד הֵאָסֵף	הַעֲמֵד	הָעֳמֵד
Prefix/vav conversive					וַיַּעֲמֹד		

1st א

			Qal	Nif'al	Hif'il	Hof'al
Affix	Sg.	3 m.	אָכַל	נֶאֱכַל	הֶאֱכִיל	הָאֳכַל
			etc.	etc.	etc.	etc.

Most 1st א verbs follow the 1st Guttural patterns, but five 1st אs deviate in some stems and forms, most notably the Qal prefix.

אהב אבד אמר אכל אפה

			Qal	Nif'al	Hif'il	Hof'al
Prefix	Sg.	3 m.	יֹאכַל	יֵאָכֵל	יַאֲכִיל	יָאֳכַל
		3 f.	תֹּאכַל	etc.	etc.	etc.
		2 m.	תֹּאכַל			
		2 f.	תֹּאכְלִי			
		1 c.	אֹכַל			
	Pl.	3 m.	יֹאכְלוּ			
		3 f.	תֹּאכַלְנָה			
		2 m.	תֹּאכְלוּ			
		2 f.	תֹּאכַלְנָה			
		1 c.	נֹאכַל			
Imperative	Sg.	2 m.	אֱכֹל	הֵאָכֵל	הַאֲכֵל	
		2 f.	אִכְלִי	etc.	etc.	
	Pl.	2 m.	אִכְלוּ			
		2 f.	אֱכֹלְנָה			
Participle	Sg.	m.	אֹכֵל	נֶאֱכָל	מַאֲכִיל	מָאֳכָל
		f.	אֹכְלָה	etc.	etc.	etc.
	Pl.	m.	אֹכְלִים			
Infinitive	Construct		אֱכֹל אֲכֹל	הֵאָכֵל־	הַאֲכִיל	הָאֳכַל
Infinitive	Absolute		אָכוֹל	הֵאָכֹל		

Prefix/vav conversive וַיֹּאכַל וַיֹּאמֶר

			Qal	Nif'al	Hif'il	Hof'al
Affix	Sg.	3 m.	יָשַׁב	נוֹשַׁב	הוֹשִׁיב	הוּשַׁב
		3 f.	like the	נוֹשְׁבָה	הוֹשִׁיבָה	הוּשְׁבָה
		2 m.	strong	נוֹשַׁבְתָּ	הוֹשַׁבְתָּ	הוּשַׁבְתָּ
		2 f.	verb	נוֹשַׁבְתְּ	הוֹשַׁבְתְּ	הוּשַׁבְתְּ
		1 c.		נוֹשַׁבְתִּי	הוֹשַׁבְתִּי	הוּשַׁבְתִּי
	Pl.	3 c.		נוֹשְׁבוּ	הוֹשִׁיבוּ	הוּשְׁבוּ
		2 m.		נוֹשַׁבְתֶּם	הוֹשַׁבְתֶּם	הוּשַׁבְתֶּם
		2 f.		נוֹשַׁבְתֶּן	הוֹשַׁבְתֶּן	הוּשַׁבְתֶּן
		1 c.		נוֹשַׁבְנוּ	הוֹשַׁבְנוּ	הוּשַׁבְנוּ
Prefix	Sg.	3 m.	יֵשֵׁב	יִוָּשֵׁב	יוֹשִׁיב	יוּשַׁב
		3 f.	תֵּשֵׁב	תִּוָּשֵׁב	תּוֹשִׁיב	תּוּשַׁב
		2 m.	תֵּשֵׁב	תִּוָּשֵׁב	תּוֹשִׁיב	תּוּשַׁב
		2 f.	תֵּשְׁבִי	תִּוָּשְׁבִי	תּוֹשִׁיבִי	תּוּשְׁבִי
		1 c.	אֵשֵׁב	אִוָּשֵׁב	אוֹשִׁיב	אוּשַׁב
	Pl.	3 m.	יֵשְׁבוּ	יִוָּשְׁבוּ	יוֹשִׁיבוּ	יוּשְׁבוּ
		3 f.	תֵּשַׁבְנָה	תִּוָּשַׁבְנָה	תּוֹשֵׁבְנָה	תּוּשַׁבְנָה
		2 m.	תֵּשְׁבוּ	תִּוָּשְׁבוּ	תּוֹשִׁיבוּ	תּוּשְׁבוּ
		2 f.	תֵּשַׁבְנָה	תִּוָּשַׁבְנָה	תּוֹשֵׁבְנָה	תּוּשַׁבְנָה
		1 c.	נֵשֵׁב	נִוָּשֵׁב	נוֹשִׁיב	נוּשַׁב
Imperative	Sg.	2 m.	שֵׁב דַּע	הִוָּשֵׁב	הוֹשֵׁב	
		2 f.	שְׁבִי	הִוָּשְׁבִי	הוֹשִׁיבִי	
	Pl.	2 m.	שְׁבוּ	הִוָּשְׁבוּ	הוֹשִׁיבוּ	
		2 f.	שֵׁבְנָה	הִוָּשַׁבְנָה	הוֹשֵׁבְנָה	
Participle	Sg.	m.	יֹשֵׁב	נוֹשָׁב	מוֹשִׁיב	מוּשָׁב
		f.	יֹשְׁבָה	נוֹשָׁבָה	מוֹשִׁיבָה	מוּשָׁבָה
	Pl.	m.	יֹשְׁבִים	נוֹשָׁבִים	מוֹשִׁיבִים	מוּשָׁבִים
Infinitive	Construct		שֶׁבֶת	הִוָּשֵׁב	הוֹשִׁיב	הוּשַׁב
Infinitive	Absolute		יָשֹׁב		הוֹשֵׁב	
Prefix/vav conversive			וַיֵּשֶׁב		וַיּוֹשֶׁב	

			Qal	Qal "E"	Hif'il
Affix	Sg.	3 m.	יָטַב	יָרֵא	הֵיטִיב
		3 f.	like the	note changes יָֽרְאָה	הֵיטִיבָה
		2 m.	strong	for 3rd א ⟶ יָרֵאתָ	הֵיטַבְתָּ
		2 f.	verb	יָרֵאת	הֵיטַבְתְּ
		1 c.		יָרֵאתִי	הֵיטַבְתִּי
	Pl.	3 c.		יָֽרְאוּ	הֵיטִיבוּ
		2 m.		יְרֵאתֶם	הֵיטַבְתֶּם
		2 f.		יְרֵאתֶן	הֵיטַבְתֶּן
		1 c.		יָרֵאנוּ	הֵיטַבְנוּ
Prefix	Sg.	3 m.	יִיטַב	יִירָא	יֵיטִיב
		3 f.	תִּיטַב	תִּירָא	תֵּיטִיב
		2 m.	תִּיטַב	תִּירָא	תֵּיטִיב
		2 f.	תִּיטְבִי	תִּירְאִי	תֵּיטִיבִי
		1 c.	אִיטַב	אִירָא	אֵיטִיב
	Pl.	3 m.	יִיטְבוּ	יִירְאוּ	יֵיטִיבוּ
		3 f.	תִּיטַבְנָה	תִּירֶאנָה	תֵּיטֵבְנָה
		2 m.	תִּיטְבוּ	תִּירְאוּ	תֵּיטִיבוּ
		2 f.	תִּיטַבְנָה	תִּירֶאנָה	תֵּיטֵבְנָה
		1 c.	נִיטַב	נִירָא	נֵיטִיב
Imperative	Sg.	2 m.	יְטַב	יְרָא	הֵיטֵב
		2 f.	יִטְבִי		הֵיטִיבִי
	Pl.	2 m.	יִטְבוּ	יְראוּ	הֵיטִיבוּ
		2 f.	יְטַבְנָה		הֵיטֵבְנָה
Participle	Sg.	m.	יֹטֵב	יָרֵא	מֵיטִיב
		f.	יֹטְבָה	construct יִרְאַת־	מֵיטִיבָה
	Pl.	m.	יֹטְבִים	יְרֵא־	מֵיטִיבִים
Infinitive	Construct		יְטֹב	יִרְאָה יִרְאָת	הֵיטִיב
Infinitive	Absolute		יָטוֹב	יָרֹא	היטב
Prefix/vav conversive					וַיֵּיטֶב

			Qal		Nif'al	Hif'il	Hof'al
Affix	Sg.	3 m.	נָגַשׁ	נָפַל	נִגַּשׁ	הִגִּישׁ	הֻגַּשׁ
		3 f.	like the		נִגְּשָׁה	הִגִּישָׁה	הֻגְּשָׁה
		2 m.	strong		נִגַּשְׁתָּ	הִגַּשְׁתָּ	הֻגַּשְׁתָּ
		2 f.	verb		נִגַּשְׁתְּ	הִגַּשְׁתְּ	הֻגַּשְׁתְּ
		1 c.			נִגַּשְׁתִּי	הִגַּשְׁתִּי	הֻגַּשְׁתִּי
	Pl.	3 c.			נִגְּשׁוּ	הִגִּישׁוּ	הֻגְּשׁוּ
		2 m.			נִגַּשְׁתֶּם	הִגַּשְׁתֶּם	הֻגַּשְׁתֶּם
		2 f.			נִגַּשְׁתֶּן	הִגַּשְׁתֶּן	הֻגַּשְׁתֶּן
		1 c.			נִגַּשְׁנוּ	הִגַּשְׁנוּ	הֻגַּשְׁנוּ
Prefix	Sg.	3 m.	יִגַּשׁ	יִפֹּל	יִנָּגֵשׁ	יַגִּישׁ	יֻגַּשׁ
		3 f.	תִּגַּשׁ	תִּפֹּל	תִּנָּגֵשׁ	תַּגִּישׁ	תֻּגַּשׁ
		2 m.	תִּגַּשׁ	תִּפֹּל	תִּנָּגֵשׁ	תַּגִּישׁ	תֻּגַּשׁ
		2 f.	תִּגְּשִׁי	תִּפְּלִי	תִּנָּגְשִׁי	תַּגִּישִׁי	תֻּגְּשִׁי
		1 c.	אֶגַּשׁ	אֶפֹּל	אִנָּגֵשׁ	אַגִּישׁ	אֻגַּשׁ
	Pl.	3 m.	יִגְּשׁוּ	יִפְּלוּ	יִנָּגְשׁוּ	יַגִּישׁוּ	יֻגְּשׁוּ
		3 f.	תִּגַּשְׁנָה	תִּפֹּלְנָה	תִּנָּגַשְׁנָה	תַּגֵּשְׁנָה	תֻּגַּשְׁנָה
		2 m.	תִּגְּשׁוּ	תִּפְּלוּ	תִּנָּגְשׁוּ	תַּגִּישׁוּ	תֻּגְּשׁוּ
		2 f.	תִּגַּשְׁנָה	תִּפֹּלְנָה	תִּנָּגַשְׁנָה	תַּגֵּשְׁנָה	תֻּגַּשְׁנָה
		1 c.	נִגַּשׁ	נִפֹּל	נִנָּגֵשׁ	נַגִּישׁ	נֻגַּשׁ
Imperative	Sg.	2 m.	גַּשׁ	נְפֹל	הִנָּגֵשׁ	הַגֵּשׁ	
		2 f.	גְּשִׁי	נִפְלִי	הִנָּגְשִׁי	הַגִּישִׁי	
	Pl.	2 m.	גְּשׁוּ	נִפְלוּ	הִנָּגְשׁוּ	הַגִּישׁוּ	
		2 f.	גַּשְׁנָה	נְפֹלְנָה	הִנָּגַשְׁנָה	הַגֵּשְׁנָה	
Participle	Sg.	m.	נֹגֵשׁ	נֹפֵל	נִגָּשׁ	מַגִּישׁ	מֻגָּשׁ
		f.	נֹגְשָׁה	נֹפְלָה	נִגָּשָׁה	מַגִּישָׁה	מֻגָּשָׁה
	Pl.	m.	נֹגְשִׁים	נֹפְלִים	נִגָּשִׁים	מַגִּישִׁים	מֻגָּשִׁים
Infinitive	Construct		גֶּשֶׁת	נְפֹל	הִנָּגֵשׁ	הַגִּישׁ	הֻגַּשׁ
Infinitive	Absolute		נָגוֹשׁ	נָפֹל	הִנָּגֵשׁ	הַגֵּשׁ	הֻגֵּשׁ
Prefix/vav conversive						וַיַּגֵּשׁ	

Middle Guttural

			Qal	Nif'al	Pi'el	Pu'al
Affix	Sg.	3 m.	גָּאַל	נִגְאַל	בֵּרַךְ בֵּרֵךְ	בֹּרַךְ
		3 f.	גָּאֲלָה	נִגְאֲלָה	בֵּרְכָה	בֹּרְכָה
		2 m.	גָּאַלְתָּ	נִגְאַלְתָּ	בֵּרַכְתָּ	בֹּרַכְתָּ
		2 f.	גָּאַלְתְּ	נִגְאַלְתְּ	בֵּרַכְתְּ	בֹּרַכְתְּ
		1 c.	גָּאַלְתִּי	נִגְאַלְתִּי	בֵּרַכְתִּי	בֹּרַכְתִּי
	Pl.	3 c.	גָּאֲלוּ	נִגְאֲלוּ	בֵּרְכוּ	בֹּרְכוּ
		2 m.	גְּאַלְתֶּם	נִגְאַלְתֶּם	בֵּרַכְתֶּם	בֹּרַכְתֶּם
		2 f.	גְּאַלְתֶּן	נִגְאַלְתֶּן	בֵּרַכְתֶּן	בֹּרַכְתֶּן
		1 c.	גָּאַלְנוּ	נִגְאַלְנוּ	בֵּרַכְנוּ	בֹּרַכְנוּ
Prefix	Sg.	3 m.	יִגְאַל	יִגָּאֵל	יְבָרֵךְ	יְבֹרַךְ
		3 f.	תִּגְאַל	תִּגָּאֵל	תְּבָרֵךְ	תְּבֹרַךְ
		2 m.	תִּגְאַל	תִּגָּאֵל	תְּבָרֵךְ	תְּבֹרַךְ
		2 f.	תִּגְאֲלִי	תִּגָּאֲלִי	תְּבָרֲכִי	תְּבֹרְכִי
		1 c.	אֶגְאַל	אֶגָּאֵל	אֲבָרֵךְ	אֲבֹרַךְ
	Pl.	3 m.	יִגְאֲלוּ	יִגָּאֲלוּ	יְבָרֲכוּ	יְבֹרְכוּ
		3 f.	תִּגְאַלְנָה	תִּגָּאַלְנָה	תְּבָרֵכְנָה	תְּבֹרַכְנָה
		2 m.	תִּגְאֲלוּ	תִּגָּאֲלוּ	תְּבָרֲכוּ	תְּבֹרְכוּ
		2 f.	תִּגְאַלְנָה	תִּגָּאַלְנָה	תְּבָרֵכְנָה	תְּבֹרַכְנָה
		1 c.	נִגְאַל	נִגָּאֵל	נְבָרֵךְ	נְבֹרַךְ
Imperative	Sg.	2 m.	גְּאַל	הִגָּאֵל	בָּרֵךְ	
		2 f.	גַּאֲלִי	הִגָּאֲלִי	בָּרֲכִי	
	Pl.	2 m.	גַּאֲלוּ	הִגָּאֲלוּ	בָּרֲכוּ	
		2 f.	גְּאַלְנָה	הִגָּאַלְנָה	בָּרֵכְנָה	
Participle	Sg.	m.	גֹּאֵל	נִגְאָל	מְבָרֵךְ	מְבֹרָךְ
		f.	גֹּאֲלָה	נִגְאָלָה	מְבָרֲכָה	מְבֹרָכָה
	Pl.	m.	גֹּאֲלִים	נִגְאָלִים	מְבָרֲכִים	מְבֹרָכִים
		f.	גֹּאֲלוֹת	נִגְאָלוֹת	מְבָרֲכוֹת	מְבֹרָכוֹת
Infinitive	Construct		גְּאֹל	הִגָּאֵל	בָּרֵךְ	
Infinitive	Absolute		גָּאֹל	הִגָּאֵל נִגְאוֹל	בָּרֵךְ	בֹּרֹךְ
Prefix/vav conversive						

Hollow

			Qal		Qal	Qal	Qal "E"
Affix	Sg.	3 m.	קָם	note	בָּא	שָׂם	מֵת
		3 f.	קָמָה	changes	בָּאָה	שָׂמָה	מֵתָה
		2 m.	קַמְתָּ	for 3rd א	בָּאתָ	שַׂמְתָּ	מַתָּה
		2 f.	קַמְתְּ	→	בָּאת	שַׂמְתְּ	מַתְּ
		1 c.	קַמְתִּי		בָּאתִי	שַׂמְתִּי	מַתִּי
	Pl.	3 c.	קָמוּ		בָּאוּ	שָׂמוּ	מֵתוּ
		2 m.	קַמְתֶּם		בָּאתֶם	שַׂמְתֶּם	מַתֶּם
		2 f.	קַמְתֶּן		בָּאתֶן	שַׂמְתֶּן	מַתֶּן
		1 c.	קַמְנוּ		בָּאנוּ	שַׂמְנוּ	מַתְנוּ
Prefix	Sg.	3 m.	יָקוּם		יָבוֹא	יָשִׂים	יָמוּת
		3 f.	תָּקוּם		תָּבוֹא	תָּשִׂים	תָּמוּת
		2 m.	תָּקוּם		תָּבוֹא	תָּשִׂים	תָּמוּת
		2 f.	תָּקוּמִי		תָּבוֹאִי	תָּשִׂימִי	תָּמוּתִי
		1 c.	אָקוּם		אָבוֹא	אָשִׂים	אָמוּת
	Pl.	3 m.	יָקוּמוּ		יָבוֹאוּ	יָשִׂימוּ	יָמוּתוּ
		3 f.	תָּקוּמְנָה		תָּבוֹאנָה	תָּשֵׂמְנָה	תָּמֹתְנָה
		2 m.	תָּקוּמוּ		תָּבוֹאוּ	תָּשִׂימוּ	תָּמוּתוּ
		2 f.	תָּקוּמְנָה		תָּבוֹאנָה	תָּשֵׂמְנָה	תָּמֹתְנָה
		1 c.	נָקוּם		נָבוֹא	נָשִׂים	נָמוּת
Imperative	Sg.	2 m.	קוּם		בּוֹא	שִׂים	מוּת
		2 f.	קוּמִי		בּוֹאִי	שִׂימִי	מוּתִי
	Pl.	2 m.	קוּמוּ		בּוֹאוּ	שִׂימוּ	מוּתוּ
		2 f.	קֹמְנָה		בֹּאנָה	שֵׂמְנָה	מֹתְנָה
Participle	Sg.	m.	קָם		בָּא	שָׂם	מֵת
		f.	קָמָה		בָּאָה	שָׂמָה	מֵתָה
	Pl.	m.	קָמִים		בָּאִים	שָׂמִים	מֵתִים
		f.	קָמוֹת		בָּאוֹת	שָׂמוֹת	מֵתוֹת
Infinitive	Construct		קוּם		בּוֹא	שִׂים	מוּת
Infinitive	Absolute		קוֹם		בּוֹא	שׂוֹם	מוֹת
Prefix/vav conversive			וַיָּקָם			וַיָּשֶׂם	וַיָּמָת

Qal "O"	Nif'al	Hif'il	Hof'al	Pol'el
בּוֹשׁ	נָקוֹם	הֵקִים	הוּקַם	קוֹמֵם
בּוֹשָׁה	נָקוֹמָה	הֵקִימָה	הוּקְמָה	קוֹמְמָה
בֹּשְׁתָּ	נְקוּמוֹתָ	הֲקִימוֹתָ	הוּקַמְתָּ	קוֹמַמְתָּ
בֹּשְׁתְּ	נְקוּמוֹת	הֲקִימוֹת	הוּקַמְתְּ	קוֹמַמְתְּ
בֹּשְׁתִּי	נְקוּמוֹתִי	הֲקִימוֹתִי	הוּקַמְתִּי	קוֹמַמְתִּי
בּוֹשׁוּ	נָקוֹמוּ	הֵקִימוּ	הוּקְמוּ	קוֹמְמוּ
בּוֹשְׁתֶּם	נְקֹמוֹתֶם	הֲקִימוֹתֶם	הוּקַמְתֶּם	קוֹמַמְתֶּם
בָּשְׁתֶּן	נְקוּמוֹתֶן	הֲקוּמוֹתֶן	הוּקַמְתֶּן	קוֹמַמְתֶּן
בֹּשְׁנוּ	נְקוּמוֹנוּ	הֲקִימוֹנוּ	הוּקַמְנוּ	קוֹמַמְנוּ
יֵבוֹשׁ	יִקּוֹם	יָקִים	יוּקַם	יְקוֹמֵם
תֵּבוֹשׁ	תִּקּוֹם	תָּקִים	תּוּקַם	תְּקוֹמֵם
תֵּבוֹשׁ	תִּקּוֹם	תָּקִים	תּוּקַם	תְּקוֹמֵם
תֵּבוֹשִׁי	תִּקּוֹמִי	תָּקִימִי	תּוּקְמִי	תְּקוֹמְמִי
אֵבוֹשׁ	אֶקּוֹם	אָקִים	אוּקַם	אֲקוֹמֵם
יֵבוֹשׁוּ	יִקּוֹמוּ	יָקִימוּ	יוּקְמוּ	יְקוֹמְמוּ
תֵּבֹשְׁנָה	תִּקּוֹמְנָה	תָּקֵמְנָה	תּוּקַמְנָה	תְּקוֹמֵמְנָה
תֵּבוֹשׁוּ	תִּקּוֹמוּ	תָּקִימוּ	תּוּקְמוּ	תְּקוֹמְמוּ
תֵּבֹשְׁנָה	תִּקּוֹמְנָה	תָּקֵמְנָה	תּוּקַמְנָה	תְּקוֹמֵמְנָה
נֵבוֹשׁ	נִקּוֹם	נָקִים	נוּקַם	נְקוֹמֵם
בּוֹשׁ	הִקּוֹם	הָקֵם		קוֹמֵם
בּוֹשִׁי	הִקּוֹמִי	הָקִימִי		קוֹמְמִי
בּוֹשׁוּ	הִקּוֹמוּ	הָקִימוּ		קוֹמְמוּ
בֹּשְׁנָה	הִקּוֹמוֹת	הָקֵמְנָה		קוֹמֵמְנָה
בּוֹשׁ	נָקוֹם	מֵקִים	מוּקָם	מְקוֹמֵם
בּוֹשָׁה	נְקוֹמָה	מְקִימָה	מוּקָמָה	מְקוֹמְמָה
בּוֹשִׁים	נְקוֹמִים	מְקִימִים	מוּקָמִים	מְקוֹמְמִים
בּוֹשׁוֹת	נְקוֹמוֹת	מְקִימוֹת	מוּקָמוֹת	מְקוֹמְמוֹת
בּוֹשׁ	הִקּוֹם	הָקִים	הוּקַם	קוֹמֵם
בּוֹשׁ	הִקּוֹם	הָקֵם		
		וַיָּקָם		

			Qal		Nif'al
Affix	Sg.	3 m.	סָבַב תַּם		נָסַב נָמֵס
		3 f.	סָבֲבָה תַּמָּה		נָסַבָּה
		2 m.	סַבּוֹתָ		נְסַבּוֹתָ
		2 f.	סַבּוֹת		נְסַבּוֹת
		1 c.	סַבּוֹתִי		נְסַבּוֹתִי
	Pl.	3 c.	סָבֲבוּ תַּמּוּ		נָסַבּוּ
		2 m.	סַבּוֹתֶם		נְסַבּוֹתֶם
		2 f.	סַבּוֹתֶן		נְסַבּוֹתֶן
		1 c.	סַבּוֹנוּ		נְסַבּוֹנוּ
Prefix	Sg.	3 m.	יָסֹב יִמַּל יֵקַל	יִסֹּב	יִסַּב
		3 f.	תָּסֹב	תִּסֹּב	תִּסַּב
		2 m.	תָּסֹב	תִּסֹּב	תִּסַּב
		2 f.	תָּסֹבִּי	תִּסְּבִי	תִּסַּבִּי
		1 c.	אָסֹב	אֶסֹּב	אֶסַּב
	Pl.	3 m.	יָסֹבּוּ	יִסְּבוּ	יִסַּבּוּ
		3 f.	תְּסֻבֶּינָה	תִּסֹּבְנָה	תִּסַּבֶּינָה
		2 m.	תָּסֹבּוּ	תִּסְּבוּ	תִּסַּבּוּ
		2 f.	תְּסֻבֶּינָה	תִּסֹּבְנָה	תִּסַּבֶּינָה
		1 c.	נָסֹב	נִסֹּב	נִסַּב
Imperative	Sg.	2 m.	סֹב		הִסַּב
		2 f.	סֹבִּי		הִסַּבִּי
	Pl.	2 m.	סֹבּוּ		הִסַּבּוּ
		2 f.	סֻבֶּינָה		הִסַּבֶּינָה
Participle	Sg.	m.	סֹבֵב		נָסָב
		f.	סֹבְבָה		נְסַבָּה
	Pl.	m.	סֹבְבִים		נְסַבִּים
		f.	סֹבְבוֹת		נְסַבּוֹת
Infinitive	Construct		סֹב		הִסֵּב
Infinitive	Absolute		סָבוֹב		הִסּוֹב הִמֵּס
Prefix/vav conversive			וַיָּסָב		

Hif'il	Hof'al	Pol'el
הֵסֵב הֵסַב	הוּסַב	סוֹבֵב
הֵסֵבָּה	הוּסַבָּה	סוֹבְבָה
הֲסִבּוֹתָ	הוּסַבּוֹתָ	סוֹבַבְתָּ
הֲסִבּוֹת	הוּסַבּוֹת	סוֹבַבְתְּ
הֲסִבּוֹתִי	הוּסַבּוֹתִי	סוֹבַבְתִּי
הֵסֵבּוּ הֵחֵלּוּ	הוּסַבּוּ	סוֹבְבוּ
הֲסִבּוֹתֶם	הוּסַבּוֹתֶם	סוֹבַבְתֶּם
הֲסִבּוֹתֶן	הוּסַבּוֹתֶן	סוֹבַבְתֶּן
הֲסִבּוֹנוּ	הוּסַבּוֹנוּ	סוֹבַבְנוּ
יָסֵב יַסֵּב	יוּסַב יֻסַּב	יְסוֹבֵב
תָּסֵב	תּוּסַב	תְּסוֹבֵב
תָּסֵב	תּוּסַב	תְּסוֹבֵב
תָּסֵבִּי	תּוּסַבִּי	תְּסוֹבְבִי
אָסֵב	אוּסַב	אֲסוֹבֵב
יָסֵבּוּ יַסֵּבּוּ	יוּסַבּוּ	יְסוֹבְבוּ
תְּסִבֶּינָה	תּוּסַבֶּינָה	תְּסוֹבֵבְנָה
תָּסֵבּוּ	תּוּסַבּוּ	תְּסוֹבְבוּ
תְּסִבֶּינָה	תּוּסַבֶּינָה	תְּסוֹבֵבְנָה
נָסֵב	נוּסַב	נְסוֹבֵב
הָסֵב		סוֹבֵב
הָסֵבִּי		סוֹבְבִי
הָסֵבּוּ		סוֹבְבוּ
הֲסִבֶּינָה		סוֹבֵבְנָה
מֵסֵב	מוּסָב	מְסוֹבֵב
מְסִבָּה		מְסוֹבְבָה
מְסִבִּים		מְסֹבְבִים
מְסִבּוֹת		מְסֹבְבוֹת
הָסֵב	הוּסַב	סוֹבֵב
הָסֵב		סוֹבֵב
וַיָּסֶב		

3rd Guttural

			Qal	Nif'al	Pi'el
Affix	Sg.	3 m.	שָׁלַח	נִשְׁלַח	שִׁלַּח
		3 f.	שָֽׁלְחָה	נִשְׁלְחָה	שִׁלְּחָה
		2 m.	שָׁלַחְתָּ	נִשְׁלַחְתָּ	שִׁלַּחְתָּ
		2 f.	שָׁלַחַתְּ	נִשְׁלַחַתְּ	שִׁלַּחַתְּ
		1 c.	שָׁלַחְתִּי	נִשְׁלַחְתִּי	שִׁלַּחְתִּי
	Pl.	3 c.	שָֽׁלְחוּ	נִשְׁלְחוּ	שִׁלְּחוּ
		2 m.	שְׁלַחְתֶּם	נִשְׁלַחְתֶּם	שִׁלַּחְתֶּם
		2 f.	שְׁלַחְתֶּן	נִשְׁלַחְתֶּן	שִׁלַּחְתֶּן
		1 c.	שָׁלַחְנוּ	נִשְׁלַחְנוּ	שִׁלַּחְנוּ
Prefix	Sg.	3 m.	יִשְׁלַח	יִשָּׁלַח	יְשַׁלַּח
		3 f.	תִּשְׁלַח	תִּשָּׁלַח	תְּשַׁלַּח
		2 m.	תִּשְׁלַח	תִּשָּׁלַח	תְּשַׁלַּח
		2 f.	תִּשְׁלְחִי	תִּשָּֽׁלְחִי	תְּשַׁלְּחִי
		1 c.	אֶשְׁלַח	אֶשָּׁלַח	אֲשַׁלַּח
	Pl.	3 m.	יִשְׁלְחוּ	יִשָּֽׁלְחוּ	יְשַׁלְּחוּ
		3 f.	תִּשְׁלַחְנָה	תִּשָּׁלַחְנָה	תְּשַׁלַּחְנָה
		2 m.	תִּשְׁלְחוּ	תִּשָּֽׁלְחוּ	תְּשַׁלְּחוּ
		2 f.	תִּשְׁלַחְנָה	תִּשָּׁלַחְנָה	תְּשַׁלַּחְנָה
		1 c.	נִשְׁלַח	נִשָּׁלַח	נְשַׁלַּח
Imperative	Sg.	2 m.	שְׁלַח	הִשָּׁלַח	שַׁלַּח
		2 f.	שִׁלְחִי	הִשָּֽׁלְחִי	שַׁלְּחִי
	Pl.	2 m.	שִׁלְחוּ	הִשָּֽׁלְחוּ	שַׁלְּחוּ
		2 f.	שְׁלַחְנָה	הִשָּׁלַחְנָה	שַׁלַּחְנָה
Participle	Sg.	m.	שֹׁלֵחַ	נִשְׁלָח	מְשַׁלֵּחַ
		f.	שֹׁלְחָה	נִשְׁלָחָה	מְשַׁלְּחָה
	Pl.	m.	שֹׁלְחִים	נִשְׁלָחִים	מְשַׁלְּחִים
		f.	שֹׁלְחוֹת	נִשְׁלָחוֹת	מְשַׁלְּחוֹת
Infinitive	Construct		שְׁלֹחַ	הִשָּׁלַח	שַׁלַּח
Infinitive	Absolute		שָׁלוֹחַ	נִשְׁלוֹחַ	שַׁלֵּחַ

Prefix/vav conversive

3rd Guttural

Pu`al	Hif`il	Hof`al
שֻׁלַּח	הִשְׁלִיחַ	הָשְׁלַח
שֻׁלְּחָה	הִשְׁלִיחָה	הָשְׁלְחָה
שֻׁלַּחְתָּ	הִשְׁלַחְתָּ	הָשְׁלַחְתָּ
שֻׁלַּחַתְּ	הִשְׁלַחַתְּ	הָשְׁלַחַתְּ
שֻׁלַּחְתִּי	הִשְׁלַחְתִּי	הָשְׁלַחְתִּי
שֻׁלְּחוּ	הִשְׁלִיחוּ	הָשְׁלְחוּ
שֻׁלַּחְתֶּם	הִשְׁלַחְתֶּם	הָשְׁלַחְתֶּם
שֻׁלַּחְתֶּן	הִשְׁלַחְתֶּן	הָשְׁלַחְתֶּן
שֻׁלַּחְנוּ	הִשְׁלַחְנוּ	הָשְׁלַחְנוּ
יְשֻׁלַּח	יַשְׁלִיחַ	יָשְׁלַח
תְּשֻׁלַּח	תַּשְׁלִיחַ	תָּשְׁלַח
תְּשֻׁלַּח	תַּשְׁלִיחַ	תָּשְׁלַח
תְּשֻׁלְּחִי	תַּשְׁלִיחִי	תָּשְׁלְחִי
אֲשֻׁלַּח	אַשְׁלִיחַ	אָשְׁלַח
יְשֻׁלְּחוּ	יַשְׁלִיחוּ	יָשְׁלְחוּ
תְּשֻׁלַּחְנָה	תַּשְׁלַחְנָה	תָּשְׁלַחְנָה
תְּשֻׁלְּחוּ	תַּשְׁלִיחוּ	תָּשְׁלְחוּ
תְּשֻׁלַּחְנָה	תַּשְׁלַחְנָה	תָּשְׁלַחְנָה
נְשֻׁלַּח	נַשְׁלִיחַ	נָשְׁלַח
	הַשְׁלַח	
	הַשְׁלִיחִי	
	הַשְׁלִיחוּ	
	הַשְׁלַחְנָה	
מְשֻׁלָּח	מַשְׁלִיחַ	מָשְׁלָח
מְשֻׁלָּחָה	מַשְׁלִיחָה	מָשְׁלָחָה
מְשֻׁלָּחִים	מַשְׁלִיחִים	מָשְׁלָחִים
מְשֻׁלָּחוֹת	מַשְׁלִיחוֹת	מָשְׁלָחוֹת
	הַשְׁלִיחַ	
	הַשְׁלֵחַ	הָשְׁלֵחַ
	וַיַּשְׁלַח	

			Qal	Qal "E"	Nif'al	Pi'el
Affix	Sg.	3 m.	מָצָא	מָלֵא	נִמְצָא	מִצֵּא
		3 f.	מָצְאָה	מָלְאָה	נִמְצְאָה	מִצְּאָה
		2 m.	מָצָאתָ	מָלֵאתָ	נִמְצֵאתָ	מִצֵּאתָ
		2 f.	מָצָאת	מָלֵאת	נִמְצֵאת	מִצֵּאת
		1 c.	מָצָאתִי	מָלֵאתִי	נִמְצֵאתִי	מִצֵּאתִי
	Pl.	3 c.	מָצְאוּ	מָלְאוּ	נִמְצְאוּ	מִצְּאוּ
		2 m.	מְצָאתֶם	מְלֵאתֶם	נִמְצֵאתֶם	מִצֵּאתֶם
		2 f.	מְצָאתֶן	מְלֵאתֶן	נִמְצֵאתֶן	מִצֵּאתֶן
		1 c.	מָצָאנוּ	מָלֵאנוּ	נִמְצֵאנוּ	מִצֵּאנוּ
Prefix	Sg.	3 m.	יִמְצָא	follows 3rd א pattern	יִמָּצֵא	יְמַצֵּא
		3 f.	תִּמְצָא		תִּמָּצֵא	תְּמַצֵּא
		2 m.	תִּמְצָא		תִּמָּצֵא	תְּמַצֵּא
		2 f.	תִּמְצְאִי		תִּמָּצְאִי	תְּמַצְּאִי
		1 c.	אֶמְצָא		אֶמָּצֵא	אֲמַצֵּא
	Pl.	3 m.	יִמְצְאוּ		יִמָּצְאוּ	יְמַצְּאוּ
		3 f.	תִּמְצֶנָה		תִּמָּצֶאנָה	תְּמַצֶּאנָה
		2 m.	תִּמְצְאוּ		תִּמָּצְאוּ	תְּמַצְּאוּ
		2 f.	תִּמְצֶאנָה		תִּמָּצֶאנָה	תְּמַצֶּאנָה
		1 c.	נִמְצָא		נִמָּצֵא	נְמַצֵּא
Imperative	Sg.	2 m.	מְצָא	מְלֵא	הִמָּצֵא	מַצֵּא
		2 f.	מִצְאִי	מְלֵאָה	הִמָּצְאִי	מַצְּאִי
	Pl.	2 m.	מִצְאוּ	מְלֵאִים	הִמָּצְאוּ	מַצְּאוּ
		2 f.	מְצֶאנָה	מְלֵאוֹת	הִמָּצֶאנָה	מַצֶּאנָה
Participle	Sg.	m.	מֹצֵא		נִמְצָא	מְמַצֵּא
		f.	מֹצְאָה		נִמְצָאָה	מְמַצְּאָה
	Pl.	m.	מֹצְאִים		נִמְצָאִים	מְמַצְּאִים
Infinitive	Construct		מְצֹא		הִמָּצֵא	מַצֵּא
Infinitive	Absolute		מָצֹא		נִמְצֹא	מַצֹּא

Prefix/vav conversive

3rd א

Pu`al	Hif`il	Hof`al
מֻצָּא קֹרָא	הִמְצִיא	הֻמְצָא
מֻצְּאָה	הִמְצִיאָה	הֻמְצְאָה
מֻצֵּאתָ	הִמְצֵאתָ	הֻמְצֵאתָ
מֻצֵּאת	הִמְצֵאת	הֻמְצֵאת
מֻצֵּאתִי	הִמְצֵאתִי	הֻמְצֵאתִי
מֻצְּאוּ	הִמְצִיאוּ	הֻמְצְאוּ
מֻצֵּאתֶם	הִמְצֵאתֶם	הֻמְצֵאתֶם
מֻצֵּאתֶן	הִמְצֵאתֶן	הֻמְצֵאתֶן
מֻצֵּאנוּ	הִמְצֵאנוּ	הֻמְצֵאנוּ
יְמֻצָּא	יַמְצִיא	יֻמְצָא
תְּמֻצָּא	תַּמְצִיא	תֻּמְצָא
תְּמֻצָּא	תַּמְצִיא	תֻּמְצָא
תְּמֻצְּאִי	תַּמְצִיאִי	תֻּמְצְאִי
אֲמֻצָּא	אַמְצִיא	אֻמְצָא
יְמֻצְּאוּ	יַמְצִיאוּ	יֻמְצְאוּ
תְּמֻצֶּאנָה	תַּמְצֶאנָה	תֻּמְצֶאנָה
תְּמֻצְּאוּ	תַּמְצִיאוּ	תֻּמְצְאוּ
תְּמֻצֶּאנָה	תַּמְצֶאנָה	תֻּמְצֶאנָה
נְמֻצָּא	נַמְצִיא	נֻמְצָא
	הַמְצֵא	
	הַמְצִיאִי	
	הַמְצִיאוּ	
	הַמְצֶאנָה	
מְמֻצָּא	מַמְצִיא	מֻמְצָא
מְמֻצָּאָה	מַמְצִיאָה	מֻמְצָאָה
מְמֻצָּאִים	מַמְצִיאִים	מֻמְצָאִים
	הַמְצִיא	
	הַמְצֵא	
	וַיַּמְצֵא	

			Qal	Nif'al	Pi'el
Affix	Sg.	3 m.	גָּלָה	נִגְלָה	גִּלָּה
		3 f.	גָּֽלְתָה	נִגְלְתָה	גִּלְּתָה
		2 m.	גָּלִיתָ	נִגְלֵיתָ נִגְלִיתָ	גִּלִּיתָ
		2 f.	גָּלִית	נִגְלֵית	גִּלִּית
		1 c.	גָּלִיתִי	נִגְלֵיתִי	גִּלִּתִי
	Pl.	3 c.	גָּלוּ	נִגְלוּ	גִּלּוּ
		2 m.	גְּלִיתֶם	נִגְלֵיתֶם	גִּלִּיתֶם
		2 f.	גְּלִיתֶן	נִגְלֵיתֶן	גִּלִּיתֶן
		1 c.	גָּלִינוּ	נִגְלִינוּ	גִּלִּינוּ
Prefix	Sg.	3 m.	יִגְלֶה	יִגָּלֶה	יְגַלֶּה
		3 f.	תִּגְלֶה	תִּגָּלֶה	תְּגַלֶּה
		2 m.	תִּגְלֶה	תִּגָּלֶה	תְּגַלֶּה
		2 f.	תִּגְלִי	תִּגָּלִי	תְּגַלִּי
		1 c.	אֶגְלֶה	אֶגָּלֶה אִגָּלֶה	אֲגַלֶּה
	Pl.	3 m.	יִגְלוּ	יִגָּלוּ	יְגַלּוּ
		3 f.	תִּגְלֶינָה	תִּגָּלֶינָה	תְּגַלֶּינָה
		2 m.	תִּגְלוּ	תִּגָּלוּ	תְּגַלּוּ
		2 f.	תִּגְלֶינָה	תִּגָּלֶינָה	תְּגַלֶּינָה
		1 c.	נִגְלֶה	נִגָּלֶה	נְגַלֶּה
Imperative	Sg.	2 m.	גְּלֵה	הִגָּלֵה הִגָּל	גַּלֵּה גַּל
		2 f.	גְּלִי	הִגָּלִי	גַּלִּי
	Pl.	2 m.	גְּלוּ	הִגָּלוּ	גַּלּוּ
		2 f.	גְּלֶינָה	הִגָּלֶינָה	גַּלֶּינָה
Participle	Sg.	m.	גֹּלֶה	נִגְלֶה	מְגַלֶּה
		f.	גֹּלָה	נִגְלָה	מְגַלָּה
	Pl.	m.	גֹּלִים	נִגְלִים	מְגַלִּים
Infinitive	Construct		גְּלוֹת	הִגָּלוֹת	גַּלּוֹת
Infinitive	Absolute		גָּלֹה	נִגְלֹה הִנָּקֵה	גַּלֵּה
Prefix/vav conversive			וַיִּגֶל	וַיִּגָּל	וַיְגַל

Pu`al	Hifil	Hof`al
גֻּלָּה	הִגְלָה	הָגְלָה
גֻּלְּתָה	הִגְלְתָה	הָגְלְתָה
גֻּלֵּיתָ	הִגְלֵיתָ הִגְלִיתָ	הָגְלֵיתָ
גֻּלֵּית	הִגְלֵית הִגְלִית	הָגְלֵית
גֻּלֵּתִי	הִגְלֵיתִי הִגְלִיתִי	הָגְלֵתִי
גֻּלּוּ	הִגְלוּ	הָגְלוּ
גֻּלֵּיתֶם	הִגְלֵיתֶם	הָגְלֵיתֶם
גֻּלֵּיתֶן	הִגְלֵיתֶן	הָגְלֵיתֶן
גֻּלֵּינוּ	הִגְלִינוּ	הָגְלֵינוּ
יְגֻלֶּה	יַגְלֶה	יָגְלֶה
תְּגֻלֶּה	תַּגְלֶה	תָּגְלֶה
תְּגֻלֶּה	תַּגְלֶה	תָּגְלֶה
תְּגֻלִּי	תַּגְלִי	תָּגְלִי
אֲגֻלֶּה	אַגְלֶה	אָגְלֶה
יְגֻלּוּ	יַגְלוּ	יָגְלוּ
תְּגֻלֶּינָה	תַּגְלֶינָה	תָּגְלֶינָה
תְּגֻלּוּ	תַּגְלוּ	תָּגְלוּ
תְּגֻלֶּינָה	תַּגְלֶינָה	תָּגְלֶינָה
נְגֻלֶּה	נַגְלֶה	נָגְלֶה
	הַגְלֵה	
	הַגְלִי	
	הַגְלוּ	
	הַגְלֶינָה	
מְגֻלֶּה	מַגְלֶה	מָגְלֶה
מְגֻלָּה	מַגְלָה	מָגְלָה
מְגֻלִּים	מַגְלִים	מָגְלִים
גֻּלּוֹת	הַגְלוֹת	
גֻּלֹּה	הַגְלֵה	הָגְלֵה
	וַיֶּגֶל	

Particles

Single letter particles are always attached to another word.

1	אֵת אֶת	sign of definite direct object
2	אֵת	with, near
3	בְּ	in, by, with, from, against
4	הַ ּ	the (definite article)
5	הֲ	? (interrogative)
6	וְ	and, but, then, or
7	כְּ	as, like
8	לְ	to, for, of
9	מִן	from, out of, of, than
10	שֶׁ ּ	who, which, that

The rest of the vocabulary is listed in terms of its frequency in the Hebrew Bible. Verbs list the stem(s) most commonly appearing. Primary stem(s) meaning(s) are <u>underlined.</u>

1	יהוה	The LORD
2	כֹּל	all, every, any
3	אֲשֶׁר	who, whom, which, that
4	אֶל	to, toward, into, at
5	אָמַר	Q: <u>say</u>, command
6	לֹא	not
7	בֵּן	son, youth
8	עַל	on, upon, concerning, on account of, against
9	כִּי	for, that, because, when, but
10	הָיָה	<u>Q: happen, become, be</u> N: be done, come to pass
11	עָשָׂה	<u>Q: make, do</u> N: be done, be made
12	אֱלֹהִים	God, gods
13	בּוֹא	<u>Q: enter, come</u> H: bring, bring in
14	מֶלֶךְ	king
15	יִשְׂרָאֵל	Israel
16	אֶרֶץ	earth, land, country
17	יוֹם	day
18	אִישׁ	man, husband, each
19	פָּנִים	face, appearance, presence
20	בַּיִת	house, dwelling, temple
21	נָתַן	Q: <u>give, put</u>, set, permit
22	עַם	people
23	יָד	hand, strength
24	הָלַךְ	<u>Q: go, walk</u> H: lead, bring Ht: walk, walk about
25	דָּבָר	word, thing, affair
26	הוּא	he, that one, that

27 רָאָה Q: see, look at
N: appear, be seen
H: show, cause to see

28 עַד as far as, until, while

29 אָב father, ancestor

30 שָׁמַע Q: hear, listen to, obey
H: proclaim, announce

31 דִּבֵּר P: speak

32 זֶה this one, this

33 עִיר town, city

34 יָשַׁב Q: sit, remain, dwell
H: set, place, cause to dwell

35 יָצָא Q: go forth, come out
H: bring out, take out

36 דָּוִד David

37 שׁוּב Q: turn back, return
P: bring back, restore
H: bring back, turn back

38 הֵן הִנֵּה behold! lo! see! here! now! look!

39 עִם with, beside

40 לָקַח Q: take, receive
N: be taken

41 אֶחָד one, first, once, each

42 יָדַע Q: know
N: be known
P: cause to know
H: make known, declare

43 אִם if

44 עָלָה Q: go up, ascend
H: bring up, offer
N: be brought up, taken away

45 שָׁנָה year

46 שֵׁם name, fame

47 אֲנִי I

48 עַיִן eye, spring

49 שָׁלַח Q: send
P: send forth, send away

50 מוּת Q: die
H: kill, execute

51 יְהוּדָה Judah

52 שָׁם there

53 אָכַל Q: eat, consume
N: be eaten
H: feed, cause to eat

54 עֶבֶד slave, servant

55 אִשָּׁה woman, wife

56 שְׁנַיִם two (m.)
שְׁתַּיִם (f.)

57 גַּם moreover, also, even

58 מֹשֶׁה Moses

59 נֶפֶשׁ self, person, life

60 אַיִן is not, are not

61 אָדוֹן master, lord,
אֲדוֹנָי Lord

62 כֹּהֵן priest

63 אֵלֶּה these

64 מָה what? how?
65 אַתָּה you (m. sg.)
66 קָרָא Q: call, proclaim
N: be called
67 אַחַר behind, after
68 אַל not
69 דֶּרֶךְ way, road, manner
70 כֵּן thus, so
71 מִצְרַיִם Egypt
72 רָעָה evil, distress, harm
73 נָשָׂא Q: lift, carry, take
N: be lifted up, rise
P: lift, take up
Ht: lift oneself up
74 יְרוּשָׁלַםִ Jerusalem
75 אָח brother
76 קוּם Q: arise, stand
P: confirm
H: raise, set up
77 לֵב heart, mind, will
78 רֹאשׁ head, chief, top
79 בַּת daughter
80 מֵאָה hundred
81 זֹאת this one, this (f.)
82 שִׂים Q: put, place, set
83 מַיִם water, waters
84 כֹּה thus, here
85 גּוֹי nation
86 אָדָם man, humankind, Adam
87 הַר mountain, hill
88 עָבַר Q: pass over, pass by
H: cause to pass over
89 עֶשֶׂר ten (m.)
עֲשָׂרָה (f.)
90 גָּדוֹל great, big (adj.)
91 עָמַד Q: stand, stop, take one's stand
H: erect, make stand
92 הֵם they, those (m.)
הֵמָּה
93 קוֹל voice, sound
94 נָכָה H: smite, strike
95 יָלַד Q: bear, give birth to
H: beget, father
96 אֶלֶף thousand, military unit
97 תַּחַת under, below, in place of
98 חַי alive, living (adj.)
99 עוֹד still, yet, again
100 פֶּה mouth
101 צָבָא army, war[fare], host
102 צִוָּה P: charge, command
103 הִיא she, that
104 קֹדֶשׁ sacredness, holiness
105 שָׁמַר Q: keep watch, preserve
N: be on guard, be guarded

106 מָצָא Q: find, reach, attain to
N: be found, be left
H: present, bring into contact

107 עוֹלָם eternity, antiquity

108 עַתָּה now

109 נָפַל Q: fall, lie
H: fell, cause to fall

110 שָׁלֹשׁ three (m.)
שְׁלֹשָׁה (f.)

111 רַב much, many, great

112 מִי who? whoever?

113 מִשְׁפָּט justice, judgment, custom, manner, norm

114 שָׁמַיִם heaven(s), sky

115 שַׂר ruler, chieftain

116 תּוֹךְ midst, middle

117 חֶרֶב sword

118 שָׁאוּל Saul

119 כֶּסֶף silver, money

120 נָא "please," "now"

121 מִזְבֵּחַ altar

122 מָקוֹם place (noun)

123 שֶׁבַע seven (m.)
שִׁבְעָה (f.)

124 יָם sea, west

125 זָהָב gold

126 יָרַד Q: go down, descend
H: bring down

127 יָרֵא Q: fear, be awed
N: be awe inspiring

128 רוּחַ wind, spirit, breath

129 אֵשׁ fire

130 נְאֻם utterance, oracle

131 בָּנָה Q: build
N: be built

132 שַׁעַר gate

133 נָגַד H: declare, tell, inform

134 דָּם blood

135 אָנֹכִי I

136 יַעֲקֹב Jacob

137 אַהֲרֹן Aaron

138 מָלַךְ Q: reign, rule, be king
H: make king, cause to rule

139 אֹהֶל tent

140 חָמֵשׁ five (m.)
חֲמִשָּׁה (f.)

141 טוֹב benefit (noun)
טוֹבָה good, pleasant

142 סָבִיב round about, circuit, surrounding

143 עֵץ tree(s), wood

144 בָּרַךְ Q: kneel, bless
N: bless oneself
P: bless
Ht: bless oneself

145 כְּלִי vessel, utensil, article of a general sort

146 אוֹ or

147 מִלְחָמָה battle, war

148 שָׂדֶה field, country

149 אַרְבַּע four (m.)
אַרְבָּעָה (f.)

150 עָנָה Q: answer, respond

151 עֶשְׂרִים twenty

152 נָבִיא prophet

153 מִשְׁפָּחָה clan, family

154 פָּקַד Q: visit, attend to, observe
N: be missing, be visited
P: muster
H: appoint, deposit

155 סוּר Q: depart from, turn aside
H: take away, remove

156 מְאֹד very, exceedingly, strength

157 עֵת time, season

158 לֶחֶם bread, food

159 חַטָּאת sin, sin offering

160 שְׁלֹמֹה Solomon

161 חָזַק Q: be/grow strong, be firm
P: strengthen, harden
H: strengthen, seize
Ht: strengthen oneself

162 כָּרַת Q: cut off/down, make a covenant
N: be cut off, cut down
H: cut off, destroy

163 לֵוִי Levi, Levite

164 עָבַד Q: work, serve
H: compel to labor

165 פְּלִשְׁתִּי Philistine

166 עֹלָה burnt offering

167 בְּרִית covenant, agreement

168 אֹיֵב Q: be hostile to, treat as an enemy (N.B.- participle form)

169 חָיָה Q: live
P: preserve, revive
H: preserve, revive

170 חֹדֶשׁ month, new moon

171 קָרַב Q: draw near, approach
P: bring near
H: bring, bring near

172 אַתֶּם you (m. pl.)

173 אַף anger, nostril, nose

174 פַּרְעֹה Pharaoh

175 אֶבֶן stone

176 צֹאן flock (sheep and goats)

177 לְמַעַן for the sake of, in order that, on account of

178 מִדְבָּר wilderness, plain

179 בָּשָׂר flesh, meat

180 רָשָׁע wicked, guilty

181 בָּבֶל Babel, Babylon

182 בֵּין between

183 לֵבָב heart, mind, will

184 מַטֶּה rod, staff, tribe

185 מָלֵא Q: be full, fill
N: be filled
P: fill, complete

186 חֶסֶד kindness, goodness

187 יְהוֹשׁוּעַ Joshua

188 רֶגֶל foot

189 אַמָּה cubit

190 חַיִל strength, wealth, army

191 לַיְלָה night

192 אֵל El, God, god

193 גְּבוּל border, boundary, territory

194 נַעַר boy, youth, servant

195 חָטָא Q: sin, miss
P: purify, make a sin offering
H: cause to sin

196 שָׁלוֹם welfare, peace, wholeness

197 מַעֲשֶׂה deed, work

198 זָכַר Q: remember, call to mind
N: be remembered
H: remind, cause to remember

199 יָרַשׁ Q: take possession of, inherit
H: inherit, dispossess

200 עָוֹן sin, guilt, punishment

201 קֶרֶב midst, among, inward part

202 זֶרַע seed, offspring

203 רָבָה Q: be/become many, much
H: make many, great

204 אֲדָמָה ground, land

205 בִּקֵּשׁ P: seek, desire

206 נַחֲלָה property, share, inheritance

207 כָּתַב Q: write
N: be written

208 מוֹעֵד appointed time, place, or meeting

209 אֵם mother

210 תּוֹרָה Torah, teaching, law

211 כּוּן N: be established, ready
H: establish, prepare

212 שָׁתָה Q: drink

213 אָהֵב Q: love

214 שֵׁשׁ six (m.)
שִׁשָּׁה (f.)

215 נָטָה Q: stretch out, extend
H: turn aside, incline, pervert justice

216 בֹּקֶר morning

217 יָסַף Q: add
H: add to, increase, do again

218 מַחֲנֶה camp, encampment

219 מַלְאָךְ messenger, angel

220	עָזַב	Q: leave, abandon N: be forsaken
221	יוֹסֵף	Joseph
222	נָצַל	N: deliver oneself P: strip off, plunder H: deliver, take away
223	שָׁכַב	Q: lie down
224	בֶּגֶד	garment
225	כָּלָה	Q: be complete, be finished P: complete, finish
226	צַדִּיק	just, righteous
227	יָשַׁע	N: be liberated, saved H: deliver, save, give victory to
228	אֲרוֹן	ark, chest
229	אָסַף	Q: gather, remove N: assemble, be gathered
230	כָּבוֹד	glory, splendor, honor
231	רוּם	Q: be high, exalted; rise H: raise, lift up, erect
232	יָכֹל	Q: be able, prevail
233	כַּף	palm of hand, sole of foot
234	לָכֵן	therefore
235	שֶׁמֶן	oil, fat
236	גָּלָה	Q: uncover, depart, go into exile N: be uncovered, revealed P: uncover, disclose H: take into exile
237	שֵׁבֶט	rod, staff, tribe
238	אֹזֶן	ear
239	בְּהֵמָה	cattle, beast
240	רֵעַ	friend, companion
241	שָׁבַע	N: swear, take an oath H: cause to swear
242	סֵפֶר	letter
243	שָׁפַט	Q: judge, govern N: plead one's cause, be judged
244	אָבַד	Q: perish, be lost P: destroy, kill H: destroy, put to death
245	בָּקָר	cattle, herd, ox
246	יַרְדֵּן	Jordan
247	רִאשׁוֹן	former, first
248	מִצְוָה	commandment
249	אֶפְרַיִם	Ephraim
250	מוֹאָב	Moab
251	זָקֵן	old man, old, elder
252	שָׂפָה	lip, speech, edge
253	שְׁלֹשִׁים	thirty
254	חָוָה	prostrate oneself in worship
255	קָדַשׁ	Q: be set apart N: show oneself sacred P: set apart, consecrate Ht: purify oneself H: consecrate
256	בָּחַר	Q: choose N: be chosen
257	לָחַם	N: wage war, fight

258 שָׁאַל Q: ask, inquire

259 בִּין Q: perceive, understand
N: be intelligent
H: teach, understand, cause to understand

260 דּוֹר generation, era

261 מְלָאכָה work, business, occupation

262 רָעָה Q: pasture, tend, graze

263 בִּנְיָמִין Benjamin

264 בַּעַל Baal, owner, lord

265 הָרַג Q: kill, slay

266 חוּץ outside, street

267 לָמָּה why?

268 אַחֵר another, different, other

269 חֲמִשִּׁים fifty

270 פֶּתַח doorway, opening, entrance

271 דָּרַשׁ Q: seek, consult
N: let oneself be consulted

272 זֶבַח sacrifice (noun)

273 סָבַב Q: turn around, surround
N: turn around
H: turn, cause to turn, lead around

274 אַךְ surely, only

275 מָוֶת death

276 טָמֵא Q: be, become unclean
N: defile oneself, be defiled
P: defile
Ht: defile oneself

277 נוּס Q: flee, escape

278 גִּבּוֹר warrior, mighty man

279 צְדָקָה righteousness

280 שֵׁנִי second (m.)
שֵׁנִית (f.)

281 אַיִל ram

282 לְבַד alone, by oneself

283 חָכְמָה widsom, skill

284 צִיּוֹן Zion

285 שָׂמַח Q: rejoice, be glad
P: gladden

286 מִנְחָה offering, gift, tribute

287 צָפוֹן north

288 כָּסָה P: cover, conceal

289 כְּמוֹ as, like, when

290 נֶגֶד in front of, opposite

291 רֹב multitude, abundance

292 שָׁחַת P: spoil, ruin, corrupt
H: spoil, ruin, corrupt

293 נָגַע Q: touch, harm, reach
H: cause to touch or reach

294 אֲרָם Aram (Syria)

295 אַשּׁוּר Ashur (Assyria)

296 עֵדָה congregation, gathering

297 שָׁבַר Q: break
N: be broken
P: break, shatter

298 יִרְמְיָהוּ Jeremiah

299	נָסַע	Q: set out, journey H: lead out
300	חָצֵר	court, enclosure
301	יוֹאָב	Joab
302	עֲבֹדָה	labor, service
303	שָׂנֵא	Q: hate P: hate
304	אָז	at that time, then
305	חָנָה	Q: encamp
306	נוּחַ	Q: rest, be quiet H: give rest to, leave
307	פָּתַח	Q: be open N: be opened P: set free, open, loosen
308	הָלַל	P: praise Ht: glory, boast
309	יַיִן	wine
310	רָדַף	Q: pursue, persecute P: pursue vigorously
311	מַעַל	upward, above
312	שְׁמוּאֵל	Samuel
313	מִשְׁכָּן	tabernacle, dwelling
314	יָחַד	be united
	יַחְדָּו	together (adv.)
315	נַחַל	stream, wadi, torrent
316	סוּס	horse
317	חָכָם	wise, skillful, clever
318	יָמִין	right hand
319	יֵשׁ	there is, there are
320	נְחוֹשֶׁת	copper, bronze
321	קָרָא	Q: meet, encounter, befall
	לִקְרַאת	(infinitive)
322	אַרְבָּעִים	forty
323	מְנַשֶּׁה	Manasseh
324	פָּנָה	Q: turn, look P: turn away, clear away H: turn
325	גִּלְעָד	Gilead
326	זָבַח	Q: slaughter, sacrifice P: sacrifice
327	חוֹמָה	wall
328	כִּסֵּא	throne, seat
329	מִסְפָּר	number
330	פֶּן	lest
331	שָׁאַר	N: be left over, behind H: leave over, spare
332	שֶׁמֶשׁ	sun
333	אַף	also, indeed, even
334	פַּר	bull, young bull
335	קָבַר	Q: bury N: be buried
336	חִזְקִיָּהוּ	Hezekiah
337	עֶרֶב	sunset, evening
338	שָׁכַן	Q: dwell, tent P: establish, settle H: place, cause to dwell
339	חָלַל	P: defile, profane, pollute H: begin

340 נָשִׂיא chief, prince
341 חֹק statute, ordinance
342 כֹּחַ strength, power
343 קָבַץ Q: gather, collect
N: assemble, be gathered
P: gather together
344 אֱמֶת faithfulness, truth, stability
345 נָגַשׁ Q: draw near, approach
N: draw near
H: bring near
346 עֶצֶם bone, substance, self
347 שָׁלַךְ Q: throw, cast
H: throw, cast
348 חָשַׁב Q: think, account, plan
N: be reckoned
P: consider, devise
349 יְהוֹנָתָן Jonathan
350 חֲצִי half, middle
351 קָהָל assembly, congregation
352 בְּכוֹר first-born
353 אוֹר light
354 אֲנַחְנוּ we
355 חֵמָה heat, rage, fury
356 בָּטַח Q: trust, be confident
357 לָכַד Q: capture, seize
N: be captured, caught
358 נָהָר river, stream
359 רֶכֶב chariot, chariotry

360 יָשָׁר upright, just, straight (adj.)
361 פְּרִי fruit
362 אָמַן N: be confirmed, faithful
H: trust, believe
363 חַיָּה living being, animal
364 פַּעַם time, occurrence, foot
365 צֶדֶק righteousness, rightness
366 לָשׁוֹן tongue, language
367 שָׂרַף Q: burn
N: be burned
368 תּוֹעֵבָה abomination
369 מַמְלָכָה kingdom, dominion
370 קָדוֹשׁ sacred, holy
371 גָּדַל Q: grow up, become great
P: raise, rear (a child), make great
H: make great, magnify
372 קָטַר P: burn sacrifices, incense
H: burn sacrifices, incense
373 אָחוֹת sister
374 בָּכָה Q: weep, bewail
375 יָדָה H: give thanks, praise
Ht: confess, give thanks
376 נָבָא N: prophesy
Ht: prophesy
377 בִּלְתִּי not, except
378 כָּבֵד Q: be heavy, honored
N: be honored
P: honor, glorify
H: make heavy

379	שָׁפַךְ	Q: pour out N: be poured out
380	שֶׁקֶר	lie, falsehood
381	יִצְחָק	Isaac
382	רַק	only, surely
383	שַׁבָּת	Sabbath
384	כִּפֶּר	P: reconcile, cover over
385	לָבַשׁ	Q: dress, put on clothes H: clothe (someone)
386	נֶגֶב	southland, Negev
387	עַמּוּד	pillar, column
388	בּוֹשׁ	Q: be ashamed H: put to shame
389	כָּנָף	wing, extremity, skirt
390	שְׁמֹנֶה	eight (m.)
	שְׁמֹנָה	(f.)
391	שֹׁמְרוֹן	Samaria
392	עָפָר	dust, dirt
393	שְׁלִישִׁי	third
394	יָתַר	N: be left over, remain H: leave over, leave
395	כֶּבֶשׂ	lamb
396	סָפַר	Q: count, number N: be counted, numbered P: recount, relate, tell
397	נָחַם	N: be sorry, repent, be comforted P: comfort, console
398	עֳנִי	affliction, poor (one)
	עָנִי	afflicted, poor (adj.)
399	עַמּוֹן	Ammon
400	צָרָה	distress, trouble, narrow
	צַר	
401	בַּעַד	through, behind, on behalf of
402	בָּמָה	high place, ridge, back
403	גָּאַל	Q: redeem, act as kinsman N: redeem oneself, be redeemed
404	חֻקָּה	statute, enactment
405	יָרָבְעָם	Jeroboam
406	אַבְשָׁלוֹם	Absalom
407	רוּץ	Q: run
408	שָׁלֵם	Q: be complete, sound P: complete, make good, reward
409	תָּמִיד	continually, daily
410	יָטַב	Q: be well, be pleasing H: do good to, make good
411	מַרְאֶה	sight, appearance, vision
412	שָׁכַח	Q: forget N: be forgotten
413	מְעַט	a little, a few
414	רֹחַב	breadth, width
415	רָעָב	famine, hunger

Word	
אָב	29
אָבַד	244
אֶבֶן	175
אֲבְשָׁלוֹם	406
אָדוֹן	61
אָדָם	86
אֲדָמָה	204
אָהֵב	213
אֹהֶל	139
אַהֲרֹן	137
אוֹ	146
אוֹר	353
אָז	304
אֹזֶן	238
אָח	75
אֶחָד	41
אָחוֹת	373
אַחַר	67
אַחֵר	268
אֹיֵב	168
אֲיִל	281
אַיִן	60
אִישׁ	18
אַךְ	274
אָכַל	53
אַל	68
אֵל	192
אֶל	4
אֵלֶּא	63
אֱלוֹהִים	12
אֶלֶף	96
אִם	43
אֵם	209
אַמָּה	189
אָמַן	362
אָמַר	5
אֶמֶת	344
אֲנַחְנוּ	354
אֲנִי	47
אָנֹכִי	135
אָסַף	229
אַף	173, 333
אֶפְרַיִם	249
אַרְבַּע	140
אַרְבָּעָה	
אַרְבָּעִים	322
אֲרוֹן	228
אֲרָם	294
אֶרֶץ	16
אֵשׁ	129
אִשָּׁה	55
אַשּׁוּר	295
אֲשֶׁר	3
אַתָּה	65
אַתֶּם	172
בָּבֶל	181
בֶּגֶד	224
בְּהֵמָה	239
בּוֹא	13
בּוֹשׁ	388
בָּחַר	256
בָּטַח	356
בִּין	259
בֵּין	182
בַּיִת	20
בָּכָה	374
בְּכוֹר	352
בִּלְתִּי	377
בָּמָה	402
בֵּן	7
בָּנָה	131
בִּנְיָמִין	263
בַּעַד	400
בַּעַל	264
בָּקָר	245
בֹּקֶר	216
בָּקַשׁ	205
בְּרִית	167
בָּרַךְ	144
בָּשָׂר	179
בַּת	79
גָּאַל	403
גְּבוּל	193
גִּבּוֹר	278
גָּדַל	371
גָּדוֹל	90
גּוֹי	85
גָּלָה	236

325 גִּלְעָד
57 גַּם

31 דִּבֶּר
25 דָּבָר
36 דָּוִד
260 דּוֹר
134 דָּם
69 דֶּרֶךְ
271 דָּרַשׁ

26 הוּא
10 הָיָה
103 הִיא
24 הָלַךְ
308 הָלַל
92 הֵם
הֵמָּה
38 הִנֵּה הֵן
87 הַר
265 הָרַג

81 זֹאת
326 זָבַח
272 זֶבַח
32 זֶה
125 זָהָב
198 זָכַר
251 זָקֵן
202 זֶרָה

170 חֹדֶשׁ
169 חָוָה
266 חוּץ
327 חוֹמָה
161 חָזַק
336 חִזְקִיָּהוּ
195 חָטָא
159 חַטָּאת
98 חַי
254 חָיָה
363 חַיָּה
190 חַיִל
317 חָכָם
283 חָכְמָה
339 חָלַל
355 חֵמָה
269 חֲמִשִּׁים
140 חָמֵשׁ
חֲמִשָּׁה
305 חָנָה
186 חֶסֶד
350 חֲצִי
300 חָצֵר
341 חֹק
404 חֻקָּה
117 חֶרֶב
348 חָשַׁב

141 טוֹב
טֹבָה
276 טָמֵא

23 יָד
375 יָדָה
42 יָדַע
51 יְהוּדָה
1 יהוה
349 יְהוֹנָתָן
187 יְהוֹשׁוּעַ
301 יוֹאָב
17 יוֹם
221 יוֹסֵף
314 יַחַד
יַחְדָּו
410 יָטַב
309 יַיִן
232 יָכֹל
95 יָלַד
124 יָם
318 יָמִין
217 יָסַף
136 יַעֲקֹב
35 יָצָא
381 יִצְחָק
127 יָרֵא
405 יָרָבְעָם
126 יָרַד
246 יַרְדֵּן

74	יְרוּשָׁלַיִם
298	יִרְמְיָהוּ
199	יָרַשׁ
15	יִשְׂרָאֵל
319	יֵשׁ
34	יָשַׁב
227	יָשַׁע
360	יָשָׁר
394	יָתַר
378	כָּבֵד
230	כָּבוֹד
395	כֶּבֶשׂ
84	כֹּה
62	כֹּהֵן
211	כּוּן
342	כֹּחַ
9	כִּי
2	כֹּל
225	כָּלָה
145	כְּלִי
289	כְּמוֹ
70	כֵּן
389	כָּנָף
328	כִּסֵּא
288	כָּסָה
119	כֶּסֶף
233	כַּף
384	כִּפֶּר
162	כָּרַת
207	כָּתַב
6	לֹא
77	לֵב
183	לֵבָב
282	לְבַד
385	לָבַשׁ
163	לֵוִי
257	לָחַם
158	לֶחֶם
191	לַיְלָה
357	לָכַד
234	לָכֵן
267	לָמָּה
177	לְמַעַן
40	לָקַח
366	לָשׁוֹן
156	מְאֹד
80	מֵאָה
178	מִדְבָּר
64	מָה
250	מוֹאָב
208	מוֹעֵד
50	מוּת
275	מָוֶת
121	מִזְבֵּחַ
218	מַחֲנֶה
184	מַטֶּה
112	מִי
83	מַיִם
185	מָלֵא
219	מַלְאָךְ
261	מְלָאכָה
147	מִלְחָמָה
138	מָלַךְ
14	מֶלֶךְ
369	מַמְלָכָה
286	מִנְחָה
323	מְנַשֶּׁה
329	מִסְפָּר
413	מְעַט
311	מַעַל
197	מַעֲשֶׂה
106	מָצָא
248	מִצְוָה
71	מִצְרַיִם
122	מָקוֹם
412	מַרְאֶה
58	מֹשֶׁה
313	מִשְׁכָּן
113	מִשְׁפָּט
153	מִשְׁפָּחָה
120	נָא
130	נְאֻם
376	נָבָא
152	נָבִיא
386	נֶגֶב
133	נָגַד

290 נֶגֶד
293 נָגַע
345 נָגַשׁ
358 נָהָר
306 נוּחַ
277 נוּס
315 נַחַל
206 נַחֲלָה
397 נָחַם
320 נְחֹשֶׁת
215 נָטָה
94 נָכָה
299 נָסַע
194 נַעַר
109 נָפַל
59 נֶפֶשׁ
222 נָצַל
73 נָשָׂא
340 נָשִׂיא
21 נָתַן

273 סָבַב
142 סָבִיב
316 סוּס
155 סוּר
396 סָפַר
242 סֵפֶר

164 עָבַד
54 עֶבֶד
302 עֲבֹדָה
88 עֵבֶר
28 עַד
296 עֵדָה
99 עוֹד
107 עוֹלָם
200 עָוֹן
220 עָזַב
48 עַיִן
33 עִיר
8 עַל
44 עָלָה
166 עֹלָה
22 עַם
39 עִם
91 עָמַד
387 עַמּוּד
399 עַמּוֹן
150 עָנָה
398 עָנִי
392 עָפָר
143 עֵץ
346 עֶצֶם
337 עֶרֶב
11 עָשָׂה
89 עֶשֶׂר
עֶשְׂרֵה
151 עֶשְׂרִים
157 עֵת
108 עַתָּה

100 פֶּה
165 פְּלִשְׁתִּי
330 פֶּן
324 פָּנָה
19 פָּנִים
364 פַּעַם
154 פָּקַד
334 פַּר
361 פְּרִי
174 פַּרְעֹה
307 פָּתַח
270 פֶּתַח

176 צֹאן
101 צָבָא
226 צַדִּיק
365 צֶדֶק
279 צְדָקָה
102 צָוָּה
284 צִיּוֹן
287 צָפוֹן
400 צַר
צָרָה

335 קָבַר
343 קָבַץ
370 קָדוֹשׁ
255 קָדַשׁ
104 קֹדֶשׁ
351 קָהָל

קוֹל 93
קוּם 76
קָטַר 372
קָרָא 66, 321
קָרַב 171
קֶרֶב 201

רָאָה 27
רֹאשׁ 78
רִאשׁוֹן 247
רַב 111
רֹב 291
רָבָה 203
רֶגֶל 188
רָדַף 310
רֹהַב 414
רוּחַ 128
רוּם 231
רוּץ 407
רֶכֶב 359
רֵעַ 240
רָעֵב 415
רָעָה 72, 262
רַק 382
רָשָׁע 180

שָׂדֶה 148
שִׂים 82
שָׂמַח 285
שָׂנֵא 303
שָׂפָה 252
שַׂר 115
שָׂרַף 367

שָׁאַל 258
שָׁאוּל 118
שֵׁבֶט 237
שָׁבַע 241
שֶׁבַע 123
שִׁבְעָה
שָׁבַר 297
שַׁבָּת 383
שׁוּב 37
שָׁחַת 292
שָׁכַב 223
שָׁכַח 412
שָׁכַן 338
שָׁלוֹם 196
שָׁלַח 49
שְׁלִישִׁי 393
שְׁלֹשִׁים 253
שָׁלַךְ 347
שָׁלֵם 408
שְׁלֹמֹה 160
שָׁלֹשׁ 110
שְׁלֹשָׁה
שָׁם 52
שֵׁם 46
שְׁמוּאֵל 312
שָׁמַיִם 114
שֶׁמֶן 235
שְׁמֹנֶה 390
שְׁמֹנָה
שָׁמַע 30
שָׁמַר 105
שֹׁמְרוֹן 391
שָׁנָה 45
שֵׁנִי 280
שֵׁנִית
שְׁנַיִם 56
שְׁתַּיִם
שַׁעַר 132
שָׁפַט 243
שָׁפַךְ 370
שֶׁקֶר 380
שֵׁשׁ 214
שִׁשָּׁה
שָׁתָה 212

תּוֹךְ 116
תּוֹעֵבָה 368
תּוֹרָה 210
תַּחַת 97
תָּמִיד 409

Noted are those locations where the discussion of a word goes beyond simple dictionary information.